THE BOARD OF FOREIGN MISSIONS
OF THE
PRESBYTERIAN CHURCH IN THE U. S. A.
PACIFIC DISTRICT OFFICE
228 McALLISTER ST.
SAN FRANCISCO

THE FOREIGN MISSIONARY

The Foreign Missionary

An Incarnation of a World Movement

By
AUTHUR JUDSON BROWN
*For Thirty-four Years Secretary of the Presbyterian
Board of Foreign Missions, New York*

THIRTEENTH PRINTING—REVISED EDITION

With Introduction by
SAMUEL MARINUS ZWEMER
*Professor of the History of Religion
and Christian Missions in Princeton Theological Seminary*

NEW YORK   CHICAGO
Fleming H. Revell Company
LONDON   AND   EDINBURGH

Copyright, 1907-1932 by
FLEMING H. REVELL COMPANY

BOOKS BY ARTHUR JUDSON BROWN

THE NEW ERA IN THE PHILIPPINES
THE MASTERY OF THE FAR EAST
JAPAN IN THE WORLD OF TODAY
RUSSIA IN TRANSFORMATION
NEW FORCES IN OLD CHINA
THE CHINESE REVOLUTION
THE EXPECTATION OF SIAM
A TOUR OF ASIA
UNITY AND MISSIONS
THE FOREIGN MISSIONARY
THE WHY AND HOW OF FOREIGN MISSIONS
RISING CHURCHES IN NON-CHRISTIAN LANDS
A SECOND VISIT TO CHINA, JAPAN AND KOREA
THE NEARER AND FARTHER EAST (Joint Author)

New York: 158 Fifth Avenue
Chicago: 851 Cass Street
London: 21 Paternoster Square
Edinburgh: 99 George Street

TO MY WIFE

To whose happy companionship, wise counsel, and sympathetic understanding of missionaries and their problems I owe more than words can express.

INTRODUCTION

THE foreign missionary not only but the church which sends him abroad are today under fire of criticism. Titanic forces are assaulting the very principles that lie at the foundation of the missionary enterprise. The supremacy of Christ, the authority of the Word of God, the validity of the great commission, the adequacy of the message and of the methods hitherto followed and found fruitful are called in question. Why does the Church send out missionaries? Are they still needed? What is the aim and the goal of all their effort?

Some voices declare that the Gospel message of the Apostles, and of the missionaries who laid the foundations of the younger Oriental churches in Asia and Africa, needs modification by subtraction or addition, by way of compromise or syncretism. Others would shorten the Bible by omitting for example, in Luke XV, the reference to the " fatted calf," because it is a stumbling-block to Hindus, and would call Christ " by some more distinctively Indian title than ' Lamb of God '—a name which meant much to a pastoral nation but means nothing at all in India." Above all, there is the spirit of secularism and naturalism which denies the idea of absolute ethical standards, a supernatural revelation and the validity of Christianity as a universal message.

Amid this confusion of ideas the pronouncements of the Lausanne Conference on Faith and Order and of the Jerusalem meeting of the International Missionary Council agreed that the heart of the Christian message and the secret of our power is Jesus Christ Himself; that power and that message are the same yesterday, today, and forever. We do not, therefore, so much need to discover new values in the non-Christian religions as to share the old values and the new values which are in Christ. We need not so much a new interpretation of the Christian message as its proclamation with its ancient power. It is less important to nationalize Christianity than it is to Christianize the nations. We should never confuse the substance with the form, nor the message with the language in which it is presented. The gift of God in Jesus Christ remains the same by whatever human terminology we try to express the fact that " in Him dwelleth all the fulness of the God-head bodily." The inadequacy of the stammering messenger does not change the essential worth of the Divine message. A missionary is still one who is sent with a message; and that message is still the Gospel of Christ.

It is therefore not less, but more important and urgent to understand the foreign missionary's task; what his qualifications are, what he is trying to do, what difficulties must be overcome and what are the human conditions for that success in the realm of the spirit where, in the last analysis, all depends not on man's device or wisdom but on the power of the Holy Spirit. This book deals with these questions frankly and fundamentally. We live in a changing world, but there are things so fundamental and simple as to be unchanging, principles that abide forever. The ancient civilized world believed that there were four elements, earth, air, fire, and water. The modern world knows that there are scores of known elements and some yet to be discovered. But earth, air, fire, and water are what they always were, and behave as they always did. Greater knowledge of nature has only added greater mystery. Thus it is in the realm of evangelism. The spiritual seed still grows secretly in the soil of the human heart. The wind still " bloweth where it listeth." God's Spirit is not bound by any missionary council or program. Revivals of religion follow the same laws that they did at Pentecost or in the days of Luther, Savonarola, Wesley, and Moody. The human heart everywhere responds to the cry of Isaiah: " Ho, every one that thirsteth," and to the promise of Jesus Christ: " Whosoever drinketh of the water that I shall give him shall never thirst." The

Introduction

Christian message and mission, its aim and dynamic, are as simple as the common things of life.

As Dr. Robert E. Speer says: " The fundamental question is as to whether we know what Christianity really is and mean really to give our lives to its claim. *This is all there is to the foreign missions appeal and argument.* Everything else is secondary or irrelevant. If Christ is the only Lord and Saviour then He must be shared with all mankind. If the present methods of sharing Him are inadequate or ineffective, then let the men who believe in Christ rise up and correct them and pour out in the enterprise a new flood of power and accomplishment."

Dr. Brown's book keeps to the middle of the great historic highway. Its chapters are based on principles that have governed the missionary enterprise for over a century. The author writes after a long and intimate experience of all yesterday's and today's problems. He has not only repeatedly visited the great mission fields but has come into the closest friendship with many hundreds of missionaries of every type through personal and official relationship. As a missionary statesman he has gained not only a broad and sympathetic outlook, but insight into the deeper problems of missionary administration and strategy, impossible to a novice. When the book was written it was admittedly not abreast but ahead of the times. The chapters that deal with missionary co-operation and the essential unity of Christendom and of the church are still a challenge, for a divided church cannot save the world.

When the first edition was published Dr. John R. Mott affirmed: " It is the strongest thing which has ever appeared bearing on the life and work of the missionary." Dr. Eugene Stock of the Church Missionary Society of England wrote:

"It is simply admirable. Dr. Brown has brought his wide and lengthened experience to bear upon every branch of the subject, and has treated every one with a rare combination of lofty principle and practical common sense. The highest spiritual standard is set up and other matters are discussed with a fullness of knowledge and a ripeness of judgment that never fail. We really do not see where criticism could be successfully offered. . . . Every member of a missionary board ought to read and pass an examination in this book, before he presumes to take his part in missionary administration; and every missionary should go through the same experience before he sets sail for the foreign field."

All through the book, the emphasis is on quality and not on quantity. We need more and better missionaries. The final chapters on the Real Strain of Missionary Life, on the Spirit of the Missionary, and on his Reward could only have been recorded after long and sacrificial contact with those who in lonely stations and dangerous out-posts wrote their record on human hearts in tears and blood.

For several semesters THE FOREIGN MISSIONARY was used as a basis for class-room discussion in the Theological Seminary at Princeton, New Jersey, with increasing appreciation of its value. The book has passed through twelve editions and, at the instigation of Professor J. de Rougemont of Neuchatel, a French translation by Caroline Barbey Boissier appeared in 1910. Naturally a book so long before the public needed certain changes and corrections. The revision has been thorough. But the message and the spirit of the book remain unchanged. There is breadth of charity, but no surrender to syncretism; a sound theology, evangelical and evangelistic, but no narrowness of dogmatism. Dr. Brown is not ashamed of the gospel of Christ, or of trying to win disciples for Him.

THE FOREIGN MISSIONARY was largely used by the last generation of students as a text-book; it is a challenge to the present generation of students for a new missionary leadership. This can only come, as in the past, by prayer and sacrificial obedience to Jesus Christ. He was, as David Livingstone put it, "The first Foreign Missionary." Those who feel called of God to such high fellowship and office will therefore with deep humility use words similar to those of Albert Schweitzer in an African forest: " Jesus is Lord, our Lord. What is decisive is not the theories we are teaching about Him, but the obedience with which we are serving Him."

To preach and to practice Christianity, that is the true missionary ideal; the bold proclamation of the Word of God, once for all revealed in His gospel, and the silent eloquence of a hidden life, hid with Christ in God and yielding the fruit of the Spirit.

SAMUEL M. ZWEMER.

The Theological Seminary,
   Princeton, New Jersey.

FOREWORD

WHETHER one sympathizes with Foreign Missions or not, no thoughtful person can be indifferent to a movement that is now represented by 29,188 foreign missionaries and 151,735 national workers who are conducting Christian work in 4,598 stations and 50,513 outstations; 36,246 churches with 3,614,154 communicants and a Christian community of 8,342,378; 2,440,148 pupils in 50,079 schools ranging from kindergartens to great universities; 858 hospitals and 1,686 dispensaries treating in a recent year 4,788,258 patients; hundreds of millions of pages of tracts, books and periodicals annually published; the distribution of the Bible in 853 languages and dialects at the rate of over 11,000,000 copies a year; 104 leper asylums, 32 schools for the blind and deaf, and 361 orphanages—a vast and varied enterprise to which the Protestant Christians of America and Europe contributed $69,555,148 in a recent year, and which has received the warm commendation of intelligent supporters and of such public men as former Presidents Theodore Roosevelt and William H. Taft, Lord James Bryce, several viceroys of India, British and American ambassadors in lands where missionaries work, and many Asiatic officials of high rank.

The purpose of this book is to describe the missionaries who incarnate this great work, who and what they are, their motives and aims, their policies and methods. Are they wise in their dealings with proud and ancient peoples and their social and religious customs? Do they make trouble for their own and other governments? What are their real difficulties? What progress is being made? How are the boards organized? How do they select missionaries and administer mission funds? Is money being spent to the best advantage?

etc. Most criticisms of missionaries are based upon misapprehensions as to these and similar questions. Many supporters of the cause have never heard them answered. They give when their pastors ask them to, but they often have only vague conceptions of the work, and when they hear objections they are unable to meet them. Indeed, some missionaries have not made a careful study of policies and methods.

The changes that have taken place since the publication of the first edition in 1907 have not altered the essential character and purpose of the missionary enterprise which were then discussed. There have been, however, changes in details, and I have taken advantage of the call for another printing to make an extensive revision, incorporating later facts and dates, and, in general, seeking to bring the discussion abreast of present-day knowledge of missionary work and problems and to emphasize the fundamental principles that are unchanged and unchangeable. But I do not agree with those who would banish all use of the term "native." It is a sensible word, implying no inferiority but simply designating that which belongs to a given country as distinguished from that which is foreign; just as we talk of native Americans and native Englishmen.

The term "heathen" was in universal use when this book was first published. Its original meaning was simply "a dweller on the heath," and Webster's Dictionary gives its present primary meaning as "an individual of the pagan or unbelieving nations" as distinguished from those who believe in "the true God"; and adds: "now used of all people except Christians, Jews and Mohammedans." Nothing offensive therefore need be implied in its use. If I were rewriting the entire book, I would probably substitute "national" for "native" and "non-Christian" for "heathen"; but with this explanation of the legitimate sense in which I use the latter terms, it appears unnecessary to incur the expense of changing plates for merely verbal alterations.

I gratefully acknowledge the assistance that I have re-

Foreword

ceived from the Rev. Samuel M. Zwemer, D. D., who, after forty years as a missionary in Arabia and Egypt, became Professor of Missions in Princeton Theological Seminary in 1930. He has been using the book as a text-book in his classes, and out of his practical experience on the mission field and in the class room he has written an Introduction and made valuable suggestions which I have gladly adopted.

And now this revised edition is sent forth, with warm appreciation both of the kind words and the helpful criticisms regarding earlier editions, and with humble hope and prayer that it may serve to make the lives and work of devoted missionaries better understood and to strengthen interest in the cause to which I have devoted many years of my life.

THE AUTHOR.

156 Fifth Avenue, New York,
  January 1, 1932.

CONTENTS

I. THE MISSIONARY MOTIVE.................... 13

> Primary motives: a valid Christian experience, world's need of Christ, command of Christ; world evangelization His supreme thought; heresy of disobedience; missions main work of church; scope and grandeur of Divine purpose; secondary motives: philanthropic, intellectual, commercial, civilizing, historical; disposition unduly to exalt secondary motives; missions now conducted under changed conditions; no changes affect central fact that Christ is for all men and that Christians should make Him known to all.

II. THE MISSIONARY AIM....................... 29

> To present Christ for intelligent acceptance; all forms of work tributary to this; converts to be organized as church; missionaries cannot reach all unevangelized; church in each land to be trained to self-propagation, self-support and self-government.

III. MISSIONARY ADMINISTRATION 44

> Should be commensurate with scope and dignity of aim; boards necessary; varying types of relationship and organization; how boards do their work; business methods; administrative expenses; uncertainty of income; special objects; gifts for objects outside budget; "Station plan"; primacy of gifts for budget; criticism often unintelligent; missionary policy; church board a faith work.

IV. QUALIFICATIONS FOR MISSIONARY APPOINTMENT 67

> High standard; varieties of candidates desired; points inquired into—age, health, education, executive ability, steadiness of purpose, temperament, doctrinal views, freedom from

xvii

Contents

debt, Christian experience; how one should know whether to apply; comparative home and foreign needs; assignment of field.

V. FIRST IMPRESSIONS AND LANGUAGE STUDY..... 85

Travel arrangements; outfit; the voyage; impressions on arrival; determination of station; language study.

VI. THE MISSIONARY AT WORK.................. 97

Variety and scope of duties; comparatively small force; typical instances; educational work; literary work; medical work; evangelistic work; when converts should be baptized; vital themes of the Gospel needed; mistakes to be avoided; reform movements; missions not a crusade but a long pull; increasing opposition of non-Christian faiths.

VII. THE MISSIONARY'S FINANCIAL SUPPORT........119

Salary; cost of living; children's allowances; servants; "Why not live as natives do?" salaries of independent and Roman Catholic missionaries; necessity of salary from home church; houses of missionaries; handling of trust funds; borrowing from mission treasurer.

VIII. THE MISSIONARY'S PHYSICAL LIFE..........140

Care of health indispensable; responsibility of medical missionaries; losses from disease in war; laws of health; medical training for laymen; exposure to sun; food; drinking water; location and screening of buildings; disposition of refuse; clothing; inoculation for typhoid and smallpox; layman's medical kit; available hospitals.

IX. THE MISSIONARY'S INTELLECTUAL LIFE....162

Missionary an educated man; books to be taken; courses of study; periodicals; much of missionary's work intellectual; literary work; contributions of missionaries to world's knowledge; prestige of scholarship in Orient; intellectual recreation; cultivation of love of nature.

X. THE MISSIONARY'S SPIRITUAL LIFE.........177

Vital element in missionary life; dangers to spirituality; many duties "secular"; tempta-

Contents　　　　　　　　　　xix

tion to professionalism; helps to spirituality—
Bible study, prayer, conferences for devotion;
reliance upon Holy Spirit; difficulty of maintaining spiritual life in non-Christian lands;
influence of consecrated lives.

XI. THE MISSIONARY AND THE BOARD........197

Alleged alienation unfounded; boards seek
views of missionaries; difficulties involved;
board decisions often relieve missions of embarrassment; responsibility of boards to home
church; types of boards; manuals; distribution of funds; boards and missionaries coworkers; relations should be friendly, frank,
loyal, magnamimous; priority of "regular
grants"; special gifts.

XII. THE MISSIONARY AND THE HOME CHURCH 216

Letters and reports; furlough addresses; reciprocal duty of home church; need of better
support; increasing efficiency in promoting interest; activities of women and laymen; per
capita gifts; example of Antioch church;
methods of raising money; "diversion" of
gifts from home causes; responsibility of pastors; "people not interested"; responsibility
of theological seminaries; place of missions in
public and private prayer; relation of church's
spiritual power to missionary zeal.

XIII. THE MISSIONARY AND HIS ASSOCIATES.....236

Seriousness of problem; privacy difficult; associates perhaps uncongenial; importance of
starting right; factor of temperament; new
missionary should be slow to criticize; older
missionary should be considerate; gossip; insisting upon rights; elimination of the cantankerous; complaints against fellow workers;
votes on return after furloughs; respect for
policy of mission; use of gifts; relation to
work of other denominations; avoidance of
sectarianism; principles of comity; relations
with non-missionary white men.

XIV. THE MISSIONARY AND THE NATIVES........260

Difficulty of the problem; race prejudice; political and commercial aggressions by western
nations; Asia has learned of the white man's
vices; Orient no longer cringes before western

nations; Oriental objection not so much to Christianity as to its identification with foreigners; selection of consuls, diplomats, and commercial agents; disaffected servants; western manners; respecting native etiquette; example of missionary's family; should native dress be adopted; native ideas of right and wrong; position of single women; reasons for seclusion of women in some countries; avoidance of political questions; mission architecture; sympathetic relations with people as brother men; non-Christian peoples not inferiors; their religions should never be ridiculed; study of ethnic religions; example of Christ in dealing with men.

XV. THE MISSIONARY AND THE NATIVE CHURCH . 291

Problem, easy in pioneer days, now difficult; financial embarrassment in different scale of support; larger rewards in secular positions; educated Christian leaders require higher salaries; problem not solved by increased appropriations; aiding Oriental students in America; rising nationalistic feeling; loyalty to missionary aim to establish a self-supporting, self-propagating and self-governing church; independent spirit of Japanese churches; creed and polity of national churches; when should self-government be advised? mistaken fears of independence; problem of relationship acute with high grade native leaders; why mission membership restricted to missionaries; danger of obscuring fundamental principles; sphere of national leaders in church; objections considered; should the missionary join the national church? organizing a church out of foreigners before there are national Christians; sympathy for position of national leaders.

XVI. THE MISSIONARY AND HIS CRITICS 319

Criticism reasonable; sources of criticism; superficial impressions mislead travellers; current criticisms—missionaries inferior, converts not genuine, missionaries responsible for antiforeign feeling, missionaries interfere in law suits, hated by natives, make trouble for governments, denationalize converts, preach sectarianism, evils at home, introduce destructive civilization, missionaries' children usually bad,

Contents

missionaries in trade, do more harm than good, single women cause scandal, force alien civilization on already civilized peoples, higher Christian standards increase moral responsibility, religions of other races good enough for them, no right to force Christianity on other peoples, expense of converting "heathen," missionaries accomplish little.

XVII. THE REAL STRAIN OF MISSIONARY LIFE....355

Physical hardships less than commonly supposed; but conditions in many fields not pleasant; mental hardships great — loneliness; depressing influence of environment; separation from children; distress as see unrelieved suffering and debasing forms of sin; spiritual burden for needy souls—the strain that broke Christ's heart.

XVIII. THE SPIRIT OF THE MISSIONARY..........369

Missionary not a saint on a pedestal, but a practical Christian worker; wives of missionaries; single women; missionaries who reject worldly rewards; fortitude in emergencies; why missionaries remain at posts in times of peril; the "thin red line"; home support contrasted with support of soldiers in war; instances of self-sacrificing devotion; graves on the picket line; missionaries true heroes of modern life; deserve all honour.

XIX. THE MISSIONARY'S REWARD..............386

Reward not object of missionary; but is reward of men, of conscience, in using life to best advantage, in laying moral foundations, in uplifting men temporally, in helping men spiritually, in seeing results, in a vision of the Kingdom of God; reward of the Master; not in worldly things to buy the joy of the missionary; poem on the Lienchou massacre.

REFERENCES FOR SUPPLEMENTARY READING.402A

INDEX 403

The Foreign Missionary

I

THE MISSIONARY MOTIVE

WHY do missionaries go forth? This question is fundamental. The motives must be powerful, for weak motives would not lead thousands of earnest men and women to spend their lives among uncongenial people, far from the associations and opportunities of home and country, nor would they induce the Christians of Europe and America to give millions of dollars annually for the maintenance of the enterprise. In fact, various motives are involved. Some operate upon one class of minds and some upon another, and all of them do not appeal with equal force to the same person. For convenience they may be divided into two main classes, primary and secondary, though this classification is arbitrary and though there may be difference of opinion as to the class to which certain motives properly belong. Something depends upon the viewpoint.

The primary motives may be reduced to three.

(a) A Valid Christian Experience.—In proportion as this is genuine and deep, will we desire to communicate it to others. Propagation is a law of the spiritual life. The genius of Christianity is expansive. Its inherent tendency is to propagate itself. A living organism must grow or die. The church that is not missionary will become atrophied. All virile faith prompts its possessor to seek others. Ruskin reminds us of Southey's statement that no man was ever yet convinced of any

momentous truth without feeling in himself the power as well as the desire of communicating it.[1] That was an exquisite touch of regenerated nature and one beautifully illustrative of the promptings of a normal Christian experience which led Andrew, after he rose from Jesus' feet, to find first his own brother, Simon, and say unto him: "We have found the Messias; and he brought him to Jesus." No external authority, however commanding, can take the place of this internal motive. It led Paul to exclaim,—"Woe is me if I preach not the gospel!" It made him plead "with tears" that men would turn to God; and become "all things to all men, that 'he' might by all means save some."

People who say that they do not believe in foreign missions, are usually quite unconscious of the indictment that they bring against their own spiritual experience. The man who has no religion of his own that he values of course is not interested in the effort to make it known to others. It is true, one may be simply ignorant of the content of his faith or the real character of the missionary movement, but as a rule those who know the real meaning of the Christian experience are conscious of an over-mastering impulse to communicate it to others.

(b) *The World's Evident Need of Christ.*—He who has knowledge that is essential to the welfare of his fellow men is under solemn obligation to convey that knowledge to them. It makes no difference who those men are, or where they live, or whether they are conscious of their need, or how much inconvenience or expense he may incur in reaching them. The fact that he can help them is reason why he should help them. This is an essential part of the foreign missionary impulse. We have the revelation of God which is potential of a civilization that benefits man, an education that fits him for higher usefulness, a scientific knowledge that enlarges his powers, a medical skill that alleviates his sufferings, and above all a relation to Jesus Christ that

[1] Modern Painters I, xx.

The Missionary Motive

not only lends new dignity to this earthly life but that saves his soul and prepares him for eternal companionship with God. "Neither is there salvation in any other." Therefore, we must convey this gospel to the world. There is no worthy reason for being concerned about the salvation of the man next to us which is not equally applicable to the man five thousand miles away. "It is hard to realize this concerning those who are so distant?" Precisely, foreign missionary interest presupposes breadth of soul. Any one can love his own family, but it takes a high-souled man to love all men. He who has that which the world needs is debtor to the world. The true disciple would feel this even if Christ had spoken no command. The missionary impulse would have stirred him to spontaneous action. Christ simply voiced the highest and holiest dictates of the human heart when He summoned His followers to missionary activity and zeal. The question whether the heathen really need Christ may be answered by the counter question: Do we need Him? and the intensity of our desire to tell them of Christ will be in exact proportion to the intensity of our own sense of need.

We do not hear as much as our fathers heard of the motive of salvation of the heathen. Our age prefers to dwell upon the blessings of faith rather than upon the consequences of unbelief. And yet if we believe that Christ is our "life," it is impossible to avoid the conclusion that to be without Christ is death. Reason as well as revelation tells us that man has sinned, that "the wages of sin is death," and that this truth is as applicable to Asia and Africa as to Europe and America. We grant that it is possible that some who have never heard of Christ may be saved. The Spirit of God is not shut up to the methods that have been revealed to us. He works when and where and how He pleases. In ways unknown to us, He may apply the benefits of redemption to those who, without opportunity to accept the historic Christ, may live up to the light they have. Missionaries tell us that they seldom find such

[1] Cf. Foreword, p. xiv on use of word "heathen."

cases; but we should not dogmatize regarding every individual of the millions who have never been approached. Taking the heathen as we know them, however, it is sorrowfully, irrefutably true that they are living in known sin, and that by no possible stretch of charity can they be considered beyond the necessity for the revealed gospel. Various statements and figures are used in the New Testament to express the condition of those who know not Christ, but whether they are interpreted literally or figuratively, their fundamental meaning is plain. Jesus came "to save," and salvation is from something. A charitable hope that some are living like the pious Hebrews before the incarnation does not lessen our duty to give them the clearer knowledge which, like Simeon of old, they would eagerly welcome, nor does it modify in the least our obligation towards the masses who are living on a lower level. The light shines for all and those who see it must spread the tidings, for every man, however degraded, is

> "Heir of the same inheritance,
> Child of the self-same God.
> He hath but stumbled in the path
> We have in weakness trod."

(c) *The Command of Christ.*—The circumstances in which He expressed His wish were inexpressibly solemn. He had risen from the dead and was about to ascend to the Father. But ere He left His disciples, He said unto them: "All power is given unto Me in heaven and in earth. Go ye therefore, and teach all nations, baptizing them in the name of the Father, and of the Son, and of the Holy Ghost; teaching them to observe all things whatsoever I have commanded you: and lo, I am with you alway, even unto the end of the world." [1] A little later, He reiterated the charge: "Ye shall be witnesses unto Me both in Jerusalem, and in all Judea, and in Samaria, and unto the uttermost part of the earth." [2] "And He lifted

[1] Matt. 28: 18-20.   [2] Acts 1: 8.

up His hands, and blessed them."[1] "And a cloud received Him out of their sight."[2]

There is no gainsaying that command. Whether we consider the Person who gave it, the circumstances in which it was given, or the duty imposed, we must regard it as the weightiest of utterances. If it were the only motive, foreign missionary work would be a mechanical performance of duty, the missionary merely an obedient soldier; but taken in connection with the preceding motives, it adds the impressive sanctions of divine authority. It is the bugle call which to the true soldier never loses its thrilling, response-compelling power. It is not a request; not a suggestion. It leaves nothing to our choice. It is an order, comprehensive, unequivocal, a clear, peremptory, categorical imperative: "Go!"

No one can read the New Testament without seeing that the evangelization of the world was the supreme thought of Christ. He came into the world to save it. He sought, not merely for the rich and the influential, but for men as men, irrespective of their wealth or position. When the blind beggar cried out to Him for help, He said unto him: "Go thy way; thy faith hath made thee whole."[3] When He saw the famishing multitude, He "had compassion on them, because they were as sheep not having a shepherd."[4] He could not bear to see men perish, and the very thought of it caused Him keenest agony. He was Himself a missionary and His entire ministry was a missionary ministry. While His earthly life was confined to Palestine, He made it clear that the scope of His purpose was world-wide. He plainly said, "Other sheep I have, which are not of this fold: them also I must bring, and they shall hear My voice."[5] He declared that "God so loved the world that He gave His only begotten Son, that whosoever believeth in Him should not perish, but have everlasting life."[6] He taught the sublime truth of the fatherhood of God and the

[1] Luke 24: 50. [2] Acts 1: 9. [3] Mark 10: 52.
[4] Mark. 6: 34. [5] John 10: 16. [6] John. 3: 16.

brotherhood of man. He broke down the partition wall between Jew and Gentile. In an age when men regarded men of other races as foes, He said, "Love your enemies." He showed the race-proud Jews that the Samaritan was their "neighbour." Going "into the borders of Tyre and Sidon," He saved a poor Syrophenician woman.[1] From heaven He gave Paul his commission to the Gentiles. With a vision of world conquest, He exclaimed: "I say unto you that many shall come from the east and west, and shall sit down with Abraham, and Isaac, and Jacob, in the kingdom of heaven."[2] "And I, if I be lifted up from the earth, will draw all men unto Me";[3] while John declared that on Patmos he heard a voice saying, "I, Jesus, have sent Mine angel to testify unto you these things in the churches. . . . And the Spirit and bride say, Come. And let him that heareth say, Come. And let him that is athirst come. And whosoever will, let him take the water of life freely."[4]

And still the world's evangelization is His supreme thought. He is "the same yesterday, and to-day, and forever." He knows no distinction of race or caste. He loves men, and, as Phelps has said, the most attractive spots to Him are "those which 'are' crowded with the densest masses of human beings." Now, as of old, the Son of Man looks upon a sorrowing, dying world with pity unutterable. The author of "Beside the Bonnie Brier Bush" represents Lachlan Campbell as grieving over his erring daughter. Yet sinful though she was, he longed for her return, and in faith that she would come back, every evening when the shadows fell, he tremblingly lighted his best lamp, which was only used on special occasions, and set it in the window, that its light might shine "down the steep path" up which he fondly believed that Flora would yet come. In like manner, the Father of us all longs for our home coming. Indeed Christ says that when the

[1] Mark 7: 24-26. [2] Matt. 8: 11. [3] John 12: 32. [4] Rev. 22: 16, 17.

The Missionary Motive

prodigal "was yet a great way off, his father saw him and had compassion, and ran and fell on his neck, and kissed him." Seeing him "a great way off" of course means that He was looking for him, gazing often and with fatherly yearning far down the road on which He hoped and prayed and knew that the wanderer would soon come. Mrs. Browning truly says:

> "He's better to us than many mothers are,
> And children cannot wander beyond reach
> Of the sweep of His white raiment."[1]

His love comprehends and seeks the most distant. We complacently imagine that God loves us more than any other people, but the Shepherd who left the ninety and nine sheep in the wilderness and sought the one that was lost is surely most tenderly solicitous, not about us in our comfortable, gospel-lightened homes, but about the oppressed blacks of Africa and the starving millions of India. Whoever fancies that God does not love all men and that Christ does not desire the salvation of all men but dimly sees the truth. Jehovah is the God of the whole earth. Christ " is the propitiation for our sins; and not for ours only, but also for the sins of the whole world."[2]

Since the salvation of men is Christ's supreme thought, it should be ours. How is it possible for one who professes to follow Christ not to believe in missions, when missions is simply the organized effort to carry out the will of the Master? Has the Church entered into the mind of Christ regarding this matter? Men talk about heresy as if it related only to creed. Jesus said, "I and My Father are one;" but He also said, "Go ye into all the world and preach the gospel to every creature." Is it not as heretical to deny one statement as the other? Failure to do the will of Christ emasculates the essential idea of the Church. There may be a noble edifice, a large congregation, brilliant oratory, inspiring music, but if the Mas-

[1] "Aurora Leigh," Book Third.   [2] 1 John 2: 2.

ter's call is not heard and heeded, it cannot be a church of the living God.

Those who are solicitous about the salvation of the millions who die without having heard of Christ may well add some concern about the salvation of professed Christians who, with the Bible in their hands and the condition of the lost world before their eyes and the command of Christ sounding in their ears, manifest but languid interest in the effort to save the world. "Son of man, I have made thee a watchman; . . . therefore hear the word at my mouth. . . . When I say unto the wicked, 'Thou shalt surely die,' and thou givest him not warning; . . . the same wicked man shall die in his iniquity; but his blood will I require at thine hand."[1] It is difficult to understand how those who profess to serve Christ can be indifferent to the most important work which Christ has committed to His followers, or how they can expect His blessing while they neglect His specific injunction! "If a man love Me, he will keep My words," said Christ,[2] and the word is "go—preach." If we believe in Christ, we must believe in foreign missions.

Foreign missions, therefore, is not a side issue, the object of an occasional "collection"; it is the supreme duty of the Church, the main work of the Church. So the first disciples understood it, for they immediately went forth as missionaries. It is interesting to note that the word "apostle" is derived from a Greek word which means one sent forth, a messenger, and that the word "missionary" comes from an original which is simply the Latin equivalent of the Greek apostle. Therefore the modern apostle is the missionary, and while men at home are disputing over apostolic succession, the foreign missionaries, who are the real apostles of the present, are doing what their lineal predecessors did—"going away" from home to preach the gospel to the scattered nations of the

[1] Ezek. 3: 17, 18. [2] John 14: 20.

earth. The words "Go ye" surely mean that He intended every one of His disciples to have some part in the effort to make the gospel known to all men, either by personally going or by giving towards the support of those who do go. The obligation is squarely and heavily laid upon the conscience of every Christian. This majestic enterprise is therefore of divine authority. When a young clergyman asked the Duke of Wellington whether he did not deem it useless to attempt to convert India, the great general sternly replied: "What are your marching orders, sir?"

We may well be awed by the majesty of Christ's declaration. A lonely Nazarene, surrounded by a handful of humble followers, calmly bidding them carry His teaching to the most distant nations. They were not to confine their efforts to their own country. "Every creature" must be reached. We are to begin with the man on our right hand and belt the globe until we come back to the man on our left hand. No exceptions are to be made. Christ did not say: "Teach all nations save those that you deem beneath you"; nor did He say: "Preach to every creature, except the Hindu and Buddhist and Mohammedan, who have religions of their own." He made the scope of His command absolutely universal.

It is the purpose of God, said Paul, "to reconcile all things unto Himself." We should never lose sight of the grandeur of this conception. Christianity is not a life-boat sent out to a sinking ship to rescue a few passengers and let the rest go to the bottom. It will save all the passengers, unless they refuse to be saved, and it will save the ship. The Bible looks to a redeemed earth. Let us hope and pray and work for nothing short of that stupendous consummation. Limiting the grace of God, doubting its adequacy for all men, acting as if it were for America and not for Africa and the islands of the sea, are sins against the Holy Ghost.

These are and ever must remain the primary motives of the missionary enterprise. There are others, however, of a secondary character, which are influential with many people and which may be briefly enumerated:

(*a*) *The Philanthropic Motive.*—This is stirred by the consciousness of human brotherhood and the natural desire to relieve the appalling suffering and ignorance which prevail throughout the heathen world. Christ is the Great Physician now as of old. As we see the prevalence of disease and misery, the untended ulcers, the sightless eyes to which the surgeon's skill could bring light, the pain-racked limbs pierced with red-hot needles to kill the alleged demon that causes the suffering, and the fevered bodies that are made ten times worse by the superstitious and bungling methods of treatment, our sympathies are profoundly moved and we freely give and labour that such agony may be alleviated. Medical missions with their hospitals and dispensaries strongly appeal to this motive, as do also the educational missions with their teaching of the principles of better living. The gospel itself is sometimes preached and supported from this motive, for it is plain that the sufferings of men are diminished and the dignity and the worth of life increased by the application of the principles of Christianity to human society.

(*b*) *The Intellectual Motive.*—Missionaries have vastly increased the world's store of useful knowledge. They have opened vaguely known lands. They have probably done more than any other class of men to extend a knowledge of the earth's surface and its inhabitants. Geography and ethnology, entomology and zoology, botany and kindred sciences gratefully enroll the names of missionaries among their most successful explorers, and many thoughtful men appreciate this and give their sympathy to the cause which the missionaries represent.

(*c*) *The Commercial Motive.*—The missionary is the representative of a higher civilization. His teaching and his manner of living incidentally, but none the less really, create wants and introduce goods. He lights his house with a lamp, and straightway thousands of the natives become dissatisfied with a bit of rag burning in a dish of vegetable oil. So foreign lamps are being used by millions of Chinese, Japanese, and Siamese and East Indians. The missionary marks time with a clock, and German, English and American firms suddenly find a new and apparently limitless market for their products. He rides a bicycle on his country tours, and the result is that to-day the bicycle is as common in the cities and many of the villages of Siam and Japan as it is in the United States. His wife makes her own and her children's dresses on a sewing-machine, and ten thousand curious Chinese, Japanese, and Laos are not satisfied till they have sewing-machines. And so the missionary opens new markets and extends trade. He has been one of the most effective agents of modern commerce, not because he intended to be, not because he reaped any personal profit from the goods that he introduced, but because of the inevitable tendencies that were set in motion by the residence of an enlightened family among unenlightened people. And this appeals to some minds as a motive of missionary interest. It begets hundreds of addresses on the reflex influence of foreign missions and it undoubtedly secures some support for the cause from those who might not be responsive to the other arguments.

(*d*) *The Civilizing Motive.*—This is closely allied to the preceding motives. In the ways that have been indicated and in others that might be specified, the missionary is "the advance agent of civilization." As the product of centuries of Christian civilization with all its customs and ideals, he appears in a rude village in Africa. He opposes slavery, polygamy, cannibalism and infanticide. He teaches the boys to be honest, sober and thrifty; the girls to be pure, intelligent and industrious. He induces the natives to cover their nakedness, to build houses and to till the soil. He inculcates and exemplifies the social and civic virtues. His own home and his treatment of his wife and daughters are object lessons in a community which had always treated woman as a slave. The inertia of long-established heathenism is hard to overcome, but slowly it yields to the new power and the beginning of civilized society gradually appears. Volumes might be filled with the testimonies of statesmen, travellers, military and naval officers to the value of missionary work from this viewpoint. Ask almost any public man to speak at a missionary meeting, and he will probably respond with an address in which he enlarges upon this aspect of missionary effort. The British officials in India have been outspoken in their praise of the civilizing influence of missionaries in that country. Darwin's testimony to the usefulness of missionary work in the South Seas is a classic illustration and hundreds of others might be cited. Dr. James S. Dennis has collected a vast mass of facts bearing on this subject in his noble volumes on "Christian Missions and Social Progress" and the cumulative power of this class of evidence is doubtless a large factor in the growing respect for missions in the public mind.

(*e*) *The Historical Motive.*—With many people of the utilitarian type, the argument from results is the most decisive. They want to see that their money accomplishes something, to know that their investment is yielding some tangible return. They eagerly scan missionary reports to ascertain how many converts have been made, how many pupils are being taught, how many patients are being treated. To tell them of successes achieved is the surest method of inducing them to increase their gifts. Mission boards often find it difficult to sustain interest in apparently unproductive fields, but comparatively easy to arouse enthusiasm for fields in which converts are quickly made. The churches are eager and even impatient for results. Fortunately, in many lands results have been achieved on such a scale as to satisfy this demand. But in other lands not less important, weary years have had to be spent in preparing the soil and sowing the seed, and hard-working missionaries have been half disheartened by the insistent popular demand for accounts of baptisms before the harvest time has fairly come.

There is, apparently, a growing disposition to exalt this whole class of motives. The basis of the missionary appeal has noticeably changed within the last generation. Our humanitarian, commercial and practical age is more impressed by the physical and temporal, the actual and the utilitarian. The idea of saving men for the present world appeals more strongly than the idea of saving them for the next world, and missionary sermons and addresses give large emphasis to these motives. We need not and should not undervalue them. They are real. It is legitimate and Christian to seek the temporal welfare of our fellow men, to alleviate their distresses, to exalt woman and to purify society. It is, moreover, true and to the credit of the missionary enterprise that it widens the area of the world's useful knowledge, introduces the conveniences and necessities of Christian civilization, and promotes wealth and power, while it is certainly reasonable that those who toil should desire to see some results from their labour and be encouraged and incited to renewed diligence by the inspiring record of achievements.

But these motives are nevertheless distinctly secondary. They are effects of the missionary enterprise rather than causes of it, and the true Christian would still be obliged to give and pray and work for the evangelization of the world even if not one of these motives existed. Moreover with the wider diffusion of knowledge, some of these considerations are becoming relatively less important. Men who are not Christians at all can, and as a matter-of-fact do, travel and study in non-Christian lands. Trade, as we have seen elsewhere,[1] disseminates vices as well as virtues. Japan, India and the Philippines have educational systems which give excellent secular training. As for civilization, some non-Christian lands

---

[1] "New Forces in Old China," pp. 124*sq.*

already have civilizations of their own, more ancient than ours and, so far as moral questions are not involved, quite as well adapted to their needs, while our own civilization is not by any means wholly Christian. Whether men are civilized or not, and whether they trade with us or not, we must continue our missionary work. The achievements of a hundred years of missionary effort are encouraging; but if they were not, our duty would not be affected. We are to do what is right, though we never see visible results. Christ's life was a failure, from the viewpoint of His own generation; so were the efforts of Paul and Peter and Stephen; but later generations saw the rich fruitage. Like them, the true missionary toils from motives that are independent of present appearances. He knows that he is working with God, for God and in obedience to God, and, with Faber, he is confident that in the end,

> "He always wins who sides with God;
> With Him no chance is lost."

Still less do the changes in the political and economic life of the world, in the attitude of the Christian nations towards the non-Christian and their attitude in return towards us, impair the primary missionary motives. Rather do they increase it. There may indeed be a change of emphasis in the motives that prompt men to engage in it. Some that stirred our fathers are not as strongly operative to-day, but others have emerged that were then but vaguely discerned.

It is generally recognized now that, in the future, mission work must be prosecuted amid changed conditions. Our constituency has a knowledge of the non-Christian world that in the past it did not have. Men in our churches are no longer so ignorant of other peoples. Books and magazine articles have dissipated the mystery of the Orient. Electricity enables the newspapers to tell us every morning what occurred yesterday in Seoul and Peking, in Rangoon and Teheran. Our treatment of the Chinese and the Negro testify to the fact that race prejudice is still strong. Nevertheless, the white man does not look down upon the man of other races as he did a century ago. He recognizes more clearly the good qualities that some of the non-Christian peoples possess. He hears more of the industry of the Chinese and the intellect of the Hindu. This recognition is not unmingled with fear. No white man of to-day despises the Japanese, certainly not in Russia, nor can any one view with unconcern the evidences of awakening and powerful national life among the teeming myriads of the Oriental world.

The transition from the first century of Protestant missions to the second century is attended by no more significant change than this. People at home are no longer under illusions as to what the non-Christians are, and non-Christians are no longer under illusions as to what we are. The romance of missions in the popular mind has been dispelled. The missionary is no longer a hero to the average Christian, but a man with a message to his fellow man.

There are, too, certain movements of theological thought which must be considered. Whatever we may think of them, we cannot ignore their prevalence, nor should we argue that they are inconsistent with missionary interest. No man should be allowed to feel that he is exempt from the missionary obligation because he is not influenced by our particular motive, or because he adopts a different interpretation of the Bible teaching regarding certain doctrines. We may deplore his interpretation, but we cannot admit that it releases him from the duty of coöperating in this work. Every man who believes in God and who finds joy in Christ, aye, every man who receives the benefits of Christianity, whether he is personally a disciple of Christ or not, is bound to aid the effort to communicate those benefits to races that do not have them.

No changes that have taken place or that can possibly take place can set aside the great central facts that Jesus Christ means the temporal and eternal salvation of men; that it is the duty of those who know Him to tell others about Him; that no matter how distant the ignorant may be, no matter how different in race, we must get to them. There may be questions as to method, but no objection lies against the essential enterprise that does not lie with equal force against the fundamental truths of the Christian religion. Through all the tumult of theological strife, the one figure that is standing out more and more clearly and commandingly before men is the figure of the Son of Man, the Divine and Eternal Son of the Ever-Living God. In Him is the true unity of the race and around Him cluster its noblest activities. No matter how much Christians may differ as to other things, they will be more and more agreed as to the imperative duty and the inspiring privilege of preaching Jesus Christ to the whole world.

II

THE MISSIONARY AIM

IT is important that both the missionary abroad and the Church at home should have a clear idea of the aim of the missionary enterprise. The motives stated in the preceding chapter prompt gifts and prayers for the cause and perhaps a strong desire to go to the foreign field. But what object is the missionary to seek when he gets there and by what methods is he to accomplish his purpose? Of course all know in a general way that it is proposed to convert the heathen; but beyond that, many who support the work and even some who apply for appointment appear to have only vague ideas. But the missionary movement is not a mere crusade. It has certain definite aims, and these aims must be kept clearly in mind if the work is to be intelligently and efficiently done.

We need not repeat the negative considerations in the first chapter further than to state that as it is not the motive, neither is it the aim of the missionary to improve men's physical condition as such or to increase the world's knowledge or to extend trade or to civilize the heathen. These are concomitants and results of the missionary enterprise, but they are not what the missionary primarily seeks. His aim is something more fundamental.

First of all, the aim is to present Christ so intelligently to men that they will accept Him as their personal Saviour. More is involved in this than might at first be supposed. He who would achieve this immediate aim must first know Christ himself, must exemplify the spirit of Christ in his daily life, must know the language of the people to whom he is to preach and must know how to win and hold the attention of men of a different race and temper of mind. Some of these points are so important that they require the special consideration that will be given in later chapters. Other points will doubtless occur to the thoughtful reader.

Emphasis should be laid upon the words intelligently known. This idea excludes the hurried and the superficial presentation of the gospel. It is not enough to go into a heathen community, proclaim Christ for a few days or even for a few months, and then pass on in the belief that we have discharged our responsibility. Even Americans and Europeans with all their general knowledge do not grasp new ideas so quickly as that and we cannot reasonably expect other races to do so. To a large part of the non-Christian world, Christ is still unknown even by name, and a large majority of those who have heard of Him know Him only in such a general way as most people in this country have heard of Mencius or Zoroaster. Of his real character and relation to men, they know nothing, nor does it ever occur to them that they are under any obligation to Him. Moreover, what little they have heard of Him as a historical personage is beclouded and distorted by all the inherited and hostile presumptions of age-old prejudices, superstitions and spiritual deadness. In such circumstances, to make Christ intelligently known is apt to be a long and perhaps a wearisome effort. Carey in India and Morrison in China toiled seven years before their hearts were gladdened by one solitary convert. Tyler in South Africa saw fifteen laborious years pass before the first Zulu accepted Christ, while Gilmour preached for twenty years in Mongolia before visible results appeared. After the heathen mind once fairly grasps the new truth, progress usually becomes more rapid, but at first and sometimes for long periods, it is apt to be painfully slow. The missionary and the church that supports him often have need of patience.

This becomes more clear when we remember that our immediate aim includes conversions. We are to make Christ so

The Missionary Aim

intelligently known to men *that they will accept Him as their personal Saviour*. We cannot agree with those who urge that the worker has no responsibility for results. It is true that regeneration is the work of the Holy Spirit and that the number of converts is not always a safe criterion of the faithfulness of Christian work. Stephen preached as earnestly as Peter, but instead of seeing three thousand converts, he was stoned. Paul preached magnificently on Mars Hill, but only a few believed. It is also true that the effect of missionary work is to be seen, not simply in accessions to the Church, but in the changed spirit of communities, and that schools, hospitals, printing presses and churches may accomplish much for God in undermining evils, purifying society and edifying those who are already Christians.

Whatever we may say, however, of the Holy Spirit as the sole author of regeneration, it is undoubtedly true that as a rule God associates conversions with the faithful preaching of His Word and with personal work for the unsaved, and that if conversions do not follow such effort, workers should seek the reason upon their knees. If it be replied that much of missionary work is necessarily preparatory, we grant it. Seed-sowing is not only a necessary but sometimes a long and toilsome process. And yet Christian workers both at home and abroad have sometimes unduly solaced themselves for delayed harvests by the thought that they were sowing the seed. "Must we be forever and forever preparing the way and sowing the seed and devising processes, while the centuries roll by? Believe mightily in the things God has promised. Give tremendous emphasis to the idea of expecting and commanding immediate results. 'Say not ye, There are yet four months and then cometh harvest.' The harvest is now—is *now*, is always NOW."[1]

In urging large emphasis on the evangelistic phases of the

---

[1] The Rev. Dr. Herrick Johnson.

work, we are not unmindful of the value of other forms of missionary activity. The missionary is following the example of Christ in alleviating the bodily sufferings of men, while it is absolutely necessary to translate and print the Bible, to create a Christian literature, to teach the young and to train them for leadership in the coming Church. Man must be influenced at every stage of his career and shown that Christianity is adapted to his present state as well as to his future life. Nevertheless, hospitals and schools and presses are means, not ends. The aim is not philanthropic or educational or literary, but spiritual. The boards do not send out mere physicians or school-teachers or business men, but missionaries, and those who are engaged in healing or teaching or translating or printing should take special care to keep the spiritual object uppermost, so that they may be as distinctively missionaries as the ordained ministers of the Word.

The missionary may be of inestimable service to heathen lands and to the world in intellectual ways. He may increase our knowledge of ancient languages and literature. He may introduce the science and civilization and learning of the Occident and so contribute to the material and social awakening of the nations. He may make a name for himself in ethnology or botany, in ornithology or entomology. But whatever he may or may not do in these directions, he should never forget that the supreme need of men is the knowledge of Jesus Christ and that he goes as the bearer of that knowledge.

Every missionary, therefore, whatever his special department, should make a direct, earnest, prayerful effort to lead souls to Christ. Every teacher should seek the conversion of scholars; every physician the cure of souls; every wife the salvation of heathen mothers and children. In the home, in the school, in the hospital, by the wayside, in the marketplace, anywhere and everywhere that opportunity offers or can be made, the gospel should be set forth. No thought of the next generation should blind him to his duty to this one, nor

The Missionary Aim

should the missionary be content with any mere civilizing or educating or healing which, however indispensable as means, yet as ends only make man a more comfortable and respectable animal and leave him on the same moral plane on which he was before. It is a new birth, an internal, not an external transformation, that men most vitally need.

This personal presentation of Christ with a view to men's acceptance of Him as Saviour is to issue as soon as possible in the organization of converts into self-propagating, self-supporting and self-governing churches. This is a vital part of the missionary aim. In the words of Lawrence: "God's great agent for the spread of His kingdom is the Church, and missions exist distinctly for the Church. . . . Then the Church of each land, thus planted, must win its own people to Christ."[1] Christianity will not control a nation's life as long as it is an exotic. It must become an indigenous growth. To this end, effort must be put forth to develop the independent energies of the converts. The new convert is usually a spiritual child, and like the physical child, he must be for a time "under tutors and governors;" but the instruction looks to the development of self-reliant character. Missionaries may, at first, do the local preaching, but as fast as suitable natives develop, they should be set to work as helpers, Bible-readers, colporteurs, while the most capable should be put in charge of churches.

Self-propagation, therefore, should be insisted upon as soon as converts appear. They should be taught from the beginning that as soon as they become Christians, the missionary motive should become operative within them, and that they are under precisely the same obligation as Christians in Europe and America to give the knowledge of Christ to others. The missionaries who have most clearly discerned and effectively acted upon this principle have witnessed the most gratifying progress of the work.

[1] "Modern Missions in the East," p. 31.

This was the way Christ Himself worked during His earthly ministry. He preached both to individuals and to multitudes wherever and whenever He had opportunity; but one of His chief efforts was to train up a band of disciples to perpetuate and extend the work after His departure. Paul also worked in this way. He would go to a city, preach the gospel, gather a band of disciples, organize them into a church, remain long enough to get them fairly started and then go elsewhere.

The modern missionary will have to remain a good deal longer than Paul did, for he does not find such prepared conditions as the great apostle found in the Jews of the dispersion. A land may be evangelized in a generation, but the Christianizing of it may be the toilsome process of centuries. Moreover, when the object has been attained in one country, the responsibility of the missionary and of the home Church will not cease, but simply be transferred to other populations. It is a long campaign upon which we have entered, but we should resolutely keep our purpose in mind.

This is not only wise in itself from the viewpoint of the success and permanency of the work, but it is absolutely necessary from the viewpoint of the men and money that are available. It is impossible for the churches of Europe and America to send out and maintain enough missionaries to preach the gospel effectively to each one of the thousand millions of the unevangelized world. To attempt this would be as foolish as it would be for a government to make an army out of major-generals while making no provision for subalterns, non-commissioned officers and privates.

The mission boards are studying this question with a care not unmingled with anxiety. Letters from the field indicate that the outlook is more encouraging than ever before. Doors of opportunity are opening on every side and there appears to be no limit to the work that might be done if the men and the means could be had. Naturally, therefore, the missions are calling for reinforcements. In a single year, the calls upon the Presbyterian Board alone aggregated no less than two hundred and fifteen new missionaries, exclusive of wives. It is painfully apparent that the boards are not likely to get anything like the sum that would be needed to send out and maintain such an enlarged force. Nor are the men available. In the year referred to, the Presbyterian Board did its utmost to secure them and appointed every qualified candidate. Yet the total number was only forty-two out of the two hundred and fifteen asked for.

Some may wonder why the Student Volunteer Movement, of whose thousands we hear so much, does not supply this need. It must be remembered, however, that the Student Volunteers include young people of all denominations and in all stages of education, so that the number of any one denomination graduating in a given year is not so great after all. Moreover, many of them find that, on account of conditions that could not be foreseen, they are unable to go to the foreign field, while others have to be declined by the boards because they are found to lack the necessary qualifications. The Movement enrolls only those who give reasonable promise of usefulness, but of course it cannot always know what a student may develop by the completion of his course. The Movement is doing a splendid work. It is supplying a large majority of the new missionaries and has undoubtedly saved the boards from what would otherwise have been a disastrous lack of candidates.

Taking the situation as a whole, it is plain that the boards cannot get enough new missionaries to meet all the demands that are coming from the foreign field, that if they could get them, they could not secure the money to cover such a large expansion of the work and that it would not be wise to flood the foreign field with a host of missionaries even if they could be found and supported. An India missionary writes:

"The force that we have in the station at present is such that the united touring possibilities are probably one person for one hundred days each year. At this rate, with the present force, it would take one hundred and eighty years to preach the gospel once to the present inhabitants of the district. . . . We need at once, in order to preach the gospel till all have heard it, forty-five new missionaries. Fewer than these will not properly man the field."

Such an appeal ignores the part that the native Church is to play in the evangelization of India. It apparently assumes that the Indian Christians have no responsibility in making Christ known to their countrymen, or that they will not discharge it, and that the entire burden of evangelizing India rests so exclusively upon foreigners that the people will never hear the gospel unless great numbers of white men are sent to preach it. All missionaries do not fall into this error, for one of the oldest and wisest of the India missionaries wrote about the same time that there was danger that the mission would feel that such appeals were the easiest way to deal with its great responsibilities, when the divine plan would be for it to pursue the harder but more lasting method of raising up native workers. The native worker is better for this direct evangelism anyway. He can live far more economically than a foreigner and he has a knowledge of native idioms and ways of thinking and manners and customs that no foreigner can ever obtain. Moreover, there is no gulf of race between him and his countrymen. There is much about the Asiatic and the African that will ever remain inscrutable to the American and the European. The former, in particular, is apt to be secretive and to make his outward manner a mask behind which there may be thoughts wholly unsuspected to a foreigner. A man of the same race is able to get behind that mask, and just because he is a native and probably one of superior force of character, the people will be more influenced by him than by the missionary.

Most converts are made by such evangelists. Dr. John Ross, of Manchuria, in reporting 1,200 conversions to one of the Shanghai Conferences, said that " the first principles of

The Missionary Aim

Christian instruction were implanted almost invariably by the natives," and that he could not "trace more than four and twenty who were directly the converts of the foreign missionaries." Others at the conference declared that five hundred native evangelists would be a far greater power in China than five thousand foreigners.

This is not meant to minimize the need of reënforcements. The present force is far too small for effective superintendence in many fields. The home Church should not relax its efforts to provide a more adequate supply of foreign workers; but while it is doing this, the missions should give more persistent effort to the development of a native agency. The Rev. Dr. Albert A. Fulton, after an experience of nearly a quarter of a century in China, writes:

"I would require every missionary to raise up a large body of able native preachers. Every missionary worth his passage should be able to superintend the labours of fifty native evangelists. Granted that some of them will prove to be failures. So some missionaries and editors and doctors are failures. If you are going to wait for native preachers until you can find in every one an Apostle Paul, you will wait until the sun grows cold before China will be evangelized."

We are not unmindful of the practical difficulties that beset this problem. In hardly any other part of the mission work is there so much need of prudence. Hundreds of natives want employment who are quite unfit for it. Nor is every one who is willing to work without pay qualified for efficient service. But these difficulties, and others that might be mentioned, can and should be overcome. The more successful the work, the more essential it is to develop the native ministry that is indispensable to conserve the evangelistic results already attained and which we hope to attain in yet larger measure in the future. A foreign missionary represents an annual expenditure sufficient to maintain nearly a dozen native ministers, even when they are paid by the mission. The work will not be self-supporting in any proper sense, but on the contrary will become ruinously expensive if so large a part of it must continue to be performed by foreign missionaries instead of by a native ministry supported by the people. It has been well said that ordinations, and not baptisms, are the real guage of missionary success, and that if the work fails to produce them, something is wrong.

It will thus be seen that it is a serious mistake to regard evangelistic and educational work as rivals. They are simply phases of the common work and each is necessary to the success of the other. The teaching and the preaching missionary should therefore keep in close touch, and the former should train the kind of men that the other can use to advantage.

The native Church should be led to self-support as well as self-propagation. Here, also, the difficulties are formidable. The missionary goes to the heathen representing not only a superior, but a more expensive type of civilization. His scale of living, while moderate from our viewpoint, appears to them princely. Centuries of abject poverty and of despotic government have predisposed most Orientals to accept with eagerness whatever is given them. Accustomed to living, or rather half-starving, on an income of from thirty to one hundred dollars a year, the native regards the missionary on a salary of $1,500 or $2,000 not only as an individual of wealth, but as the representative of untold riches in America. He is therefore tempted to go to him for the sake of the loaves and fishes, and this temptation is enormously strengthened if he gets the impression that the missionary may employ him as a helper, or that some individual or society in America may support him.

The missionary, in turn, is tempted to the free use of money by the wretchedness of the people and by the prospect of the visible results which may be secured by a liberal financial policy. Would-be converts flock to him in such circumstances, many converts can be hired to apparent advantage, and buildings can be cheaply rented and furnished. But if he yields to the temptation, "he puts himself and the young church in a false relation at the outset. It is better to teach the converts to make their own arrangements, the missionary guiding by advice from his larger experience of their probable requirements, and only in the last resort giving pecuniary help." [1]

Experience has shown that a Church that is chiefly developed on foreign money is built on sand, and that when the storms come, it does not endure. In a few fields, one of the greatest obstacles to the development of the native Church lies in the past mistaken use of money. A whole generation of dependent Christians has been developed, Christians who resent pressure towards self-support as an infringement upon their rights and who do not appear to realize their obligation to live the Christian life without being paid for it by the foreigner. There are indeed some fields, notably Japan, where these difficulties do not exist, and other lands, like Korea and Uganda, where the policy of self-support has been so followed from the beginning that the native Christians have never had an opportunity to form the habit of financial dependence. But in some other fields, the difficulty is keenly felt.

The native pastors are not infrequently half-hearted in their advocacy of self-support, because they find that a salary paid by the mission is more regular and more easily secured than a salary raised by their own people, and that it gives them independence of restless members.

On this point we must be increasingly firm. To lead an able-bodied man to Christ does not involve responsibility for his temporal support. He made his living before his conversion; why should he not do so after it? Persecution may hinder him for a time; but better far that he should suffer a little than that he should be pauperized at the outset. Christianity does not unnerve a man. It increases his ability to

---

[1] Gibson, "Mission Problems and Mission Methods in South China," p. 193.

fight the battles of life. No native should ever be allowed to get the impression that if he becomes a Christian, he will be given a job and a salary, even though the job be so sacred a one as the preaching of the gospel.

Our duty is to start Christianity in Asia, not to run it, to give the gospel, to found its institutions, to aid them so far as necessary in their infancy, but to insist that as soon as practicable they shall stand upon their own feet. We must be patient and reasonable, for now, as of old, it is the common people who hear Him gladly, and in Asia the common people are pitifully poor. We must not withdraw aid so rapidly as to injure the work. But the spirit of self-help is as vital to character abroad as it is at home. Strength comes with independence, and we must not pauperize the Christians of Asia by an indiscriminate and unnecessary charity. They paid heavily for the support of their old religions, and there is no reason why they should not in time support their new faith.

It is important not to discourage the infant Church by unnecessary expenditures at the start. In planting Christianity in heathen lands, where, as a rule, the people are very poor, it is indispensable to project it upon a plane of inexpensiveness on which the people themselves can perpetuate it. Native preachers must do the great future work, and they must, as in other lands, live on salaries which their people can pay. This is not inconsistent with what was said about the importance of raising up an adequate number of native helpers. Some of these agents should undoubtedly be employed by the missions, but many should be maintained by their fellow Christians, while others should do Christian work in connection with their present occupations, just as thousands of consecrated men and women at home do. The votaries of other systems adopt this method. The Mormons and Christian Scientists in our own land, the Arya Somaj in India and the Mohammedans in India and Africa are conspicuous examples. "In a list of India missionaries (Moslem) published in the journal of a religious and philanthropic society of Lahore, we find the names of schoolmasters, government clerks in the canal and opium departments, traders, including a dealer in camel carts, an editor of a newspaper, a bookbinder, and a workman in a printing establishment. These men devote the hours of leisure left them after the completion of the day's labour to the preaching of their religion in the streets and bazaars of Indian cities, seeking to win converts from among Christians and Hindus, whose religious belief they controvert and attack."[1]

Some missionaries write that unless the board can send them more money, they might as well come home, as they "cannot make bricks without straw." Such missionaries always have their full salaries, house rent, medical attendance, furlough expenses and at least a small appropriation for their work.

We have scant sympathy with the idea that in such circumstances they cannot do enough to justify their presence on the field unless they have imported "straw." Adequate appropriations are, of course, highly desirable; but they are not indispensable. Any missionary can accomplish much that is worth while if he has nothing beside his own support, for he can get into sympathy with the natives, speak to them the message of Christ and exemplify that message by a life of loving helpfulness.

There is of course a legitimate use of foreign money in the earlier stages of the work. Infancy must be helped. The boards should make such appropriations as an equitable distribution of funds will permit for the employment of native evangelists and teachers; but the number should be limited to real needs and the salary should be only that which will enable them to live near the plane of their countrymen, while they should be made to understand clearly that this pecuniary arrangement is temporary. We must insist, in season and out of season, line upon line and precept upon precept, that while

[1] Arnold, "The Preaching of Islam."

the missionary, being a foreigner, will be maintained by the people of America, the native pastors must not look to the boards, but to their own people, for their permanent support. It will take a long time to reach it, but the ideal should be foreign money for foreign missionaries and native money for native workers.

Consider the example of Paul. He gave the infant churches under his care rich moral support and splendid spiritual leadership. He wrote them letters of Christian counsel. He revisited them as he had opportunity; but save in some temporary emergency, he left them financially to care for themselves and they had to stand on their own feet from the start or fall. We know that those early Christians did not fall, that they held their services in one another's houses or in the open air, that each man was a missionary for Christ among his friends and neighbours, and that they got along in that way until they were able to set apart one of their own number as a pastor and build a little church. And yet the Church grew mightily.

The apostolic method is as good now as it was then. We confidently preach that Christianity is inherently adapted to every people. Then it ought to be able to live among them, particularly in the Orient where it started. The Holy Spirit is not limited in His operations by the sums that are sent from the home land. Experience, from the days of the apostles down, has shown that the best missionary work has been done with very little money beyond that which was necessary to maintain the missionary himself. We should resist the temptation to an artificial numerical growth which the free use of money can beget, and remember that one vigorous, self-reliant church is worth more to the cause of Christ than a dozen that are dependent upon foreign money. There must, of course, be due regard to local conditions. Neither the missions nor the boards should violently revolutionize in fields where the opposite policy has been long pursued. Self-support cannot be attained by immediately discharging all aided workers, or by so reducing the work that nothing will be left to support. Change must be gradual; but no land will ever be evangelized until it has a self-propagating, self-governing native Church. Let us work and give and pray for this essential aim of missionary effort.

The self-government of the native Church will be considered in the chapter on the Missionary and the Native Church.

III

MISSIONARY ADMINISTRATION

WORLD evangelization being the supreme work of the Church, the method of administration should be commensurate in scope and dignity with the task to be performed. Such a work cannot be properly done by individuals or by congregations acting separately. It is too vast, the distance too great, the single act too small. Local churches do not have the experience in dealing with missionary problems or the comprehensive knowledge of details necessary for the proper conduct of such an enterprise. Moreover, the individual may die or lose his money. The single church may become indifferent or discouraged. Even if neither of these alternatives happened, the work would lack stability. It would be fitful, sporadic, too largely dependent upon accidental knowledge or temporary emotion. A chance newspaper article or a visit from some enthusiastic missionary might direct a disproportionate stream of gifts to one field, while others equally or perhaps more important, would be neglected. The wise expenditure of large sums of money in far distant lands, the checks and safe-guards essential to prudent control, the equitable distribution of workers and forms of work, the proper balancing of interests between widely-scattered and isolated points, the formulation of principles of mission policy—all these require a central, administrative agency.

This is a spiritual warfare on a vast scale, and war cannot be prosecuted by individuals fighting independently, however numerous or conscientious. There must be an army with its centralization of authority, its compactness of organization, its unity of movement, its persistence of purpose. The Japanese defeated the Chinese, not because they were abler, but because they were better organized. A church or a conference can, with comparative ease, supervise the simpler and more homogeneous work within its bounds and therefore under its immediate oversight; but the foreign missionary work is in distant lands, in different languages, among diverse peoples. It is, moreover, a varied and complex work, including not only churches, but day-schools, boarding schools, industrial schools, normal schools, colleges, academic, medical and theological, inquirers' classes, hospitals, dispensaries, the translation, publishing and selling of books and tracts, the purchase and care of property, the health and homes and furloughs of missionaries, fluctuating currencies of many kinds, negotiations with governments, and a mass of details little understood by the home Church. Problems and interrelations with other work and workers and questions of mission policy are involved, which, from the nature of the case, are entirely beyond the experience of the home minister and which call for an expert knowledge only possible to one who devotes his entire time to their acquisition. Missionary work has passed the experimental stage, and an apparently simple question may have bearings that even friends may not suspect. The experiment of having each state control its own regiments in a national war has been tried and with such disastrous results that it is not likely to be repeated. Dr. Cust says that "the conduct of missions in heathen and Mohammedan countries has already risen to the dignity of a science, only to be learned by long and continuous practice, discussion, reading and reflection; it is the occupation of the whole life and of many hours of each day of many able men selected for the particular purpose by the turns of their own minds, and the conviction of their colleagues that they have a special fitness for the duty."

Dr. William N. Clarke, of Colgate University, expresses the opinion that "the interdenominational societies that have arisen do not prove to bring any great contribution to this problem. They bring individuals from various denominations to their aid, but they generally hold such special views or employ such special methods as to be virtually denominational after all. No undenominational movement has arisen, or seems likely soon to arise, that is capable of standing as successor to the great denominational agencies."[1]

Mr. Wm. T. Ellis, who made a special investigation of missionary work in 1907, wrote from Asia:

"My own observation leads me to conclude that they (independent missionaries) make more stir in the home land, where their money is being raised, than they do here. They are usually temporary, since they depend upon one man, and cannot continue beyond the term of his personal residence here. He, in turn, is so busy keeping alive the interest of his supporters that he has little time left for actual work among the Japanese. . . . The only effectual missionary work that can be pursued is that conducted on a broad basis and a long continued plan by the great churches of Japan and of Christian lands."

The wise student volunteer will bear these considerations in mind, and make his application to an established agency, which has a broader basis and more permanent guarantees than the enthusiasm or peculiar doctrines of an individual.

It is interesting to remember that prior to the organization of their board, Presbyterians thoroughly discussed the question whether missionary operations should be carried on by independent societies or by the Church itself. The result was the decision of the General Assembly of 1837, "that the General Assembly shall superintend and conduct by its own proper authority the work of foreign missions of the Presbyterian Church by a board appointed for that purpose and directly amenable to said Assembly." This was clearly the wise course under the Presbyterian system. A denomination would be

[1] "A Study of Christian Missions," p. 160.

false to its highest duty, it would abdicate its claim upon Christ's promise to be with His disciples "alway," if it confined its organized energies to its own land and relegated its most important activities to outside societies, characterized perhaps by doctrinal vagaries and irresponsible leadership, and, however ably and conscientiously led, with no guaranty for responsibility or permanence but the personal character of the men who for the hour control them. It is fundamental to any sound thinking on this subject that the foreign missionary enterprise is not something outside and voluntary, but that it is the inherently vital work and obligation of the Church itself.

It is neither safe nor businesslike for the Church to leave such an undertaking to outsiders. The Lord's work calls for business methods as well as man's work. The Church must take up this matter itself. It must form some responsible agency, whose outlook is over the whole field, and through which individuals and churches can work collectively and to the best advantage; some lens which shall gather up all the scattered rays of local effort and focus them where they are needed; some institution which, though "men may come and men may go," shall itself "go on forever." Recognizing these things, each of the leading denominations has constituted a board of foreign missions as the great channel through which it shall unitedly, wisely, and systematically carry on this work for humanity and God.

All auxiliary denominational agencies are supposed to cooperate with this board, sending their money to it for administration. There is no exception to this in most churches; but in a few, as for example, the Methodist Episcopal Church, the woman's societies are separately organized and administer their own funds. Every secretary could speak warmly appreciative words of the loyalty and efficiency of many of these organizations. The increasing intelligence and zeal with which they are prosecuting their work are among the encouraging signs of the time.

The organic relation of a board to the Church that it represents is naturally affected by the ecclesiastical system that is involved. The Methodist Episcopal, Protestant Episcopal, Presbyterian and other bodies that have an authoritative denominational organization, have created boards that are directly amenable to the supreme judicatories of the Church. Churches like the Baptist and Congregational, that do not have such denominational organization, or that, like the Church of England, have more than one board of foreign missions, act through missionary societies which, though having no formal relation to an ecclesiastical body, are nevertheless distinctively church agencies with the same scope and authority as other boards. The societies of these churches are not, therefore, " independent," in the sense in which we have used that term.

Usage differs as to name. Some denominations prefer the term society. Others vest administration of their missionary work in Executive Committees. The Congregational Church employs the term Prudential Committee, while the Presbyterian and Reformed Churches use Boards. But whatever the name, the functions are practically the same, except that in the churches whose form of government is episcopal, the local bishop on the field exercises some of the powers that are committed to the boards of the non-episcopal churches.

The method of selection also varies. In churches that have a governing judicatory, the members of the board are chosen by that judicatory. In the Methodist Episcopal Church, the General Conference appoints a Board of Managers consisting of thirty-two ministers and thirty-two laymen together with thirty-two bishops who are ex-officio members, making the total membership ninety-six. In the Protestant Episcopal Church, the Presiding Bishop and the National Council of twenty-four members are charged with the " unification, development and prosecution of the missionary, educational and social work of the Church." The Presbyterian General Assembly elects a Board of forty members, fifteen ministers, fifteen women and ten laymen. In churches of the Congregational polity, the method is, of course, different. The nine original members of the American Board were appointed by the General Association of Massachusetts in June, 1810. The membership now consists of 225 corporate members who are elected by the Board from representative men all over the country, though to avoid confusion it should be borne in mind that the term board as used by the Congregational Church does not refer to the executive body that is styled board in this book, these functions being discharged by a Prudential Committee of thirty-eight elected by the American Board. In the Northern Baptist Church, the corresponding body is called the Foreign Mission Society, composed of men and women appointed by Baptist churches and accredited delegates to each annual meeting of the Northern Baptist Convention. The Board of Managers consists of twenty-eight members, including the president of the Society. The Managers appoint several standing committees with responsibility for various phases of work, but all matters relating to missionary policy, appointment of missionaries, etc., are determined by the Managers. This Board, like the Prudential Committee of the American Board, is the real board in the sense in which the term is popularly understood. With the Southern Baptists, the board is an administrative body of the Southern Baptist Convention. As a rule, all the boards or committees are divided into three classes, each class serving three years. Usually too, the majority of the members live in or near the city in which the board is located, because " experience has proved that a few men, each of whom can be easily reached, all of whom have a vital interest in the trusts confided to them, will perform any given labour more efficiently than a large board whose members are so diffused as to be seldom collected, or as to forget the claims of a duty whose immediate field is far away." [1]

---

[1] Presbyterian General Assembly, 1870.

But though the members of a board are chosen from one part of the country, they are not sectional in spirit. There are no wiser ministers in the country than those who are on our boards of foreign missions. There are no more sagacious business men than the lay members of those boards. Those who sneer at mission boards forget that they are composed not only of distinguished clergymen, but of bank presidents, successful merchants, railroad directors, great lawyers, managers of large corporations—men who in the commercial world are recognized as authorities and are implicitly trusted. Is their judgment of less value when they deal with the extension of the Kingdom of God?

These men devote much time and labour to the affairs of the boards, leaving their own work, often at great inconvenience, to attend board meetings and committees, earnestly and prayerfully considering the things that pertain to this sacred cause. Yet they receive no compensation whatever, freely giving the Church the benefit of their ripe experience and business capacity. It would be necessary to pay a large sum to command their services for any other cause, if indeed they could be commanded at all. One of them has said: "I could not be hired to do this work for $5,000 a year, but I will do it gratuitously for the sake of Christ and my brethren." The churches owe much to their boards. Whatever their shortcomings, they are unselfishly and self-sacrificingly administering the great trust that has been committed to them, and though they may make an occasional mistake, their loyalty, devotion, and intelligence are a reasonable guaranty that they will wisely serve the cause that is as dear to them as to others.

The executive officer of a board is the secretary, the larger boards having several secretaries. Some make the treasurer also an executive officer, but others do not. These officers are usually elected by the board, but sometimes, as in the Methodist Church, by the General Conference. The editor of *The Interior*, in discussing the personnel of the mission

Missionary Administration

boards, says that "so far from a ministerial life unfitting a man for practical affairs, the Church has command of the best brains in the country for the least money, and makes fewer business mistakes than the great corporations of which we hear so much." Devoting their entire time to the great interests entrusted to their supervision, secretaries of course receive a salary, though it is modest compared with the salaries paid by the larger city churches. It may interest some who imagine that a secretaryship is one of the soft seats in Zion to know that Dr. Wm. N. Clarke says that "in respect of responsibility and laboriousness, there is scarcely any other Christian service that is comparable to that of the officers of such societies. Missionary secretaries have to conduct a work of which the delicacy and difficulty are very largely unappreciated. It can scarcely be otherwise, for very few persons know missionary operations from the inside, and most Christians have no experience that would help them to enter into the problems of the missionary board."[1] Dr. Henry H. Jessup, of Syria, testifies out of his personal experience as a substitute during the illness of a secretary: "Among the hardest-worked men in the missionary ranks are the secretaries and treasurer of the board. After three months of the mental and physical strain of a secretary, the dread nineteenth century malady, nervous prostration, laid me aside."

The boards meet regularly once or twice each month. The docket often includes forty or fifty items and comprehends phases of Christian work which in America are usually distributed among half a dozen different boards, besides several undenominational and philanthropic agencies. Each denomination, however, has but one foreign board, and that single agency must concern itself not only with informing the churches and developing their interests and gifts, but with a multitude of details incident to the conduct of so vast and

---

[1] "A Study of Christian Missions," p. 127.

varied an enterprise and its related financial, industrial, political, educational, medical, and diplomatic problems.

"The offices of one of our great societies are as busy a hive of workers as any financial or mercantile institution. Receipts of sums varying from a few cents to thousands of dollars, and in many cases aggregating over a million, are recorded, acknowledged, cared for; accounts are kept with every variety of manufacturer and merchant; payments are made through the great banking houses of Europe and Asia to thousands of agents in every country, American and foreign; correspondence affecting not merely the spiritual but temporal welfare of millions upon millions of people is carefully considered and filed away for reference at any moment; books are published in widely different languages; large investments in real estate and in buildings are made; diplomatic questions, sometimes of immense importance, are considered. In fact, there is probably no other organization in the world, except a national government, that carries on so varied and as important lines of business as does a foreign missionary society." [1]

Regarding the Methodist Board, the Rev. Dr. James M. Buckley writes: "To be conversant with its work is to have a liberal education on the subject of missions. The Committee is made up for the most part of leaders of the Church. It would be impossible to find a better place for the study of national and international facts, tendencies and forces. Within the Committee's membership are men who can speak with definite personal knowledge concerning the conditions of life in every part of the inhabited world. Detailed information is given concerning each field both at home and abroad. Under the Committee's careful scrutiny from year to year passes the consideration of the important events that transpire upon the wide, wide field upon which universal Methodism is carrying forward her ministries of blessing. The significance of these events, especially

---

[1] The Rev. Edwin M. Bliss, D. D.

their relation to the growth of the kingdom of God, is taken into account and becomes the basis of the ever-watchful policy of the Society. Here are scholars, diplomats, statesmen; here are also wise, far-seeing business men of great good sense, of large and successful experience. Great world movements are discussed in the most intelligent and edifying manner by broad men of foresight, insight, and outlook. Provincialism has no bearing. Narrowness may not survive in an atmosphere like this."

The board is divided into committees representing the various mission fields, and there is, in addition, a finance committee to advise with the treasurer on the details of his office. The administration of the larger boards is divided into departments, each officer conducting the correspondence relating to his own department. Of course, much of that correspondence is with the individual missionary, for the secretary tries to keep in close touch with him and to form the channel through which the interest and cheer and love of the home churches flow out to the lonely workers far away. Questions affecting mission expenditure and policy, however, and all official requests to the board, the secretary takes into the "executive council" which is composed of all the officers of the board. In that council each question is discussed and a judgment reached, which at the next meeting of the board is presented to that body by the secretary in charge, and the action is not complete until it has been ratified by the board. Questions of special importance are considered by a committee of the board in conjunction with the council. It will thus be seen that there is little opportunity for one-man power in the workings of a board, inasmuch as each secretary must submit his conclusions for the approval, first, of the council, and, second, of the board itself, and, in special cases, of a committee besides.

In the handling of money great care is taken. Not only is every sum received promptly acknowledged to the giver, but a public report is made in the annual report of the board which is printed and mailed to each minister in the denomination, while extra copies are freely given to any layman who requests them. Some boards, in addition, print their receipts each month in their missionary magazines. An annual contract is made by many of the boards with a firm of certified public accountants, whose representatives walk into the office at any time, take possession of all books and vouchers and audit all accounts, making their report, not to the treasurer, but directly to the finance committee of business men. In this, as well as in other ways, every possible precaution is taken to secure entire accuracy, and so great is the care exercised and so complete is the system, that it is not believed that any serious mistake could escape prompt detection. In 1897, a Buffalo banker and a Pittsburg merchant made an exhaustive examination of the financial methods of the Presbyterian Board, and they bore "testimony to the complete and businesslike methods that are followed in the office management, which we believe are fully up to the best practice in the leading financial and industrial institutions of the country, and give assurance that the business entrusted to this office is promptly, efficiently, and economically conducted." Like testimony would have followed an inquiry into the methods of other boards. The editor of *The Interior* declares that "it can be proven that no trust company handles more money at a less expense, with smaller per cent. of loss, than the benevolent agencies of our Church."

Several of the members and officers of the board are or have been pastors, and the others are members and contributing lay officers of churches. They know, therefore, apart from the board's correspondence, that the money they receive comes not only from the rich but from the poor; that it includes the widow's mite, the working man's hard-earned wage, and that it is followed on its mission of blessing by the prayers of loving hearts. "I went without breakfast for a week to save this money," wrote a poor washerwoman as she sent her offering. "I am sorry that I cannot give more, but I have been sick

Missionary Administration

and obliged to hire some one to take my place," wrote an aged coloured woman, who earned a scanty living by sweeping offices, and who enclosed two dollars. So the boards regard that money as a sacred thing, a trust to be expended with more than ordinary care.

Each mission is required to make an estimate of its needs for the year, not in a lump sum, but in an itemized statement. These estimates are carefully scrutinized by the executive officers of the board. Then the probable income is carefully computed on the basis of average receipts for a series of years, and any "signs of the times" that may indicate an increase or a decrease, and the grant is made, such a "cut" being imposed upon the total estimates as may be necessary to bring them within the limits of expected income.

Some expenditure for administration is, of course, indispensable. The work could not be carried on without it, for a board must have offices and the facilities for handling its responsibilities. The scale of administration is largely determined by the ideas of the Church that the board represents and the work that it is required to do. It is hardly fair to cite the low administrative expense of certain independent agencies, for they do not assume such responsibilities for the maintenance of their missionaries as the church boards. The churches want their missionaries adequately supported for a life-work, and that involves an administrative agency commensurate in expensiveness with the obligations that it must assume. Still, the cost of administration of the denominational boards is surprisingly low. The exact percentage varies, as some have free rentals and unpaid agents, and as the cost of stimulating the churches is not always considered administrative. In general, it may be said that the percentage of administration proper ranges from five to eight per cent. That is, it takes but little more than the value of a foreign postage stamp to send a dollar to Asia or Africa.

Is there any mercantile concern doing a great business and

requiring the services of a large number of persons scattered all over the world, whose percentage of expenditure for administration is so low? Dr. Henry Van Dyke once made inquiries of several large corporations, railway, manufacturing, and mercantile, and he found that the average cost of administration was 12.75 per cent., while in one great establishment it rose to twenty per cent. The manager of one of the large department stores in New York told me that his expense for administration was twenty-two per cent., and he expressed astonishment that the board's cost was only about one-quarter of that. The cases are not entirely parallel; but after making all reasonable allowance for differences, the essential fact remains that the cost of missionary administration is remarkably low. About ninety-five cents out of every dollar go to the work in some form. The Rev. Dr. John Hall of New York once said: "I have been closely connected with the work for more than a quarter of a century, and I do not hesitate to say that it would be difficult to find elsewhere as much work done at so moderate a cost as in our mission boards."

It is more difficult than many might imagine to manage a great board so as to avoid debt. The work, being conducted on so large a scale and over so vast a territory, cannot be hurriedly adjusted to financial changes in the United States. It has been gradually developed through a long series of years and must from its nature be stable. A board cannot end its work with the year and begin the next year on a different basis. It operates in distant lands, some so remote that from four to six months are required for the mere interchange of letters. Plans and pledges must therefore be made far in advance. In these circumstances, it is not easy to forecast the future; but the boards must do so, or try to.

Moreover, missionaries are sent out for a life service. They cannot be discharged at any time as a merchant discharges a clerk. True, the board reserves the right of recall; but it justly feels that it should not exercise it save for serious cause in the missionary himself. Foreign missionaries, too, are not situated like home missionaries—among people of their own race, with partially self-supporting congregations behind them and with larger churches within call in case the board fails them. They are thousands of miles away, among different and often hostile races and with absolutely no local resource. In such circumstances, the board simply cannot abandon them. It must pay their salaries and pay them promptly—and it does so. The boards have retrenched in many other ways, but the foreign missionary has received his full salary, and that, too, the very day it was due. We believe that the home churches will sustain the boards in that policy, that they do not want them to send a forlorn hope into Asia and Africa and then desert it. This policy, however, while only just to the missionaries, involves risk to the boards.

Another difficulty experienced by the boards is the uncertainty of income. The churches will not pay in advance. The average church does not even make pledges and has no adequate system of raising money. The tide of beneficence ebbs and flows in the most startling ways, and of course the board is often in danger of debt. The wonder is that the debts are not larger. Within sixty days of the close of its last fiscal year, one board lacked $513,000 of the sum needed to meet its pledges to the missions, ten months having brought less than half of the amount needed for the year.

The perplexities of administration are so greatly increased by the special object system that a fuller explanation appears to be necessary. At first, contributors were content to give to the general fund; but as the work grew, an increasing number began to ask for particular objects. This practice has grown until now in many organizations a large majority of the missionaries are thus supported. A few years ago, twenty-nine boards reported that twenty-five per cent. of their native work was assigned to special object givers, and as they also reported that the proportion was increasing from year to year, it is probable that the present percentage is considerably larger.

The basal reason for giving should not, of course, lie in a particular person or institution, but in the considerations that were stated in the chapter on "The Missionary Motive." However, giving to objects assigned from the authorized work by the boards themselves can be so safe-guarded as to be helpful. It often makes the cause concrete and strengthens the sense of responsibility for its maintenance. It is true that the missionary supported sometimes proves to be an unsatisfactory correspondent, and that occasionally a church fails to keep its part of the agreement, on account of a change of pastors or the death or removal of the members who were the chief financial dependence. As a rule, however, the plan works satisfactorily, and the churches that have tried it have made large advances in missionary interest and gifts.

In the support of the native work, too, "there is a power in the concentrated individual interest that must be reckoned with and, if possible, encouraged frankly and honestly." The inclinations of multitudes of earnest and friendly people to maintain it by special object giving should not be indiscriminately opposed, but wisely guided. Within proper limits, they may be made to subserve wise ends. But when the giver insists on having a particular native pupil or helper assigned to him and to have letters from or about the native thus supported, serious difficulties emerge. The larger boards have from thirty to fifty thousand of such scholars and helpers. These myriads of individuals are constantly changing, and their comings and goings and habits and progress are subject to greater fluctuations than in a like number of people at home. Imagine the plight of a teacher of a primary school in America if, in addition to her labours in and out of the classroom, she were expected to correspond with the parents of all her pupils, tell each pupil what he should write to his parents and correct every letter that he sent. The plight of the missionary is rendered far worse by the fact that the children are not accustomed to write letters and do not know our language, so that when a letter has been laboriously gotten into shape, the unhappy teacher must add to her assistance in composition the toil of translating it into English, writing it out by hand and mailing it. Such demands upon a missionary are altogether unreasonable, and when the giver adds a demand for a photograph of a scholar or helper, who never had a picture taken in his life, with no photographer within a hundred miles and no money to pay one if he were available, patience is apt to be exhausted.

There are, moreover, administrative perplexities involved in such excessively specialized giving. Suppose a citizen should refuse to contribute towards the expenses of his community unless his money could be applied to the grading of the street in front of his house, or to the salary of the teacher who instructs his children. How could the administration of any municipality be conducted if each man insisted on having some particular item of city expenditure assigned to him? The donor does not usually suspect the difficulties in his selection of a special object. He naturally chooses the most attractive phases of the work, while others less attractive but equally important are ignored. Still less does it occur to him that it has an unfortunate influence on native helpers to know that they are specially supported from America. Centuries of poverty and oppression have predisposed most Asiatics and Africans to undue reliance upon the missionary and experience has shown that extraordinary care must be exercised in the distribution among them of foreign money, lest they be pauperized in spirit and led to a dependence upon America demoralizing to themselves and incompatible with that spirit of self-reliance that we are earnestly endeavouring to inculcate. "It has been found by experience, as our knowledge of human nature should have taught us in the beginning to expect, that the spirit of self-help is much more easily developed when the financial help it is necessary to give comes from a general fund administered by the mission, so that the amount given to any individual can be increased, diminished, or withdrawn entirely according to the actual need, than it is when the help comes from individuals in this country directly to those who are helped." [1]

Sometimes, too, the scholar supported does not turn out well. All children in mission schools are not saints; if they were, missions would not be necessary. Some have to be dismissed for bad conduct. Some are taken away by their heathen parents, while in Africa it is not uncommon for a father to sell his daughter to a licentious white trader. Even the Christian helper may prove to be incompetent or mercenary and have to be dismissed. The heritage of centuries of heathen license and deceit is not easily overcome in a few years. The missionaries exercise great care in selecting helpers and lapses are exceptional, but they do occur, and when they do, the resultant harm is greatly augmented if particular givers in America are involved.

Such special object giving, too, frequently produces embarrassment in the adjustment of appropriations to the needs of the work. Missions must be given large discretion in matters of detail, and sometimes the boards do not know what changes have been made on the field until the mission reports are received at the close of the year. The requirements, too, of a specified object may not always equal what appeared to be necessary at the beginning of the year. The native helper's salary is, of course, paid in the currency of his own country; but the gold value of that currency fluctuates, so that a given number of coins may, in the course of a year, cost several dollars more or less than the original estimate. Since, too, the constant effort is to induce the native Christians to support him, the amount paid by the mission may and should become smaller as the gifts on the field increase.

[1] The Rev. Dr. S. H. Chester.

Still further, readjustments in appropriations are frequently necessary because the boards are unable to furnish sufficient funds to carry on every department of the work as estimated by the missions. It is seldom practicable for a mission to adjust a cut on the basis of special contributions from home. It cannot develop envy and irritation by reducing one native helper's salary and leaving another untouched, maintain one department of work at full strength and almost annihilate another. The distribution of funds must be equitable, each form of work bearing its proper share of retrenchment and the guiding principle must be the interest of the cause. This being the case, it is possible that the exigencies of the work may at any time require an increase or decrease or even the total discontinuance of the expenditure for any specific object.

It would be impossible for a board to make each one of these changes the subject of correspondence with the givers, for the reason that the objects thus supported are thousands in number, that they are scattered all over the world, that the distances are so great that long periods are required for the mere interchange of letters, and that the givers also are numerous and widely distributed.

Constituents and missionaries should understand that the object of the boards in desiring to control gifts is simply in the interest of the work, that they wish to have the Lord's money used to the best advantage, and that they have no disposition to alter the direction of a designated gift, but only to safeguard the interests of the cause and to provide for emergencies and for necessary changes.

These perplexities of special object giving are increased by the disposition of many people to give to objects outside of the authorized budget. The missionaries, assembled in annual meetings, carefully consider the work that should be done and forward their estimates to the board. On the basis of these estimates, the board makes "the regular grants," pledging in them the largest sum that there appears to be a reasonable probability will be received. Plainly, therefore, the first duty of givers and their first interest, if they would truly serve the work, is towards these grants, since they include the objects which the missionaries themselves have decided to be of first importance. Therefore, to demand that money shall be applied to some other purpose is virtually to insist upon giving to the less, rather than to the more important work.

"It is a singular fact," observes Dr. E. E. Strong, "that so many donors fancy that they can get information as to the best use to be made of their gifts through individual appeals, rather than by taking the united judgment of the missionaries on the ground and the executive committees at home." The effort to evangelize the world must not degenerate into a sporadic and spasmodic individualism. A board cannot spend $50,000 this year on a mission which has happened to have several good speakers home on furlough, and $30,000 the next year because the furloughed missionaries from that field are sick or ineffective on the platform. The scale on which money should be expended in a given field cannot be wholly determined by the amount of money offered for it, or the varying degree of success which a missionary may have in presenting it to home audiences, or the newspaper articles that may happen to interest a reader; but it must be decided by the relative needs of that field, the funds that are available for the whole enterprise and the policy that has been adopted by the board. Otherwise, demoralizing elements of uncertainty and inequality are introduced.

It ought to be generally understood that the disposition of givers to send money directly to the field, with the request that it be not counted as a part of the regular grants, is based on radically wrong views of the object for which the boards exist, of the responsibility which they have incurred by the authority of the churches, of the paramount importance of the regular work as compared with outside objects, of the economy of the board's administration, of the risks that are incident to enterprises depending on the wisdom or life of individuals and of the relation of church members to the boards which are their own agencies for the disbursement of missionary funds. However sincere the intentions of the donor, the boards have the real responsibility for the maintenance of the work, and must, after his death or in the event of his inability or disinclination to continue his gift, eventually assume the financial burden of its support. It is, therefore, only just that the approval of the board should be deemed a prerequisite to the inauguration of work.

The boards have tried various expedients in the effort to harmonize the proper wishes of special object givers with the interests of the work. One of the best is called the "share" or "station plan," which assigns the giver a part of the budget which must be raised for the station in which the donor wishes his gift applied. Money is received, not for an individual scholar or native worker or school, but for the station. This plan is proving satisfactory alike to givers, boards and missionaries. It allows a flexible use of mission funds in accordance with the best judgment of the missionaries and the changing necessities of the work, provides a support for all departments and not simply for a few, makes it possible to furnish adequate information, gives room for steady advance of interest and gifts, instead of fixing limits, and insures the continuance of the gift to the permanent work uninfluenced by changes in personnel.

On this whole subject of special object giving, it is well to bear in mind "that each donor who gives what he can to the treasury of any mission board, without direction as to the specific use to be made of his gift, has a share in all the multiplied activities of that board, a share in every missionary, in every native teacher and preacher, in every school and scholar, in every book printed as well as every church established through the treasury of that board. No church and no individual should fail to be thus connected with the wide work of missions. When this is done, then special objects may well be selected and maintained by extra offerings, in this way getting the breadth which comes from taking in the whole field and also the intensity which may spring from direct touch with some particular enterprise."[1]

Viewing missionary administration as a whole, there is undoubtedly occasional ground for criticism. Every board would admit that, in deciding a myriad perplexing questions, many of them delicate and difficult and on which good men differ, some errors of judgment occur. The attitude of officers and members should be one of openness of mind towards such modifications of policy or method as God in His providence may direct. The fact that they did a thing last year is not a conclusive reason why they should do it next year. Emerson says that consistency is the virtue of small minds. We should do what we believe to be right before God to-day, whether or not it is what we did yesterday. The man who cannot change his mind when conditions have changed is not fit to be an administrator of a great enterprise. He is worse than a weak man, for the latter is amenable to advice, while the former is as inaccessible to reason as a mule.

It is probable, however, that if any one were to make a list of the real defects in present administrative methods, he would readily learn on inquiry that the boards already know those defects and that they are earnestly striving to remedy them. Dr. William N. Clarke expresses the following opinion:

"The sharpest criticism usually comes from those who know the work only from the outside, and have no idea either of its real magnitude or of the immense complications that it involves. Large parts of the work of missionary boards imply matters that are confidential in their nature. A certain amount of reserve is absolutely required by justice and by the interests of the work. Matters that can be openly discussed

[1] The Rev. E. E. Strong, D. D.

are often fully intelligible only to those who know great classes of surrounding facts. When a society or board is blamed about some occurrence on the foreign field, there is almost sure to be involved some personal matter in which prejudice for or against some one may easily mislead an outside judgment, and even in the inner circle a just and wise judgment requires the utmost caution. All administrative work is of course justly open to candid and reasonable criticism, and no missionary society expects or asks to escape it; but there are comparatively few persons who are thoroughly qualified to criticise the administration of the great missionary organizations except in a very general way. Even for those who have intimate knowledge enough to be capable of intelligent criticism, it often proves far easier to see faults in the policy of the great societies than to propose radical improvements upon their general method of administration. It is a case where correction even of acknowledged faults, though it be ever so much desired, is often beset with unsuspected difficulty. Hence the case is one that evidently calls for mutual confidence and loyal coöperation among those who are interested together in missions. . . . The fact ought to be taken more closely home to the popular Christian heart, that a missionary society is conducting a work of exceptional magnitude and difficulty, under conditions that render misjudgment of its doings extremely easy; and that its officers deserve sympathetic and respectful judgment from all their brethren." [1]

All the boards are giving increasing attention to the principles of an intelligent and comprehensive policy. They feel that the days of sentimentalism in foreign missions have passed. They are not conducting a crusade but a settled campaign, and they are planning it with such skill and prudence as they possess. They study the broad principles of missions, read the lessons that they have been taught by a hundred years of mis-

---

[1] "A Study of Christian Missions," pp. 128, 134, 135.

sionary effort, abandon plans that have been found defective and adopt new ones which promise better results. Every year, the officers and representatives of over sixty boards of the United States and Canada meet for conference as to the best methods for carrying on missionary operations, and an amount of care and thought is given to the whole subject that would surprise the average critic. The boards are earnestly trying to administer this great trust wisely, economically and effectively, and on sound business and scientific as well as religious principles.

It will be seen from all that has been said that there is no ground for the assumption of some that the work of a church board is not a faith work. At the beginning of each year, the board makes and guarantees its appropriations solely on the faith that God will move the Church to provide the necessary money. Since He has ordained that this work shall be supported by the gifts of His people, it is fair to assume that He will bless them when they move unitedly and prayerfully for the accomplishment of the chief work that He has laid upon them, and that He is quite as apt to guide the men whom the Church "looks out" as "of honest report, full of the Holy Ghost and wisdom" and appoints "over this business," as He is to guide any individual, however sincere or enthusiastic. These men regard the work as of divine authority and beneficent character. They reverently look to the Holy Spirit as the administrator of the enterprise, believing that their chief reliance must be upon His guidance. They realize that God is not limited to human methods and that the failure of a cherished plan may not argue injury to the cause but only defects in the plan. They feel that their only safety is to keep close to Christ and to seek to know His will. Prayer, therefore, begins and pervades all deliberations and wings every appeal for funds. Heavy as are the anxieties and responsibilities, every board counts it an honour and a privilege to represent the Church of God in the administration of this noblest of all Christian activities.

IV

QUALIFICATIONS AND APPOINTMENT

IT has recently been said that it is now easier to secure an appointment in the diplomatic service of the country than in the foreign missionary service of the Protestant boards. This is an extreme statement, but it is undoubtedly true that the standard of foreign missionary appointment is higher than that of the military and naval service. The government commissions all who graduate at West Point and Annapolis, but the boards take only the picked men of the colleges and universities. No other profession guards its doors more carefully. It is a mistake to suppose that any nice and apparently pious youth can become a foreign missionary. A pastor who had recommended such a youth was much surprised when the board began an investigation which ran through several months and which disclosed facts which his pastor had never suspected. If any one imagines that weaklings or milksops can be appointed, he might apply for appointment and see. Large churches, after spending a year or more in considering scores of highly recommended ministers, sometimes give a unanimous call to an unworthy man. So a board occasionally errs. But as a rule, the rigorous methods now employed quickly reject incompetent candidates, while the increasing missionary interest in colleges and seminaries gives the choicest material to select from. The boards do not send the pale enthusiast or the romantic young lady to the foreign field, but the sturdy, practical, energetic man of affairs, the woman of poise and sense and character. The New York *Tribune*, in commenting on the fact that a recent graduating class at Princeton Theological Seminary included some of the most brilliant men that had ever passed through the institution, noted that four of the most prominent had decided to go to the foreign field. This was not exceptional. Imitating the example of the Church at Antioch in setting apart as foreign missionaries Paul and Barnabas, the modern Church selects its best for this service. The result is that foreign missionaries are fast becoming a picked class, far above the average in intelligence, character and devotion.

We would not give the impression that the boards insist upon an impracticable standard, nor should modesty deter any young man or woman from applying. The tests imposed, as we shall presently see, are not merely scholastic. Sometimes the honour members of a graduating class have been rejected and men of lesser academic distinction appointed because investigation has shown that the latter gave better promise of real usefulness. High grades sometimes coexist with serious defects of character. Many of the prize men of our colleges are never heard of in after life, while others who, like General Grant, made no special mark as students have developed splendid qualities.

It may be well to indicate the qualifications that are required, partly for the guidance of young men who are contemplating application and partly for the information of friends and students of missions.

Health.—Foreign missionaries often live and work in such trying climates, amid such unsanitary surroundings, exposed to such malignant diseases and under such nervous strain, that only men and women of sound constitution and vigorous health should be appointed. It is important therefore to ascertain whether one is free from physical defects or tendencies that might shorten life. Experience has taught the boards the necessity of being particular in this respect and a large number of the candidates fail at this point. Unless, however, a given candidate is certain that he is physically disqualified, he should not hesitate on this account to apply. Ordinarily, the question is one to be determined not by the applicant but by a physician. The family physician, if there is one, will naturally be chosen for this purpose. But the boards sometimes find that a family physician, with a desire to please and with little knowledge of the conditions of missionary life, makes a perfunctory examination; so they usually prefer to have the examination made by their own physicians wherever possible. In addition, the candidate himself is expected to inform the board whether there is anything in his family or personal history or habits that might affect his usefulness as a missionary.

Age.—After thirty, one's ability to acquire a free, colloquial use of a foreign tongue rapidly diminishes, and after thirty-five it usually ceases altogether. One may learn to read or write a language after that, but he will probably not learn to speak it well. Moreover, one's ability to adapt himself to a different environment becomes less easy as the years pass. It is better that the transfer to new conditions and the study of a difficult language should begin before either the physical or intellectual life becomes so fixed that it is hard to acquire new things. The probable duration of effective service, also, shortens rapidly as one moves towards middle life. For these reasons, the boards do not like to accept any one over thirty-three, unless other qualifications are exceptionally high, in which case the age of acceptance is occasionally extended to thirty-five.

Education.—Graduation from both college and professional school is ordinarily required in men and at least a high school training in women. The boards insist, too, that the student's record shall be such as to show that he possesses more than average intellectual ability, so that there may be reason to believe that he can acquire a difficult language and become a useful missionary. A considerable part of the work of the missionary is intellectual, as we shall see in a later chapter. His daily problems require a trained mind. Moreover, in many fields he comes into contact with natives whose mental acumen is by no means contemptible. "Men of superior training are needed," says President W. A. P. Martin; "weak and ignorant men are out of place." While, therefore, a board will not reject a candidate because he does not stand near the head of his class, it will reject him if his grades indicate mediocrity. The considerations that occasionally lead the Church at home to ordain a man who has not had a full course may lead a board to send one to the foreign field, but such cases are exceptions.

Graduates of technical schools and trained nurses often inquire whether they can be appointed. Men and women of this kind are needed every year by some of the boards. Physicians are nearly always in demand. Colleges and boarding schools frequently call for recruits who are specially qualified for teaching. Sometimes mechanical and electrical engineers are needed for special chairs. Several boards have sought graduates of industrial and agricultural colleges for industrial schools. Hospitals often ask for trained nurses to act as matrons and head nurses. Mission presses occasionally call for superintendents who understand printing, while some of the larger missions can use to excellent advantage laymen of business experience as treasurers, builders and business agents. Of course, however, the number that can be used in some of these ways is not great. The all-around candidate who can do anything that he is assigned is in chief demand. The volunteer, therefore, who desires to prepare for missionary life with the largest probability of appointment should, if a man, take a college and seminary course, if a woman, fit herself for evangelistic or educational work. Those, however, who did not form the missionary purpose until late in some technical course should not on that account be discouraged. A knowledge of engineering or nursing or architecture or business is often of great advantage to a missionary whose main work is along other lines. Such knowledge adds not a little to one's value to a board, provided he does not insist that he shall be given that particular kind of work on the foreign field. Mackay of Uganda did comparatively little as an engineer, but his skill in his profession largely increased his general missionary usefulness. The force at a given station is usually so small that there is not much demand for those who can do only one thing.

Executive Ability and Force of Character.—The boards make careful inquiry as to this. Many a man can do good service in the home-land who could not succeed on the foreign field. The duties of a missionary are not like those of a pastor at home, who usually succeeds to an established work, who finds methods already so largely determined that his duty is rather one of modification than of origination and who has wise counsellors in his church officers. The missionary's functions are rather those of a superintendent. He must be a leader and organizer. Mere piety will not make a missionary, any more than mere patriotism will make an ambassador. The boards lay stress on energy, initiative and self-reliance. They inquire whether the candidate has qualities of leadership and whether, in general, he is a strong man.

Common Sense.—This is a much rarer quality than might be supposed and not a few candidates go down under the searching inquiries that the boards make regarding it. Some brilliant men lack the balance of judgment, the homely good sense, that are indispensable in a useful missionary. The foreign missionary must deal with a variety of problems and conditions that call for the practical man as distinguished from the visionary. The direction of a large work, the expenditure of considerable sums of money, the superintendence of building operations, the settlement of the questions that are constantly arising among the native Christians, the adjustment of himself and others to all sorts of persons and conditions, these and other matters that might be mentioned cannot be prudently committed to unbalanced men, however pious or healthy or intellectual. Governor Brown of Georgia used to say that "if the Lord has left judgment out of a man, there is no way of getting it in." The mission field is not the place for the visionary, the crank, the mere enthusiast. "Young man," said an old judge to a new member of the bar who had just made a bombastic plea, "young man, you need to pluck a few feathers from the wings of your imagination and stick them in the tail of your judgment." The home-land is the best place for that operation. The quality of good sense is so often developed in the school of privation that some of the best missionaries have been men who were forced by poverty to work their own way through college, for the necessity that was thus laid upon them developed those qualities of alertness, self-reliance and good sense that are of high value in missionary life.

Steadiness of Purpose.—The missionary movement is not a spasmodic crusade. It is not an easy life. The romantic halo about it is chiefly in books. It should not be entered upon, therefore, by those who are prone to rapid alternations of feeling, or who are easily discouraged, or who are incapable of persevering toil. The student who has volunteered under the impulse of emotional excitement should give his new purpose reasonable testing period before making application for appointment. The man who is always conceiving great projects and never carrying them out is another type that is not desired. Most of the boards have had experience with such missionaries and they do not want any more. The writer recalls one of that kind—a man of faith and prayer, earnest, self-sacrificing and spiritually minded, but whose usefulness was destroyed by the fitfulness of his enthusiasms. He would launch a new scheme every few weeks, champion it with fiery zeal, but before he had brought anything out of it, get discouraged and abandon it for some other scheme. Thus he was always busy, but never accomplishing anything, dwelling on the heights of exaltation one day and in the depths of depression the next, frittering away his time, wasting the board's money and keeping his colleagues in a constant state of uneasiness as to what he was going to do next. Finally, in one of his periodical fits of depression, he offered his resignation. He was sorry the next week and wanted to recall it; but the board would not permit him to do so, and he retired, leaving the field strewn with the wrecks of his fruitful but ill-regulated imagination. The man of patient persistence in well-doing, who does not easily lose heart, who courageously and inflexibly sticks to his work however discouraging it may be, the man who, like General Grant, "proposes to fight it out on this line if it takes all summer," is the type that is wanted for missionary service. Missionary employment is expected to be for life and no one should apply who is not willing to consecrate himself irrevocably to it, who cannot make light of hardships and "endure hardness as a good soldier of Jesus Christ." A veteran missionary, in asking for an associate, wrote: "Send us a despiser of difficulties, who will not be discouraged under the most adverse circumstances, who will unite unflinching courage with consummate tact, know how to do impossible things and maintain a pertinacity that borders on stubbornness with a suavity of manners that softens asperity." That is expecting a good deal of human nature, but it indicates the ideal that we have in mind.

Temperament.—Ability to work harmoniously with others is a prime qualification. The mission circle is the very worst place for a stubborn or quarrelsome man or woman. One such missionary will wreck the happiness and perhaps the efficiency of a whole station. No degree of ability or force of character can make a missionary of that type tolerable. Indeed, the stronger he is the more trouble he makes. We have known a large majority of a mission to acquiesce in an action that they did not approve, simply because they could not bring themselves to oppose a cantankerous associate who, they knew, would never cease fighting until the matter had been settled his way. Then there is the man, or more often here the woman, who takes personal offense when his or her plans are opposed. Most troublesome of all is the type of Christian who is so certain that God has, in answer to prayer, shown him what ought to be done, that he is wholly inaccessible to the arguments of others. It does not occur to him that his associates also pray and that God may guide them as well as him. A vast amount of unregenerate pugnacity and narrow-mindedness in this world passes for "fidelity to the truth as I see it."

A cheerful spirit is as essential as ability to work with others. Some otherwise very excellent people are by temperament despondent. They magnify difficulties and imagine them where they do not exist at all. Present to them any proposal, and they will see all the objections to it first. They never weary in bemoaning the shortcomings of their fellow Christians. They walk about Zion and mark the defects thereof and tell them to the public. They remind one of the old Scotch elder who lugubriously said of his church of three hundred members: "There be no real Christians here—except myself and Sandy, and sometimes I hae' my douts aboot Sandy." "Good Lord, deliver us!" is the prayer of the missionaries already on the field regarding all these types.

Doctrinal Views.—The candidate who holds opinions of doctrine or polity that are not in accord with those of the Church with which he would be associated as a missionary falls under this general head of incompatibility. Variance of this kind may be, and ordinarily is, held from thoroughly praiseworthy motives, and it is not the province of a board to attempt to convince the candidate that he is wrong or to bring any pressure whatever to bear upon him to change his views. It simply notes the fact that the candidate probably could not harmonize with missionaries who hold a different position. This objection would not, of course, apply to those variations of belief that are within the recognized limits of evangelical faith as held by the Church to which the candidate belongs. In no denomination is the ministry entirely homogeneous as to questions of doctrine, nor do the boards insist that the missionary body shall be. There are the same differences of this kind among missionaries that are to be found at home. We are referring now to those questions that would differentiate a candidate from the whole body of his associates and introduce embarrassing complications among them. The man who feels that he ought to baptize his own infant children and the infant children of the native Christians should not expect a Baptist board to appoint him as one of its missionaries, and, conversely, if one cannot conscientiously sit at the Lord's table with fellow missionaries who were baptized in infancy, he should not blame a Methodist or Presbyterian board for being unwilling to commission him. In such cases, a board does not wish to be understood as expressing any opinion as to the correctness of the candidate's belief, but as simply taking the position that the advent of such a man into a small mission circle would impair the harmony of the station and create an unfortunate impression upon native Christians. For the same reason, the boards do not usually like to appoint candidates who believe in what is commonly known as "faith-healing." Such a missionary would contradict, by example if not by precept, the position and influence of every medical missionary in the mission. Hobbies or eccentricities of any kind are considered more or less objectionable as tending to divide those who ought not to be divided and to affect injuriously the influence of the missionary body upon the natives, who are always quick to observe and to comment upon such differences.

Marriage.—It is a mistake to suppose that the boards insist upon marriage. Indeed, some boards require their men to go out single, but permit them to marry after learning the language and proving their fitness for missionary life. Other boards advise this course, but leave it to the judgment of the candidate. The objections to deferring marriage do not, as a rule, relate to the work, but come from families on the field who do not feel prepared to board young men. Traders and Roman Catholic priests usually keep "bachelors' hall," and where a couple of young missionaries are together, there is no valid reason why they cannot do so for a year or two if necessary. No Protestant board advocates the celibacy of missionaries. All appoint married men; but almost all have certain forms of work that can better be done, for a time at least, by single men. A candidate, therefore, who has not already arranged for marriage, need not feel that he is under any pressure to do so. If, after a few years on the field, he wishes to marry, the board will have pleasure in sending his fiancée to him, provided, of course, she is found to possess the necessary qualifications for missionary life. So many missionaries and friends are constantly coming and going, that there is seldom any difficulty in finding suitable companionship for the young ladies.

"The wives of missionaries are regarded as associate missionaries, uniting with their husbands in desire and effort to give the gospel to the unevangelized. It is expected that, so far as is consistent with their strength and household duties, they will learn the language and take part in missionary work." [1]

The fiancée must make a separate application and it will be as carefully investigated as that of the man whom she is to marry. No woman should go to the foreign field simply because she is the wife of a missionary. Life in a heathen land is so trying, from the viewpoint of home standards, that the wife who is not in deep spiritual sympathy with her husband's missionary work and purpose will almost certainly become lonely, discontented and depressed. She may successfully fight against this for a time, but in the end she will not only become unhappy herself, but she will probably make her husband unhappy, while it is not improbable that her health will give way and that he will be compelled to give up his life's plans and return home with an invalid wife. Most of the boards have had such costly experiences of this kind that they are disposed to make careful inquiry regarding the qualifications of those who expect to become the wives of missionaries.

So many candidates have to be declined on account of their families that it is proper to add that, while the boards cordially recognize their privilege and duty in relation to children that are born on the field, the boards hesitate where there are

[1] Manual of the Presbyterian Board.

Qualifications and Appointment

children prior to application for appointment. It costs much more to transport such families to the field and more to house them after their arrival. A mother finds it difficult to get the time and strength for language study and there is always a possibility that such missionaries will have to resign because they find the foreign field unfavourable to the health of their children. Ordinarily most boards, therefore, do not like to appoint candidates who already have children, though they do this in exceptional cases.

Freedom From Financial Obligations.—If one is seriously in debt, or if he has relatives dependent upon him for support, it is doubtful whether he should apply. The salary of a foreign missionary is designed to cover only the cost of his own living and it will not permit him to send back money to pay debts or to help relatives, without forcing an economy or causing worries that may impair health.

Christian Character and Experience.—It need hardly be said that if any one of the qualifications that have been mentioned is more indispensable than the others, it is this. No matter how healthy or able or well educated, the successful candidate must have a sound, well developed Christian character. It is unnecessary to enlarge upon this here since to do so would be repeating in substance much that was stated in the first chapter. The boards do not commission mere physicians or school-teachers, but missionaries. The medical graduate who simply wishes to practice his profession in a great mission hospital in Asia, the professor whose ambition is only to build up a flourishing school, the youth who wants to see strange lands and peoples or who is animated by the spirit of adventure, are not wanted. Missionary work in all its forms is distinctly spiritual in spirit and aim. David Livingstone, when asked what were the chief requirements of a successful missionary, gave as the first "a goodly portion of God's own loving yearnings over the souls of the heathen." The boards, therefore, place great stress on the candidate's spiritual experience and his motives for seeking missionary service. The missionary should be above everything else a spiritual guide. He is expected to preach Christ and to live Christ and to lead men to Christ. Inquiries on this point are carefully made, and if there is reason to doubt the spiritual influence of a candidate, he is certain to be declined. The boards covet candidates who are the children of prayer, "lent to the Lord," like Samuel, from their infancy, whose spiritual life indeed began, like Timothy's, before they were born in " the unfeigned faith" that dwelt first in grandmother and mother, candidates who from their earliest years have been taught to reverence the Bible, to kneel at the family altar and to listen for the call of God. Such men get large ideas of the relation of Christ to the world and when they give their hearts to God, they do it in no half-hearted way. The step is taken freely, deliberately, sincerely, unreservedly and forever.

Other considerations may emerge in the consideration of particular cases. Some experience in teaching or Christian work, and a knowledge of music in women candidates and of bookkeeping in men, while not usually required, add to the attractiveness of an application. The qualifications that have been mentioned, however, are those that are generally sought for by the boards. Taken together in this way, they may appear to constitute a formidable list ; but this enumeration should not ease the conscience of any young man or woman who is considering the question of going to the foreign field.

Ill-health, imperfect education, dependent relatives, inability to work harmoniously with others and age that forbids hope of acquiring a difficult language are valid reasons for not applying ; but unless some such positive disqualification is known to exist, the proper course is to correspond with the secretary of the board and he will gladly give all needed counsel. A general sense of unfitness for so noble a calling is not a valid reason for failure to apply. Such modesty is apt to be the refuge of those who are quite willing to have an excuse to stay

Qualifications and Appointment

at home. One should not be deterred because of reports that men are being rejected for want of funds or for any other reason. The financial situation may have changed, or an unexpected vacancy may have occurred. The fact that an apparently good man of one's acquaintance has been declined is not necessarily a reason for discouragement, for the board may have discovered some defect that his friends did not suspect, or the trouble may have been with his fiancée. No matter what one hears, if he feels that he ought to go to the foreign field, he should send in his application and place upon the board the responsibility of dealing with it.

There is no disgrace in being rejected, for it will readily be seen that a number of the reasons mentioned above may be providential in character, and, while hindering one's going to the foreign field, might not hinder a successful life for Christ in the home-land. Moreover, the boards consider all applications as confidential, so that the fact of rejection need not be known beyond the limited circle of the friends whose private opinions it is necessary for the board to seek.

How may one know whether he is called of God to be a missionary? The divine summons is made known in a variety of ways. Some men are conscious of a call almost as distinct and commanding as that of the Apostle Paul. But probably few have such an experience and the lack of it should not be regarded as an indication that one has no call to missionary service. God's will is often made known in quieter ways.[1] Many theological students make the mistake of assuming that the absence of an external peremptory call means that they should stay at home. The result is that scores look for home pastorates because they "have no call to go abroad." The assumption should be just the reverse. If God calls a man to preach the gospel at all, surely the presumption is in favour of the field where the work is the greatest and the workers are

---

[1] Cf. "Candidates in Waiting," published by the C. M. S.

fewest. With an average of one minister for every 700 people at home and candidates thronging every vacant pulpit, while abroad there is an average of but one for every 100,000 of the population, with all the doors of opportunity wide open and the mission boards vainly appealing for more men,—it is preposterous for the average student to assume that he should stay in America unless a voice from heaven summons him to go to the needy millions of Asia or Africa. In the language of Keith-Falconer: "While vast continents are shrouded in almost utter darkness, and hundreds of millions suffer the horrors of heathenism or of Islam, the burden of proof lies upon you to show that the circumstances in which God has placed you were meant by Him to keep you out of the foreign mission field."

The plea that there are needs at home is mere quibbling, in view not only of the facts already stated but of the further fact that about ninety-eight out of every hundred students are staying at home. It is probably fair to say of any given student that there is no need of him in the home field that is at all commensurate with the need of him on the foreign field. His proper attitude therefore should not be, "Why should I go as a foreign missionary," but "Why should I not go?" The late James Gilmour, the famous itinerant missionary to the Mongol tribes, wrote of this period in his student life: "Even on the low ground of common sense I seemed to be called to be a missionary. Is the kingdom a harvest field? Then I thought it reasonable that I should seek the work where the work was most abundant and the workers fewest." "This was the plain common-sense process by which that apostle to Mongolia reached a decision as to duty."

The procedure in making application is simple—write to the secretary of the board and he will send a set of application blanks and all needful information. The usual time for application is in the autumn or early winter preceding graduation from the professional school, though the secretaries are cordially willing to correspond with intending applicants at any time in order to give them any desired counsel. In some cases, boards will make an appointment a year in advance, if there are special reasons. Such appointments, however, are apt to be made without designation of field and subject to any emergencies that may affect the board's ability to send out new men, as it is usually difficult to forecast the financial situation so far ahead.

The secretary of the board, on receiving the formal application, corresponds with those who know the candidate. Some boards have a printed list of questions for this purpose, as they have learned from experience that, while most people will tell the truth, they will not tell all the truth unless definite questions are asked and a specific answer insisted upon. Even then, it is not always easy to get a candid judgment. We know a distinguished professor who almost invariably writes in superlatives regarding his students. He does not mean to deceive, but his kindness of heart and his ardent desire to help his students to a start in life unconsciously affect his judgment. Others shrink from putting into writing an unfavourable opinion of a young man or woman with whose families they are perhaps related in business or social ways. In these circumstances, a board, in spite of all its care, is sometimes deceived, but the secretaries are so thorough that they are seldom led astray. The time required for this investigation is ordinarily about two or three months, though in special cases it may be shorter or longer. Sometimes the financial condition of a board causes delay, as of course a board must know whether it can support a missionary before it appoints him. In the event, however, of delay on this account, the board usually informs the candidate at once whether the way is clear so far as his qualifications are concerned, so that he is not kept in suspense.

As a further precaution, a few of the boards have adopted the plan of bringing newly appointed missionaries to their headquarters for a conference of a week or ten days. These conferences, inaugurated by the Presbyterian Board in 1898, have proved to be of great interest and value, enabling the secretaries to pass the appointees in careful review before going to the field, establishing at the outset relations of personal friendship, acquainting the new missionary with some of the lessons of missionary experience and the main features of missionary policy, and clarifying his opinions on a number of important matters.

Assignment of field is ordinarily made at the time of appointment, as a given application is usually considered in connection with the needs of some particular mission. It is not uncommon, however, especially among the larger boards which send out forty or fifty new missionaries each year, to leave the assignment of field until most of the intended appointments have been made and then take up the question of distribution. This enables the board to make the assignments more intelligently, since it can select for a given position that one of the available men who is best suited to it. The new missionary's preferences, if he has any, are respected as far as practicable, but of course they cannot always be determinative. Half a dozen physicians may wish to go to Korea when that mission needs only one, or a candidate who is fitted for teaching may desire to go to North India which has asked that year for evangelistic workers but not for educational, or a death or resignation may have created a vacancy in Persia that is more urgent than the addition of another man to the force in Japan. A board must make assignments with primary reference to the field needs, which may not coincide with the preferences of candidates. There are, too, considerations as to the kind of work for which a candidate is best qualified and the question of his physical adaptations as made known by his medical examination. Some men, who could stand any amount of work in temperate North China, might quickly succumb to disease in tropical Africa. Of course a candidate may have convincing reasons for going to the field of his choice, and then the board gladly acquiesces, if the relative needs of that field justify the assignment. Experience has shown, however, that the preferences of candidates are apt to be based upon some casual circumstance like the reading of a book or a conversation with a furloughed missionary or a general idea that he would like to work among a particular people.

The candidate of the right spirit will be willing to take into serious and prayerful consideration the claims of the field that the board may deem to be most needy at the time or better adapted to his qualifications. Need, adaptation to it and request to go to it are surely more apt to be in accord with the divine ordering of a life than a more or less hasty and unintelligent notion as to where one would like to go. God not only calls missionaries, but He assigns their fields of labour, nor does He hesitate to overrule personal preferences. We read of Paul and Timothy that they "were forbidden of the Holy Ghost to preach the word in Asia," that "they assayed to go into Bithynia, but the Spirit suffered them not," and that from the vision of "a man of Macedonia," Paul "assuredly gathered that the Lord had called us for to preach the gospel unto them."[1] The tenth chapter of Acts makes it plain that the Holy Spirit not only directed the three men to seek Peter but in turn sent Peter to Cæsarea.

Many modern illustrations might be cited. Adoniram Judson felt bound in the Spirit to go to the foreign field, but he had not intended to go to Burma, a country extremely unattractive to him. He wanted to labour in India and he tried twice to go there, but God barred the way and literally drove him to Burma, where he entered upon that marvellous missionary career among the Burmans. Barnabus Shaw was wellnigh discouraged when he saw that he could not preach the gospel in Cape Town. Buying a wagon and a yoke of oxen, he started for the interior, without any definite idea as to where

[1] Acts 16.

he was going. After 300 miles of apparently aimless wandering, he met a band of Hottentots who were journeying to Cape Town for a missionary to teach them "the great word" regarding the true God. Who brought that missionary and those Africans together? Do such things happen, or does the Spirit of God order them? William Carey, influenced by Captain Cook's reports of the Pacific Islands, "assayed to go" to Tahiti, "but the Spirit suffered" him not and sent him to India, where he was so mightily used of God. David Livingstone studied and planned for years to go to China, but in ways very strange to him and only explicable on the supposition of the Spirit's immediate direction, he was led to Africa.

The reader only needs to be reminded how much better it was in all these instances that God overruled the preferences of individuals. Save, therefore, in exceptional cases, it is better for the candidate to keep an open mind regarding his field until he has learned from the board all the facts that should enter into a decision and is sure that he is following the leadings of Providence. The final decision may involve a change in some cherished plans; but there will be no mistake and no regrets in going with God.

FIRST IMPRESSIONS AND LANGUAGE STUDY

THE sailing dates vary according to convenience and climatic conditions; but as a rule, new missionaries sail in the late summer or early fall so as to reach the field at the most favourable season and in time for the annual meetings of the missions. Arrangements for railway and steamship tickets are made through the board, which can ordinarily secure reduced rates. Necessary travelling expenses from the missionary's home to his destination are paid by the board on the basis of the most direct route. Variations may be made, if desired, but the additional cost is met by the missionary personally. He is expected to keep a memorandum of his expenditures of the board's funds and to render an itemized account to the mission treasurer on his arrival on the field.

Suggestions as to outfit, furnished by the mission to which the missionary has been assigned, will be sent by the board and should be consulted before making purchases. Some boards make no grant for outfit, leaving it to be provided by the family or friends of the missionary. Others furnish an allowance for this purpose. The amount varies, but is usually about $200, except in fields where heavy household furniture is provided by the board, the allowance then being proportionately reduced. To a medical missionary an additional allowance is sometimes made for instruments, unless they are already at his post. In any event, as much as possible of the allowance should be reserved for use on the field. New missionaries are apt to buy articles that are not needed. They should purchase before sailing only what they are sure that they will require and leave everything else until after arrival. The board will be glad to fill any order that may be sent from the field. Purchases may usually be made to advantage through the board's office, which can often secure discounts from regular prices. Correspond with it also regarding the packing and shipping of freight. The board allowance for freight charges is about forty cubic feet (two measured tons) for each person, and all articles should be reduced to the smallest possible compass, as bulk, not weight, is counted.

The farewells are apt to be of mingled joy and sorrow. A new missionary is often lionized by friends and churches, and not infrequently newspapers write him up as a prominent character. No one knows, however, until he has experienced it, what it means to part from relatives, friends and country, not for a holiday trip, but for a life work. Such a departure is a virtual expatriation. That is hard enough to one who loves his native land; but there are even closer ties which must be broken. Father and mother may be left at an age which renders it probable that parents and child will never meet again in this world. Sometimes it is an invalid sister, always there are some dear ones who must be left behind. The strain of such partings is often severe. Nor should the pain of those loved ones be overlooked. Pleased as they may be with their child's choice of a missionary's life, it is hard for them to see a son or daughter go so far away for such a long absence. "I have thought so many times," writes a young wife from China, "that if the friends in the home-land understood the real situation, there would be more thought of and prayer for the brave mothers who give their very own to the mission work. The hardest part of the past months has been little mother's part in the agony of the good-bye."

The voyage, after perhaps the first few days, is usually enjoyable. Great changes in ocean travel have taken place since the pioneer missionaries suffered untold hardships on wretched sailing vessels. The modern steamships, on the Pacific as well as the Atlantic, are thoroughly comfortable.

Much has been said of the contemptuous treatment of mission-

First Impressions and Language Study

aries by ships' officers, but the author saw nothing of it in his own long voyages on many different steamers. Where such treatment is encountered, the facts should be sent to the board from the first port of call. Missionary travel has come to be too profitable to the companies to make them indifferent to reasonable complaints. But the missionary who conducts himself quietly and sensibly will probably have little trouble. He may indeed find that the people whom he meets on shipboard are not in sympathy with the work to which he has consecrated his life. Fellow passengers may even say and do many things that surprise and wound; but tact and good sense will usually prevent embarrassment. If there are several missionaries on board, it is proper that they should hold meetings for prayer and Bible study; but it is neither necessary nor wise to be constantly singing hymns when others want to converse or read or sleep, nor is it always expedient to attempt to conduct a series of revival meetings on the steamer deck. One missionary did harm rather than good by bluntly telling a fellow traveller that he was going to hell and ruining his son because he played cards in the cabin and drank a bottle of beer at meals, while a large party of missionaries on another steamer aroused resentment by monopolizing the deck games to the exclusion of other passengers. The missionary, on shipboard as well as everywhere else, should of course exemplify the Christ life and take advantage of all reasonable opportunities to testify for the Master; but he should appreciate the necessity for great tact in dealing with those whom he meets en route to his field. A missionary should be preëminently a gentleman and carefully avoid anything that savours of cant or assertive professionalism.

The first impressions of a heathen land are not always pleasant. There are, of course, the hearty greetings of the missionaries already on the field and the charm of strange scenery, of picturesque dress and architecture, and perhaps the glamour of "the gorgeous East." He will soon find, however, that the reality is not as attractive as the first appearance. Raw heathenism may grossly obtrude itself at the outset. The sensitive mind may shrink from the narrow streets, the squalid houses, the unintelligible speech, the odd dress and manners and customs, the heat, the filth, the vermin, the unspeakable moral abominations of a heathen city. Save, too, in the older stations, there is apt to be a lack of some conveniences that are deemed indispensable in America. Fresh milk and butter may be unobtainable and the canned article may be distasteful. Fresh meat is a rarity at many stations, and tinned meats are the staple dependence. The lot of the missionary is far more comfortable than formerly, but it is not to be expected that all the advantages which can be commanded by the average minister at home can be provided for the foreign missionary in Asia or Africa. The boards believe that they act in accordance with the wishes of the home churches when they do all that their funds will permit to lighten the hardship of missionary life, and yet in many respects a foreign missionary is practically a soldier, and a soldier, too, not in garrison, but on the picket line. He must therefore prepare himself for the absence of some things that men in other circumstances can have. A veteran missionary writes:

"Our new missionaries have had to undergo some disappointments. The nice house they were to occupy is a dismal place without a bit of furniture in it. The teacher who was to impart to them a working knowledge of the language is a native who knows only his own mother tongue and who is willing, for $5.00 a month, to let them dig out of him all they can. The trolley they were to ride on to and from their preaching stations proves to be 'shanks' mares.' The fine roads are paved with dust or mud through which they must wade with the cattle, buffalos and elephants. The electric lights that were to illuminate the city prove to be but the spark on the end of some passing native's cigarette. The railroads are several hundred miles away, and the telegraph system cannot be guaranteed to deliver a message within five days. The delightful climate was the only thing that was not a disappointment from the very first, but it was just getting good and ready, and in due time showed no let-up on ninety-five and one hundred degrees in the shade night and day for months, and when relief came in a refreshing shower, it was to only resuscitate nature in the form of myriads of tormenting insects which are the bane of our lives night and day. The markets that were to furnish everything needed prove to be in America or England, a whole year away from the immediate need."

Something, however, depends upon the point of view of the new missionary. Hainan is as hard a field as any, but after a year's residence one new missionary wrote:

"I don't believe I could have been sent to a place I would love more than I do Hainan. It is a beautiful island, with its magnificent banyan trees, cocoanut palms and luxuriant bamboo, which make such pretty hedges and enclose nearly every village. The natives are a very lovable people and it is a pleasure to work among them. I can't understand why the young people at home hold back so from this glorious work. I wish you could see the great mass of people as yet unreached by the gospel within a very few miles of us. I can't tell you the great longing there is in my heart to go to them with the message of salvation. Our little handful of Christians are a constant source of inspiration. While we have difficulties to face and many discouragements at times, yet we also have great cause for gratitude to God for the blessings of the past year and for the bright outlook for the future."

New missionaries of that type are not apt to be unhappy; but an experienced worker urges all to lay in large stores of charity and patience before going to the field, declaring that it takes all the grace that Christians can command to get through the first year or two safely, while becoming adjusted to the new conditions.

While the board determines the mission to which the new missionary is assigned, as a rule the station is determined by the mission or bishop, usually after his arrival on the field. The recruit should not have a voice in this matter. He is personally interested, of course, but he is not in a position to judge wisely of the conditions and needs of the various stations, nor can he intelligently weigh the considerations that are involved in the question of housing him conveniently. Let him accept the decision gracefully, whether he likes it or not, assured that his associates have done the best that was practicable in view of all the circumstances. A change can be made in due time, if good reason for it develops. The fact that the new man was sent out on account of a vacancy or the opening of new work does not necessarily imply that he is to go to that particular place, as the mission may send an experienced man to that post and have the new man go to the place which has thus been vacated. It is seldom wise for new work to be opened by new men, nor is it reasonable for a raw recruit to expect to be given the headship of important work because his predecessor filled it. The prominent post should ordinarily be assigned to some missionary who by years of faithful service has fairly earned promotion and the new man should begin where others did—at the bottom.

The first formidable undertaking is the language. It is a task to try men's souls, for, save in Spanish and Portuguese speaking countries, native speech is a fearful thing to a foreigner. The difficulty is not so great as it once was, for the earlier missionaries compiled grammars, lexicons and phrase books which are a great help to those who come after them; but no amount of apparatus can make it easy to acquire a strange tongue. The ear must be trained to recognize new sounds, the voice to produce them accurately, the memory to hold them and the vocal organs to express them. Moreover, the native language may have no words for some of the fundamental conceptions of Christianity. The term "God" may suggest to the native the wooden god in the temple, "sin" merely a breach of custom. It appears simple enough

First Impressions and Language Study

to translate, "I am the bread of life;" but the Korean had no bread. "I am the good Shepherd and know My sheep," is eloquently suggestive to us, but it means nothing to a peasant Japanese who never saw a sheep. The missionary must therefore devise some circumlocution to convey his meaning. One sorely tried young wife wrote:

"Can anything be more bewildering to a new missionary than the thought of having to swallow whole some two thousand of these complicated characters which mock one all day long by refusing to stay put in one's memory, and then sit on the bed posts at night pointing a finger of scorn at the poor, tired missionary who tries to get to sleep? I wish there were some way in which a self-respecting Christian could express in forceful language his opinion of the study of Chinese."

It has been repeatedly demonstrated, however, that one need not be an intellectual prodigy to acquire a difficult language. Patience and perseverance will do it. The famous Dr. John Nevius of China is an instance of this. He did not consider himself a linguistic genius, but he toiled so faithfully and conscientiously that, nine months after his arrival, he could help at the street chapel, and at the end of the year could preach. This is exceptional, but what Lawrence calls "a solemn purpose to take possession of the language in the name of the Lord" will do wonders. No earnest missionary need fear failure. "Some languages are harder than others; but any one who is worthy to be a missionary, can, if he sets himself steadfastly to the task, learn any language in the world." [1]

It is well for the new missionary to limit for a time his English reading and conversation. It may not be wise to go so far as Dr. Nevius, who, for the first decade, would not permit himself to look into an English book, unless it was a commentary or other working volume that was necessary to his studies; but so far as practicable, the missionary should force

---

[1] The Rev. Dr. Calvin W. Mateer of China.

himself to use the native language in both reading and speaking until he can make it the easy channel for receiving and communicating ideas.

Experience has shown that if one does not obtain a working knowledge of the language during the first few years, the probabilities are that he will never become an efficient missionary. Care should be taken to learn correctly as one goes, so as to avoid falling into slovenly habits that, when fixed, will long trouble one. Imagine with what amusement not unmingled with contempt, we would listen to a Buddhist priest who tried to convert us in broken accents, misplaced words and jumbled idioms. Even the scholarly Dr. Philip Schaff, when beginning to preach in English, convulsed his congregation and destroyed the effect of a prayerfully studied sermon by telling his hearers that they could "be whitewashed in the blood of the Lamb," instead of "washed white." The liability to such blunders is far greater in Asia, where the meaning of words often varies with the inflection. One young missionary, blissfully unconscious that the Arabic word for "bereavement" differed by only an easily mispronounced consonant from the word for "rooster," sympathetically said to a weeping widow: "I am very sorry that a rooster has come to you; but it is a comfort to know that we are in the hands of God, and that when He sends roosters upon us, He gives us grace to bear them!" A wife, who had recently arrived on the field, charged her astonished cook to beat up too girls and put them into a cake, when she meant two eggs. Another called for a small pail of hot water, only to receive to her dismay a small puppy. A young minister, who was making his first effort to preach in the vernacular, intended to refer to the pearly gates of Heaven. But the word, "chu," unless very carefully used, may mean either pearl or pork, and he understood the eager interest of his auditors when, at the close of the service, an old woman soberly informed him that she would do her best to reach that place where pork was so plentiful, as she was very fond of it.

The inflection of the Chinese word, "kwai," makes the difference in meaning between home and devil, so that a dignified missionary, who wanted to tell some boys to go home, calmly bade them go to the devil. Another preached eloquently about his "Heavenly Father" (T'in Foo); but he failed to get in the aspirate, and the omission made him say his "crazy father." His hearers pitied him, but, of course, saw no reason why they should worship the deranged parent of a missionary. The Oriental is more outwardly impassive than the American, but his emotions are not essentially different when a missionary, as one is said to have done, uses the word for "geese" when he means "sorrow," or when, as another did, he closes a service by solemnly pronouncing the form for baptism instead of the benediction.

The new missionary is usually eager to undertake work at once, and he finds it trying to sit quietly down and study the language while loud calls are sounding on every side; but he should remember that he has come for a life service and that nothing vill be gained by skimping the initiatory studies. Christ waited until He was thirty years of age, before He began His ministry. No time is wasted that is spent in careful preparation for this great work. This initial delay is really necessary, for in going into a new country, among people whose manners and customs are unfamiliar and where the methods of work are novel, it is well to have a little time to adjust oneself to the new conditions before entering upon public work.

"If," says Dr. Henry H. Jessup, of Syria, "the recruit could plunge into his work on his first arrival, knowing the language, but knowing nothing of the habits, prejudices, customs, courtesies, proprieties, religions, tenets, superstitions and national tastes of the peoples, he would make more enemies in a month than he could unmake in years." "The study of the language compels the study of the people; the study of the people brings adaptation to them, and all this results in that practical wisdom which is one of the secrets of success."

Each mission has laid out a regular course of language study, covering, in most fields, three years and with stated examinations. Sometimes young missionaries are inclined to resent these examinations. But it is wiser to recognize both their necessity and their helpfulness. Both the missions and the boards are insisting more and more strictly upon the completion of this course. One missionary who failed for three years in succession to pass his first year's examination was informed by his board that his failure was equivalent to a resignation. Illness or premature pressure of work due to the furloughs of colleagues may, of course, hinder studies for a time. Physicians are peculiarly exposed to interruptions, for the sick and injured will sometimes make appeals that it is almost impossible to refuse. But, as far as possible, missions should see that language studies are not interfered with, and the new missionary should resolutely concentrate his mind upon his task and not allow other things to break in, unless they are absolutely imperative. He need not, however, go to the extreme of refusing to do anything whatever except to study the language. There are various little things that the new missionary can do almost from the beginning that will help his over-burdened associates without interfering with his studies. These things he should of course do, but the language should be the main thing.

The completion of the prescribed course should not be deemed the end of language study; this should never end. The missionary should set apart a little time each day for reading in the native language, watch for new words and idioms in conversation, and steadily add to his vocabulary. Sir Mortimer Durand, after a residence of many years in Asia, said: "To master an Oriental language, as you must master it if you are to be of any use, is itself a labour of years. Judson used often to sit and study his Burmese for twelve hours out of the twenty-four, and it took him twenty-seven years to complete his translation of the Bible. That is the kind of toil you must be ready to face."

First Impressions and Language Study

"Even married women with little children," says Mrs. Baird of Korea, "can accomplish much. I know a missionary who reached the field with several small children. Other little ones came to her and her health was never robust, yet little by little she added to her knowledge of the language, and by and by when her children grew older and strength and leisure were hers once more, she was able to take her place in the missionary work of the station." The veteran Dr. Calvin W. Mateer of China adds this further word from his experience:

"A special word needs to be said with regard to ladies. Other things being equal, they generally at the start learn the language with greater facility than men. What they need is the ambition and the perseverance to keep on. Married ladies are, of course, more or less handicapped with household cares. Nevertheless, with reasonable health, it is quite practicable for them to learn the language. Many have done conspicuously well in this regard, not always those who have had the best opportunities or the highest gifts, but always those who had a high sense of their duty in this regard and who had a mind to succeed. In most heathen lands, domestic service is plentiful and cheap, so that ladies may generally be relieved of much of the work of housekeeping, though not, of course, of its cares. Every woman who marries a missionary ought to do it with the distinct purpose that she is going to be a missionary herself. She is generally so regarded and so called and she ought to fulfill her calling, which she cannot do without the language."

There are, of course, many difficulties beside the language. The natives may receive the message with open ridicule or dull incomprehension. Tedious iteration for many years may be necessary before a lodgment is effected for the new idea. This stolid immobility is one of the most serious obstacles which the missionary has to encounter. It takes so long to make an impression on the native mind that, if the missionary is not the most patient and persistent of men, he will be quite discouraged. It is hardly reasonable, however, to sit down and cry, as one young wife did, because "the people do not appreciate our motives in leaving comfortable homes to work for them," or, as one young husband did, become censorious and disgusted because "the natives have so many imperfections and vices." Even the native Christians are sometimes disappointing. One sorely tried new missionary wrote, after a hard year's work: "This is the most discouraging work I have ever been in. There seems to be no return for the efforts put forth to help the people. What the native lacks is stability of character and honesty." Precisely; that is why the missionary was sent there. If the people were ideal, there would be no need for his presence. Their imperfections are his opportunity. The harder the field, the more evident is it that the gospel of Christ is needed there. No one worthy to be a missionary should want an easy place. Difficulty should beget inspiration to more resolute endeavour.

VI

THE MISSIONARY AT WORK

THE variety and scope of the foreign missionary's work are in sharp contrast with the work of the minister at home. The latter hardly realizes to what an extent the effort of the Church is reinforced by the social results of centuries of religious teaching. These helps do not exist in most non-Christian lands and therefore the missionary must create them. He must found not only churches, but schools, hospitals, printing presses, kindergartens, orphanages, and the various other kinds of Christian and benevolent work carried on in this country. He must train up a native ministry, erect buildings, translate and print books and tracts and catechisms. The gospel must be so presented as to touch the lives of men at many points and they must be helped in making the adaptation to new conditions. In some lands, the missionary must even teach the men how to make clothing, to build houses and to cultivate the soil; while his wife must show the women how to sew and to cook, to care for children and to make a decent home.

The phrase "missionary at work" is therefore not a misnomer. Those who imagine that "missionaries have an easy time" little realize the heavy and persistent toil that is involved in missionary effort. The fact is that foreign missionaries are among the hardest worked men in the world. It sounds large to state that the total number is 29,188; but this includes wives and mothers with the same family cares as women at home, those at home on furlough, the sick, the aged and recruits who are learning the language. The number available for actual service at a given time is therefore considerably smaller.

This force must conduct all the vast activities of Protestant

Christianity among the thousand millions of the non-Christian races. Much of this work, too, is done in unfavourable climates and amid conditions that tell heavily upon the strength and nerves. The typical hospital, with work enough for two or three physicians, has but one medical missionary and he must perform every operation and attend every sick patient, save for such native assistants as he may be able to snatch a little time to train. Schools, which at home would have a half dozen or more teachers, have but one or two. The ordained missionary often finds himself obliged to unite the adaptability of a jack-of-all-trades to the functions of an archbishop. One missionary in China, for example, in addition to the care of a large native church and the teaching of a class of inquirers, had to supervise eleven day schools and thirteen out-stations, draw the plans for and superintend the erection of a brick residence, a schoolhouse and several small houses for native helpers. His masons had never seen a foreign house or built a chimney and his carpenters had never made a stairway, so that he had to direct personally every detail from the sawing of the logs and the burning of the brick to the laying of the last roof-tile and the painting and papering. Another missionary has the oversight of six organized churches, forty-five out-stations scattered over a wide territory and including 1,000 communicants and 200 inquirers. He superintends forty-six day schools with 460 pupils, a single circuit of these schools involving a journey by cart or litter of 500 miles. During a famine, he employed all the natives who were willing to work in rebuilding dykes and bridges which had been swept away by a flood. His annual report showed 139 sermons, 116 days spent away from home in country work, and 1,780 miles travelled on missionary duties. He was treasurer of the station and clerk of the Presbytery, and a summer lecturer to a class of pastors on the Old Testament and on recent Egyptian and Assyrian discoveries, a subject in which those twenty Christian natives manifested keen interest. He prepared weekly Bible-lesson leaflets throughout the year, while importunate appeals to settle quarrels and lawsuits and a voluminous correspondence demanded many weary hours. These are typical, not exceptional, cases. The work is so exhausting that, as a rule, the missionary comes home on furlough completely exhausted and, not infrequently, ill. Students who are contemplating application for appointment should realize these things and be prepared to say:

> "We are not here to play, to dream, to drift,
> We have hard work to do and loads to lift;
> Shun not the struggles, 'tis God's gift." [1]

The ordinary work of the foreign missionary is along four main lines. Probably the first impression of the traveller is of the

EDUCATIONAL WORK

This is partly because it is represented by institutions that are more conspicuous, partly because children are much in evidence in a typical heathen city. They are sweet-faced, bright-eyed children to whom one is instinctively drawn. One hears the patter of their wooden sandals in the streets of Japan. He sees their quaintly grave faces in the rice-fields of China. He never wearies of watching their brown, chubby little bodies on the river banks of Siam. His heart aches as he sees their emaciated limbs and wan looks in India. Everywhere their features are so expressive, that he feels that they ought to have a better chance in life and that he ought to help them to get it, while new meaning irradiates the words: "It is not the will of your Father that one of these little ones should perish."

In this spirit, one of the first and most loving duties of the missionary is to gather these children into schools and to teach them for this life and the life to come. Day schools of primary grade are, of course, the most numerous and they

[1] Maltbie D. Babcock.

reach myriads of little ones. Above them are the boarding-schools, where children are under the continuous care of the missionary. If he be a benefactor of the race who makes two blades of grass grow where one grew before, what shall be said of the missionary who takes a half-naked urchin out of the squalor of a mud hut, where both sexes and all ages herd like pigs, teaches him to bathe himself, to respect woman, to tell the truth, to earn an honest living and to serve God. It means even more for the girls than for the boys, for heathenism, which venerates animals, despises women. In sacred Benares, India, I saw a man make reverent way for a cow and a little farther on roughly push a woman out of his path. I saw monkeys, too, in the protected luxury of a temple, while at its gates starving girls begged for bread. Is there any work more Christlike than the gathering of these neglected ones into clean dormitories and showing them the meaning of virtue, of industry, and of that which does not exist throughout all the pagan world, except where the gospel has made it, a pure, sweet, Christian home? The contrast between the boarding-school graduate and the heathen woman is so marked that in some lands, like Korea and Africa, the former can be easily identified anywhere by the unmistakable signs of superior neatness, self-respect and character.

Colleges and normal, medical and theological schools take the more promising graduates of the boarding-schools and train them for special work among their own people. The equipment of these institutions is often very humble as compared with the magnificent buildings of many of our home colleges; but we may safely challenge Europe and America to show colleges which have achieved more solid results with such limited resources. Many a mission college turns out well-trained men on an income that would hardly keep a home university in lights and fuel, and amid conditions as primitive as those of the famous Log College.

These schools and colleges are exerting an enormous influence.

They lead many students to Christ. They undermine the superstitions and dispel the prejudices of many who are not immediately converted. They give the missionary access to new villages and zenanas and familiarize the heathen mind with Christian conceptions. They often form the most effective means of reaching the upper classes. Scores of mission schools are educating the sons and daughters of officials, noblemen and, in some countries, of royal princes. An interesting illustration of the opportunities thus created occurred in Bangkok, Siam. A nobleman, whom the missionary had vainly tried to lead to Christ, sent his only son to the Christian Boys' High School. A year or two later, in an epidemic of cholera, the boy died. The missionary gently told the stricken parents of the Good Shepherd, who sometimes took a lamb in His arms to induce the sheep to follow Him. Deeply moved, the father sketched an outline of the incident and bade an artist paint it. He showed us the picture: a shepherd, with a face kindly and sweet, carrying a lamb in his bosom, while afar off two sheep, which had been walking away, were turning with wistful eyes to follow their loved one. "Now," said the nobleman, "I want to give 10,000 ticals to build a church in recognition of God's dealings with me through my boy." And we said: It is as true now as of old that "a little child shall lead them."

Mission schools should be uncompromisingly Christian. The Bible is the chief text-book. Jesus is the great Teacher. Prayer is the atmosphere. Japan tested missionary fidelity to this position. All avenues of preferment lead from the schools which have government recognition. The mission schools were thus recognized; but one day, the Minister of State for Education issued an order forbidding any religious instruction in schools approved by the government. The missionaries had to choose that day whom they would serve. Severance from the government system of education meant that students would be, in effect, debarred from the university and from many positions that are coveted by the patriotic Japanese; but the missionaries and the boards said: "We cannot use missionary funds to give the young people of Asia a purely secular education; we are here for Christ's sake, and for His only." The result was that some schools had to be closed and that the attendance of others dwindled from hundreds to dozens. It looked for a time as if the end of mission educational work in Japan had come; but a mighty protest went up from the Christian people of all lands. The public opinion of Christendom, to which Japan is keenly sensitive, made her statesmen feel that a backward step had been taken. The order was not enforced, and to-day the mission schools are fuller than ever and with a tremendously enhanced influence, because in the hour of emergency, they would not buy the favour of the state at the cost of their faith. The missionary repudiates the statement of a professor at home that "the university is not responsible for the character of its graduates." Character is precisely what mission institutions are responsible for, and in the schools and colleges on the foreign field, the Protestant churches are producing it.

The hope of the future is largely in these schools. In many lands, the missionary encounters an opposition from adults that can only be compared to a wall. It is often difficult to break down that wall by direct attack, for inherited prejudices, social, business and religious associations and that fixity of character which usually comes with mature years in every land, combine to make it hard to induce an adult to abandon the faith of his ancestors. But in the mission school, that wall is undermined, for character is taken at a plastic period and shaped for the future.

The opening of Asia to the influences of the modern world and the development of the native churches give special emphasis to the question of higher education. The need is emphasized by the fact that leading Asiatic nations are beginning to appreciate the importance of western learning and are establishing colleges of their own. Hindu, Buddhist and Moslem institutions will not, of course, train men for Christian leadership. The churches must provide the needed facilities or see their young men go to schools dominated by anti-Christian influences. That the boards and the missions realize this is seen in the fact that there are now on the foreign field no less than 50,079 mission schools, of which about a thousand are of the higher grades, the total number of pupils being 2,440,148.

Another department of missionary activity is

Literary Work

Protestantism believes that a knowledge of the Word of God is indispensable to intelligent and permanent faith. Therefore one of the duties of the missionary is to translate the Bible into the vernacular. The American Seminary at Beirut, Syria, preserves with sacred care the upper room where Drs. Eli Smith and C. V. A. Van Dyck toiled for weary years translating the Bible into Arabic. There are many such rooms in various parts of the world and in them patient scholars have felt like Robert Moffat, who, when he had written the last verse in the tongue of the Bechuanas, said: "I could hardly believe I was in the world, so difficult was it for me to realize that my work of so many years was completed. My heart beat like the strokes of a hammer. My emotions found vent by my falling on my knees and thanking God for His grace and goodness in giving me strength to accomplish my task." We often hear that the Bible is now accessible to practically all the nations of the earth. It is true, and the missionary is the one who has made it so.

Bible translation, however, is not all of this work. Many books and tracts must be prepared. Most of the literature of the mission lands is unclean. There are, indeed, some excellent writings in the sacred books of Hinduism, Buddhism and Confucianism; but at their best, they are merely ethical and are intermingled with a vast mass of error, puerility and superstition. The books in common circulation are usually saturated with heathenism, if not actual immorality. The missionary, therefore, must create a Christian literature. This involves both translation and original composition. The chapter on The Missionary's Intellectual Life will show more in detail how extensive and how valuable is this form of missionary labour.

Publishing has to follow preparation. Many lands had no types or presses when the missionary arrived; so he had to create and operate them. He was among the first to see the providential significance of movable type and the application of steam to the printing press. To-day, 160 presses are conducted by the Protestant mission boards in various parts of the world, and they issue annually about 400,000,000 pages of a Christian literature and the Word of God. The Presbyterian and Methodist presses in Shanghai are exerting an enormous influence on the thought of a quarter of the human race, the former alone printing over 97,000,000 pages a year. An interesting illustration of this occurred when 10,000 Christian women of China presented a copy of the New Testament, bound in silver and gold, to the Empress Dowager on her sixtieth birthday. The gift excited so much interest in the Imperial Palace that the Emperor purchased a copy for his own use. That Chinese Bible has gone into many a yamen as well as into myriads of humble homes. A medical missionary, calling on the late Viceroy Li Hung Chang, found that great statesman reading a Testament printed on the Shanghai mission press, and when a servant took the book away as the physician entered, the Viceroy said, "Do not put that in the library; take it to my bedroom; I will read it again." The mission press in Beirut, Syria, is probably doing as much as all other agencies combined to influence the Mohammedan world, for there the Bible is printed in the language that is spoken by more than 40,000,000 souls. Scriptures and explanatory books and tracts go forth from that unpretentious building, which are read not only in Syria and Palestine, but in Asia Minor, Arabia, Egypt, Tunis, Algiers, Morocco, India and among the Arabic speaking colonies of North and South America.

The Bible Societies give valuable coöperation in this department of mission work, paying the cost of printing the Scriptures, and, through their agents and colporteurs, aiding greatly in distributing them. These Societies should therefore be considered an integral and a very important part of this large development of missionary effort.

Greater emphasis should be laid upon literary work as a missionary agency. The peoples of Asia are not so much accustomed to public discourse as Western races. The priests of the native religions seldom or never preach, and it is much more difficult to influence people in that way than it is in England and America. The Chinese, in particular, are preëminently a people of books. Buddhism converted them, not by preaching, but by literature. The essay, the pamphlet, the placard, and more recently the newspaper, are the common means of disseminating ideas. Christianity must make a larger use of this method if it is to supersede Buddhism and Confucianism.

The printed word goes where the living voice cannot be heard. It brings its truths to men in the quiet hour. The force of its message is never lessened by controversy or perverted by error. "If," said Archbishop Longley, "I must choose between sending the man without the Book, or the Book without the man, then I say send the Book. The man may make mistakes, but the Book can make none." Within a century, over 200,000,000 copies of the Bible have been printed in 853 languages and dialects. If every missionary were to be banished, God's Word would remain in Asia, a mighty and indestructible power, operating as silently as the sunshine, but containing within itself the stupendous potency of a world's regeneration. To-day, the Persian and the Hottentot, the Korean and the Siamese are reading in their own tongues that "He is able to save them to the uttermost that come unto

God by Him," and we know that God's Word shall not return unto Him void.

A phase of missions that touches all hearts is the

MEDICAL WORK

Christ Himself set the example by ministering to the sick. Indeed, He cited among the proofs of His Messiahship that "the blind receive their sight, the lame walk, the lepers are cleansed and the deaf hear."[1] Of His thirty-six recorded miracles, twenty-four were of physical healing, and there must have been scores of others, for we read that "all they that had any sick brought them unto Him, and He laid His hands on every one of them and healed them."[2] So medical work is not a mere humanitarian addition but an essential part of our Christian service in heathen lands. We cannot "pass by on the other side" those countless sufferers or shut our ears to their cries of agony.

Every non-Christian land is a land of pain. All the diseases and injuries common in America and others far more dreadful are intensified by ignorance, by filth and by superstition. An Oriental tour fills the mind with ghastly memories of sightless eyeballs, scrofulous limbs and festering ulcers. If our child is ill, our physician's understanding of the case and its remedy, the sympathy of friends and the sweet comforts of the gospel, make the sick chamber a place of peace and probable recovery. But in most heathen lands, illness is believed to be caused by a demon that has gotten into the body, and the treatment is an effort to expel it. Drums are beaten or horns blown beside the sufferer in the hope that they will frighten away the demon. Hot fires are built to scorch it out, and of course the fierce heat adds to the distress of the patient. Sometimes even worse methods are employed. "What are those scars which so thickly dot the body?" we asked Dr. Neal, in China, as he

[1] Matt. 11 : 5.   [2] Luke 4 : 40.

examined a wan, pitiful little girl who had been brought in. "Places where hot needles have been thrust in to kill the spirit which is believed to have caused the pain," was the startling reply. "What a horrible foot!" we ejaculated, as we looked with Dr. Avison in Korea on a poor fellow who had hobbled in. A fall had made a bruise. A native doctor had told him to smear it with oil and set it on fire. Dirt and flies had aggravated the resultant sore, till the whole foot was literally rotting away.

The horrors of superstitious mal-treatment of the sick and injured are relieved in many lands only by medical missionaries who walk through those regions of pains in the name and spirit of the Great Physician, cleansing filthy ulcers, straightening deformed limbs, giving light to darkened eyes, healing fevered bodies, robbing death of its sting and the grave of its victory and showing to weary multitudes that

> "Thy touch has still its ancient power,
> No word from Thee can fruitless fall."

In the Syrian city of Hums, we saw the sick flock to Dr. Harris as of old they doubtless flocked to Christ. He had with him only a pocket case of instruments and a few medicines. The receiving room was the little church, the operating table a board laid across a couple benches. But amid those primitive conditions, the missionary gave such relief to scores of sufferers that wonder and gratitude knew no bounds and men who would have stoned a preacher reverently listened to the physician while he talked to them of Christ. The day we entered Allahabad, India, 170 people died of the plague. Corpses were hourly carried through the streets. Shops were closed. The authorities, finding that preventive measures provoked dangerous riots, helplessly allowed the pestilence to run unchecked. Half the population had fled; but the medical missionary stood heroically at her post, freely going among the sick and dying, responding both by day and night to every appeal for help, giving what aid was possible in that swiftly fatal scourge and telling all of the healing of the soul in Christ. Few men anywhere will touch a leper, but the medical missionaries lovingly seek them in a score of places, mitigating the horrors of disease for which no cure is known and faithfully applying the remedy for the soul's leprosy.

Twenty-five hundred and forty-four hospitals and dispensaries are now being maintained on the foreign field by the Protestant boards, and they treated last year 2,347,780 patients. No other phase of mission work has done more to soften hearts and to open doors, no other been more fruitful in spiritual results. Standing in one of those humble buildings and watching the tender ministries to suffering, one feels sure that God loves that place and he rejoices that in Asia as well as in America, men can say:

> "The healing of the seamless dress
>   Is by our bed of pain;
>   We touch Him in life's throng and press,
>   And we are whole again."

An unqualified statement that the fourth department of missionary activity is

EVANGELISTIC WORK

might give a wrong impression, for all forms of work are supposed to be evangelistic in spirit and in aim. Educational work is designed to reach the children for Christ and to train men for the ministry and other forms of Christian work. Literary work prepares and publishes the Bible and a helpful literature that all may know the gospel by the printed page as well as by the spoken word. Medical work is intended not only to relieve suffering, but to do it in Christ's name and in such ways that the patients will accept Christ. There remains, however, much work that is distinctively evangelistic. Its magnitude may be inferred from the fact that there are now no less than 1,103 organized churches and a large number of unorganized congregations, with 3,614,154 adult communicants and a Christian community of 8,342,378, of whom more than a million are enrolled inquirers.

The direct preaching of the gospel naturally has a prominent place. There is an increasing number of churches in which there are stated sermons; but the main evangelistic work is done in less pretentious, though not less effective ways. The message is proclaimed in humble street chapels, in crowded bazaars, in secluded zenanas, from house to house and on long country tours. The itinerations often occupy several months and include the visitation of hundreds of villages. All sorts of conveyances are used. Elephants, camels, horses, mules, donkeys, canoes, launches, schooners, house-boats, wheelbarrows, jinrikishas, bandy-carts, bicycles and railroad trains all serve the missionary's purpose as occasion offers, while sometimes he travels on foot.

There are no bounds to the zeal of the itinerant missionary. A toilsome journey on elephants through the jungles of Siam brought us to Saturday night with the weary ejaculation: " Now we can have a day of rest !" The next morning we slept late; but the missionaries did not, for they spent an hour before breakfast in a neighbouring village, distributing tracts and inviting the people to come to a service at our camp at ten o'clock. It was an impressive service,—under a spreading bo tree, with the mighty forest about us, monkeys curiously peering through the tangled vines, the huge elephants browsing the bamboo tips behind us and the wondering people sitting on the ground, while one of the missionaries told the deathless story of redeeming love. The other missionary, the Rev. Dr. Daniel McGilvary, was not present. Seventy-four years old though he was, he had walked three miles under a scorching sun to another village, and was preaching there. And we said: "If that is the way the missionaries rest, what do they do when they work?"

This is but a sample of the evangelistic fidelity that we saw everywhere. Missionaries whose immediate assignments are to medical or educational work take their turns in country touring. A physician in Africa never did a better thing for Christ than on a trip of which he wrote:

"I returned last week from a tour of seventeen days through the Utum country. The wet season was at its worst. All the rivers were flooded and the swamps were terrible to get through. Almost every day, I waded in water waist-deep, sometimes for hours at a time. A large river was crossed on a raft of logs. Much of my trip was through a country from which we had never been able to get any schoolboys, as the people were afraid to let them go so far from home and with white men of whom they knew but little. I went with the determination not only to preach the gospel, but to bring back with me some boys for our school. I knew if I could get a few for a start, we would get plenty in years to come. The Lord answered my prayers and when we marched back through streams and forests, about seventy prospective pupils went with me. That long line of children, so ignorant and needy, some footsore and weary, marching away from their homes of darkness and sin towards the light of the dear Saviour who died for them, was a sight which would move a heart of stone. Sometimes a mother in parting from her child would follow along for miles and then take me by the hands and with tears rolling down her cheeks say: 'Doctor, that is my only child, you will take good care of him, won't you?' Human nature is very much the same here as elsewhere."

Such tours bring one into closer touch with the people, enable him to bring the gospel to some who might not otherwise hear of it and keep his own spiritual zeal warm and rich. Missionaries sometimes frankly write of the difficulty of securing time for these country trips. They candidly admit that the temptation is strong to become absorbed by the various phases of institutional and station work, that it is so easy to sit down in a school or hospital, to become a pastor of a native church or to stay at home and write a book, and so hard to leave one's family and endure the physical privations incident to itinerating. But more of this work must be done if the world is to hear the gospel. Christ Himself signally honoured this form of missionary effort, for He devoted no small part of His ministry to itinerating; so did Paul and his apostolic associates. Dr. S. A. Moffett assigns the first place among the factors in the remarkable development of missionary work in Korea to " the wide-spread preaching of the gospel message in its simplicity." He adds:

" There should be a perfectly frank avowal of one's mission and a presentation of the gospel message to every one as the most natural subject of conversation and interest. A method adapted to the genius of the people seems to be informal conversation with individuals and small groups of people, along the wayside, in the inns, on the street, in the shops, in the country village, anywhere and everywhere, with the invitation to visit you in your sarang. The wide-spread informal dissemination of the gospel news will result in bringing visitors from a wide territory, while the sarang work will give opportunity for a heart-to-heart dealing with individuals.

Some missionaries assert that street chapel preaching does not pay. But Dr. Hunter Corbett of Chefoo, after over forty years' experience, emphatically declares that it does pay. It must, however, have the right kind of a preacher, alert, sympathetic, and ready in extemporaneous address. It must, too, be followed up by diligent house-to-house work and by free itineration. Few may be converted at the chapel, but prejudices will be removed, hearts softened and thoughts of God aroused. Hearers are often visitors from the country, and months afterwards, the preacher, visiting some distant village, may be welcomed by a man who first heard the gospel at the city street chapel, and through him gain a foothold in a new community. It has repeatedly happened that work has suddenly sprung up in some distant village, and that the missionary has been at a loss to understand why that particular place, rather than scores of nearer ones, should yield such fruit, till he has found that the leading spirits received the Word in the city chapel.

How soon should a professed convert be baptized? This is another of the perplexing questions that confront a missionary. Manifestly, great care must be exercised lest unworthy members be received. It is desirable that some immediate commitment should be insisted on; but the purity and influence of the infant Church must be protected from those who seek membership from improper motives. Probably the best method of attaining both of these ends is the catechumenate. Dr. Moffett, who has made large use of this method, writes:

"As soon as a man gives evidence of a knowledge of sin and of an acceptance of Christ as his Saviour, he should be encouraged to make a public confession. It assists a man to reach a decision, and this helps him to cut loose from his past life; it is a formal recognition of his desire to be a Christian so that he becomes connected with the Church in a way that necessitates some provision for his systematic instruction and oversight, and it puts him in the position of at once making known to others the fact that he has identified himself with Christianity. It is particularly valuable in the early stages of work, furnishing a means of recognition and organization of first converts before the Church with its baptized membership and fuller organization becomes the more prominent exponent of Christianity."

The wise missionary selects for his evangelistic preaching the more vital themes of the gospel. There is no time for doubts or secondary truths when face to face with heathenism. Sin and atonement, repentance and faith, the dire need of man and the sovereign love of God are among the doctrines that are indispensable. No one should be misled by the idea that men are going to be converted wholesale or by any patent device. It has recently been said that present missionary methods remind one of the old time sexton who went about a church and lighted each lamp separately, and that we ought to adopt the method of the modern sexton, who simply goes behind the pulpit and touches a button. "Convert a dozen of China's leaders," it is asserted, "and you will convert China." We do not believe in that kind of conversion. We sympathize rather with James Gilmour who, in a letter shortly before his death, wrote: "I am becoming more and more impressed with the idea that what is wanted in China is not new 'lightning methods' so much as good, honest, quiet, earnest, persistent work in old lines and ways." Some changes in method are indeed required, but not those that involve the abandonment of Christ's method of dealing with men.

There are some mistakes at home that should be avoided. We rejoice in the magnificent work of several undenominational religious and philanthropic agencies at home. They are necessary here as things are. But some of them would not have been necessary if the churches had been more united in practical work. Thousands of churches largely confine themselves to sermons and prayer meetings for those who voluntarily attend, and leave much of the real application of the gospel to society to outside organizations, manned and supported indeed by Christians, but as individuals, not as churches. Experience has taught us something at home. Shall we not heed its lessons abroad? Converts should start with the idea that the Church of God comprehends all needful vows and all Christlike activities, that the Church can and should teach the young and the sick and the poor and work for temperance and purity, and that its duty is not half done when it preaches to those who seek it. Christ not only said to the people: "Come," but He peremptorily said to His disciples, "Go." The Church should touch human life at many points and be a centre from which influences and activities radiate. Its chief business is to seek those who will not come. Men used to say that "a demand creates a supply." To-day we say, "a supply creates a demand." The extraordinary development of western trade with foreign lands is largely due to this aggressive policy. In Hongkong we found American flour controlling the market. We learned that a Christian business man had created that market, working for years and spending tens of thousands of dollars to dispel the prejudice of the rice-eating Chinese against American flour. Now he sells in such enormous quantities that his numerous mills must run day and night to supply the demand. In like manner, we are taking the gospel to people who know nothing about it, explaining it to them, persuading them in Christ's stead to accept it and to organize their whole personal and social life in accordance with its precepts.

Reform movements in a community naturally grow of spiritual work, but there is a difference of opinion as to the missionary's direct relation to them. Some urge that the missionary should not concern himself at all with such movements, his efforts being to instil in the minds of men the formative principles of the Christian religion and then leave them to work their own legitimate results through saved men. They urge that Christ and His apostles followed this method, and that, inasmuch as sin is the root difficulty, the missionary in solving the problem of sin is really bringing to society the ultimate solution of its moral problems.

Others, however, insist that the missionary cannot be indifferent to the practical application of the gospel to human society; that when orphans in India are starving, his efforts should include bread as well as exhortations; that when opium-smoking in China is an effectual bar to the entrance of the gospel, the missionary should ally himself with the effort to remove that bar; and that where the blind, the insane, the deaf and dumb are entirely neglected, the missionary who passes "by on the other side" exposes himself to the indignant censure which Christ visited upon the heartless, hypocritical "priest" and "Levite."

It seems to us that extreme views in either direction are to be avoided and that the mediate course is the proper one. The gospel was intended to save men both for this life and for the life to come, and when a missionary goes among people who are wholly ignorant of the bearings of the gospel upon human life, it is surely within his province to show them how to live in time as well as eternity. This, as a matter of fact, is what the missionaries are doing. It is no small evidence of the value of mission work that missionaries have founded and are maintaining three hundred and thirty-three asylums of various kinds for the afflicted and dependent classes. Though reform movements, as we have seen elsewhere,[1] are results rather than objects of the missionary enterprise, they are nevertheless of value. Missionaries have done more than all others combined to lessen the evils of slavery, infanticide, intemperance, concubinage, opium-smoking, the degradation of woman and kindred evils.

A signal instance of the usefulness of the missionary in matters of reform occurred in Siam. Gambling is the national vice. It was licensed and even encouraged by the government. The monopoly in every town was auctioned off to the highest bidder. The successful concessionaire erected a large building in a central location. Music and theatrical performances added to the attractiveness of the place, and, in the evenings, almost the whole population assembled. There were one hundred and three large gambling houses throughout the interior, besides a great number in Bangkok, the capital. The demoralizing consequences can be readily understood. This vice was vigorously combatted by the missionaries, led by the Rev. Dr. Eugene P. Dunlap and powerfully reinforced by the Hon. Hamilton King, the American Minister. They frankly represented to the

[1] Chapters I and II.

King that gambling was inimical to the best interests of Siam and that the money that the government derived from it was obtained at a ruinous cost to character and legitimate industry. The King listened, and the result was the issuance of a royal decree, January, 1905, ordering the abolition of these gambling concessions by April, 1907.

Another illustration occurred in Shanghai, China, where there are about 20,000 Chinese prostitutes. Distressed by their pitiful lot, Mrs. George F. Fitch opened a Rescue Home to which the slave girls could flee for refuge. The Home has attracted wide attention and it witnesses powerfully for Christ. A high official visited it one day with his wife, and as he noted the sweet ministries to the fallen, he marvelled and said to his wife, "Nobody but Christians would do this."

Care should be taken, however, not to allow purely reform movements to take the place of the more direct and vital forms of missionary work. The missionary is preëminently a man who is working at the foundations of character and morals, and useful as he may be as a reformer, he will make a great mistake if he becomes a reformer only.

It is apparent from all that has been said that the working out of so vast a movement as the missionary enterprise will require time. This is not a crusade whose object is to be attained by a magnificent spurt. Error and superstition are interwoven with the whole social and political fabric of the non-Christian world and they are not to be overturned in a day. "We are in the midst of habits and institutions from which our civilization is separated by a long interval of development, where progress upward must be a long, slow process, must proceed on native lines, and must be the effect of the example and prestige of higher standards rather than the result of ruder methods."[1]

Missionary effort, therefore, must be a work of undermining

[1] Benjamin Kidd.

for a long period. In removing the Hell-Gate obstructions from New York Harbour, an army of workmen toiled for weary months in hidden tunnels, and hundreds of thousands of dollars were expended before anything could be seen on the surface. Indeed, there was no visible result whatever till that supreme moment when, in the presence of uncounted multitudes, the waters were tumultuously upheaved and with an awful roar the obstructions of ages were blown to fragments. Most great reconstructions of society have come slowly, and religious transformations have been no exception. Christianity was three hundred years in conquering Rome and even then the Roman world was far from complete conversion. The gospel has been operating on the peoples of northern Europe and their descendants for more than a thousand years, and no Christian feels that the work is done. It is to be hoped that other peoples will not take as much time as we took; but we cannot reasonably expect that a few decades will suffice.

Moreover, we must count now on more strenuous opposition from the non-Christian religions. At first, they were contemptuously indifferent to the missionaries. But as the priests see more clearly what radical changes Christianity involves, that it is "turning the world upside down," contempt and indifference are giving place to alarm. The ethnic faiths are therefore setting themselves in battle array. It would be foolish to ignore their power, foolish to imagine that we are seeing the last of Buddhism in Japan and Siam, of Confucianism in China, of Brahmanism in India, and of Mohammedanism in Turkey. Heathenism will die hard. The world, the flesh and the devil are in Asia as well as in America, and fighting more fiercely. It is no holiday task to which we have set ourselves. It is a gigantic struggle in which there are against us "the principalities, the powers, the world rulers of this darkness." Need have we of patience, of determination, of "the strength of His might and the whole armour of God." The missionary must sternly face his task in the spirit of the man of whom Browning said : He

> " . . . never turned his back, but marched breast-forward,
>   Never doubted clouds would break;
> Never dreamed, though right were worsted, wrong would triumph;
> Held we fall to rise, are baffled to fight better,
>   Sleep to wake."

The issue is not doubtful, for "if God be for us, who can be against us."

VII

THE MISSIONARY'S FINANCIAL SUPPORT

THIS is a subject that interests both the student volunteer and the layman who supports him. There is the more reason for discussing it because it is very commonly misunderstood.

The principle should be borne in mind at the outset that the missionary is not paid a salary at all, in the sense of compensation, but is simply given a support. Inquiry is made as to the cost of a reasonably comfortable living, and a sum is assigned that covers that cost. The amount varies in different fields, as the cost of living varies; but everywhere it is intended to make possible the same scale of support. The fact that salaries are higher in South America than in Africa does not mean that the missionaries in the former get more, but simply that the expense of living is greater. In accordance with this principle, a single man receives the lowest sum, because he alone is to be supported. A married man gets more, because two are to be supported instead of one. The birth of a child brings a small additional allowance, usually $200 a year, because it means an increased expenditure.

Most of the boards make a flat rate for all the missionaries of a given region, paying the same amount to the new recruit as to the veteran. Others grade salaries according to length of service, paying a minimum amount for the first term, a little larger sum for the second term and a still larger one for the third. This plan is growing in favour, as it recognizes the fact that expenses increase with enlarging work and family; but no distinction is ever made on the ground of relative ability or responsibility. The most famous preacher, the president of a great university and the superintendent of the largest hospital receive precisely the same salary as the humblest member of the mission. Evangelists, educators and physicians are all paid the same salaries. Single men usually receive a little more than single women, not because they are considered as worth more, but because it costs them more to live, as they more often require separate establishments, while single women can usually live with some family or in a school.

It will be seen that it is not possible to state any particular figure that would apply to all fields. Generally speaking, however, the average salary is about $1,000 for a single missionary and $1,800 for a married one. This is not designed to cover house accommodations, which are provided in addition. Some of the boards prefer to rent rather than to build, if suitable houses can be secured; otherwise, land is bought and a residence erected. It does not follow that the new missionary will find a residence waiting for him on his arrival. Funds for such purposes are hard to get and he may be called upon to make shift temporarily in anything that he can find, perhaps a few rooms in a school or a hastily adapted native house, until a permanent place can be secured.

The scale of support is intended to be adequate to the needs of a Christian worker who is not extravagant in his tastes, and the promised sum is promptly paid. It covers, however, only reasonable needs, and while ministers in this country may look forward to an increase, sometimes to large figures, the most eminent foreign missionary can expect only modest support to the day of his death. Other foreigners in non-Christian lands are paid far more liberally than missionaries. It is as true now as when Macaulay wrote that "all English labour in India, from the labour of the governor-general and the commander-in-chief, down to that of a groom or a watch-maker, must be paid for at a higher rate than at home. No man will be banished, and banished to the Torrid Zone, for nothing. The rule holds good with respect to the legal profession. No English barrister will work fifteen thousand miles from all his friends, with the thermometer at ninety-six in the shade, for the emoluments which will content him in chambers that overlook the Thames. Accordingly the fees at Calcutta are about three times as great as the fees of Westminster Hall; and this, though the people of India are, beyond all comparison, poorer than the people of England."[1]

Business men who have commercial dealings with Asia and Africa say that they have to pay three times the salaries that are paid in this country in order to induce their clerks and agents to stay abroad. One of the latter is reported to have said that he "would rather hang on to a lamp-post in the United States than to have an estate and a palace amid the heat and dust and snakes and dirt and fevers and fleas of a typical Oriental country." But missionaries like the Rev. Henry Jessup, D. D., LL. D., the famous scholar and former Moderator of the Presbyterian General Assembly, the Rev. Hunter Corbett, D. D., LL. D., the great evangelist and also a former Moderator of the Presbyterian General Assembly, the Rev. D. Z. Sheffield, D. D.,LL. D., President of Tung-chou College, the Rev. H. H. Lowry, D. D., LL. D., President of Peking University, Dr. J. P. Cochran, the celebrated surgeon, and dozens of other distinguished missionaries who could have commanded large salaries if they had stayed at home, received simply the ordinary missionary salary of their day, and house rent.

Nor has the missionary the local resources of the home missionary. He cannot accept money from native Christians for his personal use without exposing himself to the charge of mercenary motives in coming among them. It is hard enough at best for them to understand his disinterestedness. He must be able to say: "I seek not yours, but you." Therefore if he earns money, he turns it over to the board, so careful is he to avoid even the appearance of self-seeking.

[1] "Essays," III, p. 64.

It is said that "a dollar will go farther in a mission land than in America." It may, perhaps, in the purchase of some native supplies, but seldom in the articles which Europeans and Americans deem necessary. The average mission land does not produce the kinds of food and clothing that a white man has to use, and the missionary must usually buy in the home land, paying the same price that the average American at home pays and, in addition, the cost of freight across a continent or an ocean, usually both. True, he can sometimes purchase a part of his supplies at a local store, but, as a rule, he finds it cheaper to buy some staple foods and clothing in London, New York or Chicago. Even when his necessary supplies can be secured locally they may be expensive. In Colombia, some years ago, potatoes were $3.60 a bushel, kerosene was $1.10 a gallon, beef fifty cents a pound, lard twenty-four cents, sugar eighteen cents, butter $1.00, tea $3.20 and baking powder $2.00. In Persia, the missionary must pay an eighth of his year's salary for his winter's fuel. In Africa, one paid $11.00 a barrel for flour, thirty-three cents a quart for milk and $10.00 for a goat. In Siam, butter imported in tins from Belgium was sixty cents a pound. In China, condensed milk was thirty-seven cents a tin and butter seventy-five cents a pound. Some of these prices were exceptional, and the rate of exchange sometimes favours the missionary, but prices are very apt at such times to go up in proportion, so that the gain is often apparent rather than real.

The change in economic conditions in recent years has seriously affected the missionary. The cost of living has risen even more rapidly on the foreign field than at home, but the salaries have seldom risen proportionately. A committee of the Siam Mission wrote: "The cost of vegetables, fruit, chickens, eggs, fuel and coolie hire has doubled, and in some cases trebled, within the past twelve years. There has also been a constant advance in the prices of meat and milk. We

The Missionary's Financial Support

do not mention such luxuries as Irish potatoes, which sell at $24.00 per bushel (too dear for a missionary's purse); nor ham, which sells at sixty cents per pound."

This upward movement is spreading all over the world. A missionary in South America writes: "Multiply American prices of shoes by two and a half, clothing by two, cheap cloth by three, underclothes by four, hats by three and house rent by five, and you will have the prices of the same qualities of the same articles here."

It should be borne in mind, too, that the missionary has many calls upon his charity. Pastors of large city churches know how numerous such calls are at home. But there is probably no other Christian worker in the world upon whom they press so heavily as the foreign missionary. He finds himself in the midst of multitudes of poverty-stricken people. There are no charitable agencies, as at home, to which they can be referred, and there are seldom laymen in the congregation who can help in bearing the burden. The sick and the starving are continually appealing to him. Moreover, as he organizes the converts into churches, he wishes, as we have already explained, to impress upon them the duty of giving as a Christian grace, and in order to make his teaching effective, he must set the example. We do not know of any missionary who gives less than one-tenth of his salary in these ways, and we know of many who give a much larger proportion. If Christians at home would give as liberally as the missionaries, the whole missionary enterprise would be far more generously supported.

In the light of these facts, the absurdity of the criticism that "missionaries live in luxury" will readily be seen. The people of this country can judge of the facts as well as any critic by simply considering the scale of living which an income of $1,000 or $1,800 and house rent permits in America and then reflect what added cost would be represented by the effort to maintain it in different conditions several thousand miles away.

Missionaries who can "live in luxury" in such circumstances must be remarkable financiers. The fact is that the missionary is seldom able to save anything, and if he breaks down, he becomes dependent.

The "liberal provision for the education of the children," which one critic objects to, is $100 a year, and in some cases only when the child is in America and both parents are on the field. The average parent in the United States could doubtless give that critic some valuable information as to whether it is possible to feed, clothe and educate a child on $200 a year if at home, or $300 if in college, while the larger the family, the greater the difficulty. There are a few missionaries who have private means, but manifestly their expenditure is not a fair criterion for the missionary body as a whole.

Globe-trotters who have eagerly accepted missionary hospitality have sometimes been guilty of base ingratitude in their accounts of it. Oppressed by their loneliness and hungry for tidings from the home land, the missionary and his wife heartily welcome the visitor and, in honour of the occasion, bring out their little household treasures, put on their best clothes and prepare a dinner far better than they ordinarily have or than they can really afford. Then the guest goes away to prate about the extravagance of missionaries. A friend once gave Mrs. Hepburn of Japan a large turkey, a costly gift in Japan. That very day, an American traveller called with a letter of introduction. She invited him to dinner, and he wrote home, and his statement was printed in several newspapers, that the most expensive meal he had eaten in his tour around the world was at the table of a foreign missionary!

"But I hear that a certain missionary keeps four servants, while I can afford but one!" cries a wife in America. Allow us to suggest some considerations which may not have occurred to this wife.

First: Her one servant doing general housework means as much help as four servants mean in a heathen land. A cook

The Missionary's Financial Support 125

in India will do nothing but cook; a sweeper nothing but sweep; a water-drawer nothing but draw water; and so on through the whole list, each one, moreover, performing his task in a spirit the reverse of strenuous. A cook would die rather than touch a broom, for he would break his caste. A writer in the New York *Evening Post*, discussing the question from the view-point of the English military and civil service, says that "a modest household of two in an ordinary sized bungalow (in India) will command the services of no less than twenty servants." [1]

Second: The one servant at home costs more than the missionary's four. A servant in India receives from $3.00 to $5.00 a month and boards himself. A sewing woman costs four cents a day. A Chinese cook receives $5.00 a month. A missionary mother paid the nurse who cared for her four children $4.00 a month. These are the prevailing prices and the natives are glad to get them. Miss Kingsley says that she "once had an Irish charwoman who drank, who would have done the whole week's work of an African village in an afternoon, and then been quite fresh enough to knock some of the nonsense out of her husband's head with the broom, and throw a kettle of boiling water or a paraffin lamp at him, if she suspected him of flirting with other ladies." [2] "If," writes a missionary wife, "my own pleasure were consulted, I would certainly prefer working in my own home to visiting dirty Chinese homes infested with vermin and offensive odours. It seems a little strange that the missionary who pays her servants out of her own salary is so much blamed for what she would gladly help if she could."

Third: Consider, too, that at home we all have many assistants whose services we fail to take into account in comparing ourselves with foreign missionaries. The mail carrier

[1] Cf. Maxwell, "The Bishop's Conversion," pp. 97sq.
[2] "Travels in West Africa."

delivers our mail without cost to us; but the missionary usually has to hire some one to get his mail from the post-office, which is probably miles away. We can travel on a street car or a railway train; but the missionary must employ coolies to carry him in a chair or wheel him in a barrow or row him in a boat to his preaching appointments in outlying villages. The city policeman patrols our street; but the foreigner in Asia and Africa must engage a watchman or risk having his things stolen. The grocer calls at our house for orders and delivers the goods; but the missionary must have a native to do his marketing, as in many cases the native shopkeepers will ask a foreigner several times what they would ask their own people and will come down to a reasonable figure only after hours of wearisome haggling, for time is no object to an Oriental. Our complex and highly developed civilization in Europe and America enables the average man to avail himself daily of the labours of scores of others. The missionary, living in more primitive conditions, must hire servants, or neglect his work and spend the greater part of his time doing things himself that natives can do just as well and at smaller cost.

Fourth: The foreign missionary, living as he does in lands where hotels are few and vile and where Oriental ideas of hospitality prevail, is forced to keep open house for all comers. The occasional traveller and the constantly passing and repassing missionaries of his own and other churches must be freely entertained. The natives, too, call in appalling numbers. The host, like Abraham of old, must hasten to set meat and drink before every guest, for failure to do so would be deemed a breach of hospitality and an offense which would probably end the missionary's influence. A missionary wife in Syria says that she often had twenty to meals and a hundred callers in a single day, all of whom had to be served with cakes and coffee or lemonade. Another wife in China had 4,580 women visitors in one year, besides men and children. Tea had to be provided for all that host.

The Missionary's Financial Support

Fifth: Would it be common sense to send an educated Christian woman as a foreign missionary, and then force her to spend her time in cooking meals and washing dishes, when she can hire native servants who are glad to do that work for a few cents a day? Julian Ralph, writing from Asia on this subject, says: "I demand that the missionaries keep servants. They are paid to give their time to missionary work, and, especially in the case of a wife and mother, I claim she has no right to do housework, sewing, etc., and give only her leisure from such things to that service for which she has a regular salary. Carriages, also, are a necessary saving of time and strength for their work, and not for pleasure."

It may be well, however, to add this caution to new missionaries by Mrs. Baird of Korea:

"When you reach the mission field, you may conclude that it (keeping several servants) cannot be altogether right and that you will adopt a different course. But as time passes, you will see that the cheapest and most plentiful thing under heathen skies is human labour, and that the scarcest and most precious are missionary time and strength. But having yielded the point of servants, do not go to the other extreme and employ more than are necessary. Resist the temptation to increase your style of living. Take a firm grip on your original ideas of missionary simplicity, and never let go of them. Put them to practice in the house you build, the table you set, and if I had ever known a missionary who over-dressed, I would add, in the clothes you wear. Remember that you are a city set on a hill, a target for criticism from every wandering one who may strike your station, and also, as time passes on, an example to those missionaries who come after you."

Some people innocently ask, "Why don't missionaries live as the natives do?" Such people probably do not know how the natives live. The African fastens a yard of calico around his waist, ties a string of beads about his neck, and fancies himself dressed for all occasions. Bare-headed, bare-chested and barefooted, he exposes himself to the fierce rays of the tropical sun, and when night comes with its chill air and drenching dew, he sleeps upon the ground. An American doing that would be smitten with African fever within twenty-four hours. The Chinese lives contentedly and works hard on a handful of rice a day and in a dark, unventilated room not much larger than the kennel in which the reader keeps his dog. Would the critic live that way? Could he? A typical peasant woman does all the drudgery of the household, collects fuel, tills the fields and secures and prepares the food. Do the critics at home want their wives to do such work? Burmese children run around naked until they are about ten years of age. Would we allow our children to do so?

Live as the natives do? The natives do not live. The death rate of heathenism is appalling. The men die of consumption and pneumonia and fevers and cholera and small-pox. The children are carried off in regiments by diphtheria and measles and scarlet fever and cholera infantum; while as for the women, at the age of forty, when the English and American woman is in the full splendour of her beauty, the typical Asiatic and African woman is old and withered.

If any critic really imagines that he could live as many natives live, let him try it. Let him build a hut in his back yard—no floor but the beaten earth, no windows but latticed or paper-covered openings, no bed but a hard platform, no stove but an open fire in the middle of the room, no chimney but a hole in the roof through which the smoke rises and the wind and rain and snow fall, and no fuel but manure mixed with grass, made into cakes by his wife or daughter and dried in the sun. For food, let him buy three bushels of corn. It will sustain life for several weeks and cost but a dollar. Have the wife pound it between two stones, mix it with water and bake it in the ashes. Then let him eat corn for breakfast and corn for dinner and corn for supper, and the next day eat corn for breakfast and corn for dinner and corn for supper, and before many days have passed, even the most obtuse critic will know why the foreign missionary does not and cannot live as the natives do.

No, the boards are not going to ask foreign missionaries to live as the natives do. The missionary is a civilized man and he needs some things that the uncivilized man does without. Making all due allowance for compensations and exceptions, it still remains true that the average foreign missionary lives and works under a strain which few at home realize, and it would be folly to compel him to adopt a mode of life that would wreck his constitution in a few years. Common sense dictates that, having incurred the expense of sending him out, he should be so equipped that he may be able to do the work for which he was sent. The disastrous experience of the American army in Cuba taught the government that it is poor policy to economize in the support of soldiers. A division of invalids is worth little in a campaign. Shall the Church be less wise in taking reasonable care of its men?

We grant that there are richer natives who live on a much better scale; but their expenditures are so great that a missionary could not possibly equal them. The Chinese mandarin and the East Indian noble often spend money lavishly; but even then, their ideas of comfort differ so widely from ours that their home could scarcely be deemed ideal by the average American. Thousands of young men in England have pleasanter bedrooms than a governor in China, and the average mechanic in the United States has a more comfortably warmed house than a Samurai of Japan, in spite of the costly furs that lie on his floor and the elaborate carvings that adorn his room. The food and general manner of life of the wealthier classes in Asia would quickly undermine the health of a European or American.

The fact should be borne in mind that centuries of Christian civilization on the one hand and of heathen barbarism on the other have created a wide gulf between the methods of living of heathenism and Christendom. A white man who is the product of these centuries of civilization simply cannot bridge that gulf and live as his ancestors did five hundred years ago. Man, like a lower animal or a plant, becomes adjusted to his physical environment. Generations of arctic life have adapted the Laplander to intense cold, and generations of tropical life have adapted the African to intense heat; but interchange them and both will probably die. When Peary brought a party of Esquimaux to New York, every one was soon taken ill and one died of pneumonia. In like manner, nature has fitted the American to the conditions of American soil and climate, and if we transplant him to Asia or Africa, we subject his health to a strain. Therefore for him to be careful and for the boards to equip him so that he can be careful is not luxury or extravagance but common prudence.

It is said that the missionaries of certain independent organizations are not maintained as are the missionaries of the denominational boards. This is an error, so far as the best of these societies are concerned. The actual salary may be smaller, but there are allowances that the denominational boards do not make, so that the net result to the missionary is practically the same. There are, however, independent societies of which the statement is true; but the frequent result is suffering that ought to have been avoided, or else, as one missionary writes, "the independent missionary cultivates friendly relations with some neighbouring board missionary, his calls, by a singular coincidence, usually happening about meal-time." A disregard of means that God has provided is neither religion nor business. The Christian at home has no right to demand all the good things of life for himself—comfortable house, abundant food, adequate clothing—and then insist that his personal representative in preaching the gospel abroad shall be half-starved. If it is a Christian's duty to live like a tramp without visible means of support, let the home pastor and layman set the example. It is easier to do it here than in a heathen land and less dangerous to health.

The Missionary's Financial Support

It is also true that it costs more to maintain the Protestant missionary than to maintain the celibate Roman Catholic priest; but Protestantism long ago decided for itself the question of marriage versus celibacy, and we are not afraid that the sensible people of England and America will join the critics who condemn Protestant missionaries for any such reason. The author saw a large number of Roman Catholic priests in Asia, and many of them impressed him as being quite as well fed and clothed as the Protestant missionaries. As for the others, we should not overlook the fact that, while some Roman Catholic priests in non-Christian lands are men of fine ability and culture, there are thousands of ignorant friars in such lands as Brazil and Mexico, the Philippines and Central and South America, who have been fairly described as "oleaginous monks who need no outfit but a snuff box, a string of beads, a broad-brimmed hat and a long gown which is a bed by night and a chest of drawers by day, and who wash once in six months, sleep on the ground and grow fat." The condition of the lands mentioned shows that after a hundred years of such missionary work, the natives are as degraded as ever. The Protestant missionary who does not "live as the natives do" costs more money; but he is the cheaper man in the long run, because he does a far higher and more permanent grade of work.

It should be remembered, too, that the missionary represents not only a superior religion but, in some lands at least, the more decent style of living which has resulted from that religion. It is, though a subordinate, yet a real part of his mission to exemplify this. His better house and mode of living are themselves an object lesson of the uplifting influence of Christianity. He would be untrue to his faith if he abdicated the function of a Christian gentleman and lived like an East Indian villager. He goes out to bring the people up to his level, not to go down to theirs.

Nor would personal degradation be more likely to win the natives to Christianity. The Rev. John Forman, of India, made a persistent effort in three different places. He rented a small room, wore cheap clothes and ate the simplest food. He writes:

"What I had longed for was to get near the people, to convince them that I really was working only for their salvation and that I was denying myself for them. I was never more thoroughly earnest about anything I undertook, and I entered upon it with great hopefulness and confidence, and never have I felt that I made a more dismal failure. Everything turned out just as I had not expected. They seemed to regard me as nothing but poor white trash. The idea that I had voluntarily given up anything or was denying myself never occurred to them. I was still the same government official, only had not succeeded in getting a very remunerative position. I had less influence instead of more. I met with a great deal of opposition, a vast amount of ridicule, and had no end of yelling, hooting and hand-clapping from the small boys, but my success seemed to end there."

The Salvation Army has tried the same experiment, as far as it was possible to carry it; but with no better success. The health of their officers has been impaired and they have made no more converts than missionaries who have lived as other foreigners do.

The fact is that an American simply cannot equal an East Indian fakir in his mode of living. The latter sprinkles himself with ashes, begs his frugal meals, wears nothing but a loin cloth, subjects himself to frightful austerities, performs his devotions in public places and never washes himself. The plainest living possible to a foreigner impresses the natives as luxurious in comparison with their own devotees, and therefore has absolutely no good effect upon them.

Some missionaries, who do not believe in boards or fixed salaries, have gone out independently, with the intention of supporting themselves by teaching or some other kind of work, or of subsisting on the direct spontaneous gifts of individuals or local churches at home. The results have usually been disastrous. Dr. Lawrence said that it seemed to him "that India was literally strewn with the wrecks of mission work begun by such independent missionaries, but for one reason and another abandoned. Much the same is proving true of Africa."[1]

A missionary who has no means of his own cannot live in Asia or Africa without a salary. He cannot reasonably expect the poverty-stricken natives to support him. If he supports himself, he must toil in a way that will undermine his health, secularize his life and probably expose him to the charge of mercenary motives. If he depends upon a salary from home, a board is the best agency for its collection and payment. A missionary once declined to receive further salary from his board on the ground that the Holy Spirit had directed him "to trust the Lord to support him by the voluntary gifts of his people." Such a request indicates a confusion of ideas. Does not the Lord provide money that His people send through a board? It is not a question whether a missionary shall receive money for his support; it is whether he shall receive it in the orderly way that the people of God, led by His Spirit, have instituted. A Christian worker who refuses a salary either receives a larger sum than he ought to have, with the attendant injustice to givers and waste of the Lord's money, or he receives less than he ought to get, with the attendant injury to his own health and wrong to those who are dependent upon him. When Mr. Moody conducted a series of meetings in a certain city, he agreed to a definite payment for his services, and all believed him to be both pious and sensible. Another evangelist, a year or two later, refused to enter into any financial compact or to allow any collections or subscription papers, stating that he would take only what the Spirit of God prompted the people to give. The result was not only embarrassment for the

[1] "Modern Missions in the East."

committee in charge but, in the end, a considerably larger sum than he ought to have had.

It appears reasonable to insist that if a missionary ought to go to the foreign field at all, the home Church ought to send him and maintain him, unless he has a personal income that suffices for his wants, and that gifts for his support should be sent through the established agency of the Church to which he belongs. Faith and piety are consistent with common-sense.

The question has often been mooted whether a board, instead of guaranteeing the missionary a fixed salary, should not simply send him his proportion of whatever sum it may receive. This has been advocated as more in accord with the principle of faith in God which underlies the missionary effort and as a justification for sending out larger reinforcements than a board would dare to assume full responsibility for. This plan, however, would subject the missionary to grave uncertainty as to his support. The receipts of all the boards come in very irregularly. They seldom equal expenditures for the first eight months of a fiscal year, and not infrequently half the entire receipts of the year come in during the last sixty days. If the board simply distributed its receipts as they came in, the missionaries would not have enough to live upon for two-thirds of the year. They would suffer for the necessaries of life, or they would have to run up debts that would seriously compromise their missionary reputation.

The plan impresses us as visionary and unbusinesslike. No sensible layman would dream of conducting his business on any such basis. Nor should we expect grocers and butchers and clothiers of heathen or Christian lands to supply missionaries with the necessaries of life with the understanding that they will be paid for them if the Lord moves His people to provide the funds. If that scheme is a good one, why should it not be made equally applicable to ministers at home? There is no valid reason why it should be confined to the foreign missionaries. That some of the missionaries are willing to accept it.

is not an argument in its favour; for the typical missionary is of such stuff that he will accept almost anything as far as he is personally concerned. But this is something that he ought not to be asked to accept. We believe that the only sound principle, both in faith and in business, is that the Church should, through a duly constituted board, assume responsibility for the support of the missionaries that it sends out. When God calls men to go, He calls His people to send. If there is financial risk to be taken, the Church should take it. It is neither fair nor Christian to unload its proper responsibilities upon the already overburdened missionaries.

Information about the houses of missionaries is frequently desired, especially by those who have been disturbed by statements that they are equal to the houses of native noblemen. A similar statement might be made about the houses of many American mechanics. We do not deny that the missionary's dwelling often appears palatial in comparison with the wretched hovels in which the natives herd like rabbits in a warren. Shattered health and rapidly filled cemeteries have taught missionaries that, if they are to live, they must go a little apart from the malodorous, unsanitary, human pigsty, with its rotting garbage and open cesspools, select a site high enough to afford natural drainage, and build a house with a sufficient number of cubic feet of space for the persons who are to occupy it. Then the natural taste of the husband leads him to make a little lawn and to set out a few shrubs and flowers, while indoors his wife sensibly makes everything as cozy and attractive as she can with the means at her disposal. As it is supposed to be a home for life, articles by gift and purchase are gradually accumulated and it really becomes a pretty place in time. Contrasting as it does with the miserable habitations of a heathen city, it attracts attention; but its attractiveness is not due to the lavish expenditure of money, but to the good taste and inventiveness of a cultivated, intelligent family.

A great ado has been made by some travellers about the missionary residence of Dr. Hunter Corbett at Chefoo, China, which looks from a distance like a marble mansion. The real story is told as follows by Dr. Corbett's daughter, Mrs. Hays: "When Dr. Corbett and his young wife arrived at Chefoo, they rented a native house in the city. In that little dismal house with mud walls and narrow windows, surrounded with cesspools and garbage heaps, with the nearest neighbour perhaps dying of smallpox or typhus fever, their first child was born. Is it any wonder that when the missionary had the chance of buying land up on the hill above the filthy city, he thought it a special dispensation of Providence? The board was unable to provide money for a home, so the missionary built a modest, one-storied building of gray brick at his own expense. As the years rolled by, rooms were added to the ends of the house to accommodate the increasing family, and as a protection from heat and storm a veranda was built along one side of the house. Alas! it is this veranda which causes all the trouble. Arches of brick were found to be less expensive than pillars of wood, and when the rash missionary overlaid the brick with plaster and a coat of whitewash, there stood the 'palace' with arches of 'white marble gleaming in the sunlight.'"

The visitor approaching Fusan, Korea, is apt to remark upon the buildings that stand conspicuously upon the hill, and to hear a sneer about the selfishness and ostentation of missionaries in selecting the best sites. The facts are that when the missionaries went to Fusan, they could not afford to buy in the city and they took the hill site because it was unoccupied and cheap, paying just $75 for the whole tract on which church, hospital and residences now stand. The owner was glad to get that price, as the land was then practically valueless. That time has proved it to be the best site in Fusan and that the mission occupation of it led others to seek the neighbourhood so that the place is now valuable is simply a tribute to the good judgment of the missionaries. Another illustration occurred in Persia, where the missionaries were accused of having for a summer resort at Lake Urumia "one of the finest palaces in all the land." The "palace" referred to was an old, abandoned one-story and basement mud building which the owner was delighted to sell to the missionaries for $80. They fixed it up as best they could with a private gift of $170 from a kind-hearted lady in St. Louis, and then the several missionary families of Urumia took turns in occupying it a few weeks during the heated term.

A few missionary residences in different lands have been built by wealthy relatives for particular missionaries, and occasionally one is built as a memorial for a deceased friend. But the average missionary residence costs from $4,000 to $5,000, including land. As building in most fields is quite as expensive as at home, the reader can judge for himself how "palatial" such a place must be. The average missionary residence is about like the home of a country clergyman or school-teacher in England and America; though in the tropics, the fertility of the soil, the luxuriance of palms and foliage plants and the cheapness of labour make it easier for the missionary to have beautiful grounds.

There is another phase of this financial question that deserves consideration on the field, and that is the missionary as the handler of trust funds. We do not refer to his salary but to the money that he is called upon to expend for mission work. We have already discussed missionary administration so far as it relates to the board;[1] but the board must administer its funds through the missionaries. The erection and maintenance of schools, hospitals, and printing-presses and the employment of native helpers involve the handling of considerable sums. Some missions receive for this purpose as high as $80,000 a year. This money goes from the board to the treasurer of the mission and is by him paid out through the

[1] Chapter III.

station treasurers to the individual missionaries, who, in turn, disburse it for the work that is under their immediate care. The boards have, of course, certain rules governing these expenditures. They provide blank forms for this purpose and they expect a strict accounting, certified by an auditing committee and approved by the mission.

Missionaries sometimes complain about these rules and occasionally one is offended by them. The difficulty ordinarily is that such a missionary has gone to the field directly from a theological or other professional school, with little or no business training. Unaccustomed to the methods of business life, he chafes under the "red tape" that is required of him. We knew a missionary who, when asked to sign a receipt, indignantly inquired whether the board distrusted him. It is unfortunate when a missionary is so ignorant of business principles and methods. The missionary is, in an important sense, a business man, charged with fiduciary responsibilities. The fact that he is a missionary does not absolve him from those obligations that rest upon those who administer trust funds anywhere else. No degree of piety or devotion can take the place of straightforward business habits. No man is morally justified in handling other people's money as a trustee, without taking the precautions that are accepted by business men everywhere as indispensable to the intelligent and safe conduct of such enterprises. The boards have a right to demand vouchers for all missionary expenditures, and they are forced to have them, for those expenditures are checked over by auditing committees. Everything about a missionary's financial methods should be above the suspicion of carelessness. He should be conscientious in making out the estimates for his work, and his associates should be equally conscientious in passing upon them. He should never borrow mission funds, except in health emergencies, and then only in ways authorized by the rules of the board and approved by the mission. The mission or station treasurer who accommodates missionaries by personal loans of the money committed to his care is guilty of a breach of trust, and the missionary who asks him to do so shares in the wrong. A broad distinction should be observed between personal and mission funds, and any use of the latter that would be improper in a bank cashier is improper in a mission treasurer. A great enterprise cannot be wisely conducted without business rules, and when a missionary is called upon to observe them, he should not imagine that the board has any want of confidence in him.

VIII

THE MISSIONARY'S PHYSICAL LIFE

HEALTH is indispensable to the missionary. An invalid may manage to be useful in the home-land, but a sick missionary is almost as useless as a sick soldier. When, as often happens, he needs a well person to take care of him, the loss is doubled. The chances of recovery, too, are usually less than in the home-land where the climate and facilities for treatment are better, and if the health becomes seriously impaired, there is no alternative but a return which involves not only a heavy expenditure of missionary money but perhaps the breaking up of the missionary's life plans. "Nothing hinders a man half so much as dying." Therefore every consideration of prudence as well as of duty dictates reasonable care in the preservation of health.

There are undoubtedly diseases and accidents that cannot be prevented, and if they befall the missionary, he should accept the situation with faith and courage and resignation. His colleagues will ungrudgingly give all needful time to him, and the board will not hesitate to make the necessary grant, if a return to America becomes necessary. The missionary should understand, however, that the means for controlling or preventing measles, malaria, diphtheria, smallpox, dysentery, cholera, typhoid fever, yellow fever and several other maladies are now well known and practically applicable. Moreover, if the general tone of the system falls below a certain point so that one becomes anæmic or depressed, the door of welcome to a half-dozen diseases is thrown wide open, and germs which ordinarily would not find lodgment enter and rapidly propagate themselves. The change of climate and diet and the mental and physical conditions incident to life far from home and accustomed environment tend to invite disease. In such circumstances, that care of health which is essential to every one is doubly so to the foreign missionary. He should endeavour to keep his physical vigour at a point that will make him immune, and he should constantly bear in mind the saying, "break nature's laws and she will break you."

This care of health is not only the dictate of prudence but of religion. "Know ye not," says Paul, "that your body is a temple of the Holy Ghost which is in you, which we have from God? And ye are not your own; for ye were bought with a price; glorify God therefore in your body."[1] This involves the use of reasonable means, and as God has provided them so abundantly, it is fair to assume that He meant to have us use them. Why did God give to the bark of the cinchona tree, and to many herbs which have no other uses whatever, such medicinal qualities if He did not intend to have them employed for our healing? Indifference to physical laws and neglect of the remedies for disease which the Creator has placed at man's disposal are not evidences of faith and fidelity but of poor judgment and unreliability of character. God's care for His servants will not exempt them from the penalty for carelessness or disobedience.

The medical missionary has a special responsibility in this matter. He should set an example by taking reasonable care of his own health. He should feel that it is his duty not only to treat the sick but to educate both missionaries and natives to adopt those measures that will prevent illness. The surgeons of the Japanese army were models to physicians the world over during the Russia-Japan war. There are many who believe with Dr. Seaman that "the real triumph of Japan" lay not so much in her victory over the Russians as in her conquest of disease. Indeed, it was the latter that helped powerfully to make the former possible. In almost every other great war, eighty per

[1] 1 Corinthians 6: 19, 20.

cent. of the losses were from disease. This meant that the chances were four to one that a soldier would be stricken by illness rather than by a bullet. This frightful proportion was not lessened even in the later wars of the two most highly civilized nations of the earth, England and America. The mortality from disease in the British-Boer war was appalling, while in the Spanish-American war of 1898, fourteen were incapacitated by disease for every one who was killed in battle. The account of the wars of white men for centuries is a sickening record of soldiers dying off like flies from diseases that ordinary common sense might have prevented. It was reserved for the Japanese to show a skill and forethought which have revolutionized modern warfare, not so much by treating sick men, as by preventing men from getting sick. They reduced disease to such a point that whereas in her war with China, one Japanese soldier in every nine suffered from an infectious disease, in the war with Russia only one in every eighty suffered. Including all diseases, only one and two-tenths per cent. of the entire army died of sickness and out of twenty-four per cent. wounded, only one and one-half per cent. died.[1] This unparalleled result was attained simply by the resolute and common-sense application of that knowledge which is now the common possession of all intelligent people.

We cannot go into the details of the methods by which this splendid result was accomplished. Suffice it here that it places tremendous emphasis upon the statement that most diseases are preventable and that the physician should regard himself as a sanitary officer, whose duty it is to educate the community in health matters.

In trying to avoid illness, one should not go to the opposite extreme of being fussy. The missionary, like the soldier, is not sent out for his health, and he must occasionally take some risks. It is not necessary to be frightened every time one gets

[1] Dr. Louis L. Seaman, "The Real Triumph of Japan," pp. 5 and 184.

his feet wet or has a headache or feels depressed, nor is it good to be continually testing one's temperature with a thermometer and brooding morbidly over every little symptom that may develop. There is a superstition that night air is injurious, and so some timid people sleep with their bedroom windows closed. The fact is that one must breathe night air every night anyway, for the simple reason that there is no other air to breathe. The only question is whether it shall be pure night air or impure. Keep the windows open, both from the top and the bottom, and you will not waken in the morning with a headache and a bad taste in the mouth. Equally baseless is the idea that malaria is caused by exhalations from swamps or freshly dug ground and that one can ward off colds by swathing himself in flannels and huddling over a stove. Others imagine that they can kill germs by drinking whiskey, the result being an injury to the system that invites a million germs for every one that the alcohol kills. While one should not unnecessarily expose himself to a contagious disease, it does not necessarily follow that exposure will result in infection. Physicians are continually coming in contact with diseases of this sort, and it is comparatively seldom that they are infected. The right course is to avoid, as far as practicable, violations of the laws of health, and then with a cheerful spirit and a courageous heart perform the duty that needs to be done. If a contagious case has been handled, take a bath and hang the clothing in the open air. Reasonable care in keeping the health at a proper point of vigour and a mind that is kept sweet by faith in God and the consciousness of duty being performed will ordinarily result in good health anywhere in the world.

In order that the missionary may intelligently adapt himself to the physical conditions of life on the foreign field, he should, if possible, acquire some knowledge of elementary hygiene, nursing, medicine and surgery before going to the field. It is true that the average missionary of to-day is within reach of medical attendance. Besides the medical missionaries at the stations, the larger cities of Asia are, as a rule, well supplied with foreign physicians and surgeons in private or government practice, while Japan, Mexico and South America have native physicians, some of whom were trained in the best medical colleges of Europe. Still, the missionary will often be far from professional attendance and forced to rely, temporarily at least, upon his own knowledge. Moreover the non-professional missionary is often besieged, especially on his itinerating tours, by natives who wish him to treat all sorts of diseases and injuries. Babies with foul ulcers will be brought to him with faces that pitifully appeal for help. Broken bones will have to be set, decayed teeth extracted and a score of other ills attended to. No matter how much the missionary may protest that he is not a physician, the people will often refuse to believe that he cannot help them. As a matter of fact there is considerable assistance that he can give. Crude it may be from a professional viewpoint, but it is better that he should do what he can than to let the people die in neglect. Such a minister as the Rev. Dr. E. P. Dunlap, of Siam, was often compelled to do a large dispensary work on his tours, while other missionaries have frequently been called to attend women in confinement. The non-professional missionary should be very cautious in attempting difficult cases, for if he fails, he may do more harm than good and the people may turn furiously against him. He should confine himself strictly to the simpler remedies and operations. But there are many of these that he ought to understand.

Good opportunities for this lay training are now to be found in both England and America at medical colleges where special courses for laymen are given.[1] Many of the English

---

[1] Livingstone College in London gives an excellent course of this kind. Missionaries who desire lay medical instruction in America should consult the medical secretaries of their respective boards.

missionaries avail themselves of these courses for a few months, either before sailing or during a furlough. Those who have done this are emphatic in their testimony to the benefits that they have received, declaring that they understand better how to take care of their own health and that they can often give great relief to native sufferers when no trained physician is available. If none of these institutions can be reached, perhaps an elementary course could be taken in some ordinary medical college or with the aid of a friendly physician. There are, too, books that might be studied to advantage and that any physician can suggest.[1]

There are, however, certain methods and precautions that are so self-evident that one can adopt them himself. For convenience we will enumerate some of these.

Sun. While sunlight is as important to health on the foreign field as anywhere else, greater caution is necessary in exposing the head to the direct rays. In tropical climates, one should invariably wear a cork or pith helmet. Get one that is longer behind, so that it will protect the back of the neck, which is a vulnerable point. In the middle of the day during the hot season, it is well, in addition, to carry a white umbrella. It is easy to have a white removable cover put over an ordinary black umbrella, so that it can be taken off and washed as desired. Pay no attention to any one who tells you that he does not bother to protect himself from the sun and that it has never hurt him. "There are some people whose brains are so well protected that they can stand any heat; but do not be led to think that you are made that way." Coloured glasses should

---

[1] *Personal Hygiene Applied,* by Jesse Feiring Williams, M. D.; *Personal Hygiene For Women,* by Clelia Duel Mosher, M. D.; *Handbook on Positive Health,* by Woman's Foundation for Health; *The Maintenance of Health in the Tropics,* by W. J. Simpson, M. D.; *The Home and Health in India and the Tropical Colonies,* by Kate Platt, M. D.; *Essentials of Medicine,* by Charles Phillips Emerson, M. D.

be at hand, for the brain is often affected by the sun's glare on the eyes.

Food. This should be adapted to the climate. It is idiotic for a man in the tropics to live on the saleratus biscuit, corned beef and cabbage and mince-pie of a Maine lumberman, and then solemnly confide to his friends that he feels "bilious" and fears that the climate does not agree with him. It is equally idiotic for a woman to lunch on a piece of pie or cake, washed down by tea or coffee, and then wonder why she is sallow, listless and anæmic. If both of them would eat wholesome food and masticate it thoroughly, they would quickly improve. A meat diet may be wholesome in a temperate region, but the farther south one goes, the more prominent in his daily fare should be fruit, nuts and vegetables. Avoid over-ripe and under-ripe fruits, and also jellies, shell-fish and cold meats that have been standing in exposed places. Canned food should be eaten only so far as necessary; even then it is not as healthful as fresh. Many tinned meats and vegetables are preserved by acids that are injurious to health. The best diet is one of hot, freshly-cooked foods. The amount should be well distributed through the day. The "no-breakfast" plan is a mere fad, with no rational basis whatever. It is absurd, and in time injurious, to take no food whatever for eighteen hours and then load in the entire amount for the day in the remaining six hours. It is better to take light meals frequently than to take heavy meals at longer intervals. Do not go out in the morning on an empty stomach. When urged to do so, it is well to follow the advice of Mark Twain who said that if he had any work to do before breakfast, he always ate his breakfast first.

Water. This is the most vital precaution of all. Physicians agree that the average person does not drink enough water. It is an excellent health habit to take one or two glasses on rising in the morning and on retiring at night, and, in addition, to drink between meals as one has desire and opportunity. But it is not good to take too much liquid at meals. The stomach then needs its room and energy for the food and it cannot do its work to advantage if it is deluged with water at the same time. Great care, however, should be exercised to have the water pure. This is particularly necessary in non-Christian lands. The wells are apt to be old and foul with the surface drainage and accumulations of decades. The streams are often little better than open sewers or public laundries, or both. In such crowded regions as China and India, it is practically impossible to find a well or a river from which it is prudent to drink. We were occasionally assured in Asia by a missionary: "Oh, it is perfectly safe to drink this water, for it comes from a spring in the hills where there is no chance for contamination." A medical missionary once said this as we were riding through the mountains of Siam and watching the clear, sparkling stream beside us; but presently we found the half-rotten body of a dead elephant lying across that very stream. Miss Kingsley wrote from Africa:

". . . In addition to malarial microbes, the drinking water of West Africa is liable to contain a peculiar abomination, a filaria. This is a worm which gets into the white of the eye and leads there a lively existence, causing distressing itching, throbbing and pricking sensations. A similar, but not identical, worm is fairly common on the Ogowe, and is liable to get under the epidermis of any part of the body. . . . The treatment consists of getting the thing out, and the thing to be careful of is to get it out whole, for if any part of it is left in, suppuration sets in.

"Do not confuse this filaria with the Guinea worm, which runs up to ten and twelve feet in length and whose habits are different. It is more sedentary, but it is in the drinking water inside small crustacea (cyclops). It appears commonly in its human host's leg, and rapidly grows, curled round and round like a watch-spring, showing raised under the skin. The native treatment of this pest is very cautiously to open the skin over the head of the worm and secure it between a little cleft bit of bamboo and then gradually wind the rest of the affair out. Only a small portion can be wound out at a time, as the wound is very liable to inflame, and should the worm break, it is certain to inflame badly and a terrible wound will result." [1]

Do not depend upon filters to purify water. They will take out sticks and mud, but many of the most deadly germs are held in such perfect solution that no filter can remove them. Moreover, unless a filter is thoroughly cleaned every day with boiling water, it soon becomes a dangerous breeding place for microbes. Miss Kingsley says that wherever in Africa filters are depended upon, "men have died and worms have eaten them." She adds: "A good filter is a very fine thing for clearing drinking water of hippopotami, crocodiles, water snakes, catfish, etc., and I dare say it will stop back sixty per cent. of the live or dead African natives that may be in it; but if you think it is going to stop back the microbe of marsh fever, my good sir, you are mistaken."

There is only one way to purify water and that is to boil it. The new missionary should not be dissuaded by any talk about trouble or any good-natured banter by older missionaries, who ought to know better. He should insist on having his drinking water boiled. He will soon find that he cannot depend upon the native servants to do it. They can never be made to understand why it is that the foreigner wants water to boil, and if he leaves it to them, they will either lie about it or simply make it hot. When the author was journeying in the interior of Korea, he found that the only way to get boiled water was to stand beside the native cook. He is not sure that he is not known to this day among the natives of his party as "Kul-nan-mul" (water-that-bubbles-up), for morning and evening the direction was "kul-nan-mul, kul-nan-mul." A missionary wife in the Philippines developed a severe case of amœbic dysentery which compelled her to leave her husband and hurry

[1] "Travels in West Africa," Appendix II.

off to America; for amœbic dysentery, once fairly started, cannot be cured without a change of climate. She was at a loss to understand the cause, for she had bought the distilled water that can be had cheaply in Manila. But on inquiry, she learned that her native servant had used the distilled water for other purposes and had filled her pitcher with ordinary water!

The taste of boiled water will be rather flat at first, and in a land where ice is not available, it will not be cold. But one will soon become accustomed to it. The American habit of gulping down ice water is a bad one any way. Tepid water is far more healthful. The best way is to pour the boiling water into a narrow-necked jar, tie a clean cloth over the neck and then hang it up where it will be exposed to the breeze or partially immerse it in a bucket of water from the well or river. It will soon cool in this way. Shaking or a red-hot iron will relieve the insipidity caused by the distillation of oxygen in boiling. But care must be exercised to see that the jar is kept covered; for after water has been exposed for some time, it is apt to be almost as full of germs as it was before boiling.

Boiled water should be used not only for drinking but for washing fruits and vegetables that are to be eaten uncooked. It is of no use to boil drinking water and then eat unclean lettuce or radishes that have been picked by a dirty native from ground fertilized with filth. Wells should be dug as far as possible from privies, cesspools, graves and native houses; but the water should still be boiled.

Houses. The architecture should be adapted to the climate. In India, where the weather is hot and the ground is usually baked hard and dry by the scorching sun, it is customary to make the walls thick and the piazzas wide, so as to keep out the heat. In Siam and Africa, where the rainfall is heavy and the wet ground steams under a tropical sun, the houses are set up on posts from four to eight feet above the ground. In the more temperate climates, the houses are built about as at home. The site should be dry and high enough to afford natural drainage. A house should never be built on low, swampy ground or in the bottoms of valleys where fogs frequently rise, unless, of course, no other place is available. Experience in Africa has shown, however, that it is not well to build on the tops of hills or in a hollow between hills where there will be a constant draft. The ideal site is back a little from the water or the dense vegetation of a tropical bush, on moderately high ground and with the surrounding land so far cleared as to permit an abundance of sunshine. Trees are pleasant for shade, but they should not be so close as to make the house damp and gloomy.

Bathing. It is taken for granted that the missionary appreciates the importance of this; but in a heathen land, and particularly in the tropics where dust and sweat cannot be avoided, the daily bath is more than desirable; it is indispensable to health. The hot bath should be taken only before retiring so as to avoid catching cold; but such an occasional bath is not a substitute for the morning cold sponge bath followed by a brisk rubbing. A basin of water and a towel are always to be had, so that even when travelling, one need not miss this luxury. It keeps open and healthy the millions of pores, promotes the quick circulation of blood to the extremities of the body and begets an exhilarating vigour that is as delightful as it is beneficial. A handful of salt in the water, or the use of a towel that has been soaked in salt water and dried, will add to the tonic effect of the bath.

Exercise. This, needful at home, is imperative abroad. It should not be violent. It is dangerous for one who leads a sedentary life to subject himself suddenly to great physical strain, especially in the tropics. But there are dozens of things that the missionary may do moderately that will help greatly to maintain his general vigour. He may use dumb-bells or other forms of exercise in the morning in his room, after his bath. Such open-air games as tennis, croquet, quoits and basket-ball are excellent, and the missionary is fortunate indeed if he can add that king of games—golf. If there is water within a dozen miles, by all means cultivate the gentle art of fishing. If there is game, hunt, unless the field is one where the religious scruples of the natives are involved. Whether these forms of exercise are practicable or not, walking is always possible, and it is the best exercise of all, though in the tropics it should be confined to the morning or evening hours when the heat will not cause perspiration so profuse as to be enervating. The British in Asia set a good example by their fondness for athletic sports. No matter how busy an Englishman may be, he does not neglect his outdoor games, and in consequence he is the healthiest foreigner in the Far East.

Refuse. Non-Christian communities seldom have sewers, so that the question of disposing of refuse is a serious one. In some places, the natives will gladly carry away garbage and night-soil free of charge to feed their pigs and fertilize their fields; but usually the missionary must solve the problem himself. The best way is to burn as much as possible and to empty the rest into a cess-pool at a prudent distance from the house and where it cannot contaminate the water supply. Garbage pails should be kept carefully covered.

Clothing. One always needs warm clothing in crossing the ocean. In such temperate climates as Japan, Korea, North China, Persia and Syria, the missionary will wear practically the same kind of clothing that he would wear at home. He should therefore prepare his outfit about as he would if he wished to clothe himself up for two or three years in America. In the tropics, however, the foreigner usually wears white duck suits. The men wear two-piece suits, the coats buttoning up to the chin so as to afford a welcome freedom as to what is worn underneath. Ladies wear waists and skirts of the same material. Such clothing is not expensive, as the native tailors make up these white duck suits for five or six dollars apiece, and laundering costs from six to ten cents a garment. If one is particular about American shoes, he should take several pairs with him; but in the tropics he will probably find them very hot, and he will prefer the white canvas shoes made by the Chinese shoemaker for $2.50 a pair. They are light, durable and comfortable.

Opinions differ as to underclothing. Before we went to the tropics, a medical friend advised us to take only woollen underclothing, as he assured us that it was really the most comfortable in the tropics. We took his advice and have been trying ever since, we trust in a Christian spirit, to overcome a strong desire to murder that adviser. An abdominal band of thin flannel is, indeed, a prudent safeguard against the dangerous chilling of the abdomen which sometimes follows an exposure to a draft and which is particularly apt to occur in the hour preceding daylight when there is often a sudden fall of temperature. If in addition to this band, one can wear light woollens, he will find good medical support for his preference; but we found woollen underclothing intolerable, and though we continued to wear the abdominal band, we experienced inexpressible relief and no ill effects from a change to the lightest cotton gauze we could find.[1]

Inoculation for typhoid and smallpox should be attended to before leaving America. Some of the boards will not advance funds for traveling until satisfactory evidence has been presented that the vaccination has been successful, or, if not, that it has been repeated at least six times within one year. Smallpox is a common disease in Asia and Africa. Missionaries who keep vaccinated are as a rule immune; but neglect of this precaution is apt to result in a funeral. No one should interfere with the liberty of a man who does not believe in vaccination; but he should exercise that liberty in the homeland and not deny the boards the liberty of spending their money on safer risks.

Eyes and Teeth. Consult an oculist before leaving America. The eye is one of the most delicate organs of the body. It is more often out of order than is commonly supposed, and when

[1] "The New Era in the Philippines," pp. 48, 49.

The Missionary's Physical Life 153

it is disregarded, the nervous system is subjected to undue strain. The glare of the Oriental sun is severe on the eyes and quickly intensifies any tendency to headache or nervousness. If glasses are necessary, take two extra pairs, for in case of accident it may require several months to get a new supply. It is equally important to consult a dentist. An ulcerated tooth is a serious matter when one is hundreds of miles from a dentist. Dr. Nassau of Africa once had to make the long and expensive journey to the United States solely on this account, suffering all the way.

Flies and Mosquitoes. These pests are ubiquitous, particularly in the tropics. The former breed in filth, become saturated with it and then crawl over food, leaving a trail of malignant microbes. Zymotic diseases are often communicated in this way. Mosquitoes are more deadly because they are more voracious and aggressive and because they attack during sleep. It is now known that the germs of malaria do not enter the human body from marshy ground or from the atmosphere or from the morning or the evening damps, but in the bites of mosquitoes. Nor is malaria the only disease thus communicated. Dr. Finley, an American surgeon in Cuba, first suggested that mosquitoes communicate yellow fever and the medical commission appointed in 1900, of which the now famous Dr. Walter Reed was chairman, conclusively proved it. With that heroism that is so characteristic of the medical profession, young men offered themselves for experiments, and for twenty days two of them slept in an unventilated room in bedding taken directly without washing from the beds of yellow-fever patients, exposing themselves to every form of infection except the bites of mosquitoes. They were absolutely unharmed; but Drs. James Carroll and Jesse Lazear, members of the medical commission, who submitted themselves to the bites of mosquitoes which had previously been allowed to bite a yellow-fever patient, were quickly prostrated by that dread disease, the latter dying. Prompt action on these facts reduced the number of deaths from yellow-fever cases in Havana from 300 in October, 1900, to three in October, 1901. At a memorial service in honour of Dr. Reed, Major-General Leonard Wood said: "His discovery results in the saving of more lives annually than were lost in the Cuban war, and saves the commercial interests of the world a greater financial loss in each year than the cost of the entire Cuban war."

Protection against the mosquito is to be sought, therefore, not simply in the interest of comfort but of safety. Every missionary should have a mosquito-net and sleep under it. If a rent is discovered, tie a knot about it till it can be mended. Doors and windows should have screens. They are cheaper than illness. The missionary should, in addition, try to destroy the mosquitoes in his neighbourhood. They breed only in water. Large areas of swamps or stagnant water may be beyond his power; but experiments have shown that when mosquitoes infest a house, most of them come, not from distant pools or marshes, but from little puddles of water close to the house and even from water standing in tubs or barrels or cisterns or even old cans. Dr. Ronald Ross of the Liverpool School of Tropical Medicine strongly advises missionaries not to allow themselves to be misled by statements that there are no mosquitoes in their locality. He declares that the species of mosquito that does the mischief is to be found in practically every missionary field in the world, and that the most dangerous species of all does not hum and might not be noticed at all, especially by people who are not particularly sensitive to the sting. The best preventive is the destruction of the larvæ and the places where they breed. The smaller pools should be cleaned out or filled up. The larger ones may be treated once a week with kerosene oil, which will usually destroy the larvæ and wigglers. Keep cisterns and all vessels of water carefully covered and see that utensils are promptly emptied. Another wise precaution is to go through the house early every morning and kill the mosquitoes, which are then gorged and torpid.

Smoke is a good preventive at any time as mosquitoes cannot endure it. If all windows and doors are closed and a smudge of sulphur is made inside the house, the insects will quickly be killed. Mosquitoes do not fly far, and vigorous warfare against them will soon exterminate them, unless careless neighbours are too close or the conditions are too formidable to be overcome.

Stimulants. Be very conservative in resorting to them. Beware especially of patent medicines that are "guaranteed to relieve that tired feeling." Most of them contain a large proportion of alcohol. The pious soul who "feels better after a dose" does not realize that his temporary exhilaration is simply that which would follow a drink of whiskey. Some innocent persons, who were strict prohibitionists in principle, have become drunkards in this way. Medicines that are advertised to relieve pain and to "soothe irritated nerves" usually contain opium in some form. Many a mother has given paregoric to her crying baby without dreaming that its quieting effect is simply due to laudanum. Foreigners in the tropics usually assert that alcohol is necessary ; but the death rate among them is far higher than among missionaries, who are total abstainers. Geil speaks of one station in Africa where nine foreigners died in twelve years. "Meantime the missionaries in that region lived comfortably and are still living." It is better to let liquors and drugged nostrums alone. If depressed in mind or exhausted by fatigue, take a hot bath, a cup of weak tea or boiling milk, and go to bed. Nature will probably do the rest, and if she does not, send for a physician, not a bar-keeper.

Diseases. It is not possible in such a book as this even to enumerate the diseases that are to be guarded against, much less to give detailed advice regarding their treatment. Physicians should be summoned whenever possible. But there are a few of the more common diseases whose beginnings a layman can understand and there are some remedies which every missionary should know how to apply.

Diseases of the bowels are more prevalent than any others. Most foreigners have trouble with them in some form. They are usually amenable to treatment in their earlier stages, and as the trouble may occur when medical attendance is not immediately available, the missionary should know what to do for himself. The main thing to bear in mind is that a regular daily discharge is absolutely indispensable to health. Constipation should be relieved by an enema of warm water, and for this purpose a syringe should be a part of every missionary's outfit. Other forms of relief are a glycerine suppository, or a dose of Eno's Fruit Salts or Epsom or Rochelle salts or castor oil. A physician should be consulted in chronic cases. Never ignore constipation. It increases tenfold susceptibility to any prevalent disease. We all know that clogged waste pipes are a menace to the health of a household. The bowels are the waste-pipes of the system, and if they do not carry off their load, illness will inevitably follow. After his journey through Africa, Mr. W. E. Geil said that the medicine chest should contain first a good cathartic, second a better cathartic and third a first-class cathartic, and he quoted approvingly a medical expert who declared that "purgation is salvation."[1]

The opposite trouble, diarrhœa, is even more common. It is usually due to some local irritation caused by something that has been eaten or by the inflammation following a chill. In either case, the first thing to do is to cleanse the bowels thoroughly with a dose of two grains of calomel, followed, six or eight hours later, with a Seidlitz powder or a dose of salts or castor oil. If this is taken promptly, it will often suffice without further treatment; but if the diarrhœa continues, take one tablet of bismuth-opium compound every two hours, confine the diet to milk and keep as quiet as possible. The appearance of blood in the discharge means the dreaded dysentery. The same course should be taken, but the patient should go to bed and call a physician at once.

[1] "A Yankee in Pygmy Land," p. 258.

The Missionary's Physical Life

Fevers are legion, particularly in the tropics. Malaria is the scourge of heathen lands. It is far more serious than malaria at home. Official reports reveal the startling fact that "in the British army in India during the year 1897, out of a total strength of 178,197 men, no less than 75,821 were admitted into hospital for malarial fever! Among the civil population (who do not take adequate treatment), the mortality from fevers during the single year 1897 amounted to the enormous total of 5,026,725, being nearly ten times that due to any other disease. . . . Yet India on the whole is not nearly so malarious as many localities. In short, next perhaps to tuberculosis, malarial fever is admittedly the most important of human diseases."

Quinine is the great specific for all malarial fevers. It should be taken promptly in five grain doses three or four times a day until a physician can be called. If one is in a region where malaria is prevalent, it is well to use quinine as a prophylactic by taking four grains a day for two or three days each week. Such use of quinine will often prevent malaria.

It would be easy to extend this list almost indefinitely, but this is not a medical treatise and we are simply concerned to give a few simple suggestions which every one should understand. The missionary should take with him a small medicine case. Several firms in England and the United States make a specialty of preparing such cases for missionaries and travellers. The one that the author carried on his journeys through Asia was put up under the direction of David Bovaird, M. D., then medical adviser of the Presbyterian Board, New York, and proved exceedingly useful.[1] Several experienced medical

---

[1] Edward M. Dodd, M. D., formerly a medical missionary in Persia and now Medical Secretary of the Presbyterian Board, New York, has kindly given me the following suggestions for personal medical kit for new missionaries:

1. Aspirin—5 grain tablets. Headaches and other aches and pains can often be properly treated and relieved by the use of a few doses of aspirin.

missionaries commended it and I found it indispensable in several emergencies.

A word of caution, however, should be given as to the use of powerful medicines by a layman. Morphine should never be used except in cases of intolerable pain and then only as indicated. Repeated doses of phenacetine may affect the heart. Calomel is a mineral that, taken too frequently, may injure the system. Quinine is the most valuable of all medicines, especially in the tropics, and has probably done more to alleviate suffering and save human life than any other; but it is often used injuriously. Some insist that it should be taken every day in such climates as Africa and Siam, in order to ward off malaria. The result may be quinine poisoning. We have known of cases where health was almost wrecked by a prolonged use of this drug. "An excellent authority doubts whether hæmaturia (the most deadly form of Africa fever) is not, in some cases at any rate, brought on by over-doses of quinine, and Dr. Plehn (a German expert of Kamerun, Africa), asserted, and his assertions were heavily backed up

---

2. Boracic acid powder—about one ounce. One teaspoonful in four ounces, or about two-thirds of a glass of water, will give the usual strength solution of boracic acid. This can also be used for wet dressings for inflamed conditions, such as infected fingers, or wounds discharging pus.

3. Bismuth (sub-carbonate or other form)—5 grain tablets. This may be used in persistent diarrhea after a preliminary dose of castor oil or salts, using one or two 5 grain tablets three times a day, or every four hours during the day and night. It is better not to use it many days at a stretch.

4. Cascara—5 grain tablets, for mild catharsis.

5. Castor oil in desired amount, for more vigorous catharsis. Epsom salts (magnesium sulphate) may be substituted for this.

6. Cough tablets.

7. Iodine—a small rubber corked bottle, if possible with a small brush attached to the cork for application, is useful for cuts and also as a counter irritant to paint over a painful area.

8. Seiler's tablets; for throat gargle. One dissolved in a glass of water can be used as a gargle or spray.

9. Soda bicarbonate—about two ounces. This can be used with or without dissolving in water for indigestion with sour stomach or gas. Dose about one-half teaspoonful. A solution of bicarbonate of soda is also useful as a dressing for burns.

by his great success in treating this fever, that quinine has a very bad influence when the characteristic symptoms have declared themselves, and that it should not be given."[1] Miss Kingsley, who quotes this, adds: "When you know, by reason of aching head and limbs and a sensation of a stream of cold water down your back and an awful temper, that you are in for a fever, send for a doctor if you can. If, as generally happens, there is no doctor near to send for, take a compound calomel and colocynth pill, fifteen grains of quinine and a grain of opium, and go to bed wrapped up in the best blanket available. When safely there, take lashings of hot tea or, what is better, a hot drink made from fresh lime-juice, strong and without sugar—fresh limes are almost always to be had—if not, bottled lime-juice does well. Then, in the hot stage, don't go fanning about, nor in the perspiring stage, for if you get a chill then, you may turn a mild dose of fever into a fatal one. If, however, you keep conscientiously rolled in your blanket until the perspiring stage is well over, and stay in bed till the next morning, the chances are you will be all right, though a little shaky about the legs."[2]

In addition to the medicines indicated, it is well for the missionary to have some strong disinfectant like corrosive sublimate antiseptic tablets and a few simple surgical appliances such as the "first aid packet," which can be obtained through almost any druggist. One of the very best of these packets is

---

[1] "Travels in West Africa," Appendix II.   [2] *Ibid.*

10. Quinine sulphate—5 grain tablets. The chief use of this is for malaria. Five grains three times a day, or a larger dose an hour or two before the expected time of the chill, if chills are occurring regularly, are convenient ways of taking this.

11. Zinc oxide ointment. This can be used for many irritations and sores or unhealed surfaces on the skin.

12. Miscellaneous:
    Half a dozen bandages of one-inch and two-inch width;
    A small roll of Z. O. adhesive tape, one-inch width;
    A medicine dropper;
    A small amount of absorbent cotton;
    A thermometer;
    A spray for nose and throat.

prepared by the Surgeon General's Department of the Army. A description of it can be had on application and the packet can then be made up by any physician or trained nurse. An accident that breaks the skin should be promptly attended to by washing the hands in hot boiled water before touching the wound, cleansing it thoroughly with boiled water as hot as it can be borne, and applying the antiseptic bandage, which should always be carried. This treatment will probably suffice until a physician can be obtained, unless an artery has been severed, in which case the artery should be tightly tied near the wound and between it and the heart. This should be done quickly and with a scarf, or handkerchief, or strip of clothing, or anything else that may be available, taking care to have the knot over the artery. Then get to a physician as quickly as possible. In the Russia-Japan War, every Japanese soldier was provided with a first aid to the injured packet and instructed to treat himself substantially in this way in case he was wounded. The result was that a very large proportion of the wounded men recovered without any further treatment at all.

The missionary who adopts such simple precautions as those that have been indicated and exercises the common sense that ought to be expected of a reasonable person anywhere, will probably be able to live and work for many years in almost any climate. The West Coast of Africa is popularly considered the worst climate in the world for white men, but some missionaries have toiled there for a generation and have come up to the age of seventy in about as good condition as the average person in the home-land.

The necessity for returning to America on account of ill-health is far less than formerly. This is because the missionary of to-day has a more sanitary house than his predecessors, knows better how to take care of himself and has so much more frequent communication with home that the strain of loneliness is diminished and the supply of accustomed food is increased. Most of the larger cities of Asia now have as good medical and surgical skill as the average minister at home can command, and many cities in Asia and some in Africa and Latin America have well-equipped hospitals. The multiplication of steamers and railways makes these more accessible and enables many missionaries to secure a change of climate on the field. It is only right that these facilities should be exhausted before incurring the heavy expense of returning to Europe or America. In any event, the trip home should not be made except on the written certificate of one or more physicians.

On this whole subject of health, the missionary, and every one else for that matter, should remember that common sense is the best prophylactic, and that violation of it is neither smart, brave nor pious. If, in addition, he remembers that the best drink is water, that " the best tonic is fresh air, that the best restorative is sleep, that the best stimulant is exercise, that fatigue calls for rest not the spur, and that a change of occupation is more restful than idleness," [1] he will probably enjoy good health and be able to do a large amount of useful work.[2]

[1] Ellen H. Richards.
[2] Cf. the author's "The New Era in the Philippines," Chapter IV, " The Climate and How to Live in It."

IX

THE MISSIONARY'S INTELLECTUAL LIFE

THIS is a phase of missionary life that may be considered incidental, but it is far more important and far more valuable to the world than is commonly supposed. The missionary is an educated man, and his tastes are therefore the tastes of a cultivated gentleman. Being a scholar, he needs a scholar's tools. Books are even more necessary to him than they are to the home pastor. The latter lives in a land of innumerable newspapers and magazines. Books are abundant and cheap, and if he is unable to buy all that he needs, there is a public library in every considerable town. But the foreign missionary is an isolated man, and unless he happens to be located in a treaty port, he is wholly dependent upon his own shelves.

In these circumstances, there are fewer opportunities for mental stimulus than at home, and intellectual stagnation is one of the dangers against which missionaries must guard. The temptation is strong to accept the apparent necessities of the situation and, because few books are available, to be content and allow the mind to be wholly occupied by routine duties. If this temptation is yielded to, the missionary's intellectual life becomes stunted and narrow.

In order that the recruit may start right, he should take with him, not only all the good books that he already possesses, but as many more as he is able to buy. He should, moreover, add to this stock from time to time as circumstances permit. He may be able to obtain what he wants in some port of the country in which he is labouring; but if not, he can always order either direct from the publisher or through his board. The missionary needs these books for enjoyment, for culture,

The Missionary's Intellectual Life

for mental growth. They will be friends who will never fail him. Apart from the intellectual value of reading, there are few forms of recreation and mental diversion that are more delightful and wholesome than the pages of a favourite author. The brain, wearied with long thinking upon the problems of routine work, refusing to leave those problems when the tired man throws himself upon the bed, is rested and soothed by the gentle influence of a good book.

Young missionaries often ask for suggestions as to the books that they should take with them. It is difficult to make out a list that would be satisfactory to all, for tastes and purses vary. It is not wise to use much of the outfit allowance for this purpose, as that is needed for clothing and furniture. Moreover, in going to a tropical climate, there is danger that dampness and white ants may destroy books. It is not well therefore to get too many at once or to get costly bindings. But good books substantially bound in cloth are not expensive in these days, nor is freight a serious matter, as steamer charges are based upon bulk rather than upon weight and books do not take up much room.

Widely as tastes vary, there are certain books that may be classed as necessaries to the missionary. The list given below [1]

---

[1] The missionary's library should include, if possible, an English dictionary; a Bible dictionary; a concordance; Beach's Geography and Atlas; several commentaries on the Bible, if the purse will permit, so that one will not be at the mercy of one man's opinion; Greek and Hebrew Testaments, grammars and lexicons; an "Encyclopædia of Missions;" a book on comparative religions, such as Menzies' "History of Religions," or Jevons' "Introduction to the History of Religions"; and a few volumes on the country in which the missionary is to live. Gibson's "Mission Problems and Mission Methods in South China" and the Reports of such conferences as those in Shanghai, Madras, and particularly Edinburgh and Jerusalem embody a wide range of expert missionary experience that is of great value. The physician will of course need some of the best books in his special line. For those engaged in educational work, James' "Talks to Teachers" and Bagley's "Educative Process" are excellent

is, of course, only suggestive, and each individual will naturally make changes that will adapt it to his special needs; but it may serve to illustrate the general range of desirable reading. The seriousness of the missionary's calling, however, need not deprive him of a few novels like those of Hugo, Scott and that great magician of the heart, Charles Dickens. A single volume of one of these authors is worth a ton of the cheap and trashy fiction of the day. Fiction bears the same relation to the intellectual diet that pepper and mustard bear to the physical. Too much of them ruins the digestion, but a little, wisely used, adds flavour. When the mind has become jaded and anxious by toiling or worrying over some grave problem, a page or two of Pickwick Papers is a blessed relief.

It is a good plan to lay out for oneself a careful and fairly comprehensive course of study and to secure books that bear upon it. In this way the mental development may be more wisely shaped and the mind prevented from falling into ruts. There are certain important studies, particularly in philosophy and sociology, that are apt to be ignored unless a program is resolutely mapped out. With good books upon his shelves, the missionary will have the material for intellectual resource and

pedagogical helps. Standard histories of the United States and England, Guizot's "History of Civilization," and a few biographies of great missionaries like Carey, Morrison, Martyn, Livingstone, Keith-Falconer, James Chalmers, etc., are highly desirable. In the realm of poetry, the missionary will of course want Homer, Dante, Milton, Shakespeare, Wordsworth and Whittier. If he can afford some books of general literature, like the works of Carlyle, Ruskin, Macaulay and Irving, he will find as the years pass that they are among his choicest treasures. A few devotional books such as Augustine's "Confessions," à Kempis' "Imitation of Christ" and one or two of the little volumes of Meyer, Murray or Gordon will prove a helpful addition.

For more extensive lists, compare those in the reports of the quadrennial conventions of the Student Volunteer Movement and the lists prepared by the Missionary Research Library, New York.

stimulus always at hand. Indeed he may be a better furnished man mentally just because he is obliged to confine himself to a comparatively small selection. The abundance and cheapness of books in America are by no means an unmixed good. When one can hardly open his mail or take up a newspaper without finding attractive advertisements, he is apt to neglect authors of permanent value and fritter away his time on new ones of doubtful worth. Any one who has the time and patience to examine the thousands of new books that are published every year will find that the really valuable ones are like Gratiano's two grains of wheat in two bushels of chaff. The flood of fiction that is poured out of the presses of Europe and America has become a serious evil, while the missionary may congratulate himself that he is in a land where there is no Sunday newspaper with its bulky, blanket sheets crowded with accounts of theatres, horse-races, crimes, divorces and silly gossip. Such reading is intellectually debilitating. It withdraws attention from the tried and settled and concentrates it upon the flotsam and jetsam of daily happenings. An eminent author once said that he never read a book until it was a year old and had been commended to him by men whose judgment he had learned to respect. Of course he might in this way be a year late in reading some useful book; but if it was really good, the lapse of a year would not impair its usefulness. Such a rule saves an immense amount of time that would otherwise be worse than wasted, while by reading only the best, one gets the largest amount of intellectual enrichment.

The missionary will also want a few periodicals. A daily paper is an unnecessary expense on the foreign field. All the real news of the world is in the weekly edition, and one can often get from it a better idea of current events than from the more voluminous daily which mixes facts with a mass of rumours and trivial details. The missionary will also want at least one of the weekly religious journals of his Church, a missionary magazine, and one or two periodicals devoted to general literature. In making selections, bear in mind the importance of sound book reviews so that authoritative information can be had as to the most valuable recent contributions to thought. Two or three missionary families at the same station might combine in this matter, so that a few dollars from each will secure the newspapers and magazines that will keep the whole circle in touch with the important happenings of the world. In addition, the medical and teaching missionaries will each take their professional journals to keep them abreast of the best thought in their respective departments.

There is another phase of the missionary's intellectual life, and that is the amount of intellectual labour that he is called upon to perform and for which he must keep his mental faculties keen. At the outset, he must learn a difficult language, perhaps, as in India, Persia, Syria or the Philippines, more than one or, as in South China, several dialects. This alone is an intellectual task requiring an alert and well-trained mind.

The missionary may find, too, that his routine work is mental in character. We have already noted the large place of education in modern missionary work and the great number of schools, colleges and theological seminaries on the foreign field.[1] The missionary may be assigned to one of these institutions, and, if so, he will find that his daily tasks are as distinctively intellectual as those of the school-teacher or the college professor at home. In his mastery of the text-books that he uses and in the training of the students under his care, he will have need of full intellectual equipment, and he will find it necessary to be a student himself in order that he may do his work properly and keep pace with the advance of thought and method in the educational world.

Or he may be assigned to literary work. Parts of the Bible have already been published in the languages of nearly all of

[1] Chapter VI.

the non-Christian lands; but there are several languages and dialects into which some of the books have not yet been translated. Moreover, there is frequent need of revising the translations made by earlier missionaries, as many of them were imperfect. And so, for one reason or the other, most missions have committees on Bible revision. The men who are to do this work properly must be versed in the Hebrew and Greek of the original versions and in the vernacular into which the translation is to be made. Such work as that done by Dr. Eli Smith and Dr. C. V. A. Van Dyke on the Arabic Bible, Bishop Schereschewsky on the Chinese, Dr. James Hepburn on the Japanese, and others that might easily be mentioned, requires linguistic and philological ability of the highest order.

School and college text-books must also be prepared. Sometimes suitable ones can be translated from the English; but often the English text-book is not adapted to the needs of the Asiatic, and therefore the missionaries have to make text-books of their own. It would take a good-sized volume to give even a bare catalogue of the readers, grammars, dictionaries, phrase-books, geographies, arithmetics, geometries, books on surveying, trigonometry, chemistry, zoölogy, physics, philosophy, etc., that have been prepared and that are being prepared to-day by missionaries. Of periodicals alone, over four hundred are edited by missionaries.

Nor is this all; missionaries have provided good books for general reading outside of schools. They have translated into the languages of Asia and Africa some of the best literature of Europe and America and have made original contributions of no small value to that literature. The society for the Diffusion of Christian and General Knowledge Among the Chinese (now the Christian Literature Society) has been a large factor in the intellectual awakening in China. Work of the same kind, though perhaps more distinctively religious in character, is being done by the Tract Societies that have been organized in various countries as auxiliaries of the great Tract

Societies of England and the United States. As a rule, the missionary either writes or translates these books.

In many parts of Africa and the South Sea Islands and even in some fields in Asia, the people are indebted solely to the missionary for the reduction of languages to written form and the introduction of the printing press, books and newspapers. The literary fecundity of some missionaries is amazing. No less than "twenty-five volumes are attributed to Morrison; twenty-four to Milne; twenty to Legge; twenty-seven to Faber; and to Gutzlaff, sixty-one volumes in Chinese, two in Japanese, one in Siamese, five in Dutch, seven in German, and nine in English. In later years, Dr. Muirhead was the author of thirty volumes in Chinese and three in English. Dr. McCartee published thirty-four in Chinese; and to Dr. Edkins may be traced fourteen publications in Chinese, seven in English, and one in Mongolian. Dr. Van Dyck prepared twenty-four volumes in Arabic and Dr. Post is the author of seven, two of which, a Concordance and a Bible Dictionary, are works of standard excellence and value representing immense and painstaking toil."[1]

The contribution that missionaries have thus made to the intellectual development of non-Christian lands is enormous. Indeed, the remarkable awakening, that is now assuming such large proportions in some lands, began in the mission schools. The learning that the missionary body has made available to the unevangelized world is the mightiest factor in the mental progress of Asia. Until within a few years, nine-tenths of the general knowledge which has been diffused throughout China, and ninety-nine hundredths of all the modern schools, were due to missionaries.[2]

Sometimes the diplomatic or military representatives of western nations need the aid of the missionary's learning. In

---

[1] Dennis, "Christian Missions and Social Progress," III, p. 173.
[2] Dr. Arthur H. Smith, "Rex Christus," p. 234.

The Missionary's Intellectual Life 169

scores of instances, proud officials from the world powers would have been almost helpless if it had not been for the assistance of missionaries. A signal instance of this was the service of Dr. S. Wells Williams and Dr. W. A. P. Martin in the negotiation of treaties with China and of Dr. J. Walter Lowrie in adjusting the troubles at Paoting-fu after the Boxer uprising. Indeed, "it is not too much to say that up to the middle of the last century the governments of Europe and America were almost entirely dependent upon the missionaries for the direct conduct of their intercourse with Chinese officials."[1]

And what shall be said of the rich contribution that the missionary has made to the world's knowledge of non-Christian lands. The Rev. Dr. Thomas Lowrie has shown in "The Ely Volume" how remarkable has been this contribution by the missionaries of the American Board alone. Dr. James S. Dennis, in his "Christian Missions and Social Progress," presents a wealth of similar facts regarding the other boards. "Turn to the Oriental shelves in our libraries and you will be amazed to find that nearly all of the brightest and deepest and most valuable books there have been written by missionaries. To missionary pens we are indebted for the most reliable information that we have regarding the far East, as well as for the most fascinating, poetical and scholarly of the correct pictures of Oriental life that we have. There are a few exceptions to this rule, but by their very scarcity they only serve to prove the rule."[2] Such a fair-minded critic as Mr. Alexander Michie recognizes this, for he writes:

"The great service which missionaries have rendered to the cause of knowledge can never be forgotten. It is to their labours that we owe what we know of the Chinese history, language and literature. Missionaries compiled the only dic-

[1] Dr. Arthur H. Smith.
[2] Mr. Arthur L. Shumway, newspaper correspondent.

tionaries as yet in common use. A missionary translated the classics into English, laying the whole world under perpetual obligation. Missionaries have explained the Chinese religions. A missionary has quite recently made a valuable contribution to descriptive anthropology, the first attempt at a systematic analysis of the Chinese character."

It must be frankly admitted that many missionaries are not qualified for this literary work. Abroad, as at home, there are good men who cannot write good books. It is the rule of some boards that no missionary shall take time for literary work from other duties without the sanction of his mission, and that no book shall be issued by a mission press that has not been approved by a competent committee. Of course, however, there can be no objection to a missionary using such odd hours as he can command, without injustice to his work, in the private preparation of a volume that he wishes to have published at his own risk, either on the field or in the home land. Some of the most valuable books on mission fields that have appeared in Europe and America have been prepared in this way.

The missionary whose work is evangelistic will often find, too, that his highest mental facilities will be needed in dealing with the best native minds. The Occidental errs if he supposes that the Oriental is inferior to him intellectually. The Chinese have been scholars for ages. In no other country in the world is an educated man regarded with such reverence. It is true that until recently the Chinese confined their studies to the past; but the Chinese of to-day are studying modern science, and when their students come to our western universities, they are quite able to cope with our best men. The missionary who is to lead them must be a thoroughly trained man. The East Indians are the most intellectual people in Asia. They have been accustomed for centuries to brooding over the profoundest and most mystical of problems. Many of the Brahmans are natural born metaphysicians, and they often interrupt the missionary with questions so subtle, and support them by argu-

The Missionary's Intellectual Life

ments so keen, that he needs all the resources of a vigorous intellectual life to meet them. It is a colossal blunder for him to imagine that he can influence such men simply by repeating, parrot-like, the religious phrases of the West. He must understand the genius of the gospel that he preaches, something of the history, the philosophy and the mental characteristics of the people he is addressing, and he must know how to express his message in the terms of human life as he finds it.

A few words regarding intellectual recreation may properly have a place under this general subject of the missionary's intellectual life. He should have some specialty. He should not make a hobby of it and ride it to the neglect of his work and the annoyance of his associates; but every student should have some subject far removed from his ordinary tasks. The best kind of rest is in a change of occupation and it is often very helpful to make the mind work in some channel out of the accustomed one. Such work will be more than a recreation; for, if wisely conducted, it will broaden culture and perhaps add not only to reputation but to the world's knowledge. Every mission field furnishes abundant opportunities for such specialties. What shall be said of the educated man who, living among a strange people, does not familiarize himself with their quaint and often intensely interesting folk-lore; who, surrounded by rare species of flowers and plants, has no discernment of their beauty, and who looks every day upon peculiar forms of insect life with as much indifference as if he were an animal? Why should not a missionary take up some one of these branches and study it? When the Rev. Dr. Henry C. McCook of Philadelphia went to Texas nervously broken down, he threw himself upon the ground in despair. Presently, his attention was attracted by a spider that was busily at work near him. He began watching that spider. Soon his interest was aroused. Day after day he returned to the spot and made notes and sketches of what he saw. The study diverted his mind from his anxieties, and ere long his health and spirits began to improve. After a while, he wrote out his notes, completed his sketches and sent them to a scientific magazine. The result was that he awoke one morning to find himself famous. To-day, he is recognized as one of the foremost entomologists of the world, and his book on spiders, a large, beautifully bound and sumptuously illustrated volume, is one of the best works extant on that subject.

Why cannot the missionary follow such an example? As a matter of fact, some missionaries have followed it. The great museums of London, New York, Philadelphia, Washington, and other cities would be much poorer if they did not contain the additions that have been made to them by missionaries. Dr. Adolphus C. Good found both pleasure and reputation in studying the moths and gorgeously hued butterflies that abounded in his West African field, and he sent a highly valued collection of them to the museums of America. Scientists gratefully acknowledge their indebtedness to him for no less than seventy-two genera and 547 species. The Jesuits of Manila have made themselves celebrated and have earned the gratitude and homage of sailors and scientists everywhere by their skillful studies of earthquakes and typhoons in the Philippines. Mr. James Dwight Dana, in writing on the Hawaiian volcanoes,[1] frankly admits his debt to the careful and courageous observations of the Rev. Titus Coan. The Rev. John T. Gulick, Ph. D., became such an expert in biology that Dr. George J. Romanes pronounced him " one of the most profound of living thinkers upon Darwinian topics." Raymond Lull's book on " Astronomy," the Rev. Dr. Robert H. Nassau's book on " Fetichism in West Africa," the Rev. Dr. Wm. K. Eddy's studies of the long buried sarcophagi near Sidon, the Rev. Dr. H. H. Jessup's investigations of the geology of Mount Lebanon, the Rev. Dr. F. E. Hoskins' researches among the ruined cities as described in " The Jordan

---

[1] " Characteristics of Volcanoes," p. 40.

The Missionary's Intellectual Life

Valley and Petra," the Rev. Dr. George E. Post's "Flora of Syria, Palestine and Sinai," the Rev. Dr. S. B. Fairbank's "Lists" of "The Deccan Fishes" and "The Reptiles of the Bombay Presidency," and Miss Katherine N. Fleeson's "Laos Folk Lore," are a few of the many instances that might be cited.

Dr. Nevius' orchard at Chefoo, China, is an illustration of another form of recreation that is at once a satisfaction to the missionary and a help to the people. He found that the native fruits were exceedingly poor. It has been said that if one eats a Chinese pear for a turnip, it is fairly good, but that if he eats it for a pear, he will be disappointed. This is true of most Chinese fruits; they are coarse, woody, and poorly flavoured. Dr. Nevius saw his opportunity and brought from America a few seeds and saplings. He developed a fine orchard, and then gave cuttings to the Chinese and showed them the proper methods of cultivation. In this way, he greatly improved the quality of fruit all over north China to the great delight of Chinese and foreigners alike.

Every missionary should cultivate a love of nature. No other study is more enriching to the mind and heart. However far one may be from home and loved ones, the world of nature is still his. The charm of stream and meadow, of hill and valley, of flowers and trees and sky, the glory of sunrise and the mystic beauty of sunset, never fail. The splendours of the day are followed by the softer radiance of the night. No one who has ever stood on a Judean hilltop and looked upon the blazing stars of an Oriental sky can wonder that so many of the sacred writers loved God's great out-of-doors and besprinkled their pages with references to it. It was not poetic license but literal truth when Bryant wrote:

> "To him who in the love of Nature holds
> Communion with her visible forms, she speaks
> A various language; for his gayer hours
> She has a voice of gladness, and a smile

> And eloquence of beauty, and she glides
> Into his darker musings with a mild
> And gentle sympathy that steals away
> Their sharpness ere he is aware."

Now, as of old, to the reverent mind, "the heavens declare the glory of God, and the firmament sheweth His handiwork. Day unto day uttereth speech, and night unto night sheweth knowledge." In the tropics, the missionary has the privilege of studying some constellations that are hidden from the resident of colder climes. "Lift up your eyes on high," exclaims Isaiah, "and behold who hath created these things, that bringeth out their host by number."[1] Let us ever remember that God has written the book of nature as well as the book of revelation, that one may interpret the other and that a fact in one cannot be inconsistent with a fact in the other. Ruskin truly says: "The Spirit of God is in the air which you breathe. His glory is in the light which you see and the first-fruits of the earth and the joy of His creatures. He has written day by day His revelations as He has given you day by day your daily bread."

Many of the world's noblest thoughts have come from men who lived much with nature—shepherds, woodsmen, fishermen or scholars who, though nominally dwellers in cities, did most of their work in some quiet country home where the flowers grew and the birds sang. Jesus Himself loved to get away from the crowded cities into the wilderness where, among the solemn mountains and beside the murmuring streams, He could quietly commune with the Father. His favourite illustrations were drawn from trees and sowers and harvests and floods and fowls of the air. He bade His disciples "consider the lilies how they grow," and it was "to a desert place" that He invited them to "come apart and rest awhile." Emerson reminds us that Christianity can be best understood in the open

---

[1] Isaiah 40 : 26.

air. Jacob did not get his vision of God until he was alone on a hilltop. Nebuchadnezzar, made sordid and arrogant by the glare and pomp of a capital, had to be "driven from men" and have his head "wet with the dew of heaven" before his reason returned and he was able to realize that the divine "ways are justice," that there was a Sovereign mightier than the builder of "great Babylon," and that "those that walk in pride He is able to abase." Power and wealth had spoiled him; but nature brought him to his senses and made a man of him.

Frequent contact with nature is even more necessary to-day, if we are to be kept from false conceptions of life and do our best work. It is hard to think high thoughts in a steam-heated, electric-lighted room, with the rumbling of trucks and clang of trolleys coming through the window. And how petty most of our daily annoyances appear when we view them under the open sky. Fortunate the man who can say with Elizabeth Barrett Browning:

> "The little cares that fretted me,
>   I lost them yesterday
> Among the fields above the sea,
>   Among the winds at play;
> Among the lowing of the herds,
>   The rustling of the trees,
> Among the singing of the birds,
>   The humming of the bees.
>
> "The foolish fears of what may happen,
>   I cast them all away
> Among the clover-scented grass,
>   Among the new-mown hay;
> Among the husking of the corn
>   Where drowsy poppies nod,
> Where ill thoughts die and good are born,
>   Out in the fields with God."

Space will not permit a more extended consideration of this

inviting theme; but perhaps enough has been said to indicate both to the young missionary and to the reader at home that the missionary's intellectual life is important, and that for his own sake, for the better performance of his work and for the increase of the world's knowledge, he should not neglect it.

X

THE MISSIONARY'S SPIRITUAL LIFE

THIS is the most vital element in the missionary's character and influence. He is supposed to be "God's man, in God's place, doing God's work, in God's way and for God's glory." If, therefore, he is to be in any true sense a missionary at all, he must be a man of deep and strong spiritual life. Of the missionary as of the poet, " the words of Milton are true in all times and were never truer than in this: 'He who would write heroic poems must make his whole life a heroic poem.' If he cannot first so make his life, then let him hasten from this arena; for neither its lofty glories nor its fearful perils are fit for him."[1] This is because "the missionary himself is the great factor in evangelization. His deep underlying convictions have more to do in evangelization than the mere methods adopted. In fact, his convictions determine the methods and policy, not in their mere external form and nomenclature, but in their inner principles and their daily outworking."[2]

Spirituality is necessary to the missionary's own happiness as well as to the success of his work. Matthew Henry once said that the gospel ministry is a noble calling, but a wretched trade. This is preëminently true of missionary life. No man can be happy or largely useful in it unless he is inspired by considerations which render him, like Paul, comparatively indifferent to merely physical and temporal conditions.

Some may deem it strange that it is advisable to counsel the

---
[1] Carlyle, "Essay on Burns," p. 68.
[2] The Rev. S. A. Moffett, D. D.

missionary to guard his spiritual life, since the very fact that he is a missionary is supposed to mean that he has one of more than ordinary vigour. This is true, in a measure. The boards realize that if a man does not have spirituality at home, he is not likely to develop it abroad. A sea voyage does not change the character, nor is residence in a heathen land favourable to grace. The boards, therefore, will not accept candidates who do not give evidence of a real Christian experience. But no initial experience can carry one through life, least of all on the foreign field. Like the manna sent to the Israelites of old, the soul's food must be gathered fresh day by day. Unceasing effort is necessary. In the spiritual realm as in the physical, things do not grow of themselves; they must be vigilantly watched and diligently cultivated.

These cautions are the more necessary because the knowledge that one is a spiritual guide to others involves subtle dangers to himself, particularly on the foreign field. At home, the missionary probably did not realize to what an extent he was dependent upon others for spiritual stimulus. There were always meetings that he could attend, and when the fires of devotion burned low, it was easy to find some gathering of God's chosen, in conference with whom the flames were easily made to burn more brightly. On the foreign field these opportunities are fewer and perhaps wholly non-existent.

The first experience, too, is often a blow to pride. "You are a graduate of college and seminary, let us say, and feel that after years of preparation you are at last equipped for your life work. Perhaps you have had some experience in the pastorate or in a school, and have grown accustomed to deference. But you find yourself now again in the place of a beginner. Your past record counts for nothing. Your opinions, based on experience with men and things at home, may have been valuable there, but here you find no one greatly impressed with them. Add to this the fact that until you make some progress in the language, you have almost no outlet for your pent up energies, and you have a situation that is unexpected, bewildering and rather painful. How easy to feel envious and even a little spiteful!"[1]

Another danger is the temptation to a secular life. The missionary has to do with other things than the direct preaching of the gospel. The erection of buildings, the superintendence of schools and hospitals and printing presses, the keeping of mission and station accounts, and kindred duties, often require much time. Missionaries sometimes chafe under this "secular" work. "I came to ———— as a missionary," laments one; "but I have degenerated into a mere business man, a large proportion of whose time has been spent in carrying on two business enterprises, the dispensary and the press. Perhaps we might call each a business success; but as mission work they are not satisfying." Occasionally, missionaries, like the disciples of old, complain that "it is not fit that we should forsake the word of God and serve tables." So they ask the board to send out a layman "whom we may appoint over this business," that we may "continue steadfastly in prayer and in the ministry of the word."[2]

Some one, however, must do these "secular" things, for missionary work necessarily involves them. Why should any missionary regard himself as exempt from such duties? Can he not do them as well as others? The pastor of a church at home often feels that if he could only devote his whole energy to sermons and to personal work with the impenitent, what wonderful things for God he could do; but he finds that he must give a great deal of time to duties that are quite different in character. The temptation is strong for all of us to think that we could accomplish great things if we were only free from entangling cares.

Such notions are apt to be partly imaginary and partly selfish. As a matter of fact, those who are so situated that

[1] Mrs. Wm. Baird, Korea.   [2] Acts 6: 2–4.

they have freedom for big things seldom achieve them. **If** God felt that a missionary could do more for Him in some other way than in the usual missionary lines, He would probably bring about the opportunity. There is a significant lesson in the sequel to the disciples' complaint. The big things that they were going to do when they could "continue steadfastly in prayer and in the ministry of the word" were never done by most of them; but Stephen, one of the men who was set apart to "serve tables," promptly developed such extraordinary spiritual usefulness that the whole twelve fell into the background and were not heard of again until martyrdom had ended Stephen's life. Even then, the man who stood forth to do the mightiest things for God was not one of the twelve but the new convert, Paul. This is in line with our observation to-day. Some of the most useful missionaries are men who perform the "secular" duties of the mission, or who are physicians in charge of hospitals, or teachers in charge of schools.

Everywhere, life is largely made up of little things, and the measure of one's influence is the fidelity with which the little things are done. Huxley well said that the test of character and the evidence of ability and trustworthiness is the doing of the thing that ought to be done, when it ought to be done, as it ought to be done, whether you like to do it or not. It is unfortunate when a man fancies himself above any necessary work, or when he imagines that the performance of anything that ought to be done will lower his spiritual vitality. In the words of Mrs. Browning:

> " . . . let us be content, in work,
> To do the thing we can, and not presume
> To fret because it's little. 'Twill employ
> Seven men, they say, to make a perfect pin;
> Who makes the head content to miss the point;
> Who makes the point agreed to leave the joint:
> And if a man should cry, 'I want a pin,

> And I must make it straightway, head and point,'
> His wisdom is not worth the pin he wants.
> Seven men to a pin and not a man too much."[1]

And to this we may add the lines of Dr. Van Dyke:

> "Every mason in the quarry, every builder on the shore,
> Every woodman in the forest, every boatman at the oar,
> Hewing wood and drawing water, splitting stones and clearing sod,
> All the dusty ranks of labour in the regiment of God,
> March together towards His temple, do the task His hands prepare;
> Honest toil is holy service; faithful work is praise and prayer."

Do we not err anyway in drawing a line between the secular and the spiritual? Is it right to divide life into certain duties that are purely worldly and others that are purely religious, and then fret because we have to do some of the former? Such a conception dates back to the old error that matter is evil. It degenerates the modern Christian into the medieval monk who felt that he could not lead the life of the spirit unless he fled from the world and immured himself in a cell. Christ's life was just the opposite of this. He lived among men, doing the every-day things that needed to be done, but so suffusing the secular with the spiritual as to make them all the media of spiritual influence.

Why should not a missionary, in like manner, spiritualize the secular life? The superintendence of workmen in building operations affords an excellent opportunity to lead them to Christ and to exemplify some of the graces of the Christian life by fairness, honesty aud sympathy. The charge of a hospital opens wide avenues for spiritual influence among the sick and the suffering, who in their helplessness are wholly dependent upon the missionary and are prepared to receive with grateful hearts the spiritual influence that he can exert upon them. The schoolroom is a divinely given opportunity for

---

[1] "Aurora Leigh," p. 154.

spiritual work with young lives at their most plastic period. Every department of missionary activity can be and should be pervaded by the spiritual tone.

> "The trivial round, the common task
> Will furnish all we ought to ask,
> Room to deny ourselves, a road
> To bring us daily nearer God."

The temptation to professionalism is as great as to that of a secular life. What minister has not had to contend against the danger of regarding the most sacred duties of the Christian life as matters of routine? There is sad significance in the lament: "They made me the keeper of the vineyards, but mine own vineyard have I not kept." [1]

Probably most missionaries would sorrowfully admit this. The natural law that all things seek a common level operates in spiritual things as well as in physical. The spiritual level of non-Christian society is low, and the danger is that instead of lifting men up to his altitude, the missionary will allow them to pull him down to theirs. If, however, he successfully resists this downward suction, he is in danger of peevishness or callousness of soul as he comes into daily contact with the vices of heathenism, the numerous and irritating weaknesses of the natives and the foibles of fellow missionaries, who are so close to him that every little defect is plainly revealed. The following extracts from missionary letters are pathetically illustrative:

"I used to think that the spiritual atmosphere of foreign mission work would in itself be helpful and elevating, but I do not find it so. The atmosphere has to be made, and the making requires more time and care than at home."

"The things I was prepared to meet have not materialized; but every weakness, and, as I supposed, long conquered sins, temptations and trials innumerable, have beset me behind and

[1] Song of Solomon, 1 : 6.

The Missionary's Spiritual Life

before, until I sometimes wonder whether I am the same person that left America a little time ago."

"The missionary finds himself in the foreign field, too often, having had no experience in successful soul-winning. He finds a machine, 'a plant,' already existing and being 'administered' faithfully. After getting something of the language, he is given a place at the mill and takes his turn as 'administrator,' too. That he is to touch the people every day and secure some of them for Christ and initiate them into the work of soul-saving, he does not seem to realize, or he thinks he has not time for it, being so much occupied with running 'the machine'—perhaps a school, perhaps a circuit of country schools."

"Let us not deceive ourselves, the foreign mission field is not a hot-bed for saints. It is a place rather of dreadful spiritual tragedy. There men live away from all the holy influences of Christian society. They hear things daily that they ought not to hear, see things they ought not to see, and the tendency is always for what is fine in us to grow coarse."

The helps to the spiritual life are therefore of vital importance. One of these is Bible study. The missionary is supposed to have a good knowledge of the English Bible before going to the field, but he can never learn it well enough. It is not sufficient to have a general familiarity with Scriptural history, places and incidents. One should have a knowledge of the Bible's inner meaning and be able to make a personal appropriation of it. The Bible is God's direct message to men, and how can we know the will of God unless we understand that message?

The missionary will find his Bible indispensable to his own comfort. It will bring to him guidance in every perplexity, strength in every weakness, resources for every emergency. One who underscores the promises as he reads will soon find that he can hardly open his Bible anywhere without seeing the red lines which tell of the "precious and exceeding great promises" in which the Sovereign of worlds has entered into covenant with man. Stanley said that when almost overcome by loneliness and anxiety in the gloomy forests of "Darkest Africa," his Bible brought him strength and cheer. He wrote: "Before turning in for the night, I resumed my reading of the Bible as usual. I had already read the book through from beginning to end once, and was now at Deuteronomy for the second reading, and I came unto the verse wherein Moses exhorts Joshua in those fine lines, 'Be strong and of a good courage; fear not, nor be afraid of them: for the Lord thy God, He it is that doth go with thee; He will not fail thee, nor forsake thee.'"[1]

And the missionary needs the Bible for his work. He does not go to the foreign field to convey any ideas of his own but the knowledge of salvation and godly living that he has found in the Bible. The Roman Catholic missionary keeps the Scriptures in the background and gives his message on the authority of the Church; but the Protestant missionary rests his whole argument upon the Word of God. His warnings against sin, his accounts of God's love, his authoritative declaration as to what men ought to do, must rest upon the Bible. Paul reminded that young missionary, Timothy, that "every Scripture inspired of God" has a place in the personal life and the service equipment of "the man of God" who would be "complete" and "furnished completely unto every good work."[2] This accords with the general teaching of the Scriptures. They are the arsenal from which the Christian soldier obtains his weapons. In the stirring passage in which Paul warns us that we wrestle against "the powers" and "the world-rulers of this darkness," he exhorts us to take among other things "the sword of the Spirit, which is the word of God."[3]

No matter, therefore, what may be the pressure upon his time, the missionary should devote some part of each day to the study of the Word of God.

[1] "In Darkest Africa," I: 311.
[2] 2 Tim. 3: 16, 17.
[3] Eph. 6: 12 sq.

Another indispensable help is prayer. Of all men, the missionary most needs divine direction. What human intelligence can comprehend God's plan for the innumerable peoples of heathendom? Who can rightly solve all the varied and complex problems involved in the founding and developing of the Church and its allied institutions amid the peculiar conditions of non-Christian lands? Who knows what modifications of method may be necessary, how far the polity and terminology of our American churches should be pressed upon the Asiatic and African churches? It is not in man to overcome such difficulties, and the results may be disastrous if the missionary takes counsel of his pride, or ambition, or sectarianism, or a prayerless judgment of any kind, however sincere it may be. The more zeal he has, the more mischief he may do. Moses in such circumstances killed a man, and then, instead of being hailed as a leader as he had expected, had to flee for his life.

The missionary who does not pray, or whose prayers are merely perfunctory observances, is not in any true sense a missionary at all, and the sooner he is recalled, the better for the work. It is literally true that

"Prayer is the Christian's vital breath,"

and that unless he prays, his spiritual life will not only be inefficient, but it will die.

Assuming, however, that the missionary will pray, there remains the danger that in the hurry and pressure of his life, he will not pray enough. If it be asked why he should spend valuable time in private prayer when he is going to devote a considerable part of the day to prayer and preaching for others, the answer is that he needs to pray for his own sake and that his power in public will be largely increased by his private devotions. It is when one is alone with God that he gets his message for others. The missionary who prays gets more things done and done better. The promise is explicit—"If any of you lacketh wisdom, let him ask of God, who giveth to all liberally and upbraideth not; and it shall be given him." The secret of Livingstone's indomitable courage in danger and his extraordinary influence over men appeared when he said: "Nothing earthly will make me give up my work in despair; I encourage myself in the Lord my God, and go forward." When his African followers found his dead body beside the burning candle, in the gray dawn of that memorable fourth of May, 1873, it was upon its knees, for the great missionary had died, as he had lived, in prayer. The touching entry in his journal, written on the next to the last birthday of his life, told the story: "My Jesus, my King, my life, my all, I again dedicate my whole self to Thee."

Whatever else the missionary neglects, therefore, he should not neglect his private devotions. If he cannot find the time for them, he must make it. "It may mean a less quantity of work, but it must mean an immense addition to the energy of service. If we neglect this, we shall teach false lessons to the heathen, worry when we ought to be teaching peace, irritability when we ought to be teaching forbearance, passion when we ought to be teaching love." [1]

Both in Bible study and in prayer, it is well to have methodical habits. It may impress us as incongruous to associate method with prayer. It may be said that prayer is an atmosphere, "the Christian's native air," and that if anything should be spontaneous and untrammelled, it should be prayer. But we are creatures of habit. We do better and easier the things that we are accustomed to do. It is as true of spiritual things as of mental and physical, that activity follows the grooves of method. "A rule is a staff set up for a weak and inconstant impulse to lean against and to be bound to." There are some excellent precedents for methodical prayer. David says: "Evening and morning and at noon will I pray," and David was a spiritually-minded man. The writer of the One Hun-

[1] The Rev. Donald Fraser, of Africa.

dred and Nineteenth Psalm remarks: "Seven times a day do I praise Thee." Daniel "kneeled upon his knees three times a day," and he was particular about the exact spot where he kneeled and the exact point of the compass towards which his face was turned. "All of which was quite mechanical and formal; and yet we remember that Daniel was an exceedingly safe man in an emergency. . . . He was more methodical than may be poetic; but it is something to be able to forecast a man's latitude and longitude as Daniel's could be. The clock-work element in his religion was quite conspicuous, and yet it is worth a good deal to have a man in trying times that will tick the minutes as distinctly as he and strike with so full a ring when the hour comes round. It is good to have men in a community that run so close with the sun, that when it is foggy you can tell what time it is by looking in their faces."[1]

The Bible tells us to "pray without ceasing," and we ought. We probably shall when we get to heaven, where sanctification is complete; but we are not in heaven yet, neither are we already perfect. We are just ordinary Christians stumbling along on earth, and we have not gotten beyond the necessity of earthly methods. The Christian who has no settled times for family or closet prayer and who leaves it to impulse or leisure soon becomes a negligent and prayerless Christian; but the Christian who has stated seasons for his devotions is the one who is growing most rapidly in grace. The homes where the prayer hour is as regular as the meal hour are the homes of the purest influences and the holiest fragrance. So we need a method even in prayer. "Praying by the clock is not ideal, neither are we, and trying to adapt ideal methods into situations that are not themselves ideal not only gives us no perfection in the result, but a very ordinary sort of imperfection."[1]

The missionary should therefore set apart a particular time

[1] Parkhurst, "The Pattern in the Mount and Other Sermons," pp. 73 sq.

of the day or night and allow nothing to interfere with it. "The morning watch," that is observed by so many of the young people of our generation, is probably the best. It is easier to get a little time immediately after rising than after one has become involved in the duties of the day. These devotional moments, however brief, help one to begin his work in the right spirit, while there is added inspiration in the thought that one is joining the great host of those who also observe "the morning watch."

It is almost equally important not to omit frequent spiritual conferences with one's associates. There should be a regular prayer-meeting at every station. Each missionary should attend it and help to make it profitable. "Do not let anything," observes Mrs. Baird, "mislead you into 'forsaking the assembling of yourselves together' for purposes of prayer and praise in your own language, no matter how small your community may be. The whole history of missions presents no more noble picture than that of Judson and his wife sitting down alone to celebrate the Lord's Supper. You and your fellow workers, as long as you live and labour together, will need to get down on your knees at regular intervals and make humble confession of sins and shortcomings and raise earnest prayer for forgiveness and strength. It will be to the inner working of your station what the drop of oil is to the piece of machinery."

Larger conferences should be held as opportunity offers. They can always be had in connection with the annual meeting of the mission. The Siam missionaries have found great profit in occasional conferences with the native Christian leaders. In Korea, such conferences have come to be a prominent feature of the work. Then there are vacation assemblages. Large numbers of missionaries gather annually at some resorts in China, Japan and India. Of course, recreation is prominent at such times; but there ought also to be such conferences for prayer and the deepening of the Christian life as will make

The Missionary's Spiritual Life 189

the vacation a spiritual as well as physical tonic. No Christian ever needs a vacation from religion.

Prayer and Bible study will nourish that mighty faith which should characterize the missionary. The obstacles that he confronts are of the most formidable character. Without faith in God, he might well be appalled as he considers the vast numbers of non-Christians, their deeply rooted superstitions, the influence of their omnipresent priests, the obstinacy of ancient customs, and the prejudices of a self-centred people against an alien religion opposed to all the traditions of their individual and national life. How almost hopelessly formidable appears caste in India! How apparently invincible Mohammedanism in Turkey! It is hard enough to change the character of a sinful man in America, but it is far harder to change it in a heathen land, while the social ostracism of a convert tends to make even the bravest hesitate. It is a tremendous task to uproot the prejudices of centuries and revolutionize the lives of millions of people. Nothing could be more preposterous from a human viewpoint than for a handful of men and women to attempt such a transformation. God alone can do it; but "He is able," and linking ourselves to His omnipotence, we can accomplish the apparently impossible. We may labour on, with faith in the future because with faith in Him who controls it. Even when our plans prove futile, we need not lose heart. He is not limited to our schemes. We have only drifted away from Him and need but to return.

It cannot be too often or too strongly emphasized that the missionary must rely heavily upon the Holy Spirit. The missionary enterprise is preëminently a spiritual one, and if it is to be successful, it must be conducted by spiritual men. God has ever chosen for the work men of this type. We read that "the Holy Ghost said, 'Separate Me Barnabas and Saul for the work whereunto I have called them.'"[1] So marked was the

---

[1] Acts 13 : 2.

direct interposition of the Holy Spirit in the case of William Carey, that Dr. Ryland declared that "God Himself infused into the mind of Carey that solicitude for the salvation of the heathen which cannot be fairly traced to any other source"; [1] while Alexander Duff himself wrote: "When, by the grace of God, I was led to care for my own soul, then it was that I began to care for the heathen abroad. In my closet on my bended knees, I then said to God: 'O Lord, Thou knowest that silver and gold to give to this cause I have none; what I have I give unto Thee. I offer myself; wilt Thou accept the gift?'" The inner history of almost every missionary who has been largely used of God reveals similar experiences.

The missionary should not be content with a general knowledge of the Holy Spirit. Charles Finney used to say that "conversion to Christ is not to be confounded with consecration to the great work of the world's conversion." The man who receives the grace of God for his own salvation and not for the salvation of others not only learns little of the real joy of the Christian life, but defeats one of its main ends. The disciples were Christians before the day of Pentecost, but they could hardly be considered effective ones. They were staggered by the commission of Christ. A few obscure men commanded to disciple all nations! They would have ignominiously failed if they had attempted such a task in their own strength. And so, though the urgency of the field conditions was as great as it is now, Christ said to them: "Tarry ye in the city until ye be clothed with power from on high." [2] When they were thus clothed, they at once became aggressive. They preached with such irresistible fervour that men "were pricked in their heart," and cried: "What shall we do?" [3] Peter, who had cowered before a servant girl, sternly arraigned the Sanhedrin, and when he was "charged not to speak at all

---

[1] Gordon, "The Holy Spirit in Missions," p. 82.
[2] Luke 24 : 49.
[3] Acts 2 : 37.

nor teach in the name of Jesus," he replied : " Whether it be right in the sight of God to hearken unto you rather than unto God, judge ye; for we cannot but speak the things which we saw and heard." [1]

The Ephesian Christians passed through a similar experience and one that suggests much to the followers of Christ in all lands. They were not present at Pentecost and knew nothing about it. When Paul said to them: " Did ye receive the Holy Ghost when ye believed?" he did not mean that they had not experienced the regenerating influence of the Holy Spirit, for they are spoken of in the first verse of the chapter as "disciples," and in this very question as those who "believed." They could not have been "disciples" or have "believed" without the Holy Spirit. The question simply implied that they were living on a low spiritual plane, enjoying little and accomplishing little, helplessly confronting a heathenism upon which they were making no impression, and that the cause lay in their ignorance of the richer enduement of the Pentecostal outpouring. There is a touch of pathos in their position—a handful of half-discouraged believers, exerting but feeble influence, seeing the truth but dimly, and yet in their imperfect way holding on to it and refusing to go back to their former Christless state. And now the apostle opens to them the door of a larger life. Will they enter? We can almost see the eagerness in their faces as they listen. "And when Paul had laid his hands upon them, the Holy Ghost came on them." [2]

The missionary of to-day occasionally finds little companies of groping disciples who are in the spiritual state of those believers at Ephesus and, like Paul, he should have in himself the spiritual experience that will enable him to help them. He should know, both for them and for himself, that the Holy Spirit's power can be obtained just as any other spiritual bless-

[1] Acts 4 : 18–20. [2] Acts 19 : 1–6.

ing is obtained—by prayer and faith. It is not a wage to be earned, but a gift to be appropriated. It is not to be confounded with a paroxysm of emotion or with any immediate and striking change of feeling. If we have rightly sought for spiritual power, we may take God at His word and assume that we have it. The first effort to use it will show that we are not mistaken.

Other limitations may be beyond our control, but we ourselves are responsible for an impoverished spiritual life. If we do not have the power of the Holy Spirit, we ought to have it. The inspired writer exhorts us: "Be not drunken with wine wherein is riot, but be filled with the Spirit."[1] That can only mean that it is just as much our duty to "be filled with the Spirit" as it is to "be not drunken with wine." This is, therefore, no new theory, but simply the common doctrine of sanctification, the scriptural teaching that the Christian ought not to be satisfied with a weak, joyless, uncertain spiritual life, but that he should "grow in grace," "walk in the light," "press on towards the goal unto the prize of the high calling of God in Christ Jesus," in short, "receive power."

It is difficult to live a holy life amid the unfavourable conditions of a heathen land, but it is not impossible. The pond lily lifts its pure white flower out of the foulest mud. There is profound significance in Paul's reference to "the saints . . . that are of Cæsar's household."[2] The Cæsar referred to was one of the worst monarchs that ever disgraced a throne and his court was notorious for its profligacy; but even in such a place, there were those who consistently served God. This illustrates the truth that the Christian life ought to be independent of its environment. It depends, not upon conditions that are without, but upon those that are within. "The ordinary man," says Carlyle, "is forever seeking in external circumstances the help which can be found only in himself.

[1] Eph. 5 : 18.   [2] Phil. 4 : 22.

... Were he there and not here, were he thus and not so, it would be well with him. ... He expects from it (the world) what it cannot give to any man; seeks for contentment, not within himself, in action and wise effort, but from without, in the kindness of circumstances, in love, friendship, honour, pecuniary ease. ... Thus he cannot gird himself up for any worthy well-calculated goal, ... is ever and anon turned from his path; and to the last cannot reach the only true happiness of a man, that of clear decided activity in the sphere for which, by nature and circumstances, he has been fitted and appointed."[1]

The missionary may wisely take these words to heart. The fact that some of the outward incentives to the Christian life are wanting ought to drive him closer to Christ and teach him the joy of living in such constant fellowship with the Master that his inspiration will be drawn direct from its original source and become, in a measure at least, independent of other channels. The missionary of mightiest power will be the one who can say with Zinzendorf: "I have one passion and that is Christ, He only"; or with James Calvert, missionary to the Fijis: "Where Christ commands and directs, I cheerfully go; I only desire what He approves and to do what He requires for the remainder of my life"; or with David Brainerd: "This I saw, that when a soul loves God with a supreme love, God's interests and his are become one; it is no matter when or where or how Christ should send me, nor what trials He should exercise me with, if I may be prepared for His work and will"; or with that convert of the first century who is represented by Richard Watson Gilder as saying:

> "If Jesus Christ is a man —
> And only a man,—I say
> That of all mankind I cleave to Him,
> And to Him will I cleave alway.

[1] Essay on Burns.

> "If Jesus Christ is God—
>   And the only God,—I swear
> I will follow Him through heaven and hell,
>   The earth, the sea and the air."

Such a life is a wonderful power. Whatever the natives may think of the missionary's doctrines, they know as well as any one else the difference between the life that is Christlike and the life that is not. The Rev. Simeon H. Calhoun, who was for thirty years a missionary in Syria, became known throughout all that region as "the Saint of Lebanon," and he and his associate, the Rev. William Bird, gained such influence over the warlike, fanatical Druses that during the massacres of 1860, when 15,000 Christians lost their lives, the house of the latter was untouched; and when, years afterwards, Dr. Jessup asked the haughty leader of the Druses why he had spared the missionaries, he replied: "It was because of the character of Mr. Calhoun and Mr. Bird that I saved that house." At the funeral of Mr. Bird, a Sheik said to the missionaries:

"Sirs, Mr. Calhoun and Mr. Bird were our brothers and friends. They loved us, and we loved them. On behalf of the whole people of Lebanon, we entreat you to allow Mrs. Bird and her daughter Emily to remain here among us, for we need them and Abeih would be orphaned without them."

And so we affectionately charge the new missionary to enter upon his duties with a deep and humble consciousness of his dependence upon God. He should feel that he has consecrated his life to the work which, of all works, is nearest to the heart of God, and that he may absolutely rely upon the divine presence and guidance. When a minister left the pastorate that he might undertake missionary work, a brother minister prayed: "We thank Thee oh, God, that Thou hast made it possible for him to touch Thy throne with one hand and the heart of the heathen world with the other. Oh, bless him, that he may be the channel through which the divine wisdom and power may come to men!" Such a prayer finely expresses

The Missionary's Spiritual Life

both the opportunity of the missionary and the dignity of his service.

In that charming book, "Beside the Bonnie Brier Bush," Watson reminds us that "every Scotch cottage has at least two rooms—the kitchen where the work is done and where all kinds of people come—that is called the 'but'; and the inner chamber which holds the household treasures and where none but a few honoured guests have entrance—that is called the 'ben.' So we imagine an outer court of the religious life where most of us make our home, and a secret place where only God's nearest friends enter; 'and it is the highest tribute which a Scotchman can pay the spiritual life of a friend to say: He's far ben.'" This is our desire for every missionary—that he may abide in the inner chamber of divine love, remembering that he may be so "filled with the Spirit" that he will be lifted above the anxieties and trials of life into the region of calms, where "none of these things" disturb the soul. The happiness and efficiency of missionary service will be in direct proportion to the richness and fullness of the spiritual life. There is no self-denial to him who walks with God. He does not lose his sensitiveness to sin, nor is he made callous by the daily observation of heathenism and vice. No problem will be too hard for him.

> "I say, the acknowledgment of God in Christ
> Accepted by thy reason, solves for thee
> All questions in the earth and out of it."[1]

In the solemn service in which John Coleridge Patteson was consecrated Bishop of Melanesia, Bishop Selwyn gave this loving counsel, that we wish to pass on to every missionary reader of this book:

"May every step of thy life, dear brother, be in company with the Lord Jesus. May Christ be with thee as a light to

---
[1] Robert Browning.

lighten the Gentiles; may He work in thee His spiritual miracles. May you feel His presence in the lonely wilderness, on the mountain-top, on the troubled sea. May Christ be ever with thee to give thee utterance, to open thy mouth boldly to make known the mystery of the gospel.

"May you sorrow with Him in His agony and be crucified with Him in His death, be buried with Him in His grave, rise with Him to newness of life and ascend with Him in heart in the same place whither He has gone before, and feel that He ever liveth to make intercession for thee, 'that thy faith fail not.'"

XI

THE MISSIONARY AND THE BOARD

IN a long tour of Asia, the author made special inquiries of a large number of missionaries of various denominations regarding their relation to their respective boards. He is happy to report that the alienation, which is sometimes said to exist, is confined to a very few missionaries whose leadership is expressly disavowed by their associates. There are, indeed, occasional differences of opinion as to policy and the wisdom of particular actions; but of resentment or distrust there is remarkably little. The missionaries frequently referred to the great improvement in this respect in recent years. "A generation ago," they said, "the missionary was often disposed to look upon the board as his natural enemy; but to-day he regards it as his personal friend."

Some missionaries, who would be first to repudiate the charge of personal feeling, raised the question whether the boards sufficiently consulted the missionaries before making decisions. Inquiries, however, developed the fact that the missionaries did not realize what an effort the boards are already making to ascertain their views. The secretaries give much of their time to correspondence with individual missionaries and to conferences with missionaries or missionary bishops who are home on furlough. Secretaries covet such interviews, and whenever there is advance notice so that the necessary arrangements can be made, a committee of the board meets the representative from the field. In this way, the missionary has free opportunity to set forth his views, while if his visit occurs when the board is in session, he may be introduced to that body.

Besides these regular methods, there are special ones. For

example, during the Boxer outbreak in China, one secretary wrote to the forty-five China missionaries of his board, who were then on furlough, asking their counsel as to the policy that should be pursued, and in addition invited eight of them to come to New York at the expense of the board for a personal conference. Several of the boards send a secretary or a deputation to visit the field at intervals of a few years, for the express purpose of becoming more fully informed regarding mission work, while the bishops of the Methodist Church make regular visitations of foreign conferences. In these ways, many secretaries and not a few board members have personally visited the foreign field and by their studies on the ground, as well as by their wide experience in handling mission problems of an administrative character, have become experts.

Thus it will be seen that the boards have special facilities for ascertaining the judgment of the missionaries. Indeed, it not infrequently happens that the secretary has a more accurate knowledge of the real sentiment of a mission than many of the missionaries themselves, since he is the only one who has direct and confidential correspondence with every member of the mission. It is the policy of the boards to attach much weight to the judgment of the missionaries and to give them all the liberty of action consistent with the prudent administration of the trust which the Church has committed to the board. The presumption is always in favour of the requests of the devoted and trusted workers on the field. With the exception of items that involve a mistaken policy, the custom is to approve their estimates, and assign to the missions as large a lump sum as the Board's anticipated income will permit, and leave the missions considerable freedom in determining how funds can be expended to the best advantage.

Missionaries, however, do not always appreciate the difficulties that beset the effort to ascertain their views. They represent about as many different types of character and judgment as an equal number of Christian workers in the United States. Every one knows how rare unanimity is in a General Conference or Assembly. If the proposed action is one in which there is any interest at all, there are certain to be divergent opinions. This difficulty, that is experienced when several hundred ministers and laymen in the home Church meet, is enormously intensified when a question is submitted to an equal number of Christian workers scattered all over the world. A proposal from the board reaches two or three families in some remote station. They have probably given little or no previous thought to the matter. They do not know the views of missionaries in other lands, nor do they have the benefit of opinions expressed in a debate. The letter of the secretary explains as far as possible, but it cannot meet every point that arises in the mind of a reader. The result is that the missionaries cast a vote which they might not have cast if they could have profited by the views of their associates in other countries. If the matter is held for mission meeting, a long delay is usually involved, for the mission meets only once a year. Moreover, it is comparatively seldom that such opinions are expressed by yeas or nays. Each mission is very apt to suggest some amendment, so that the returns to the board are a chaos of conflicting views. One of the curiosities of the Presbyterian Board's office is the vast pile of manuscripts which resulted from that Board's effort to obtain the views of its missionaries regarding a new manual. It would puzzle any one to get a concensus of opinion out of it on many important topics. A medical missionary once wrote to the author, proposing certain changes in the manual rule affecting medical missionaries. We sent a copy of his letter with a request for an opinion to every medical missionary connected with our board, so that we might formulate a policy that would represent a general judgment. Three years later, only about half the medical missionaries had been heard from. Other illustrations could easily be given. A large number of men and women scattered over Asia, Africa, South America and Oceanica, who seldom see one another and who have no means of intercommunication except through the board, cannot possibly be made the unit of missionary administration.

A further consideration was suggested by some missionaries themselves. They protested against the policy of one board in consulting missionaries as much as it does, declaring that some matters could not be discussed in a mission meeting without embarrassment and fear of personal offense and that the mission vote was apt to represent the sentiment of those who were personally involved rather than that of the mission as a whole. One missionary frankly said: "We have difficulty enough to keep harmony on the mission field without the board throwing firebrands into our meetings. What is the board for if it cannot decide such questions? Your knowledge of the missionaries and your acquaintance with missionary problems are such that you ought to know what should be done. Do it and announce the result to us, and do not trouble us by unloading your responsibilities on our shoulders which are overloaded as it is." Another experienced missionary writes:

"In the nature of the case, perhaps there is no circle in the world, except the family circle, in which its members need to guard one another's susceptibilities so carefully, as the foreign missionary circle. The fewness, the intimacy, the parity, the isolation, the conspicuousness, the indispensable harmony, all conspire to make this so. It follows that delicate subjects affecting personal and local interests are nowhere in the world so difficult to handle, as in the mission circle. And it is often necessary, in the interest of internal harmony, to neglect or postpone important measures. Hence, in dealing with such questions, the board must often need to take the initiative, and to follow it up if necessary with no little pressure, to counteract the personal forces at work, and get beyond the compromises into which these are apt to lead, and into the region of the independent and impartial judgment of the mission as a whole."

It should be borne in mind, too, that the decision of many

questions by the board is required, not only by the necessities of the case, but by the board's relation to the Church. It has been specifically entrusted by the Church with the duty of directing the missionary enterprise. The half-dozen men who form the official board of a local church may not, as individuals, be any wiser than scores of other men in the congregation, but when they act as a body, in accordance with the powers committed to them by the constitution of the Church, their judgment prevails. In like manner, officers and members of a board, as individuals, may be no abler than many of the missionaries under their care, but when they act in their official capacity as a board, they should have authority. Certain questions must come to the home office for final decision, not because the men in it are necessarily better qualified to decide them, but because they must be decided somewhere by somebody and the board has been formed for that purpose. It has been constituted, not simply as a commissary department to send supplies to the army on the field, nor as a money-order office to receive and forward funds, but as the agency of the Church "to superintend and conduct the work of foreign missions." It is held to strict account for this supervision, and it assumes responsibilities for the maintenance of the missionaries and their work that are inseparable from the administrative control of receipts.

A home pastor has said that "it is absurd that a missionary should have to ask the board every time he wants to spend $25 or more." The multiplication table should answer that objection. If each missionary wished to do this only once in three months, and spent each time the minimum sum mentioned, that would make for the entire force of one of the larger boards from $75,000 to $100,000 a year, which the board would be expected to provide. Then that pastor would probably criticise the board for being in debt. Most of the requests from the field that are declined call for money that the boards do not have, so that compliance with the request would involve either debt or unfair discrimination between missions by lessening to that extent the grants for the regular work in other fields.

The argument that the missionaries know better than the board what ought to be done confuses ideas; for it ignores, not only the efforts that the boards make to ascertain the judgment of the missionaries, but also the fact that no one missionary is in a position to judge of all the elements that may be involved; nor is he held responsible by the Church if anything goes wrong. His experience, however extended and successful, has usually been confined to his own field and may not have included any such project as he now urges; while the board is aided in forming a judgment by its relations with all the other missions, by conferences with boards of other denominations and by long experience in dealing with missionary problems, having perhaps considered that identical scheme a dozen times. Not infrequently, too, a decision of the board, which implies a refusal to one mission, is really the expression of the majority of all the missions obtained by the board through its wide correspondence.

In the methods of support, two types of mission boards may be distinguished. The first assumes no responsibility for the maintenance of its missionaries, beyond forwarding to them such sums as are committed to it. The other makes definite pledges for the support of the missionaries and their work. Very properly, all of the Church boards belong to the latter type. Their missionary operations are intended to express, not simply the zeal of individuals, but the obedience of the denomination to the command of Christ. They are based upon the idea that the Church as a Church is the real foreign missionary agency, the board being simply its standing committee for the details of management. The home Church must therefore have a voice in the administration, if it is to feel a just responsibility for the support of the missionary enterprise.

Most of the boards have embodied their usual procedure in

relation to missionaries in a printed manual. These manuals are not contracts, for the missionary is not a contract labourer, and if a board were to hold him to the letter of a hard and fast agreement made before he reaches the field, he would often be in sore distress. Subject, therefore, to such amendments as changing conditions may from time to time prove necessary, the manual puts the missionary in possession of the principles that govern his relation to the board and in accordance with which certain classes of questions will be settled. These manuals indicate the positions which long experience has proved to be necessary to wise administration. The missionary, therefore, should carefully study his manual. Most of the embarrassments that arise in a board's dealings with missionaries result from neglect of some manual rule on the part of the missionary. Exceptions, it is true, do occasionally occur, and the board, in its regard and sympathy for the missionaries, is disposed to give them the benefit of every doubt; but the rules are believed to be not only wise and necessary, but generously appreciative of the missionary's position, and it is never safe, except in emergencies that are expressly provided for, to violate them on the assumption that the board will acquiesce, or that the conditions created by the violation will be accepted as a reason for approving the missionary's independent action. In so vast and complicated a work, there must be recognized principles of administration or chaos will result.

A question that often perplexes a board, and that probably appears inexplicable to many missionaries, relates to the distribution of funds between the various missions, each of which is apt to feel that it deserves more than it gets. The population, the readiness of the people to hear the gospel, the presence of other evangelical agencies and several other factors must be taken into consideration. We should not hastily conclude that the missions which receive the most money per capita are delinquent in pressing self-support. Some missions have an old and largely developed work; though it might be said in reply that just because of this fact they ought to be more nearly self-supporting than younger missions, for if age and enlarging constituencies bring increasing dependence upon foreign funds, when are we ever to attain our aim of a self-supporting, self-governing native Church?

Nor is the factor of poverty wholly determinative, for poverty is a relative term signifying different things in different places. What would be called poverty in America would be comfort in India. The average Syrian impressed us as better fed, better clothed and better housed than the native of any other country that we visited; but it does not follow that it is any easier for him to support his minister, for his climate and the standards of the civilization which he has inherited make it impracticable for him to confine himself to the loin-cloth of Kohlapur or the bamboo hut of Efulen. Where the scale of living is lower, the salaries can also be lower. That poverty is not a reason for larger appropriations is shown by the fact that Korea, Egypt, Brazil, and parts of China, where it is as bitter as anywhere in Asia, are among the missions which have most successfully pushed the policy of self-support.

More essential factors may be found in the extent and character of the institutional work required in a given field and in the local conditions that affect its expensiveness. For example, the situation in India justifies a large educational work. The ordinary reasons for such work that apply to all fields are intensified by the eagerness of Indian youths of the upper classes to secure an education, by their readiness to go to mission schools, by the open coöperation of the British government officials and their avowed intention of gradually leaving the educational field to private institutions. If we do not educate largely in India, we shall lose much of our best missionary opportunity and, in time, find ourselves with comparatively small influence. But despite the abject poverty of the masses of the people, Indian civilization is not primitive. Not only do the wealthy Hindus, Moslems and Parsees live on a princely scale, but generations of Englishmen have created the expensive apparatus of modern civilization. In most of the cities where mission stations are located, the traveller finds handsome residences, well-kept lawns, splendid roads and magnificent public buildings. The government, too, has set the educational standard by founding stately colleges and by creating a criterion of scholarship to which all mission institutions must conform or lose their right to send students to the government examinations. On every side, one sees great establishments, public and private, government, Roman Catholic, Hindu and Moslem, as well as Protestant.

It will at once be seen, therefore, that educational work in India requires a more expensive equipment than that in Africa, Siam or Korea, where the people know little or nothing of such high standards and where competition is on a much humbler scale. What is true in this respect of India might in substance be urged of Syria and Japan, and some other lands. In such countries, we are dealing with conditions that are far removed from the simplicity of primitive life. Varying civilizations require varying scales of expenditure, and we must adapt ourselves, in some measure at least, to circumstances, and not imagine that because a twenty dollar chapel of undressed logs, bark sides and thatched roof will do for the negroes of Elat, it will also do for the Brahmans of Saharanpur or the Samurai of Tokyo.

These considerations, however, modify rather than answer the criticism that money is not distributed equitably among the missions, and it would be well for the boards to look more fully into the matter. As a rule, the appropriations cannot be reduced without disaster. No mission has too much money. Not one that we visited has enough. Those which receive most really need and ought to have more. But there is a feeling in some quarters that the boards should content themselves with maintaining the present status in certain missions, and apply any further increase in receipts to bringing up to the same level promising fields that are now receiving less than their fair quota.

There are, moreover, strategic places and times in the development of the Kingdom of God. We see no reason, except the low one of desire to avoid offense, for the policy of dividing an increase in receipts equally among the missions, irrespective of the differing needs and opportunities. Whatever may have been true ten years ago, and whatever may be true a decade hence, the boards, as administrators of trust funds, cannot ignore the fact that the present call of God is for a more aggressive policy in certain fields, and that, so far as is compatible with justice to other fields, they should, for a time at least, place a larger proportion of men and money upon them. Some of the fields that are now comparatively unproductive would quickly be developed if more men and more money could be sent to them. A small present work is not, therefore, necessarily a satisfactory reason for small support from the board.

In order that a board may be wisely counselled and that it may do its work in the most effective way, its relation to the missionaries under its care should be friendly, as distinguished from official. True, there are and must be some official relations; but they should not be magnified. All discussions as to whether the boards are the agents of the missionaries or the missionaries the agents of the boards are unworthy of the cause and tend to irritation, even if they do not fall under the Master's rebuke to His disciples who were disputing as to who should be greatest in the kingdom of heaven. The controlling spirit should be fraternal, not formal. Boards and missionaries are co-workers in Immanuel's service, and their mutual relationship should be personal and loving. The settlement of questions is comparatively easy when each knows the heart of the other; while some written expressions, which from a stranger might give offense, are good-naturedly accepted when the recipient can read personal friendship between the lines.

The relations between the boards and the missions should be frank as well as friendly. Both parties should be above all unnecessary concealments, and both should insist upon their right to declare what they believe to be right, without offense being taken. The assumption should be that all concerned have a supreme desire to do that which is best for the cause of Christ and that all personal considerations are subordinate. The missionary, therefore, should not hesitate to write frankly to his secretary, and the board should be equally frank in its correspondence with the missionary. There cannot be mutual confidence on any other supposition. It is well that boards should be held to close accountability in the exercise of their power, and missionaries who think that their board has made a mistake should not be permitted to feel that their criticisms will be resented. Their interests are so vitally affected that they have a perfect right to watch it and, if they deem it necessary, to criticise it. If the lonely and troubled missionary is convinced that a blunder is being committed, let him say so. Perhaps he is right, and if he is not, the expression of his doubt gives opportunity for correcting his misapprehension.

The missionaries should keep the secretary fully posted regarding their work and problems. It is his duty to represent them before the board and the Church, to see that their requests are attended to and that the grants necessary for their work are made, as far as available funds will permit. He can do this only when the missionaries keep him informed. The board should not be considered outside of the mission circle but an integral part of it. Efficient and harmonious administration of the common cause is possible only when the board and the missionary are regarded as co-workers, each with a right to the confidence of the other.

For the same reason, when there are divergent views among the missionaries, it is not only just to the board but to the missionaries themselves that the secretary should be informed. Complaint is sometimes made that private letters from those who oppose a given action are unduly influential with the board. The majority does not write, but the minority does, and it is alleged that the mission action is occasionally overruled, because the board has detailed reasons against it and only an unexplained mission action for it. This suggests the desirability of correspondence that will explain the mission's position. This can be arranged by appointing a committee, including a proportionate representation of both majority and minority, to explain the case to the board.

It is sometimes said that a board cannot realize the situation on the field. We reply that it can if the missionaries will send reasonable explanations. We have scant sympathy with the idea that mission work is so complicated and esoteric that it cannot be understood by intelligent and fair minded men. There are undoubtedly details that can be grasped only by the officers who give their entire time to the work; but we believe that the boards are, as a rule, well informed and that their judgment is ordinarily sound. The questions of a given mission are not apt to be as peculiar as its members may imagine. It was not uncommon, in our tour of Asia, for missionaries to begin a conference by stating that their problems were quite distinct from those of other missions, and then go on to present the very topics that had been presented in every conference since we landed at Yokahoma. One of the dominant impressions of a world tour is the essential similarity of the problems of the mission field. The differences are superficial; the agreements are fundamental.

It is equally important that the relations of the boards and missionaries should be loyal. This means that a board should be true to the missionaries under its care, watchful of their interests, ready to defend them from unjust criticisms and eager to secure for them all possible support. And in turn the missionary should be loyal to the board, not necessarily because he owes any allegiance to its officers and members as individuals, but because it represents the home Church in the conduct of the missionary enterprise, because its regulations have been proved by experience to be for the best interests of the cause and for the welfare of the general missionary body, and because the board is the home representative of the missionaries and therefore disloyalty to it reacts upon the missionaries themselves.

The missionary needs to remember this in writing to his friends. The sole capital of a board, under God, is the confidence of its constituency. Whatever undermines that confidence infallibly diminishes gifts, and the real sufferer is not the board but the missionaries dependent upon it, since the board will have less money to send to them. All complaints should be made direct to the board itself, and not to others, unless, of course, the board's failure to do justice to a complainant necessitates an appeal to the Church. It will be found, however, that boards are quick to respond to such complaints and to give prompt and full justice to missionaries who have been wronged.

Loyalty not only to the board but to the cause will prevent appeals to home churches or individuals for special gifts to objects that have not been included in the regular budget for the year. The manuals of the boards explicitly forbid such appeals, because, as one states it: "Such applications involve unjust discriminations in favour of some missions and missionaries, subordinate the judgment of the mission to private judgment, interfere with the regular income of the board, and if right for one are right for all, and so militate against the purpose of the Church in the establishment of the board. It is expected that each missionary will aid in raising the large amount required for the work formally recommended by the missions and approved by the board."

Some of the misunderstanding on this subject probably grows out of the phrase "regular grants." Many missionaries and givers understand these words to mean money that the board actually has, or is certain to have, irrespective of effort to secure it. The result is that many missionaries feel that any money that they can secure or that is given specially for their work is "an extra," and that many givers expect any increase in their gifts to be used in this way. The misapprehension might be lessened if the word "pledges" were substituted for "grants." As a matter of fact, of the large amount of money, in some of the boards over four million dollars a year, covered by what are called the "regular grants," not a dollar is in the treasury at the time those "grants" are made. The board simply pledges them to the missions, and its ability to meet the pledge depends upon the coöperation of all the missionaries and all the friends of the cause. These pledges are based upon the expectation of special gifts as well as of general contributions. Indeed the board itself, in the effort to raise the required sums, offers to many individuals, churches and societies the privilege of making their gifts to special objects, if they prefer to do so. Such gifts are, of course, counted as an asset for the regular grants.

The alternative policy would be for the board to reduce the regular grants to a sum equivalent to its estimated undesignated gifts to the general treasury, and then appropriate special gifts as they are received. This would throw the missions into demoralizing uncertainty, for special gifts come in very irregularly; they fluctuate greatly from year to year, and sometimes promises to make them are not kept. It is better for the missionaries that the board should guarantee a total sum and then handle special gifts as a part of it.

The plea is often made that appeals for "extras" "will not interfere with the regular contributions;" but experience has proved that, unless carefully guarded, they do and weaken the giver's sense of responsibility for the maintenance of the general treasury upon which the work really depends. The principle, too, denies to the boards and the missions the benefit of natural increase in contributions. The amount that is being given to "the regular fund" is not adequate to the needs of the work. Each year, too, the work grows and calls for more money. Meantime, some givers are falling out by death, absence, business reverses or diversion of interest to other causes. Unless these losses are covered by the new givers, the work will rapidly dwindle.

The board welcomes special gifts, especially for property. It simply insists that the relations of an individual missionary to the mission and to the board are such that his work must be considered an organic part of the whole, and that it must be subject to those rules of mission and board coöperation which experience has demonstrated to be essential to the wise administration of funds. Some missionaries, like some ministers and laymen at home, are not invariably wise in the expenditure of money. The boards do not appropriate mission funds save on the collective judgment of the officers and members. Is it unreasonable to expect the same care on the field? Some zealous missionaries have used personal gifts in ways that their associates have seriously disapproved as harmful to the cause. The consideration that was stated in the chapter on Missionary Administration should be emphasized on the field as well as at home, namely, that when the mission and the board have agreed upon the work that should be done during the year, common prudence, as well as loyalty to fellow missionaries and to the cause, demand that the first care should be the raising of the money required for this purpose, and that "extras" should be deferred until the work included in the regular grants has been provided for. The Methodist Board makes this compulsory by refusing to special credit gifts, unless the quota of the congregation for the regular budget has been paid. This is a sound principle; though it might not be easy of application in some other churches.

It is fair, however, to expect missionaries to see that reciprocal obligations are implied in the fact that the board guarantees their salaries, house-rent, children's allowance, medical attendance, travelling expenses on furlough, language teachers, etc., and that, in addition, it is called upon to make special appropriations for unexpected emergencies. In these circumstances, a board is entitled to any coöperation in raising the funds thus called for, which the missionaries may be able to render. Their opportunities to secure money have been created chiefly by the fact of their appointment by the board and their relationship to the missionary enterprise of the Church. "Their powers of solicitation therefore belong to the organization which has sent them out,"[1] and when that organization needs their help in carrying out the carefully considered plans of their brethren on the field, it is hardly fair for them to use for personal plans the status which the board has given them for the strengthening of the common work. Wise missionaries cordially recognize this. The following rule of an India mission is in line with a rapidly growing sentiment among missionaries:

"Any sum of money received for mission work by a member from any church, Sabbath-school, society or individual in the United States, connected with the Presbyterian Church, shall be promptly transferred to the station treasurer, with any directions sent by the giver concerning the object of expenditure. No such gift shall be considered as cause for any excess of expenditure for any object over the board's appropriations. The mission recommends that gifts from other sources shall be likewise transferred to the treasurer, when such transfer is consistent with the conditions imposed by the giver."

It is true that the amount given by the friends of a particular missionary may be relatively small; but each one of the many missionaries has such friends, and the aggregate of these various circles forms a very important part of the board's constituency. Manifestly, if each missionary encourages or allows his own circle to send its gifts directly to him, the chief source of the board's supply would be dried up.

If it be said that people will often give for their own missionary friend when they would not give to the board, we reply that they are giving for their friend when they give to

[1] Dr. E. E. Strong.

the board upon which he depends, and that if he is loyal to the board, his friends will be. There will be no trouble, if he says to them: "Send your gifts to the board; it will provide for me, if those who love me and the work will send their money to its treasury." An experienced missionary writes: "I firmly believe that a great deal of this special object difficulty might be avoided if every missionary would not only refuse to encourage it, but use every opportunity to work up enthusiasm for 'stock in the general fund.' I have never yet met a giver whom I could not convince in five minutes on this subject when I tried to." We grant that there are occasional individuals who cannot be influenced in this way and that there are some objects which fairly call for exception; but a board is always willing to consider such cases on their merits as they arise.

Perhaps there is some danger that a board may be too exacting in its demands that all contributions should go through its treasury and that it may not allow sufficient freedom to individual effort; but, on the other hand, all missionaries and givers may not appreciate the tremendous responsibility which a board accepts in absolutely guaranteeing the prompt payment of the large sums required for the maintenance of the work and the anxieties that are involved in the knowledge that disaster will befall devoted missionaries, if the board cannot meet its pledges to them. Those who know best what a nervous strain this means will not harshly blame a board if it makes an almost desperate effort to lay hands on every possible dollar, not for itself, but for beloved workers far away who are depending upon it.

It cannot be too strongly emphasized that the interests of the boards and of the missionaries are identical, and that if they do not stand together and bring united pressure to bear upon the Church at home, the cause will suffer irreparable damage.

The relation of the board and the missionary should not only be friendly, frank and loyal, but it should be magnanmous. It is so vast and complex a work, conducted in so many lands, in such varying ways, and involving so many widely separated individuals, the possibilities of friction are numerous. A board sometimes does an unintentional, but none the less real, injustice to a missionary. On the other hand, the necessarily distant and comparatively isolated worker cannot be expected to see some questions in the same light as a board whose outlook is over the world, which is in constant communication with every part of it, which is in close touch with the home Church and which must bear the responsibility for consequences. The churches do not provide nearly enough men or money to meet the reasonable demands of the work. In an average year, one of the larger boards was asked by its missions to send out one hundred and ninety-three new missionaries, when the total number of qualified applicants was only fifty-eight, and to appropriate $1,400,000, when its income hardly exceeded $1,000,000. It is inevitable, in such circumstances, that many requests to a board should be declined, not because the board wishes to decline them, but because it is forced to do so. It is inevitable, too, that some missionaries, seeing the needs of their own field very clearly and being unable to see the needs of distant fields which they have never visited, should feel that their own work is more important. They learn that the board is doing various things that do not impress them as so vital as the undone work in their particular region, and they naturally feel perplexed and sometimes aggrieved. When a certain mission had written in this strain and the secretary of the board had easily demonstrated that the complaint had no foundation, one of the members of the mission wrote the following eminently Christian letter :

"We acted hastily, unadvisedly, and in a wrong spirit, with regard to the letter on financial matters. The truth is, our circles of interest here are exceedingly narrow and we have to fight continually against a disposition to mental short-sightedness. And it is also true that when work which we are giving our very lives for is done almost to death for lack of funds from home, the tendency is to grow sharp-tempered from anxiety and to cast about in our minds for some one to blame or for some way of rectifying matters in our own strength. As I look at the matter now, it would have been much better last fall to have followed the suggestion that was in some of our hearts and to have taken the time which was given to the agitation which resulted in the aforesaid letter, and put it in earnest prayer to God that He would touch the hearts of His stewards in the home churches and lead them to come up to His help."

It is impossible for missionaries to understand in every case what influences are being brought to bear upon the board, not only from other missions, but from home churches. All lines of information converge to the home office, but not to any particular place on the field. Standing between a Church which demands conservative appropriations and missionaries who demand liberal ones, between critics who think that missionaries are given too many privileges and friends who think that they are given too few, the boards are sometimes fired upon by both sides in a way that is rather trying. When to these considerations we add the factors of diverse temperaments, we can readily see how easy it is for a feeling of estrangement to arise. It is vital, therefore, that the relations of the missions and the boards should be characterized by mutual magnanimity; that each should have confidence in the judgment and friendship and consecration of the other, and that each should assume that the presumptions are in favour of the wisdom of the actions of the other.

The sum of the whole matter is in Peter's affectionate counsel: "Finally, be ye all likeminded, compassionate, loving as brethren, tender-hearted, humble-minded; not rendering evil for evil, or reviling for reviling; but contrariwise blessing; for hereunto were ye called, that ye should inherit a blessing."[1]

[1] 1 Peter 3: 8, 9.

XII

THE MISSIONARY AND THE HOME CHURCH

THE missionary has important relations not only on the field but in the home land. In addition to the ties of race and kindred, he is dependent in no small degree upon the Christians of America. He expects them to maintain him, and if they fail to do so, he is not slow to complain. He should, therefore, consider them joint partners in his work and frankly recognize his reciprocal obligations.

The most frequent expression of this relationship is in the form of letters and reports. It is not easy for a busy worker to find time for such correspondence, but he must do it in some way. He is on the foreign field, not as a private individual, but as an official representative of the missionary enterprise, and the Church which sends him out has a right to insist upon reports. Undoubtedly spiritual apathy, provincialism and preoccupation by nearer objects, account in large measure for indifference to foreign missions; but a great deal of that indifference is due simply to ignorance. When people really understand what the missionary is doing they are usually interested; but of course they cannot understand unless he writes.

The boards usually require an annual report; but that is not enough: there should also be a quarterly letter from each station, though it need not always be written by the same missionary. This letter should be sent to the secretary of the board, who will see that copies are made and distributed. The mission which keeps its secretary best posted will find the board and Church best informed regarding its work.

Missionaries often say that they do not know what to write. They imagine that because their daily experiences are commonplace to them, they are to people at home; but these are the very things that supporters wish to know. Let the writer be a reporter, not a correspondent. Often the most interesting letter that he can write is one that describes in a colloquial style the things that he has done and the scenes that he has witnessed during the preceding week. There are, of course, limitations to this suggestion. Recreations need not be enlarged upon in a letter that is to be read from the pulpit, nor should a whole paragraph in an official station report be devoted to a rhapsody over a baby. It is better to discuss the youngster in a personal letter to a relative or the secretary, who will be much interested. Do not begin an annual report by the solemn asseveration that another year has passed into eternity, leaving its record indelibly written upon the pages of time. Avoid moralizings. Do not complain or criticise. People at home are not pleasantly impressed when a missionary stabs his associates in the back by writing to strangers about them or by undermining confidence in the board which supports him. Never ridicule or revile the customs or religious beliefs of the natives. Not only do such letters create an unfortunate impression at home, but, if printed, they sometimes prove to be boomerangs. Japanese agents in America, with the aid of press clipping bureaus, send to Tokyo practically everything that is printed in the United States about the Japanese Empire, and the missionary who writes indiscreetly is very apt to be subjected to embarrassment. A missionary in South America aroused great resentment by a contemptuous account of some native ceremonies, which got back to the city where he lived. No people like to be traduced to foreigners.

The best letters give incidents, experiences, observations, accounts of the work and how it is being done. Laymen like a succinct, straightforward narrative with a generous admixture of the human element. They want the dark as well as the bright side; for sensible people understand that the missionary has undertaken a formidable task and that there must be discouragements as well as encouragements. The letters should have such variety that in the correspondence of a year or two, the missionary will cover the things that the people ought to know in order to have an intelligent idea of his station, the physical characteristics of the country, the people among whom he lives and his joys and difficulties and opportunities. Such letters should average about five or six hundred words, hardly ever more than a thousand. Long letters will not be printed by editors and cannot be used to advantage by pastors without an amount of editing that many will not give. It is better to write a short letter once a quarter than a long one once a year.

This question of correspondence, however, has two sides. The home Church is sometimes unreasonable in its demands upon its representative abroad. It is not fair to expect him to maintain all the missionary interest of the congregation. Churches often complain that their missionaries do not write. We have investigated many such complaints and we have usually found that neither the pastor nor any member of the Church had written to the missionary. It is not in human nature for a missionary to keep on writing letters to people who never acknowledge them or send him a word of cheer.

Donors, too, too often ask for the sensational in letters. While the lives of some missionaries abound in adventures, the lives of others, and very useful ones, too, contain few incidents of a stirring character. All missionaries are not surrounded by savage cannibals who are hurling spears at their heads, or waking them up in the night with blood-curdling whoops. Much of the best missionary work proceeds very quietly. American Christians who lose interest in a missionary because his letters are not filled with dime novel adventures should stop reading yellow journals and cultivate proper tastes. Nor should the home Church be impatient in its expectation of results. It is just to expect missionary labour to issue in converts, but there should be due recognition of the difficulties that are involved and missionaries should not be pressed to enroll natives who are not fit for baptism. Demands for artificial, exciting, highly coloured letters and for premature results are unworthy of the dignity of a great enterprise and of the sober and intelligent interest which should sustain it.

Another phase of the relationship of the missionary to the home Church appears during furloughs. He is ordinarily expected to make many addresses. The board and his friends should protect him from undue pressure of this kind, especially during the first months of his furlough. He has come home, not primarily to inspire the home Church, but to recruit wasted energies and to put himself once more in touch with the mental and spiritual forces of his native land. It is poor economy to make him exhaust himself so that he will return to the field debilitated rather than invigourated. But the missionary has a mission to the Church at home, as well as to the non-Christian world abroad. Knowing the urgency of the need and the ripeness of the opportunity as few others can, he is in a position to speak with authority. The duration of the furlough is fixed with this in mind. He should, therefore, regard deputation work as a legitimate part of his missionary duties. It is wise to plan tours in consultation with the board, as it will often be able to arrange for itineraries among contiguous churches and to make engagements at places of special value, so that time can be used to the best advantage.

As to the subject matter of addresses, much that was said about letters is applicable. We have in mind three addresses by as many prominent missionaries. One preached on the text: "Go ye into all the world and preach the gospel to every creature." It was an admirable sermon, but the pastor could have preached on that theme as well as the missionary. The people wanted the man fresh from the field to tell them things which their pastor could not know. The second missionary gave an interesting account of the geography, ethnology, resources, politics and commerce of the country from which he came; but as a missionary address it was a failure because it did not contain any missions. Said a layman afterwards: "I do not see any connection between that address and my pastor's request that I should give money to evangelize the Chinese." The third missionary devoted about ten minutes to a graphic account of the country and the natives, and then gave a vivid picture of his work. He told what the missionaries were doing and how they were doing it. He described an itinerating tour, mentioned the schools and hospitals, and showed that missionary work was a rich blessing to men. We need hardly say that his address was the most effective of the three. "It is not ancient history or the theory of missions or Scriptural arguments that the people want, so much as how God is working in the world now." The missionary who narrates the things which he has seen and heard is usually listened to with the deepest interest. Most people believe with Ruskin that "the greatest thing a human soul ever does in this world is to see something, and tell what it saw in a plain way."

While the missionary need not fear to speak of his difficulties, the dominant note should be hopefulness. Men will not subscribe to a losing cause. It is in human nature to wish to be on the winning side. The missionary should present his enterprise as one that is sure to succeed, whatever the temporary discouragements, make it plain that something is being achieved and that his part is not a lugubrious but a joyful one.

We have said that the home Church should be patient with the missionary. It is equally important that the missionary should be patient with the home Church. He probably went to the field direct from the seminary, without any experience in the pastorate, and he does not realize the pressure upon his brethren in the ministry in America, nor how much of self-denial the people before him may have to practice. His hearers are probably the most devoted friends that he has in the community. The people who need to be rebuked are probably not there; they knew that he was coming and stayed away. It is a great blunder in such cases to scold the faithful ones who have come. Even if some of the faithless ones are present, the worst possible way to enlist their sympathies is to whip them. Some missionaries have almost ruined their influence by the temper with which they have berated pastors and churches. It is easy for the missionary to be misled as to the ease with which money can be secured. He reads glittering statistics regarding the wealth of America; but that wealth may not be in the hands of the people whom he is addressing. It is seldom wise to interfere with the local methods of raising money, unless they are found to be bad, and then suggestions should be made in a tactful way. There is a great deal of ignorance and indifference on the part of many of whom better things might reasonably be expected, and the missionary will doubtless hear many criticisms ; but he should not be dismayed. Ignorance must be met with information and indifference with enthusiasm. As for criticism, most of it is based on misapprehension, or a secret desire to excuse failure to obey the voice of duty. Specific criticisms of the board should be communicated at once to the secretary, and they will be promptly investigated.

Here also, the home Church has a duty as well as the missionary. It should give him a hospitable welcome as a brother-worker, extend him the encouragement that he so often sorely needs and see that his expenses are paid. It is inexcusable to treat him as if it were a favour to let him have the pulpit and to leave him to pay his own carfare.

Many people base their poor opinion of missionaries on an alleged dull address of one on furlough. Well, General Grant could not make a speech, neither could Admiral Sampson; nevertheless they did pretty fair service for their country. Some of our most useful men in commercial and political life are poor speakers, but they are not adjudged worthless on that account. When so many other people are making dull speeches, an occasional foreign missionary may be allowed to do so. Even great orators are not always interesting. Missionary work for many years in another language, perhaps in a school or hospital or in personal dealing with individuals, does not tend to give fluency in English. Some of the best missionaries on the foreign field are therefore not always effective on the platform during their furloughs. The average missionary, however, has a story to tell that is worth the hearing. Most of the boards make large use of furloughed missionaries in deputation work, and with increasingly satisfactory results. A dozen commendations reach their offices, for every complaint. If a man is not interested in an account of what the heroic and self-denying missionaries of his Church are doing in distant lands, the fault is quite as apt to be in the hearer as in the speaker. It is not fair to expect a weary missionary visitor, on his much needed vacation, to wake the dead that the home pastor, with far better opportunities, has failed to arouse. The missionary at home is away from his work, out of his environment, and, like the naval officer off duty and in civilian dress, he does not always suggest the power that he actually wields when he is in the midst of his appointed activities.

A discussion of the relation of the missionary to the home Church would not be complete if it did not emphasize the duty of the Church to support the missionary enterprise on a more adequate scale. From this view-point, there is much to gratify the missionary. There is an increasing number of pastors who are intelligently developing the interests and gifts of their people. Missionary committees are becoming more efficient. The Young Peoples' Missionary Movement, the Women's United Study of Missions and the denominational work of the various boards are spreading missionary information broadcast. The Student Volunteer Movement has led a great host of the brightest young people in our colleges to consecrate their lives to foreign missions. The watchword of the movement, "The Evangelization of the World in this Generation," has profoundly impressed itself upon the imagination of the Christian world, and time has shown that the fears that some at first entertained were groundless. The movement is magnificently led by men of the highest ability and wisdom.

The women's societies are always a source of encouragement. They are earnest, loyal, sympathetic, and far more sensible in their methods of raising money for missions than their husbands and fathers. Indeed from this view-point, the typical business man of the Church appears to poor advantage beside the typical woman. In proportion to her means, she gets more money for missions than he does, and she gets it more systematically. The boards have come to consider the women's societies as solidly reliable assets.

One of the most encouraging signs of the times, however, is the increasing interest among the men. They are manifesting it in many practical ways. Though a painfully large number of laymen are yet uninformed as to missionary work, those who are informed are the very best men in the churches. There are now men in every city who intelligently and generously coöperate with the boards. Men are beginning to realize that the Archbishop of Canterbury spoke truly when, before a great assemblage in Boston, he characterized foreign missions as the vastest of all subjects that could occupy the thought and enlist the aggressive energy of Christian people, and declared that the time would come when it would be considered a discreditable thing for any one to be ignorant of or indifferent to the story of missionary extension, because it would be equivalent to being ignorant of the history of one's country and of what is happening in the world.

Nevertheless, our optimism should not blind us to the fact that the average annual gift for foreign missions is less than one dollar per capita. Only about half of the membership of the average church participates in the gifts for missions, and many pastors make no adequate effort to reach the other half. A committee of one denomination reported, a few years ago, that nine-tenths of the contributions were made by one-tenth of the membership. Some whole churches give nothing at all, and others give only through the women's societies, the pastor and all his officers standing helplessly or indifferently aloof. The plea that they are small and weak reminds one of some little home missionary churches, mere handfuls of poor people, who send offerings for every one of the boards of the Church. A feeble congregation is made stronger by doing what it can. The individual Christian needs to be educated as to his relation to the world-wide mission of the Son of God and to give proportionately and prayerfully towards it, whether he is rich or poor, in a small church or a large one.

If ever a congregation had reason to assign local burdens as an excuse for neglecting foreign missions, it was the little Church at Antioch when the Holy Ghost said: "Separate me Barnabas and Saul for the work whereunto I have called them." It was the only church in a large and wicked city. No church in all Europe or America has a greater work at home, in proportion to its resources. The devoted little band, however, never flinched, but "when they had fasted and prayed and laid their hands on them, they sent them away." Why should not the modern Church, with its vastly greater strength, equal the faith and courage of the Church at Antioch?

There is no ground for discouragement. From the beginning, every good cause has had to contend against the indifference or opposition of the multitude. The Church is not going to abandon the missionary enterprise. The faint-hearted should remember the Lord's rebuke of the depressed Elijah. There are many times 7,000 to-day who have not bowed the knee to the Baal of worldliness. Our task is to interest the uninterested and to get them to help. At a critical moment in the battle of Waterloo, the Duke of Wellington issued the order: "Advance along the whole line!" Prompt obedience won the battle. The Church will win, when it responds with like unity and promptness to the order of its Commander.

No sympathy should be wasted over the common excuse that

people do not have the money that is required. They have it in abundance, and they prove it by spending it freely on things that minister to their pleasure. If some have too many other burdens, they should diminish them. The evangelization of the world is too important an enterprise to take what is left after people have provided for everything else. The Moravian Church sets an excellent example to Christendom as to what can be done when Christians have the right ideas. Most of its members are poor, but it supports one missionary for every sixty of its membership; whereas among Baptists, Congregationalists, Methodists and Presbyterians, with far greater wealth, it takes an average of 6,000 members to support one missionary. Allowing for the aid that the Moravian missions receive from the members of other churches, the fact remains that, if all Protestant churches would send out missionaries in the same proportion as the Moravians, there would be half a million missionaries on the field, a number far in excess of what it would be wise to send.

We need not go into questions of method. Effective ways of doing a thing will be easily found by one who is determined to do it. The important thing is to have a method and to work it in such a way as to secure some offering from every individual, not necessarily large in amount, but proportionate in ability and reaching the absentees as well as those who are present.

We must protest, however, against the two-cent-a-week argument. It does not secure the gift of the poor, it benumbs the liberality of the rich and it belittles the whole enterprise. Fancy a minister standing before a congregation, whose typical member is wearing $50 worth of clothing and $75 worth of jewelry, whose household furniture has cost several thousand dollars, who smokes from ten to forty cents' worth of tobacco a day, and who commands not only the conveniences, but many of the luxuries of life—fancy telling such a man that his foreign missionary responsibilities are met by a gift of two cents a week! He spends more than that for blacking his shoes. A proportionate gift for the average layman is not pennies at all, nor even silver, but bills or checks.

We insist, too, that missionary operations have gone about as far as they can go in dependence upon the passing-the-hat method among those who happen to be present at a given service. Inquiry in a certain state developed the fact that only forty per cent. of the reported membership attended church on a Sunday morning of average weather conditions. Business men who are present seldom carry much cash on their persons. Large givers never have proportionate sums with them. If, in response to an appeal, they empty their pockets, they are doing all they can do, or, at any rate, all they will do under that system. This is an era of large private gifts. Almost every week we hear of some one bestowing $100,000 or $1,000,000 on a college or library or hospital. The chief dependence of most of our educational and charitable institutions is upon contributions of this character. Is it not almost farcical for the Church to endeavour to maintain hospitals, schools, colleges, theological seminaries, printing presses, churches, and a host of missionaries and native workers, by plate collections as an incident of a public service? If we are to give the gospel to the world, we must raise money for missions as we raise it for other big enterprises, by subscription. The wisest pastors are calling for pledges instead of cash. A man who would unblushingly slip a quarter into a collection basket would never dream of signing a card for such a sum. We have passed the canal-boat and stage-coach days in foreign missions as well as in transportation. We must now have money in larger sums. Our laymen are doing big things in business. Why should they not do big things for God?

Whenever an effort is made to increase gifts for foreign missions, there are some who raise a hue and cry about the alleged diversion of funds from home enterprises. A Presby-

The Missionary and the Home Church

tery not long ago refused to permit a missionary campaign within its bounds, on the ground that it would interfere with gifts for other causes. Yet official reports showed that this Presbytery was giving nearly ten times as much to home objects as to foreign. There is a great work to be done in the homeland, but it is not helped in the least by opposition to foreign missions. Giving to world evangelization enlarges the mind, broadens the sympathies and so opens the springs of benevolence that those who do most for foreign missions are usually the very ones who do most for home missions. Mr. Jacob Riis, who has toiled so indefatigably for the poor people of New York, says that "for every dollar you give away to convert the heathen abroad, God gives you ten dollars' worth of purpose to deal with your heathen at home." "A religion," adds Dr. Clarke, "cannot be really strengthened at home by declining to extend its blessings abroad. It is a complete misunderstanding of Christianity to suppose that some Christian church or country, by concentrating its attention and labours upon itself, can so accumulate power as to be able to turn in full vigour to do its Christian work for others at some later date. It was said long ago that Christianity is a commodity of which the more we export the more we have at home. It is equally true that the less we export the less we may find at home."[1]

The pastor has a special responsibility in this effort to arouse the Church. The boards, of course, will help; but they can accomplish little without the pastor. Indeed a secretary has no access to a pulpit except as he is invited. It is no part of his duty to instruct the congregation of a local church in foreign missions or anything else. Secretaries gladly do what they can to assist pastors, by publishing information and by making numerous addresses; but if one were to visit two churches every Sunday, it would take him ninety-six years to get around

---

[1] Clarke, p. 82.

the Presbyterian Church once, and a couple centuries to visit all the Baptist or Methodist Churches.

The pastor must do this work. He has entire control of the pulpit. He is the duly constituted leader of the Church, the divinely ordained means for its instruction. The people will give if he does his duty.

Appeals should not be based solely on financial necessities. The cause is cheapened by too much begging and pleading. The fact that an enterprise wants money is not a sufficient reason why it should receive it, nor is the begging argument apt to secure anything more than the beggar's temporary dole. Do not apologize or talk about "the needs of the board." As the late President Harrison pithily said: "The man whose grocery bills are unpaid might just as well talk about the needs of his butler. Present your need, the needs of the Church, the needs of the world, those claims which church membership implies and which are more than life in that personal relation with the great Head of the Church."

Some pastors excuse themselves by pleading that "the people are not interested in missions." Then the pastor should interest them. That is one thing he is there for. Demosthenes himself never had so inspiring a theme, and there is something wrong with the minister who can see nothing in it. If hearers complain: "Missions, missions, always missions;" reply in the words of Bishop Doane of Albany: "Yes, always missions, because they are the life-blood, the heart-beat, the lungs—breath of the body of Jesus Christ."

It must be admitted that, with certain classes of minds, the foreign mission cause is at some disadvantage as compared with the other enterprises in which the Church is engaged, as it cannot make so strong an appeal to patriotism or self-interest. The foreign missionary impulse is really the Christ impulse. It is prompted by no selfish motive. It summons us to toil and sacrifice for peoples that are beyond our sight and for whom we naturally feel but little concern, especially as they ordinarily cling to their old faiths and sometimes resent our well-meant efforts. In these circumstances, foreign missions can effectively appeal only to those motives of spiritual experience, unselfish love and glad obedience which prompted Christ to seek a lost race. His mission "began in disinterested love. It was sustained by the long patience of love. It triumphed by the sufferings of love. It was rewarded only by the joy of love. It is that incarnate Love which points the Church to the misery and wants of the heathen, saying: ' As My Father hath sent Me into the world, even so send I you into the world.' The cause of foreign missions must depend upon the piety of the Church and upon that only. It can appeal to little but love for souls and grateful, loyal obedience to our Lord; but to this it does appeal as the wretchedness and guilt of men of old appealed to the love of heaven!"[1]

Many pastors are needlessly afraid of their congregations in missionary matters. The daily papers and the monthly magazines teem with articles on the changes that are taking place in Asia and Africa. Intelligent people everywhere are discussing them. Why should not the minister show the hand of God in these movements and the opportunity that they present to the Church? Laymen often say to a secretary after an address: "That is wonderful. Why doesn't our pastor tell us these things?" The negligent pastor would be surprised and humiliated if he only knew how he cheapens himself in the estimation of his people when he fails to organize and lead them aright. Laymen understand perfectly what a minister is in the pulpit for. They like to see their pastor have large ideas of the relation of Christ to the world, and they think more of him when he plans big things and urges them to do big things. Hundreds of ministers can testify to this. Shortly after one became pastor of a certain church, he announced that he would preach the following Sunday on foreign missions. After the

[1] The Rev. Arthur Mitchell, D. D.

service, one of the elders told him that it would have been better to discuss that subject without previous announcement, as it was not popular. The pastor replied: "If foreign missions is not popular in this congregation, I shall try to make it popular." He found no difficulty in doing so, and after that, whenever he announced that he was going to speak on missions, the congregation was sure to be unusually large. The fact is that foreign missions is one of the live topics of the day, and there is no other subject to which business men will more promptly respond, if it is properly presented.

Every pastor should plan his pulpit work so that his congregation will be intelligently informed on missions. The missionary sermon will, of course, be occasional; but missionary magazines and the religious papers abound with facts and incidents which can be used illustratively in ordinary sermons. Such use of missionary material is often very effective, keeping missions before the congregation and at the same time adding vividness and power to the sermon itself. The pulpit prayer, too, will be broadened and enriched by including references to the world-wide mission of the Son of God and petitions for the devoted workers who are representing it. The monthly concert, or outlook night as some prefer to call it, will attract the people in large numbers, if the pastor takes reasonable pains to make the meeting instructive. The boards gladly furnish all needed information for it, including maps and charts and, if desired, stereopticon slides and lectures at a merely nominal cost.

The responsibility of the theological seminaries in creating a more intelligent missionary spirit should not be overlooked. They give pastors not only their general training, but the trend of mind which they carry into the ministry. Some seminaries assign missions due prominence in the curriculum; but inquiries made of many seminaries show that in others the subject has a very subordinate place. The professors, as a rule, have a genuine sympathy for the cause and are happy when their students volunteer; but, save in a few seminaries, there is no effective purpose to induce men to volunteer. The course is apparently laid out on the supposition that all the students will remain at home. The average student will, of course, do this, but he should not be encouraged to do so. Foreign missions should be set before him, not simply by occasional visits of missionaries and secretaries, but by the regular teaching of the class-room, in order that he may acquire a comprehensive knowledge of missionary motives, aims, methods, problems and opportunities, and will either offer to go to the foreign field or remain in the home-land as an intelligent and enthusiastic advocate of the cause. There ought to be a chair of missions in every seminary, so that the subject can be presented, not merely as a part of church history, but as a present and majestic enterprise of the Church in which every minister should have a part, either as a missionary or as a supporter. A missionary pastorate is urgently needed, ministers who understand the place of foreign missions in the Word of God, who discern the part of foreign missions in the plan of God, who get close enough to the divine heart to catch something of its yearning love for a lost world, and who are so baptized by the Spirit of God that they will be lifted above all spiritual narrowness and provincialism. We talk about "America for Christ," but the Bible thought is "The world for Christ"—a God who rules all nations, a Saviour who is the propitiation for the sins of the whole world, a Holy Spirit who broods over the race, a plan of salvation which is adequate for all men, a command to the Church to send it to all men. "Isn't it about time," asks Dr. Herrick Johnson, "that we brought the faith of our beloved Church up somewhere near to the measure of the limitless Word?"

And why should not foreign missions have a stated place in the private family prayer of every individual Christian? It already has such a place in thousands of homes. Many of the boards publish year books in which a missionary's name or some phase of his work appears in connection with each day of the year. Such daily remembrance will in time give one a sympathetic knowledge of the whole field and bring no small cheer to the lonely workers far away. Englishmen exulted in the fact that, at a given hour on the day of Queen Victoria's Jubilee, June 20, 1897, "God save the Queen" was sung in all the churches and on all the ships of the British Empire, so that with the progress of the sun, jubilant voices upraised the national anthem westward over oceans and continents until the mighty chorus rolled around the world. In like manner, if Christians in the home-land were to lift their voices in prayer for missions every morning, the entire globe would be belted daily with never-ending petitions to God.

Such preaching and praying constitute a more vital element in missionary success than is commonly supposed. The faith of the four friends who brought the palsied man to Christ was one of the essential factors in the miracle of grace that followed. "When Jesus saw their faith, He said unto the sick of the palsy, Son, thy sins be forgiven thee." Spiritual unity, enthusiasm and determination at home spell victory abroad.

The Church may well consider the relation of spiritual power to missionary zeal. It is a fundamental law of the Kingdom that power is given to be used for others.

The New Testament makes this very clear. The Holy Spirit was given in order that the disciples might become witnesses.[1] Before Pentecost, they had no interest in world evangelization; but when the Holy Spirit came upon them, they became evangelists to a man. The remainder of the book of Acts is a wonderful record of evangelistic spirit and extension. The early Church was preëminently a missionary Church and its members proclaimed the Gospel in almost every part of the then known world.

It would be interesting to cite in detail the illustrations in-

[1] John 15: 26, 27; 16: 7, 8; Acts 1: 8.

carnated in Ulfilas, Columba, Raymund Lull and Von Welz. Significant also from this viewpoint is the rise of Pietism with its luminous names of Francke and Spener. Ziegenbalg and Schwartz, Zinzendorf and Moravianism, Wesley and Methodism, have their place in such a study, for without them we could hardly understand the new era of missions which began with Carey. In America, the work of Brainerd and of Edwards was directly related to a new baptism of the Holy Spirit. It was not an accident that several of the great missionary organizations of the nineteenth century were born during the great revivals of the first two decades, or a mere coincidence that the forward movement in missions that characterized the closing years of that century dated from the extraordinary revivals of 1875-6. The teaching of history on this subject is unbroken. Every deepening of the spiritual life has been followed by a new effort to give the gospel to the world; but there is no record anywhere of the Holy Spirit's power remaining with any Church which did not use it in witnessing for Christ.

Here is one cause of the poverty of spiritual life. The Church is living too much for itself. God has already given it enough power to evangelize Europe and America half a dozen times over. Is it reasonable to suppose that He will increase that power simply for this purpose? This suggests the remedy both for a low spiritual vitality at home and the comparative failure to support the missionary enterprise on an adequate scale. The Church must be spiritually quickened. Foreign missions is primarily a spiritual movement and only spiritual people will adequately maintain it. Dr. Arthur Mitchell was wont to say: "The cause of foreign missions goes down to the roots of the spiritual life, and we need look for no abundance of fruit until that life is enriched." When Henry Martyn, as he lay burning with fever in Persia, received a letter asking how the missionary interest of the Church at home could be increased, the dying saint replied: "Tell them to live more with Christ; to catch more of His spirit; for the spirit of

Christ is the spirit of missions, and the nearer we get to Him the more intensely missionary we must become."

Never before has the summons been so imperative as it is to-day. Practically the whole non-Christian world is now accessible. Men in other spheres are recognizing the opportunity. Governments are pressing into the open doors and straining every nerve to influence these awakening nations. Business firms in Europe and America are keenly alive to the situation and are sending their agents to the remotest parts of the earth. The Greek and Roman Catholic Churches are pouring priests and brothers, monks and nuns into heathen lands and spending vast sums in equipping them with churches and schools. The Mohammedans are flooding Africa with zealous missionaries. The Protestant Churches should redouble their efforts, that they may mould these new conditions before hostile influences become established. It is not a rhetorical figure, but the sober truth that it would take treble the sum that the churches are now giving to handle the situation in any adequate way. Each church should immediately consider its distinct missionary responsibility and effectively plan to meet it. Some of the churches are already doing this, and the others should follow their example. There is no valid reason why every city and village on the planet should not hear the gospel within the next fifty years, and have, too, a native church so far developed that it could assume the chief duty of completing the work. This is the tremendous question of the day: Will the Church rise to the opportunity which confronts her? The cause of Christ is straitened, not by the Holy Spirit, not by opposition, but only by ourselves. We believe with Father Hecker that "a body of free men, who love God with all their might and yet know how to cling together, could conquer this modern world of ours." "We can do it, if we will." "May the constraining memories of the cross of Christ and that great love wherewith He loved us be so in us that we may pass that love on to those who are perishing. May He touch all our hearts with the spirit of self-sacrifice and with the inspiration of that love of His which, when He came to redeem the world, kept nothing back!"[1]

[1] Mrs. Isabella Bird Bishop.

XIII

THE MISSIONARY AND HIS ASSOCIATES

PEOPLE at home can hardly realize the seriousness of the problem which sometimes arises out of the relation of the missionary to his associates. The spirit of Protestantism promotes vigour and self-reliance. These virile qualities appear even more prominently in foreign missionaries than in ministers at home, partly because the boards take special pains to secure men who possess qualities of leadership and partly because the conditions of missionary life tend to intensify them. The result is that foreign missionaries are men and women of unusual force and independence of character. But force and independence are not conducive to humility and gentleness. "The truest steel the readiest spark discloses."[1] Many a missionary is at his best in leading and at his worst in following. He is apt to be impatient of restraint, good in initiative but poor in team work. And yet team work is indispensable to the highest success. There must be coördination where several men and women of equal authority are working together, and if this coördination is not harmonious, there will be great unhappiness and an unfortunate influence over the natives. The example of missionary lives is usually more powerful than the effect of missionary words. Friction in a mission station is a very serious matter.

> "How wearily the grind of toil goes on
> Where love is wanting; how the eye and ear
> And heart are starved amidst the plenitude
> Of nature, and how hard and colourless
> Is life without an atmosphere."[2]

[1] Whittier, "Among the Hills." [2] *Ibid.*

It is fundamental to remember that the only persons in this world who are absolutely independent are savages and hermits. The rest of us are set in relations to our fellow men. We are dependent upon them in innumerable ways and they, in turn, are dependent upon us. The higher we rise in the scale of civilization and of Christian service, the more close and complicated these relations become. Each person finds his own field of labour becoming less general and more particular. This is illustrated in our physical life. The civilized man wants many more things than he can produce unaided. He is therefore obliged to make use of the products of others, and he must render an equivalent for what he receives. The labour of a score of men is represented in the clothes he wears, of many more in the food he eats and of a still greater number in the house he occupies. The figure might easily be extended into the mental and spiritual spheres. Each individual is affected by a far greater number of influences exterior to himself than he realizes. The Christian worker, therefore, who tries to dissociate himself wholly from others and who imagines that he has a right to do as he pleases without regard to them, is simply reverting to the conditions of savagery.

In this realm of complicated relations, the missionary finds himself. Circumstances that are beyond his control associate him with others and the question of his personal adaptation to them becomes an important one. Sometimes it presents itself at the outset in a startling way. A young missionary recently lamented that one of his greatest trials came where he had least expected it—in his relations to his fellow missionaries. He had fondly believed that all missionaries were angels in disposition. He found, to his surprise and dismay, that they were not free from the common infirmities of humanity. He failed to realize that the trouble was partly in his own conceptions. He expected too much of human nature. He forgot that there are no perfect people in this world. The conditions of life in Europe and America, however, make imperfections less visible to the naked eye. The privacies of family life are more easily maintained. Some people, who have a reputation for unfailing graciousness of manner in public, are peevish and irritable to their own wives and children. The old saying that no man is a hero to his valet expresses a real truth. The world sees the hero; the valet sees the man off-guard, and has an opportunity to note all the petty and fretful words and deeds.

On the foreign field, however, there is no possibility of concealment. Distance, isolation, loneliness, pressure of surrounding heathenism and the necessities of the common work unite to force missionaries into closer relations than among an equal number of Christian workers elsewhere. It is notorious that two families had better not live in the same house and that the intimacies of camping in vacations are severe tests of character. Even more intimate are the relations of foreign missionaries. "I have missed the quiet of my own home more than any thing else," laments a new missionary. "Here everything is done in the open, everything you do or say, and I sometimes even think, is open to the whole compound. I have often longed for a hidden room or secret passage just to get away and find myself."

In such circumstances, little words and trifling deeds, which in other conditions would be unnoticed, are apt to develop irritations. Even the best of people have moments of weariness and impatience in which they are apt to say or do rash things. The new missionary, seeing and hearing all these things at close range, is in danger of forming unjust opinions of his associates.

This difficulty is apt to be intensified at the small and isolated station. A missionary who found himself with only one associate despairingly wrote: "I would rather be placed at a station alone than with one man, unless I could choose the man. Socially, I have no escape and no relief from his constant companionship. My reputation is absolutely at his mercy; for there are no eye-witnesses either to restrain or to testify, none to arbitrate, none to judge. Even if two such men are good men, the very best; yet good men may differ and good men's convictions are usually strong. One man may do all the yielding and the other one all the ruling, though the latter may be inferior in judgment and the other more fit to rule. Imagine a Republican and a Democrat made joint Presidents, and that, being gentlemen, it was thought there could be no contention. Being honourable gentlemen, and having opinions so widely different, they are bound to contend. But the imaginary instance does not begin to describe the situation we are discussing. You would need to remove all witnesses, all advisers, all pressure of public opinion and make the reputation of each absolutely dependent upon the report of the other."

The result is sometimes disastrous. Here are some extracts from letters which are all too common in a board's correspondence:

"Mrs. ——— is in a very nervous condition and must probably go home. It is not the climate; it is lack of proper associates. This does not mean that one missionary is essentially better than another, but that some persons are so diverse in their dispositions that even the indwelling Christ cannot make them live together. Health gives way under strain that comes not from without but from within the mission circle."

"It is sad but it is true that there is a lot of incompatibility between missionaries. . . . I know two men who have lived together on pins and needles for the past few years. Each man has his own peculiarity. One is lacking in humour absolutely. The other lacks in frankness. The association has proved impossible. Now both these men are genuine, good men. One of them is as near perfect as any man I have met. But pull together in the same ditch, they cannot."

Any one in the home-land who is "without sin" in this matter may "first cast a stone" at the missionary. Christians in England and America have their likes and dislikes as well as the missionaries. We once heard a New York pastor sharply declare that certain quarrelling missionaries were unfit to be on the field, when he himself was notorious for his quarrels with his brother ministers. Who does not know congregations and women's societies that have been rent by factions? Is there any reader of these pages who can truthfully say that there is not a Christian of his acquaintance with whom he could not work harmoniously in intimate relations? Those who are disposed to be harsh in judging missionaries may discreetly pause here long enough to read Christ's words in Matthew 7 : 1–5. We are not excusing missionaries who cannot agree, but simply calling attention to the wide ramifications of the problem.

The new missionary will start right in his relations to his associates, if he is determined not to have trouble with them. Even if they are not altogether congenial, he can usually find some way of getting along with them, if he is really desirous of doing so. The more trying they are, the more definite the test of his Christian grace. Tact and patience and prayer will often accomplish wonders. A friend writes that a missionary of her acquaintance "found herself in close association with a nature which was to hers as fire is to tow. The unpleasant possibility of quarrelling with a fellow worker yawned at her feet. Feeling entirely helpless in herself, she threw herself on her knees in an agony of prayer that God would keep her from anything so dishonouring to Him and His cause. He heard and answered, and from that moment, although they continued to work together in the same station, she never afterwards felt any stirrings of antagonism towards the person in question."

It will help one to be patient and forgiving, if he reflects that he himself probably has as many defects as his associates and that he is quite as trying to them as they are to him. It is easier to see the faults of others than to see our own; but we may discreetly remember that, to our associates, we are among "the others."

Temperament is often a factor that needs to be taken into consideration. Some men are naturally cold and impassive. The temptations that are attractive to others do not appeal to them at all. Their tempers are so placid or sluggish that they are not easily aroused. Such men little realize the difficulties of self-control that are experienced by their impulsive, warm-hearted, naturally demonstrative brethren, who, like Peter, mean to do right, but frequently blunder in their efforts and speech. "You should learn to control your temper as I do," said a phlegmatic minister to one who had spoken too vehemently in the heat of debate. "Control my temper!" was the reply; "I control more temper in a day than you do in a month." A thoroughbred horse may sometimes be hard to manage; but, after all, he is a more valuable animal and a safer one in an emergency, than a mongrel who has not spirit enough to shake a fly off of his nose.

The taciturn man, too, often gets more credit in this world than he deserves; for he has usually the same passions as his associates, though he is more prone by nature to hide them. "Man looketh on the outward appearance, but the Lord looketh on the heart."[1] We should not only take into consideration intention and achievement, but we should remember that there may have been unsuspected obstacles which involved more toil and pain than we realize.

> "The outward wayward life we see,
> The hidden springs we may not know.
> Nor is it given us to discern
> What threads the fatal sisters spun,
> Through what ancestral years has run
> The sorrows with the woman born.
>   *   *   *   *   *
> It is not ours to separate
> The tangled skein of will and fate,
> To show what metes and bounds should stand
> Upon the soul's debatable land,
> And between choice and Providence
> Divide the circle of events."[2]

It is equally important that one should not be quick to take offense himself. Some people are always looking for slights

[1] 1 Sam. 16:7.   [2] Whittier, "Snowbound."

and imagining them when none were intended. Such a person usually excuses himself by saying, half apologetically and yet half proudly: "I am very sensitive." He does not apparently realize that sensitiveness of that kind is the mark of a small mind. Of all disagreeable, mischievous persons, the "sensitive" person is one of the worst. Let the testy word, the irritating deed, be overlooked. It was probably not the expression of dislike but only of weariness and nervousness.

Occasional times of social relaxation help to relieve the strain and to preserve good temper and kindly relations. One who always works at solemn things is apt to become solemn himself and to find his nerves getting on edge so that little things will chafe him. Many serious personal differences have been adjusted by a dinner party, without any apologies whatever. The atmosphere of hospitality and good fellowship has made them seem small and cheap. The members of a station should get together not only for prayer but for games and music and charades and such other little entertainments as may be practicable. A good many irritations will be dissipated in this way.

Cheerfulness is nearly always a virtue. Hardships are not made easier by whining about them. We not only magnify our trials by thinking too much about them, but sometimes we invent them. A wise man has said that nine-tenths of the troubles in our lives never happen. The optimist does more work in this world than the pessimist, and does it better, while his hopeful spirit makes the work of others lighter. Annoyances, when they do come, instead of irritating, should put one upon his guard and lead him to show the real Christian manliness that is in him. It is a sign of weakness to be upset by every passing wind of disturbance.

> "It's easy enough to be pleasant,
>   When life flows by like a song;
> But the man worth while is the man with a smile,
>   When everything goes dead wrong."

The Missionary and His Associates 243

Whatever defects in either conduct or methods the new missionary may imagine that he detects, he will be wise if he is modest in expressing his views during the first years of his service. The knowledge that he was appointed because he was supposed to possess superior ability and the praises which he received before leaving his native land are very apt to give the recruit an idea that wisdom arrives when he disembarks from the steamer. He should remember that the missionaries already on the field were appointed with reference to precisely the same qualifications that he is supposed to possess, and that they have had the advantage of years of experience with the people, the language and all the conditions of life which are so new and strange to him. Some things may, indeed, need modification; but he will do well to familiarize himself thoroughly with the situation before he attempts to make it. We knew one young missionary who decided, within his first year on the field, that the methods which had been followed by his predecessors for half a century were radically wrong, and he wrote to the board that he must resign unless he could be assured that they would be immediately changed. Said a veteran missionary: "Of all the people in the world, deliver me from the crank in missions, who has a cocksure method of startling some one, after his three or four years on a mission field." Another writes: "I used to resent what I heard intimated about new missionaries; but now I think they are almost more of a hindrance than a help. So we might say of young children and of apprentices everywhere; but they are necessary to provide men of experience later."

Such expressions are not flattering to the ambitious youth; but they are sometimes necessary. Modesty is nearly always a virtue, particularly in a new missionary. In later years, he will probably look back with mingled amusement and mortification upon some of his first opinions and positions. One young man recently sent this rueful confession: "Although a year ago we were so all-wise that we would ask the advice of no old timer—for had we not just come from the seminary and the land of progress—let us say that this country has a decided effect in reducing swelled heads."

There is, however, another side to this question. Older missionaries may be unduly overbearing in their treatment of the recent arrival. Age does not always bring wisdom, and the methods that have been followed for many years are not on that account necessarily the best. It is an old saying that "the spectator gets the best view of the game," and sometimes one who sees conditions for the first time, with a mind free from the inherited prejudice of custom, is able to note defects which older men have unconsciously fallen into. The most helpful and constructive criticism on America ever written was by an English visitor, the Hon. James Bryce.[1] He, of course, brought to his task a more mature experience and knowledge of the world than any new missionary can possibly have; but even a raw recruit has a new pair of eyes, while a veteran's vision may have become dim.

Missionaries already on the field have sometimes caused unnecessary friction by telling a new missionary unfavourable things about his future associates. We have known several young missionaries whose minds were poisoned in this way, the result in each case being the development of friction that should have been avoided. If the recruit does hear such reports, he should not permit his mind to be prejudiced by them. The criticisms may be exaggerated, or the fault may be in the critic rather than in the criticised. It does not follow that he cannot get along with Mr. A because Mr. B did not. At any rate, the surest way to find trouble in this world is to look for it. If there are parties in the mission, the new missionary should not identify himself with them until he is absolutely sure of his ground, and even then he should be slow to take up the cudgels either for or against any section of the mission circle.

[1] The American Commonwealth.

The Missionary and His Associates

Gossip should be avoided as one would avoid the plague. It is a deadly foe to harmony. It is bad enough at home, but it is far worse on the foreign field where the intimacies of life make it so easy to see things about which to gossip. Said one missionary wife to another, who was pouring out a tirade of gossip: "If you should have an unfortunate experience in your family, would you go through the world publishing it? Suppose I did know that there had been any trouble in our mission, no one could induce me to speak of it, especially to strangers. We must guard the interests of our fellow missionaries as we do our own dear ones."

The gossiper stirs up strife wherever he goes. We could name two missionaries of unusual ability and devotion who are so caustic in their references to their associates that they have kept their respective missions in hot water for years. The table talk of one of these men is so notoriously cynical that it is a common saying that "he serves up a missionary for breakfast every morning." There is an old prayer which reads:

> "Oh, that mine eyes might closed be
> To what concerns me not to see;
> That deafness might possess mine ear
> To what concerns me not to hear;
> That truth my tongue might always tie
> From ever speaking foolishly;
> That no vain thought might ever rest,
> Or be conceived in my breast;
> That by each deed and work and thought,
> Glory may to my God be brought!
> But what are wishes? Lord, mine eye
> On Thee is fixed, to Thee I cry;
> Wash, Lord, and purify my heart
> And make it clean in every part;
> And when 'tis clean, Lord, keep it, too.
> For that is more than I can do." [1]

[1] Thomas Elmwood, 1639.

The habit of thinking the best of every one is a good one to cultivate. No one is likely to be sent to the foreign field as a missionary who does not have some good qualities. We should look for those qualities and when we think of that missionary, think of the good that is in him and the good that he does. It is said that a famous pastor in America was about to be driven from his church by the fault-finding spirit of his people, when a few of his parishioners entered into a covenant with one another to speak well of him wherever they went. The result was to change the whole current of feeling in the congregation and the pastor remained for many years and did his best work.

Any one who is worthy to be a missionary should be willing to give up positions or practices which grieve fellow Christians, provided, of course, no question of principle is involved. Only mules never change their minds. When Count Witte was asked at Portsmouth whether the Russian plenipotentiaries would make any concessions in the peace negotiations with the Japanese, he replied: "I have no hesitancy in saying that if we all took to availing ourselves of all our rights, there would be no living on earth. Right is often the enemy of expediency and compromise the safest mainstay of interest."

It is not enough that one is conscientious. Every superstition in the world from fetichism to Mormonism has been defended by conscientious people. Conscience includes a judgment of the mind regarding duty, and that judgment may be wrong. When one finds his conscience differing from the consciences of a large majority of equally sincere and devoted followers of Christ, he had better hurry to his closet and seek the reason on his knees.

The fourteenth chapter of the Epistle to the Romans is wholesome reading for people who are inflexible upon matters of Christian expediency. The Jewish converts, who had been brought up under a strict ceremonial law and taught that certain things were clean and others unclean, found it difficult to accommodate themselves to the new order of things in the Christian Church. The Gentile Christians, however, had no such scruples and, knowing that Christ had done away with the old ceremonial law, did not hesitate to eat and drink what they chose. Dissensions arose. The Gentiles looked with contempt upon their brethren who were yet in bondage to the law. They were, of course, perfectly right in their general position. Nevertheless, Paul writes in substance, if the exercise of your Christian liberty offends your brother or causes a weaker one to stumble, it is better to abstain from these things, even though they may be lawful. You have a right to eat any kind of meat you wish; "but if because of meat thy brother be grieved, thou walkest no longer in love. Destroy not with thy meat him for whom Christ died. . . . It is good not to eat flesh, nor to drink wine, nor to do anything whereby thy brother stumbleth."

The fair-minded man will seek to divest himself of mere personal desires and pride of position and look at questions from the viewpoint of the larger interests of the work. The man who is determined to have his own way, who rides rough shod over opposition, is simply intolerable in a mission. Peaceably disposed people shrink from the kind of fighting that such a man wages. "For where in this world is not refinement instantly beaten by coarseness, gentleness by rudeness, all delicacy by all that is indelicate? What can the finest considerations avail against no consideration; the sweet forbearance against intrusiveness; the beak of the dove against the beak of the hawk? And yet all these may have their victory; for where the finer and the baser metal are forced to struggle with each other in the same field, the finer may always leave it."

The better way is for the board to make the fighter leave it. That was good advice which was found among the papers of the lamented Gen. S. C. Armstrong of Hampton: "In the school, the great thing is not to quarrel; to pull all together; to refrain from hasty, unwise words and actions; to unselfishly and wisely seek the best good of all; and to get rid of workers whose temperaments are unfortunate—whose heads are not level, no matter how much knowledge or culture they may have. Cantankerousness is worse than heterodoxy."

It does not necessarily follow, however, that all the concessions are to be on one side. It is sometimes a serious question how far we should allow the unreasonable quibbles of some narrow but conscientious person to hem in our lives. While we need to cultivate self-denial, he needs to cultivate a broader conscience.

It is neither possible nor desirable that all should be alike or think alike. God uses a wide variety of types and methods in carrying out His purposes. He sometimes does the best things with instruments which appear very imperfect to us. That a given man is not working in our way is not necessarily evidence that he is a failure. His own way may be better for him than ours would be and he may reach some people that we could never influence in like degree. It takes different kinds of tackle and bait to catch different kinds of fish.

It may become necessary in an extreme case to make formal complaint against a fellow missionary. This is an exceedingly painful thing to a rightly constituted mind. It is a serious matter to impair the board's confidence in a missionary and perhaps compel him to give up his life's work and return to his native land under a cloud of suspicion. Manifestly, such a course should be taken only after all other efforts have been exhausted. Wait a reasonable time, so as to be sure that you are not acting under the impulse of temporary feeling and that the objectionable course of conduct is a permanent one. When it is evident that something must be done, begin by prayer and an earnest effort to divest your mind of all prejudice. Then go privately to the offender and have a frank and loving talk with him in the way that Christ prescribed.[1] These methods

[1] Matt. 18: 15-17.

may suffice to bring about the necessary improvement; but if they do not, the only course is to place the facts before the mission or the board, or both. It is not fair to do this, however, without frankly telling the missionary concerned that it is to be done, and the board should never act upon such correspondence until the person complained of has been given a copy of the complaint against him and has had opportunity to make reply.

Some missionaries, with a kind of exaggerated "senatorial courtesy," feel that, no matter what the provocation, they ought not to say anything to the board about it. "We shrink from it," said one, "as the schoolboy does from tale-bearing, and unless it is a matter of gross immorality or wickedness, we try to hold our peace and wait for a change of heart." This is a natural and proper feeling, within reasonable limits. But it should be borne in mind that the mission circle, rightly viewed, includes the board and that the interests of the cause should not be subordinated to the interests of an individual or to personal reluctance to act. If missionaries know that one of their number is persistently following a course of conduct which destroys his usefulness and is doing harm to the cause, it is their duty to represent the facts to the board, provided, of course, they do so in a fair and open manner.

The alternative suggested by some missionaries is that "no missionary should be returned to the field after any furlough unless formally requested to do so by a vote of two-thirds of the members of that mission." This, in our judgment, would be unwise and unfair, for it would make the presumption against the missionary instead of in favour of him. The missionary applied for and received appointment for a life service, and he could hardly be expected to settle down to steady work if he knew that his continuance in service was to come up as an open question every time he left the field on furlough. The number of missionaries who ought to be retired is comparatively small, and, painful as the duty may be, it is better to consider each case on its merits. It should be added, however, that if a mission becomes satisfied that a given missionary will never develop into an effective worker, it should notify the board at once. It is not right to let a man go on past middle age in a course that was clearly foreseen, and then turn him adrift. Some boards therefore wisely require a mission vote at the end of the first term.

Every missionary, whether young or old, should respect the policy of the mission. If he does not like it, he can try to have it changed in an orderly way in consultation with his associates and the board; but when a policy has once been determined, each one should be loyal to it. No matter how apparently isolated a missionary's work or position, he should remember that he is not an independent individual but an integral part of the foreign missionary operations of the Church to which he belongs, and that the policies which he adopts and the responsibilities he incurs involve others. He acts therefore in a representative capacity and both the mission and the board which he represents have a right to a voice in his policies. Most boards are unwilling to consider requests from individual missionaries or stations, until they have been passed upon by the mission. One's associates may, of course, sometimes unwisely overrule him; but it is fair to assume that the combined judgment of many is more apt to be right than that of an individual. The missionary, like the naval officer at sea, is given large discretion as to details; but on fundamental lines which involve his mission and the board and the success of the common enterprise, he should work in conference with his brethren. We have known missionaries to erect buildings according to some whim of their own, and then, leaving the field on account of ill-health, impose those whims on their successors who had to use the buildings. We have known other missionaries who held that they had a right to baptize any one they pleased, without reference to the standards of church membership which the mission had adopted; the result being to burden the mission with a considerable number of people who, in its judgment, were not proper subjects of baptism.

Another phase of this difficulty, which sometimes becomes acute, arises in connection with the use of specially designated gifts. The board invariably sends the full amount of such gifts to the mission treasurer; but, unless they are for new property, the mission, in its distribution of its available funds, may apply a part of a special gift to some other work which, in its judgment, is in greater relative need. We can understand how natural it is for a missionary to feel that when a friend gives money for his specific work, every dollar of it should be applied to that work. But here again comes in the principle that he is not an independent worker but a part of a missionary enterprise, and that the interests of the total work must have the precedence. To insist that a mission has no right to a voice in the expenditures for work under its care is virtually to insist that the judgment of the missionaries as a body may be subordinated to that of an individual, to introduce elements of inequality and perhaps injustice, and to transfer an essential part of the administration of foreign missions from the board and the missions, in which it has been lodged by the Church, to a great number of individual givers scattered over a distant country, without knowledge of the details of the situation and without opportunity to act in unison. The missionary who demands his "pound of flesh" in such circumstances may do great harm. It has repeatedly happened that such a man has used his special funds to start an enterprise which was strongly disapproved by his associates but which they were, nevertheless, compelled to assume when the founder left the field. Not infrequently, too, an individual has used special gifts of this kind in such a way as to postpone indefinitely the self-support of the native Church and thus endanger one of the objects of missionary work.

The simple fact should be borne in mind that, whereas the

missions ask in a given year for a given sum, the total receipts of the board from all sources, including special gifts, do not equal that sum, and that the difference must be distributed in the form of a "cut." There is no alternative. The only question is whether it shall be distributed equitably in such a way as to subserve the highest interests of the work and justice to all the missionaries, or whether it shall be distributed inequitably and in such a way as to ruin some work in the interest of other work not in itself any more important. The missionary whose work has a disproportionate amount of designated gifts is called upon to do what the civilized man must do everywhere in the world: namely, surrender some of his personal rights in the interest of the common good. He is getting a fair return, not only in the consciousness of right and the commendation of his associates, but in those benefits of organization and coöperation which are worth more to him than the rights that he surrenders. Society and government could not exist on any other basis.

Suppose, for example, there are four missionaries at a given station. They are jointly responsible for all the work of the station; but, for convenience and effectiveness of supervision, one takes the medical work, a second the educational, a third the city evangelistic work and a fourth the country work. One man receives from friends at home enough money to provide amply for all the work under his care; but the others, being dependent upon the general treasury of the board, do not receive enough. Shall the favoured man insist that his gifts shall be applied exclusively to his own work, while that of his associates is being crippled? Not if he is a Christian and a gentleman. He will take the position that the interests of the whole work are paramount to the interests of any part of it, that all should be supported on a proportionate scale and that all money received, whether from friends or the board and whether designated or undesignated, should be applied accordingly. The probabilities are that he will have no difficulty in persuading his friends that this is the proper course; but if he has difficulty, he should throw it upon the board, which will adjust it or refund the money to the donor.

The secret of happiness in all of one's relations to his associates both abroad and at home is that charity of which Paul wrote in his incomparable chapter to the Corinthians. It is a charity that is patient, unselfish, magnanimous, waiting not for great opportunities, which as a matter of fact seldom occur in life; but seizing the common, every-day opportunities for being good and doing good. It means kindliness in little things, the genial smile, the loving word, the sympathetic deed. It is made up, like life itself, of small things; but the aggregate is far from small. "Trifles make perfection," said Michael Angelo, "but perfection is no trifle."

Such kindliness of heart and manner adds much to one's attractiveness. Now and then, we meet a man of whom we say: "He is a gentleman of the old school." We sometimes wish that such gentlemen were more numerous. We do not plead for an excess of manner, for that veneer of elaborate politeness which carries with it a suspicion of insincerity and which, while keeping within the lines of good breeding, is careful to hold others at arm's length. We plead simply for real charity of heart expressed in real charity of manner. Charity "thinketh no evil," said Paul. Even the law counts a man innocent until he is proven guilty; but how many reverse the process and count him guilty until he is proven innocent. They are ready to think evil. Some men might be better if we better deemed of them.[1] If a word or deed is susceptible of a double interpretation, why not give it the better one? If a man makes a statement that is inconsistent with a former one, why jump to the conclusion that he is lying; he may have forgotten his former statement or there may be some explanation for the change that is not apparent to an observer.

[1] Bailey, "Festus."

Even when undoubted evidence compels us to think evil of another, it is not always necessary to express it. We often hear a man complacently say: "I am one of those men who always say what they think." Yes, and a mischievous fellow you are, too; forever and eternally making trouble. Commend us rather to the magnanimity of Washington, who, after he knew that Lee was plotting against him, never mentioned his name, unless it was absolutely necessary, and then without the slightest trace of unkindness. We need to resist the temptation to distrust men. Paul says that a man may be "overtaken" in a fault, that is, caught unawares, tripped up. "Ye which are spiritual restore such a one in a spirit of meekness; looking to thyself, lest thou also be tempted."[1]

The ideal missionary in his relation to his associates is simply the Christian gentleman, the man who is unselfish, considerate of others and actuated by the Spirit of Christ; who has strong convictions and does not hesitate to express them, but who holds the truth in love and with due regard to the convictions of his associates. A station made up of such men and women is one of the most delightful places in the world. Hard work is done easily and without friction. Mutual sympathy lightens care. Each member heeds the injunction to "bear one another's burdens,"[2] and to "be kind one to another, tenderhearted, forgiving each other, even as God also in Christ forgave you."[3]

The relations of the missionary include not only his associates in his own Church but those of the other churches. We have already referred to the fact that there is less sectarianism on the foreign field than in the home-land; but there should be none at all. Each missionary must, of course, be true to his own convictions as to the teaching of the Word of God; but he should remember that equally conscientious men, who are just as desirous as he is of knowing the will of God, differ

[1] Gal. 6 : 1.   [2] *Ibid.* 6 : 2.   [3] Eph. 4 : 32.

with him in some respects. It is a great thing to know how to be loyal to one's own conscience and yet to be tolerant of the consciences of brethren.

The wise missionary will make most prominent in his preaching the cardinal truths upon which the evangelical churches agree, and, as far as possible, he will avoid identifying Christianity with positions on which Christians themselves are not agreed. Partisan teaching is suicidal, for sooner or later the native finds out that some missionaries and a large number in the home churches hold a different opinion, and then there is danger either that his faith will be weakened or that his confidence in the missionary will be impaired. We must, indeed, frankly admit that there are questions on which we differ. We may even tell the native what those things are and why we believe that we are right. But when we present such questions, let us be manly enough and Christian enough to tell him at the same time that equally intelligent and devoted Christians think differently, so that when he learns those differences for himself, his faith will not be disturbed. Comity is not an armed truce. It simply means "kindly consideration for others, friendliness in regard to rights,"[1] and it ought to be cordially accepted as a working basis in one's relations to his associates of other churches.

> "All hearts confess the saints elect
> Who, twain in faith, in love agree,
> And melt not in an acid sect
> The Christian pearl of charity!"[2]

In its practical outworking, comity means:

First: That missionaries of one board should not enter the field of another board without a frank and mutually satisfactory understanding. The only exceptions to this are ports, capitals and other important cities which are natural centres for a terri-

---
[1] Standard Dictionary.   [2] Whittier, "Snowbound."

tory so extensive and populous that no single board is entitled to monopolize it. Even then, however, there should be consultation with the board already in the field and, if possible, a division of the territory, so that two sets of missionaries will not compete for the attention of the same people. Rivalry of this kind is often exceedingly injurious.[1]

Second: That missionaries should not baptize or receive into church membership natives who were converted by the missionaries of another Church or who, whether converted or not, are members of families belonging to another Church, without the knowledge and consent of the missionary concerned. There are, of course, reasonable limits to this. We should not deny to a native Christian the right, which we claim for ourselves, to change a church relationship which no longer represents his conscientious convictions. But experience has shown that, on the foreign field, such changes are very rare and that natives who wish to transfer their church relations are usually moved by personal pique or the hope of gain or other unworthy motives. The prudent missionary will carefully investigate the would-be proselyte and find out what his brother missionary has to say, before he takes the grave step of encouraging such transfers.

Third: That a missionary should never employ a native worker from another mission without like inquiry.

Fourth: That each mission should respect the general scale of pay of the nationals of other missions in the region. If possible, that scale should be fixed in conference. It is a serious breach of comity for a member of one mission to offer one employed elsewhere a higher wage than he is receiving. One careless missionary of that kind may demoralize the whole native force and cause great and justifiable irritation. A be-

---

[1] Cf. the author's "The New Era in the Philippines," pp. 188 *sq.*, for an account of the admirable plan of coöperation and division of territory adopted by the Evangelical Union of the Philippine Islands.

lief that the scale of pay is too low is not an adequate excuse. The proper place for consideration of that matter is in a conference of all the missionaries concerned.

Fifth: That a missionary should not take up the work of another Church on the ground that such Church is not doing it as it ought to be done. We found an American missionary in India preaching statedly to British soldiers, in spite of the fact that the regiment had a Protestant chaplain who held services every Sunday. The missionary urged in extenuation that the chaplain's services were perfunctory and without spiritual influence. But who made that missionary a judge over his brother clergyman, and why should he neglect natives, to whom he had been sent and who had never heard the gospel at all, because he felt that he could preach to British soldiers better than the regularly appointed chaplain? What would he have thought if the chaplain had begun services for the missionary's field on the ground that the latter was not working it properly?

The same considerations apply to a missionary who presses into the field of another evangelical denomination because he feels that his teaching represents a more perfect type of obedience to Christ and that he has no right to withhold it from any natives, even though they may have accepted another evangelical type. It might be worth while to argue this if such missionaries had first thoroughly evangelized their own fields so that there were no other worlds for them to conquer except those of other churches; but with multitudes in their own territory that have never accepted Christ, there is plenty of room for all their energies without making trouble for their brethren of sister missions. They might discreetly remember, too, that the most "perfect type of obedience to Christ" includes not only the teachings of Jesus but the Spirit of Jesus, and that His spirit was at a far remove from all assumptions of superior orthodoxy. In His time, the intolerant, holier-than-thou men, who imagined that they alone had the truth, were called

Pharisees, and the Master handled them more severely than He did the publicans and sinners. We are far from advocating that all creeds are equally sound or that it is a Christian's duty to regard every other man's interpretation of the Bible as beyond criticism. There are times and places for the proper discussion of such matters. We are simply considering here the relations of evangelical missionaries to one another and the unwisdom and unfairness of proselyting in the fields of Christian brethren of other churches.[1]

The relations of the missionary include not only his associates but, in many instances, other white men who are in the country either as traders, officials or travellers. We have discussed elsewhere the character and habits of most of these men.[2] It does not follow, however, that all of them are unworthy of the missionary's friendship. Some of them are splendid types of Christian character. Others are not inclined to be vicious, but are in danger of yielding to the peculiar temptations that befall those who are far away from home and the restraints of a stricter public sentiment. Tactful effort may enable the missionary to get into such relations with these men that he may become a moral force in their lives.

Men who are openly and insolently bad, he cannot of course associate with in the same way; and yet, save in extreme cases, his attitude towards them should be one of great patience. Reckless men are not apt to be won by a missionary who has nothing for them but anger and contempt. These men are sometimes in a position to help or hinder the missionary's influence both on the field and at home, and it may be unfortunate for his work, as well as for his peace of mind, if he lives at enmity with them. He should not, of course, conciliate dis-

---

[1] For a further discussion of the general subject of comity and coöperation, cf. the author's "New Forces in Old China," "The New Era in the Philippines," and "Unity and Missions."
[2] Chapter XVI.

solute men simply for the purpose of securing their good-will. The example of intimacy with those who are notorious for profanity or intemperance or immorality will do great harm among the natives; for they will be quick to note that he condones in those of his own colour what he reprimands in them. But rebuke need not be vituperation. There is a reproof that softens and attracts. The missionary who finds himself near such men may wisely make a careful study of Christ's relations to similar classes in His day.

The whole subject is beset with peculiar difficulties. It is impossible to give any specific rules, as circumstances vary so widely. We can only add in general terms that the consular and diplomatic representatives of one's own or other countries should invariably be treated with respect, that all reasonable courtesy should be shown to traders and travellers, that every effort that is consistent with fidelity to one's work among the natives should be put forth to win these men for Christ, and that only in the most extreme cases should a missionary allow himself to come to open rupture with them.

XIV

THE MISSIONARY AND THE NATIVES[1]

HOW can the missionary get into closer sympathy with the natives? This is the most perplexing question that confronts him. There appears to be a natural prejudice between men of different races. The terms Jew and Gentile, Greek and Barbarian, Roman and Enemy testify to the age-old bitterness of this jealousy. Americans are prone to boast of their freedom from it; but their treatment of the Negro and the Chinese is painful evidence that they, too, are not exempt from this common failing of humanity. Is it surprising that a race antipathy which characterizes the most enlightened Christian people of the earth should exist in the proud and self-centred Asiatic? This instinctive and deep-lying prejudice has been greatly aggravated by the aggressions of the white races. We need not go into this question here, as we have discussed it at length elsewhere.[2] Suffice it that the record is one that cannot be read by any fair-minded man without a feeling of mingled shame and indignation.

It must be remembered, too, that the missionary is far from being the only white man that the native sees. Traders and travellers have roamed through Asia and Africa for many years, and with the increasing facilities for inter-communication, their number is rapidly increasing. Their common attitude is unconsciously illustrated by the author of a certain book on Korea. He informs us that when the Korean sellers of curios became importunate, he "found the specific cure for their

---

[1] As stated in the Foreword, the word "native" throughout this book is used in its proper sense, implying no inferiority, but simply designating that which belongs to a given country as distinguished from that which is foreign.

pestiferous attentions to be administered best in the shape of a little vigorous kicking." A sorcerer so aggravated him that, "losing my temper and my reason altogether, I dropped his gongs and cymbals down a well, depositing him in it after them." "The interpreter will suggest that he requires a servant. For this remark he should be flogged." When the poor inhabitants of a poverty-stricken village declined to sell him their scanty stock of chickens, "the grooms, the servants and the interpreter at once tackled the mob, laying about them with their whips, . . . and fowls and eggs were at once forthcoming. The head groom came up to me, demanding an increase of thirty dollars. . . . I refused and thrashed him with my whip. The end of my journey for the moment had come, with a vengeance. The head groom stormed and cursed and ran raving in and out of the crowd. He then came for me with a huge boulder, and, as I let out upon his temple, the riot began. My baggage was thrown off the horses and stones flew through the air. I hit and slashed at my assailants and for a few minutes became the centre of a very nasty situation."

After having thus described the effect of his own methods upon the natives, he has the self-possession to arraign missionaries for the anti-foreign feeling which he professes to believe their "indiscretion" has caused.

The Siamese treat a foreigner with extreme courtesy; though it has not always been reciprocated. It is common to charge them with deceitfulness and with the breaking of promises; but no one who is familiar with the history of French dealings with Siam can truthfully deny that European duplicity has been as marked as Siamese. The "boy," as the Asiatic servant is universally called, whom we engaged in Bangkok for our trip through the northern jungles, unconsciously gave an illustration of the general conduct of white travellers in Siam. "Who is Master and what is he going to Laos for?" he was overheard asking before we started. "He is the father of all the missionaries there," was a boatman's reply, "and is going to see them." Upon which the boy ejaculated in a tone of relief: "Oh, then he won't kick me and throw bottles at me!" A fortnight later, he said to a friend: "Master must be a very holy man, for he hasn't beaten me or sworn at me at all!" What a side-light upon the conduct of the average foreign traveller! We felt humiliated that such treatment of a servant as is everywhere taken for granted at home should in Siam be deemed so exceptional; though it was pleasant to know that the very fact that one was connected with the missionaries was considered presumptive evidence that one was a gentleman. The incident is commended to the consideration of those critics who allege that the natives dislike the missionaries.

Most travellers in Siam exhaust their vocabularies in anathematizing the local magistrates, because they do not immediately furnish elephants and carriers. We know from experience how trying such delays are. At Pré and Utradit, we lost valuable time on this account. At Paknampo, we could not secure boatmen at all, and at Lakawn we should have been unable to get elephants if it had not been for the kindness of the agents of the British trading companies. And this, though we had, in addition to a passport, a special letter of introduction from Prince Damrong, Minister of the Interior, directing all Commissioners, Governors and Magistrates promptly to give us any assistance that we needed. We were ashamed again when we found that some of the officials wondered that we did not curse them. They had evidently been accustomed to abuse in such circumstances.

What were the facts? It was rice harvest and all the men were in the fields. Would it have been reasonable for us to complain because it took several days to find the carriers we needed? As for elephants, each animal is owned by an individual who keeps it for his own use, and when he does not need it, he hobbles it and turns it into the jungle. Securing an elephant for a traveller, therefore, means finding an owner who is willing to stop his own work or to send a man two or three days into the jungle to hunt up one. Suppose an Asiatic were to enter an American town and peremptorily order the Mayor to furnish him immediately four saddle horses and thirty men as carriers, and that the Mayor were courteously to reply: "It will be difficult for me to comply with your request, for it is harvest time and all the men are busy, while the only horses in town are kept by private individuals who may need them themselves or who may not care to lend them to a stranger; but I shall have pleasure in doing the best I can." And suppose that if the men and horses were not at once forthcoming, the Asiatic were to become insolent and abusive, and threaten to have the Mayor severely punished. That is precisely what happens when the average foreigner travels in Asia. Instead of kicking him out of doors, as an American official would do in such circumstances, the Oriental magistrate, knowing by bitter experience the trouble that the foreigner can make for him, meekly hastens to do his bidding; frequently being obliged to seize elephants needed by their owners and to compel men to leave their fields and families to bear heavy burdens for weary weeks under a hot sun. Why shouldn't they hate the foreigners—"these violent and angry men with white faces, who come from a country beyond the sea, who are always in a hurry and who blaspheme their God as no Buddhist would ever dream of blaspheming his!"

India is supposed to attract a good class of travellers; but a prominent hotel posts this significant notice: "Visitors will be good enough not to strike the servants; any complaints made against them will be attended to by the manager."

The political ascendancy of the white nations in some non-Christian lands and their notorious schemes in others are doing not a little to intensify this bitterness. In this respect, the modern missionary finds that his relation to the natives is quite different from that of his predecessors. They found non-Christian lands self-ruled, and, save on the fringes, practically closed to the foreigner; but the missionary of the present goes to an unevangelized world, large areas of which are ruled by the so-called Christian nations. Nearly one-half of Asia, ten-elevenths of Africa and practically all of the island world are under nominally Christian governments; while some other countries have come so far under western influences as to be from this viewpoint under almost the same conditions. The political idea which has been developed by Christianity is becoming well known throughout the whole non-Christian world, and is causing changes which the missionary must consider. His isolation is less and his country can protect him more effectively; but the native is more restless and jealous, more sullenly disposed to regard every white man as the representative of a domineering and conquering race.

Commercially, too, conditions have changed. The products of the Western world are now to be found in almost every part of Asia and Africa. The old days of cheap living have passed away. The knowledge of modern inventions and of other foods and articles has created new wants and an economic revolution of stupendous proportions is taking place.[1] The white man is considered the cause of this also, and between the greed of some natives who hope to benefit by it and the resentment of others who are suffering from it, his position is one of increasing delicacy.

We have noted elsewhere[2] that we know Asia better than formerly, but a more embarrassing fact is that Asia knows us better. The printing press runs day and night in India. Daily papers are published in all the leading cities of Japan. Siam and China have a vernacular press. The same steamer that brings to non-Christian nations western goods brings also western books and periodicals. The brutal, immoral trader

---

[1] For many facts on this subject, cf. "New Forces in Old China," Parts II and III and especially Chapters IX and XXIII.

[2] Chapter I.

arrives on the same ship with the missionary. Bibles and whiskey cross the Pacific in the same cargo. Chinese gentlemen visit America and are treated with shameful indignity. The Asiatic travels through Europe and America and goes back to tell his countrymen of our intemperance, our lust of gold, our municipal corruption. "The Letters of a Chinese Official" were not written by a Chinese, but unquestionably they represent the bitter contempt of the literati for the western world that they have come to know, and they probably will not see the effective reply of William J. Bryan.

And the Asiatic discovers not only our vices, but our sectarian differences and, worse still, our irreligion. He knows that multitudes in the lands from which the missionaries come repudiate Christianity and sneer at the effort to preach it to other peoples, and that while the missionaries exhort Asiatics to keep the Sabbath, Americans at home do not keep it themselves. Brahmans and Mandarins read infidel books and magazine articles, and confront the missionary with the hostile arguments of his own countrymen.

We no longer, therefore, confront cringing populations, but an aroused and militant Asia which has awakened to a new consciousness of unity and power. The old is passing away and a new-created world springs up, but a world that loves not the white man. British rule in Egypt has been of incalculable benefit to the people, but the Moslem's fanatical hatred of all Christians is so fierce as to make him forget all the blessings that the Englishman has brought to him. Practically the same feeling exists in India. Whatever criticisms may be made, the fact remains that Great Britain has abated grave evils and brought a peace and justice and security for life and property which the country had never known prior to British occupation; but the proud-spirited East Indian, even though he may admit these things, will nevertheless tell the traveller that he hates the Englishman. The reason is apparent; the Englishman is his conqueror. No people like to be subjugated, and the attitude of the East Indians towards the white man is the attitude of a haughty, sensitive race rankling under the wound to their dignity involved in the dominance of an alien ruler.

Passing to China, we find this equally proud-spirited people chafing because foreigners occupy so many of their fine harbours, and because even in the capital itself and almost under the shadow of its venerable palaces, the legations of western nations are virtual fortifications, stored with provisions and munitions of war and garrisoned by foreign troops. The Roman Catholic priests add to this burden of hatred. They are not given to abusing the natives, but they so arrogantly espouse the cause of their converts in lawsuits and quarrels, that often a magistrate dares not decide a case against a Roman Catholic. The priests, too, so openly identify themselves with the political designs of their respective countries, that officials and people alike fear as well as dislike them.

The occurrences of the last few years have done much to increase this general hostility to all foreigners and, from present signs, the coming years will do more. The American boycott, the occasional mobs and the anti-foreign propaganda in the vernacular press are illustrations of the feeling in China; and instances, usually less tragic, but no less significant, are not wanting in other lands. The outcome of the Russia-Japan war has enormously intensified this antagonism. The fact that an Asiatic nation has crushingly defeated what Asia had supposed to be the most powerful white nation of the earth has fanned into a flame the long smouldering spirit of resistance to the white man's domination. Everywhere in the Far East, "Asia for the Asiatic" is now the cry, and we must reckon with it. The myriads of Asia have awakened to the fear that the white nations mean them harm. An adaptation of the words of Shakespeare's Jew expresses the common feeling: "Hath not a heathen eyes? Hath not a heathen hands, organs, dimensions, senses, affections, passions? fed with the same food, hurt with the same weapons, subject to the same diseases, healed by the same means, warmed and cooled by the same winter and summer, as a Christian is? If you prick us, do we not bleed? If you tickle us, do we not laugh? If you poison us, do we not die? And if you wrong us, shall we not revenge?"

The gulf between the Oriental and the Occidental is therefore becoming wider and deeper. The words "foreigner" and "native" are not literally appropriate, for there is no such gulf between the Chinese and the Koreans, or between the Hindu and the Malay. In most of the cities of Siam, there is an amazing mixture of different peoples— Siamese, Cambodians, Annamese, Burmese, Chinese; but they blend about as Irish, Germans, French and English blend in an American city. The differences between them are unimportant as compared with those which separate the European and American from the Asiatic. The resultant condition must be frankly faced as a probably permanent and enlarging factor in missionary work.

As traders, travellers, sailors and priests, combined, greatly outnumber the Protestant missionaries, it will readily be seen that they, rather than the missionaries, fix the status of the foreigner in the public mind, and that they create against white men as a class an indiscriminate hostility which it is exceedingly hard to overcome. The Oriental seldom objects to Christianity as such. He usually has several religions already, and the coming of another does not itself arouse his antipathy. He probably knows that his race has more than once changed its faith and this, too, without bloodshed or revolution. Indeed Christianity in its essential aspects appeals more readily to him than to an Anglo-Saxon; for Christ was an Oriental and the Bible is an Oriental book, abounding with ideas and expressions which an Oriental naturally understands better than we do. It is Christianity's identification with the foreigner which arouses the Asiatic's suspicion. It comes to him as the religion of the white man who is despoiling him of his territory, overthrowing or menacing his national independence, upsetting all the economic conditions of his life, refusing in China to recognize his courts, and stationing gunboats in his harbours. Imagining that all white men are Christians, he blindly and furiously hates them all. This forms at once the most formidable obstacle and the most imperative need of the missionary; for his life of purity and kindness and his message of peace and good-will are the chief means by which Oriental and Occidental are to be brought into closer sympathy.

The governments of Christendom can help by greater care in selecting for consular and diplomatic posts men whose daily lives conform to those standards of uprightness which our best citizens inculcate and exemplify in public life at home. Many of the British and American representatives abroad are of this type; but there have been painful exceptions. It is deplorable when an alleged Christian nation is officially represented in a non-Christian land by a man whom common fame charges with conduct which is beneath the level of respectable heathenism. The American Government, in particular, has too often bestowed its appointments as rewards for political service, with but little regard for those qualities of personal character which ought to be considered an indispensable qualification for consular or diplomatic posts. It has recently been making an earnest effort to purge its service of unworthy types, and the standards of appointment have been made more rigid. Commercial houses should follow the example of the government. If drunken and licentious agents are not employed by reputable business firms in London and New York, why should they be employed as their agents in the Far East? Is it not reasonable to ask that governmental and commercial positions in unevangelized countries shall be given only to men whose lives are not inconsistent with those principles of righteousness upon which we pride ourselves at home?

Unfortunately, the chasm between the foreigner and the native can never be wholly bridged, even by the Protestant missionary. After he has shown all possible tact and made every practical concession to the customs of the natives, the patent fact still remains that, as an intelligent native minister said to the author, "You are of another race; your methods of living, your modes of thought and action are not ours." Dr. F. W. Baller, of the China Inland Mission, thinks that "the larger the station, the wider the separation in feeling; for social companionships and recreations become more numerous and more noticeably exclusive of natives. The life on the missionary compound is not the life of the people outside of that charmed circle. It is different not merely in degree but in kind."

Another missionary believes that the problem of servants sometimes causes irritation. "In order that we may do the missionary work for which we are sent out, we must employ natives as servants. Their indolence, uncleanliness and inefficiency compel frequent correction. They soon become wearied or offended, and leave; or the wife, after fruitless efforts to teach them neatness and how to do things, is obliged to dismiss them. In the course of decades, there gradually develops a considerable number of these sensitive or discharged employees, who know all our family secrets and whose accounts of their alleged treatment or of what they have seen and heard, told with Oriental exaggeration or adapted so as to save their own 'face,' do no small harm to missionary influence."

The foreigner's desire for some privacy still further aggravates the trouble. When we were travelling in Asia, our arrival at an interior village was often the signal for almost the whole population to gather. The women, in particular, often neither clean nor free from vermin, would crowd about my wife, feel of her dress, try to pull out her hair-pins and lift up the edge of her skirt to examine her shoes; all the time keeping up a stream of questions and comments that excited the uproarious laughter of the crowd, which usually included men. Nor was relief found when refuge was taken in an inn or a house, for the people would peer in at every door and window. Locks and curtains there were none, and if a blanket was hung up, eyes would presently be seen around the edges or glued to a crack in the wall. The people were good-natured and meant no offense; but most American women would hardly enjoy such curiosity. Europeans and Americans have been bred to the idea that their house is their castle. The missionary, far from his native land and surrounded by people of different customs, naturally values the privacy of his residence as the one bit of home in all the world that is left to him. But the natives are inquisitive, and they flock to his house in appalling numbers. They want to examine every part of it. With no idea of the value of time, they squat about it or in it for hours at a time. If he objects, they are bitterly offended. If he frequently has guests at his table, but confines his invitations to men of his own race, the natives think that they are discriminated against.

The financial support of the missionary creates another difference. We have seen that it is modest from a western viewpoint;[1] but from the native's, it is luxurious. The average annual income of the head of a Persian family is less than $100. In China, it is considerably below that. In India, "the average income is one-twentieth of the average English income. Sir Henry Cotton shows that the average per capita deposit in banks in England is $100, while the average per capita deposit in India is fifty cents; but how can the Indian be expected to have a large bank account when the average yearly income is $10?"[2] It is apparent that a missionary cannot possibly live on such a scale. His salary of $1,000 or $1,800 and house rent means a difference in the mode of living which is utterly impassable.

An insidious temptation comes to the missionary at this point

[1] Chapter VII.　　　[2] The Hon. William Jennings Bryan.

The Missionary and the Natives

and one that appeals to his higher nature. The poverty-stricken native, who is frequently in debt for which he is in danger of punishment, implores the missionary to lend him money. The missionary, in the kindness of his heart, does so, often at no small sacrifice; only to find that instead of making a friend he has made an enemy. It is true that the borrower is profusely grateful when the loan is received, but thereafter his attitude is that of a debtor towards a creditor. If he is asked to repay the loan, he resents it; and if he is not asked, he imagines that he is going to be. He avoids the missionary and more or less unconsciously begins to cherish a grievance against him. Wise missionaries therefore feel that it is well to be very cautious in lending money to natives.

The question of manner presents peculiar difficulties. The white man so instinctively feels that he is the lord of creation, that it is hard for him, no matter how thoroughly Christian he may be, to get over the idea that men of a different colour are his inferiors. He is apt to be brusque and peremptory. He is always in a hurry and is impatient of delays. His very kindness is apt to have an element of condescension of which he may not be conscious, but which the native is quick to detect. Blunders of tact may be almost as serious as want of sympathy. There is no other place in all the world where personal adaptations are more difficult and at the same time more important than in Asia. The Oriental is polite, ceremonious, leisurely. He is scrupulously careful to respect "face," that mysterious but potent force in Asia. His manners more nearly resemble that extinct species, a gentleman of the old school. A visitor in a certain city in Syria was welcomed by a fine looking Syrian as follows:

"You can easily see from the expression of our faces, that our hearts are filled with deepest joy because of your welcome presence. To what shall we liken you? To a noble tree in the midst of the luxuriant gardens of Damascus or to a brilliant star in our clear Syrian sky.

"Do you wonder at the bright expression of the many black eyes before you? It is but the electric fluid received from coming in contact with your ennobling personality and it should be sufficient to convey to you our heartfelt gratitude. . . . We are so proud to have the honour of your noble presence in our midst. We count this the happiest day of our lives, for you represent to us, that beloved society in America whose great heart is throbbing for us across the ocean. Even with the eloquence of the most celebrated Arabic orator, it would be impossible for us to express in words the gratitude and love we have in our hearts for you and your noble associates."

We smile at such an address, but it would have been unpardonable to fail in making proper response. After all, is the address any more flowery than some speeches of introduction at home? The Oriental, however, delights in such exaggerations and in a correspondingly exaggerated depreciation of himself. It is said that a Chinese gentleman, wearing his finest gown of silk, called at a house where his appearance disturbed a rat. In its sudden flight along a beam over the door, it upset a jar of oil over the luckless visitor, ruining his fine raiment. While he was still pale with rage, his host appeared, and after the customary greetings, the visitor accounted for his appearance in this wise: "As I was entering your honourable dwelling, I frightened your honourable rat. While it was trying to escape, it upset your honourable jar of oil over my poor and insignificant clothing. This explains the contemptible condition in which I find myself in your honourable presence." Could courtesy go further in trying to prevent the mortification of a host?

Since there are so many alienating influences that are beyond the missionary's control, and since he cannot possibly adapt himself to the physical standards of the Orient, it is all the more important that he should avoid everything that would unnecessarily accentuate an already grave difficulty. Indeed, some of the native's peculiarities furnish the missionary excellent opportunities. When a young missionary fretted because the natives spent so much time at his house, an old missionary asked: "What are you here for, if not to influence the natives, and what better opportunity can you possibly have than the one afforded you when they come to your home?"

Native customs and etiquette should be carefully studied and tactfully observed. They may appear absurd to us, but they are not absurd to the native, and the foreigner will only prejudice himself in native eyes by ignoring them. We know how we regard one at home who tucks his napkin under his chin, eats with his knife and drinks out of his saucer or finger-bowl. The Chinese thinks no better of the foreigner who takes the most honourable seat in the room, the one farthest from the door, or who begins to drink his tea as soon as it is served. To look at a high Chinese official through glasses was formerly disrespectful, and the missionary who was forced to wear glasses had to be careful to explain, or he might give offense. To make a social call in a sedan chair with short handles created about the sensation that would be created in America if one were to make a social call in a hearse, because a short-handled sedan chair was employed at funerals to carry the spirit of the deceased. To send presents wrapped up in the wrong way or by the wrong kind of a messenger is to deprive them of their value to the recipient. To hold one's hands behind the back while talking to an Oriental is to be discourteous. To walk rapidly is to class oneself with coolies. To inquire of a Moslem about the health of his wife is to commit an unpardonable insult. To count the children of a household in Africa is to bring bad luck upon them. To jump quickly out of a gharry in India is, in the estimation of an East Indian lady or gentleman, as undignified as it would be for a lady in New York to jump over a fence. "Propriety is an expression of the higher social and sometimes of the moral standards of a people. These standards vary, so that what is perfectly appropriate in one country is not so in another. Strict adherence in a foreign land to the rules of propriety obtaining in one's own country does not excuse one for breaches of etiquette in the land where one is a guest."[1] The missionary may well heed these words of Confucius:

"If you do not learn the rules of propriety, your character cannot be established. . . . If you are grave, you will not be treated with disrespect; if you are generous, you will win all; if you are sincere, people will repose trust in you; if you are earnest, you will accomplish much; if you are kind, this will enable you to employ the services of others."

Manifestly, great patience and self-restraint must be cultivated. Trying things will occur almost daily, but they cannot be helped by irritability. "The missionary must not shape his conduct by the law of the jungle, 'an eye for an eye.' He must be 'slow to anger.' He must teach and practice 'the gospel of the second mile.' One burst of anger may brand a man with such a name as 'Mr. Angry Face,' which ended the career of a missionary."[2] Forbearance, however, has its sure reward. The head man of a Läo village once sent for a missionary and asked him to explain the teachings of Christ, saying that he had watched the missionaries, and as he had never seen one of them lose his temper, he thought there must be something in their religion to account for their self-control.

Even a gracious thing may be done so ungraciously as to rob it of its intended influence. Many well-meant deeds in this world are neutralized by a curt expression. A man's heart may be warm, but if his manner is as repellent as a chestnut burr, few will care to prick their fingers to get at the interior.

The missionary's family should also be considered from this viewpoint. Not only the appointments of his house, but his treatment of his wife and the training of his children are object lessons in a heathen land. It is natural, perhaps inevitable,

[1] Cf. excellent address by Prof. Harlan P. Beach, D. D., F. R. G. S., in "Students and the Modern Missionary Crusade," 114 *sq.*
[2] Bishop E. R. Hendrix.

that the missionary should attempt to keep his children away from the native children, whose moral standards are lower; but care should be taken not to allow a child to assume an attitude of superiority towards them. Non-Christian parents are as quick as any other parents to resent an assumption of that kind. The missionary's son may not realize that he is subjected to practically the same standards of criticism as his parents, but he is. Every member of a missionary household has a part in making or unmaking the good influence of the station.

Whether it is wise for the missionary to adopt the native dress is a disputed question. In some lands it would be impracticable, for the native raiment consists largely of a loin cloth and the atmosphere; but in the interior of China many missionaries, particularly ladies, find that the native costume protects them from unpleasant notoriety. Wherever, either in dress or anything else, the missionary can reasonably adapt himself to native customs, it is wise for him to do so. At any rate, he should be slow to attempt to change customs that are not in themselves evil. If the native clothing is not immodest, the missionary should never try to induce converts to adopt foreign clothing. Indeed, we are of the opinion that the dress of the Chinese is more modest and more comfortable than the dress of the American. It is too bad to transpose good-looking, gracefully arrayed Orientals into stiff, unnatural, imitation Occidentals. And why teach boarding school pupils to shake hands, which they usually do clumsily and with evident embarrassment, when the native mode of salutation is more significant to them and just as sensible? Why urge them to wear leather shoes and to sit on chairs, instead of allowing them to slip off their sandals and sit on the clean native mats, as their ancestors have done from time immemorial? If they want to squat, let them squat. Why insist that they shall spread their sleeping blankets on a foreign bedstead, instead of on the floor or kang as they have always done?

We do not wish to give the impression that missionaries usually commit these mistakes, but the new missionary should be on his guard against them. He is not called upon to revolutionize the customs of the Orient, except in so far as those customs are morally wrong; and even some of the wrong customs had better be managed as Christ and the apostles managed slavery and intemperance—by giving sound principles reasonable time to work out their inevitable results in conduct. It is no part of a missionary's duty to interfere with national customs as such, or to denationalize any Asiatic. The Orient should remain Oriental and we should not try to Occidentalize it.

Special care should be taken to avoid shocking the native ideas of right and wrong. These ideas may be faulty, but it is a serious matter to ignore them. The Chinese feel that it is immodest for a woman to expose any part of her person or to dress in a way that makes the outline of her form conspicuous. A foreign woman, therefore, who appears at a dinner in China in the décolleté costume that she might wear in the United States subjects herself to very grave imputations. Chinese officials who visit America are invariably scandalized by the bare arms and low-necked dresses of ladies at public dinners. Professor Beach gives a humorous account of the effort that his wife made to paint baggy trousers on the bare legs of some men and women in a picture of a scene in the life of Joseph, sent out by the Religious Tract Society of London, because she knew that the picture would be regarded as highly improper by the Chinese. An American husband seldom hesitates to kiss his wife good-bye in the presence of others; but when a missionary in Africa did this, the watching crowd of natives burst into derisive laughter, and the missionary "lost more respect in a second than he had won for himself by his laborious cultivation of a strange tribe." A missionary in South America ruined his influence because he courted a single lady of the mission, whom he soon afterwards married, as he

The Missionary and the Natives

would have courted her in the United States. People who were themselves grossly immoral, but who kept their immorality within the bounds of native custom, made coarse jokes because this young missionary lady received her fiancé in a room when no one else was present and because they walked out together evenings without a chaperon. Native customs do not permit such things until after marriage.

We have noted elsewhere [1] that the charge that single women missionaries violate Chinese ideas of propriety in their tours has been greatly exaggerated. But it is well for the new missionary to remember that, in the opinion of such a good friend as Consul-General Fowler of Chefoo, "the practice of unmarried women travelling alone or with men is looked upon by the Chinese as improper, and that it exposes such a woman to unfavourable comment and perhaps to insult." Formerly, in Moslem lands, custom required women to wear veils when on the street, and the wise Christian woman also appeared veiled; for the Mohammedan attached the same idea of modesty to the exposure of the face that we do to exposure of the limbs. If an unveiled foreign lady in a Damascus bazaar knew the comments which men all about her were making, she would sink with mortification.

In one country that the author visited, a well-meaning missionary, who was secure in her own motives, but who had been long enough in the country to know better, described with evident satisfaction her effort to teach boys and girls in the same school. She deemed the native idea of separation nonsensical. It undoubtedly was, from the viewpoint of the standards to which she had been accustomed in her native land. She was not in her native land, however, but in a country which carefully separates the sexes, and she could hardly have done anything more unfortunate. Volumes have been written about the inhumanity of the Oriental men who will not allow their wives

[1] Chapter XVI.

and daughters to associate with, or even to be seen by other men, so that women are condemned to a secluded and narrow life. Many of these writers are apparently ignorant that this separation of women is due to the well-grounded suspicion that the average man cannot be trusted with a woman. In such circumstances, it would be folly for the missionary to try to bring women out of their seclusion, before the moral attitude of the male sex towards the female has been changed by religious teaching. Prof. Homer B. Hulbert, after many years of life in Korea, declares that "under existing moral conditions, the seclusion of woman in the Far East is a blessing and not a curse, and its immediate abolishment would result in a moral chaos rather than, as some suppose, in the elevation of society."[1] Until heathen notions have been purified, the missionary should be very cautious about advising women and girls to do what they have been taught to regard as immodest. A good example may be found in the Apostle Paul, who forbade the Christian women of his time to do a number of things which were not at all wrong in themselves and which Christian women in America to-day freely do, but which, according to the social usages of that age, would subject them to misrepresentations embarrassing to them and harmful to the cause of Christ.[2]

Care should be taken, also, not to interfere unnecessarily with political questions. The Protestant missionary does not have a political object. The boards have no relation to the government. They do not consult it and it does not consult them. In view of the relations of some European governments to the missionaries of their nationalities, the fact should be emphasized that the Protestant missionary goes out solely as a private citizen with no official status whatever. Indeed, when the Chinese Government offered to give him official status,

[1] "The Passing of Korea," pp. 349, 350.
[2] Cf. 1 Corinthians 11, and 1 Timothy 2.

he declined to accept it. It is sometimes impossible for the missionary to respect a corrupt and cruel government. He will often see instances of oppression which stir his indignation. But he should be exceedingly circumspect, remembering Christ's words: "Who made me a judge over you?"[1] The Russian priests and the European missionaries of the Roman Catholic Church are generally regarded as quasi political emissaries, and the Protestant missionary is apt to find that the natives regard him in the same way. This makes it all the more necessary that he should be careful. In some lands, one of the first evidences of the moving of a new life among the people is the formation of a revolutionary party. The principles of Christianity naturally beget a desire for civil and religious liberty. They have done so in other races and they are doing so in Asia. The missionary should steer clear of all such revolutionary movements. The temptation may be strong, as in India, Korea, and the Philippines; but it should be eschewed. The wise Dr. Henry H. Jessup, of Syria, writes:

"As we value our usefulness, let us keep out of politics. This is not our business. Let the local civil authorities understand that Protestant Christians are as amenable to the laws of their own land as are others. . . . Always pray for the 'powers that be.' Teach the people loyalty to their sovereign. Teach them to speak the truth and avoid litigation, if possible. If Christians are so persecuted or defrauded that you are obliged to interfere, do it by private interviews with the local officials and in the most respectful manner, showing confidence in his sense of justice and right. But never use threats of a foreign flag or battle-ship. Christ lived under Cæsar and Paul under Nero, and yet both taught obedience to Cæsar. Your converts can hardly have as cruel a ruler as Nero. Let them be patient and loyal, and you should be their example."

It is almost equally important to avoid an assumption of

[1] Luke 12: 14.

superiority and all unnecessarily disparaging references to native customs. Pride is as strong in Asia as in America. No man likes to hear his native land defamed. Some of the native customs which appear so odd to a foreigner are no more absurd than some of the things to be seen in Christian lands. If there is any ridiculous dress in the world, it is the uniform of the Gordon Highlanders of the British Army; if there is any slouchily dressed man, it is the American sailor; but any visitor in Edinburgh who should sneer at the uniform of that famous regiment, or in New York at the uniform of the American tar, would have a fight on his hands in a hurry. The Anglo-Saxon in Asia ridicules the fondness of the natives for ornaments and processions; but if there is any man on this planet more fond of donning regalia and parading the streets behind a brass band than this same Anglo-Saxon, deponent knoweth him not.

There are times when criticism is absolutely necessary, but it need not be made in an offensive way. Thirty years ago, one who wished to impress a Chinese official with the importance of correcting certain evils, after the customary preliminaries, introduced the delicate subject somewhat as follows: " I candidly recognize the value of much that China has given to the West, and with equal candour I deplore the injustice with which China has often been treated. But Your Excellency will agree with me that no nation is perfect. Mine certainly is not. Your Excellency doubtless sees serious defects in the United States. Some of them are painfully evident to us, and I shall be grateful if Your Excellency will point out others that may appear to you. In like manner, we study other nations, not as critics but as friends. It is not necessary for a foreigner to point out wherein China is lacking, since this has been done by a great Chinese, His Excellency Chang Chih-tung, Viceroy of Hupeh and Hunan." Then citations from the Viceroy were easily made. Experience has shown that the most dignified Chinese official will listen without remonstrance to statements of this kind which place the facts clearly before him, but in the words of those of his own race whom he would hardly care to contradict.

The missionary's observance of native ideas may wisely extend to the architecture of his house and other mission buildings. Missionaries are not agreed as to this. Some insist on keeping as close as possible to native lines, so that a mission building will be in harmony with its surroundings and will conciliate a people who dislike anything obtrusively foreign. Others prefer a building which will remind them of home, boldly foreign in every outline. Some good men believe that mission property should be severely plain, as more in harmony with the missionary purpose, the poverty of the people and the principle of self-support; while other men, just as good, insist upon a scale which will be a visible witness to the presence and dignity of the Church of God and an example to the natives of what religion should have. We believe that it is best to have the style of architecture conform as nearly as practicable to that of the country in which the building is situated. Exact similarity is not usually expedient. The Asiatic's conceptions of comfort differ from ours, while of sanitation he knows little. Missionaries should not live on damp mud or stone floors, or sleep on brick kangs, because natives do. Residences should be attractive to the lonely workers who occupy them. Schools, churches and hospitals should be adapted to their respective purposes; not mere sheds or hovels, but enough above the level of the natives to afford an example of decency and sanitation and the possibilities of their own architecture. But forms of architecture which needlessly aggravate a conservative people and which stamp the whole mission plant as something essentially and defiantly alien should not be adopted.

The white man is a foreigner in a country which is traditionally hostile to the outsider. Let him not unnecessarily increase this antipathy. The author has seen mission buildings which, if he were an Asiatic, he would resent. He would instinctively feel that the men who lived in them were not of his sort, that the religion which they typified was an exotic, and that to espouse it was in some sense to expatriate himself. We are glad to add that there are many missionaries who would not erect such buildings, even if they had the requisite funds. But there are Protestants as well as Catholics who need to remember that the Orient can never be Occidentalized. Asia will be Asia until the end of time, and not America or Europe. If China is to become Christian, her churches will not be Gothic nor will her schoolhouses be square, stiff, three-story bricks. Let us, as far as practicable, follow the flowing, graceful lines of Oriental architecture, build substantially and comfortably, but on as modest a scale as is compatible with taste, health and permanence. We believe that a large majority of the missionaries are in harmony with these views. All the easier is it, therefore, to write so plainly of the principle and to urge that it should not be allowed to break down through any failure to enforce it in particular cases.

Real sympathy, however, must have a deeper basis than outward conformity. It may help us here to remember that other races are not as inferior to us as we are wont to believe. The qualities which have given preëminence to the white man did not characterize him when he was found by the missionaries of the early Church. They have been bred into him by centuries of Christian teaching. The Anglo-Saxon of the days of Julius Cæsar was far more barbarous than the Chinese and the East Indian of to-day. Christian teaching may do as much for other races. There are excellent qualities in the natives of every field. Even

> "In men whom men condemn as ill
> I find so much of goodness still,
> In men whom men pronounce divine
> I find so much of sin to blot;
> I hesitate to draw a line
> Between the two when God has not."

The true missionary will look for the good in men. No one can win men of other races unless he is pervaded by the spirit of sympathy. Love melts what a hammer cannot break. Much is forgiven to him who loves much. If we may adapt the words of Carlyle:

"Wherever there is a sky above and a world around . . . is man's existence, with its infinite longings and small acquirings; its ever-thwarted, ever-renewed endeavours; its unspeakable aspirations; its fears and hopes that wander through eternity; and all the mystery of brightness and of gloom that it was ever made of, in any age or climate, since man first began to live. . . . The mysterious workmanship of man's heart, the true light and the inscrutable darkness of man's destiny, reveal themselves not only in capital cities and crowded saloons, but in every hut and hamlet where men have their abode. Nay, do not the elements of all human virtues and all human vices, the passions at once of a Borgia and of a Luther, lie written, in stronger or fainter lines, in the consciousness of every individual bosom that has practiced honest self-examination? . . . It is not the material but the workman that is wanting. It is not the dark place that hinders, but the dim eye. A Scottish peasant's life was the meanest and rudest of all lives, till Burns became a poet in it, and a poet of it; found it a man's life, and therefore significant to men." [1]

Surely this is the right spirit. Within reasonable limits, it does not make so much difference how the missionary lives, if he has the mind of Christ, and carries with him the warmth of Christ's faith in humanity. Said a Siamese: "It is not the kind of clothes on the body, but the spirit in the heart which the people notice and care for." No degree of ability or force of character can take the place of this vital sympathy with human nature. It is said that a missionary once wrote home to his friends that he could get along well enough if it were

[1] Essay on Burns.

not for these miserable natives who kept crowding into his house, but that he now had a bulldog and hoped to keep them off hereafter. This is probably one of those smart sayings which are invented by would-be wits, like the common flings regarding "the Vassar girl" and the "mother-in-law." But if such a missionary exists, he should be promptly recalled. "Nothing," says Dr. Moffett of Korea, "should prevent a close contact with the people, a sympathetic entrance into their inner life, their ways of thinking, their weaknesses, prejudices, preferences, their trials and sorrows and spiritual struggles; not an abstract interest in them as so many heathen to be converted, baptized and reported upon as so much in the way of mission assets, but an unfeigned love and sympathy for individuals, with a heart yearning for a transformation of their lives through a personal faith in Christ."

What if some of the natives are inferior? No people in the world can possibly be so far inferior to us as we are to Christ. But when He was upon earth, He showed the most genuine sympathy for those who were in the lowest social scale. What He did for us, we ought to be willing to do for others, and without making a fuss about it either. Dr. Goodell of Constantinople once said to a young missionary who was about to sail for Africa: "When you land in Africa and first meet those naked savages whose filth and repulsive habits fill you with utter loathing, and you say within yourself, Lord, is it necessary that I bear even this; that I spend my life among such beastly and imbruted creatures? then remember, that you every day ask the pure and ineffable Holy Spirit of the Eternal God, to whom the thought of sin is abhorrent, to come down, not simply to visit, but to abide in your sinful, polluted heart. Let this make you humble, patient, loving and contented."

The missionary should seldom attack and never ridicule the native religion. However absurd that faith may appear to us, it is the most sacred thing that the native has. Even if he cares little about it, he usually regards it as a national institution and he will resent abuse of it by a foreigner. The missionary never makes a more lamentable mistake than when he sneers at the religious ceremonies of the people. Paul set a good example to every missionary in his tactful reference on Mars Hill to the religious beliefs of his hearers. Bishop Thoburn of India says: "If I could recall some of the sermons I first preached, I would be glad to. I used to be proud of the fact that I could debate for two hours at a time with learned Mohammedans, but now I am sorry I ever did it. If I went around asserting, boastfully, that Jesus Christ is the Eternal Son of God, a dozen Mohammedans would be after me at once. But now I strive to tell of the love of Christ and of His power to save. Correct doctrine is of comparatively little account unless the missionary carries a message of love."

Rightly viewed, heathen rites are pathetic rather than amusing. They often represent the groping of the ignorant soul after the God whom he feels to be somewhere, but whose character and attitude towards man he little understands. At the great Temple of Kalighat, near Calcutta, the author saw an intelligent-looking woman prostrating herself upon the pavement and stretching her hands before her. An attendant marked the point which her finger tips reached, and then the woman rose and placed her feet upon that mark and prostrated herself again. We learned on inquiry that she had travelled in that way for forty miles, under the blistering sun of India, in order that she might ask that bloody goddess Kali to spare her child who was grievously ill. Could any humane man look upon such a pathetic scene without being profoundly moved? Manifestly, the proper approach to that woman would not have been argumentative, but a sympathetic recognition of her need and her yearning for help.

The foreigner often unconsciously offends the religious susceptibilities of the natives. He may excite the anger of a priest by tapping an idol with a cane. He may rouse a Moslem to murderous fury by entering a mosque without removing his shoes. In Siam, it is a standing grievance that travellers steal the images of Buddha from the temples. What would be thought of a visitor in a Christian land who should carry off a communion vessel as a souvenir? When the religious convictions of a Buddhist people forbid the taking of life, the foreigner who shoots pigeons from the trees of the temple precincts simply stamps himself as a ruffian in the estimation of the monks.

In China, the worship of ancestors presents one of the most formidable obstacles to missionary effort; but while the missionary feels obliged to oppose it, he needs to do so with great tact. Reverence for dead parents is woven into the very warp and woof of Chinese character, and unless the missionary is exceedingly careful, he will not only arouse the deep resentment of the Chinese, but he will expose himself to the charge of filial disrespect. The people should be made to understand that it is not reverence to parents that we object to, and that we who venerate the memory of Washington and of Lincoln, who set apart a day to decorate the graves of our fallen soldiers, who keep in our homes the portraits of our fathers and mothers and stand with full hearts beside their hallowed dust, would have the Chinese Christians pay all the respect to the memory of Confucius and of their deceased parents which should be paid to any human being and which is consistent with the worship which belongs to God alone.

It may be wholesome for us to reflect how we should feel if Buddhist priests or Moslem mullahs were to attempt missionary work in an American city. They might not, indeed, be molested as long as they quietly worshipped by themselves; but if they made any effort to win over our sons and daughters, there would probably be trouble. The reader will at once reply that Islam and Buddhism are not on the same plane as Christianity. Very true; but the point is that the Moslem and the Buddhist do not realize this, and that when the missionary first goes to them, their opposition is practically the

The Missionary and the Natives

same as an American would feel in similar circumstances. This does not mean that the missionary should be less earnest in seeking converts, but it does mean that he should be tactful and sensible and avoid everything that would unnecessarily irritate. Dr. Henry H. Jessup tells us that about ninety years ago in Tripoli, Syria, Dr. Wolff said one morning to his interpreter: "Abdullah, I am going to the bazaars to preach to the Moslems." Abdullah replied: "I beg you not to go, for they will mob us." The doctor insisted, and Abdullah himself afterwards described the trip to Dr. Jessup.

"We walked around to the bazaars and Dr. Wolff mounted a stone platform and said: 'My friends, I have come to preach to you the Gospel of Christ. He that believeth shall be saved, and he that believeth not shall be condemned.' I translated as follows: 'The Khowaja says that he loves you very much, and that the English and the Moslems are fowa sowa' (all alike). Whereupon the Moslems applauded, and Wolff thought he had made a deep impression."

Dr. Jessup exclaimed: "How could you deceive a good man in that way?" He replied: "What could I do? Had I translated literally we should have been killed; and Wolff may have been prepared to die, but I was not." Sir Mortimer Durand, formerly British Minister to Persia, says: "I once saw a missionary attempt to convert an Afghan. His manner of doing so was to walk up to the Afghan on the road and say in very bad Persian, which was not really the Afghan's language: 'Christ is the Son of God.' He repeated the remark twice, receiving each time a monosyllable answer, and then he sheered off, having apparently no more Persian at his command. This is the sort of thing which causes the enemy to blaspheme." These are excellent examples of how not to do it. Sir Mortimer gives the following instance of the better way:

"Not long ago, a missionary was invited by an influential mullah to speak in one of the oldest mosques in Persia. There was a large audience. After offering prayer and reading the story of the Prodigal Son, the missionary preached to them about repentance. He was treated with much kindness, and after the service the Mohammedan priest took the missionary home with him to tea, with a number of other priests and chief men of the town. The day was Friday, and the missionary's sermon followed the regular Mohammedan prayers. If I did not know that story to be true, it would seem to me incredible. I suppose that any ordinary white man who had found himself uninvited in that mosque would hardly have escaped with his life."

Sir Mortimer adds: "There is much religious toleration among Orientals in general for people who behave properly. Indeed, the spirit of religious toleration is at times one of the difficulties with which the missionary has to contend. . . . Even Mohammedans, whom many Christians regard as specially fanatical, can show much toleration to a man who treats their religion with respect, and asks only for an opportunity of temperately explaining his own."

Some study of the native's religion is a wise preparation for successful missionary work. Bryce truly says: "Unless you try to understand men as religious beings, you do not get on from any other side at all. For there is the root of their life, the root of everybody's life. However debased his religion may be, you can only understand a man through his religious life and benefit him by giving him a right religious idea." Every ethnic faith is rooted in some racial characteristic or some fundamental trait of the human mind, and the missionary who has to deal with that faith needs to understand the basis on which it rests. He will find that every one of these faiths has in it some good things. Let him frankly recognize them, and be able to understand why they have failed to work themselves out into character, and how they have come to be so entangled with error that they have become hindrances rather than helps to the moral uplifting of man.

The student will quickly find that actual heathenism is less attractive than when it is viewed from a comfortable library at home, but he need not on that account go at it with a sledgehammer. Even if he does succeed in destroying the native's confidence in his own faith, it does not follow that he has made him a Christian. He may simply have destroyed confidence in all religion, and left a chamber "swept and garnished" to be occupied by "seven devils worse than the first." Compromise is fatal, but lack of knowledge and tact are almost equally so.

Let us, with as little of the racial peculiarity as possible, urge the essential point that the supreme thing for all men, wherever they live, is the knowledge of God. That knowledge we desire to communicate to the world. We take no credit to ourselves for having it. We did not discover it. Our ancestors were simply so placed that during those centuries when the lack of intercommunication separated the Far East and the West by an impassable gulf, the white man heard that God had revealed Himself to sinful man as a personal Being, holy, just and wise, a Creator, a Sovereign, a Father; that He had caused His message to be written in a Book; and that He had sent His only begotten Son into the world to incarnate the divine sympathy, to show the ideal life and to make "propitiation . . . for the sins of the whole world." We have found that this faith and its necessary corollaries transform the human heart, purify society, exalt woman and develop all that is noblest in man. We therefore preach it to others, as it was first preached to us.

Christ set a good example to the soul-seeker everywhere in His treatment of those who came to Him. When some sought "the loaves and fishes," He did not turn them away, but spoke to them of the bread of heaven. When Nicodemus came by night, Christ did not rebuke him, but lovingly reasoned with him about the spiritual life. When the self-satisfied young ruler told Him that he had kept the commandments from his youth up, "Jesus beholding him, loved him." When the mother tried to use Christ for the advantage of her two sons, the disciples "were moved with indignation," but Christ taught them the nobler ideals of the Kingdom. His severest denunciations were not upon the "sinners," but upon hypocrites.[1] Even when a fallen woman came to Him, He, the purest of the pure, did not turn contemptuously away, but with divine sympathy made her feel that she was not beyond the reach of the Father's love. "Jesus was never rude. He never gave needless pain to a sensitive heart. He was considerate of human weakness. He was gentle towards all human sorrow. He never suppressed the truth, but He uttered it in love. . . . And to-day it is not science or intellect or eloquence that wins souls, but love to Christ pouring over in love to men. Love will give a delicacy of perception and ingenuity of persuasiveness which no heart shall be able to resist. Love will reconcile the profound scholar to a life among savages. It will carry the refined woman with the precious tidings into the most unattractive homes. Love will bear all, believe all, hope all, endure all, if only it may win men for Christ."[2] Then let the missionary, in the words of Whittier:

> "Give human nature reverence for the sake
> Of One who bore it, making it divine
> With the ineffable tenderness of God;
> Let common need, the brotherhood of prayer,
> The heirship of an unknown destiny,
> The unsolved mystery round about us, make
> A man more precious than the gold of Ophir,
> Sacred, inviolate, unto whom all things
> Should minister, as outward types and signs
> Of the eternal beauty which fulfills
> The one great purpose of creation, Love,
> The sole necessity of Earth and Heaven!"[3]

[1] Luke 11 : 42-44.
[2] Dr. E. P. Dunlap, Pamphlet: "How to Approach the Siamese with the Gospel."
[3] "Among the Hills."

XV

THE MISSIONARY AND THE NATIVE CHURCH

THE missionary's perplexity in dealing with the natives is not ended when they are converted. New problems then emerge. In the pioneer days, these problems were comparatively easy; for the congregations were small and composed of humble people who were usually content to follow the lead of the missionary. Now, however, a numerous and powerful native Church is developing and the problems are becoming more difficult. (Cf. footnote p. 260.)

The first problem to appear in most fields is a financial one. The policy, formerly in vogue, of freely aiding the congregations gave the native Christians a motive for leaning upon the missionary, who thus became the channel of temporal as well as spiritual blessings. The missionary of to-day pays less money to the native Church, partly because it is better able to help itself and partly because the principle of self-support is more generally recognized. This policy, while right and necessary, is not always agreeable to the native pastor. As an employee of the mission, he had the power of that body behind him and was virtually independent of his people; now he is more subject to their caprice. His support, too, becomes more uncertain; for the natives are not such prompt paymasters as mission treasurers, nor can they always pay adequate salaries. There are exceptions in almost every land, especially in Japan where the Christians have generally come from the middle and upper, rather than the lower classes; yet the great body of Christians in Asia and Africa is now, as in New Testament times, very poor. The talented native almost always makes considerable financial sacrifice by remaining in the service of the Church. The Rev.

Boon Boon Itt of Siam, who received $600 a year as a preacher, refused a government position which paid $4,000. Almost every educated native could readily earn far more in commercial or political life than in the ministry. A Siamese Cabinet official says that his Government is ready to take all the young men that the mission boarding school at Bangkok can turn out. President Bergen writes from China: "The Chinese officials are offering extravagant salaries to our men, and it is not surprising that they are tempted by the offer of an income which would make them independent in a decade."

The question is often not one of financial inducements, but of actual living, and it becomes acute in the case of native ministers of the higher grade. An educated native cannot live in a mud hut, subsist on a handful of rice, and confine his clothing to a loin-cloth. Abroad as at home, such a man "wants foreign books and magazines. He likes to have things about his home decent and clean. He likes to be a social factor in his parish. He wants to be respectably clad, his wife and children too, and he finds that his pay will not half meet his expenses. He does not demand unreasonable salaries, but he does demand enough to keep up a respectable standing among his friends."[1]

The first generations of the coolie class cannot be expected to produce many educated, capable Christian leaders. It is no reply to say that the apostles were unlearned men; for they were the product of centuries of Hebrew teaching in the Old Testament Scriptures. Nor is it just to urge that the best of our home ministers usually rise from the poorer classes; for they almost invariably come from Christian homes and are the results of generations of Christian influence. The "poor but honest" parents of England, Scotland and America are very different from the Asiatic peasants of age-long ignorance, superstition, poverty and oppression.

[1] Mr. F. S. Brockman.

The Missionary and the Native Church

We of other lands cannot withhold our sympathies, for our own churches in Europe and America are finding increasing difficulty in securing an adequate ministerial supply in less trying circumstances. We are wont to explain the falling off in candidates by referring to the spirit of commercialism which is tempting young men to a business career. Why should we wonder that the same cause produces the same effect abroad?

The difficulty cannot be wholly removed by an increase in contributions from the home churches. Any advance that may be possible from that quarter will be more than counterbalanced by the expansion of the general work, the more expensive institutions that it necessitates and the rapid rise in the cost of living. Nor is it in money, anyway, to solve this problem. Nowhere in the world does Christian work bring as high financial rewards as a secular career. The typical missionary himself could earn more money if he went into some business or profession; while the qualities that fit a man for successful religious work in Europe and America are far more liberally rewarded in other professions. We cannot offer an educated Indian as much money to work for Christ as he could earn in other ways, and we would not even if we could. The attempt would simply attract men who are influenced by "the loaves and fishes," rather than by the spiritual motives of Christian service. The best men in Asia, as in Europe and America, cannot be hired. In spite of diminished salaries and increased cost of living, the native churches are producing a larger proportion of Christian workers than the home churches. Commenting upon the fact that the theological seminary conducted by the Japanese gets more students than the one conducted by the missionaries, though offering smaller financial inducements, Mr. D. A. Murray writes:

"There is a strong strain of heroism in the Japanese character. If they can feel that they are personally sacrificing and giving something to the cause of Christ, that appeals to them. But it is quite a different thing when you approach a young man with the proposition that you will support him far more luxuriously than he has lived at home, and give him a splendid education for three or seven years, on condition that he will afterwards hire himself to work for you at less than half the salary that he could then get easily elsewhere. It is only a very limited number of young men that we would feel safe in making such a proposition to."

When we appeal to the avarice of man anywhere, we stimulate his most dangerous passion; but when we appeal to the best that is in him, we are more likely to get responses that are of permanent value, even though they may be less numerous. One consecrated man who is willing to make sacrifices for Christ in order that his countrymen may know the gospel is worth a hundred men who are simply working for money.

In this connection, it may be well to state that friends in the home-land should observe greater caution in responding to the appeals of the Orientals who are flocking to England and America in increasing numbers. We do not refer to those who have availed themselves of the facilities afforded by the mission schools in their native land and who have come here for the purpose of taking further studies with a view to supporting themselves afterwards. Such men should sometimes be encouraged. But if financial assistance is needed, it should be given as tuition is generally given to students in our home colleges, and never from missionary funds; nor should any one imagine, without inquiry, that he will serve the cause of Christ by giving money to an Oriental who appeals for it " to return and preach the gospel to his people." There are some splendid students from other lands who are taking courses in American universities and theological seminaries, but they are not begging among the churches. The difficulties involved are often independent of the question of personal character. Experience has shown that young converts can be most economically and effectively trained for Christian work in their own country, in the institutions which are now in operation in almost every mission field and which have been founded at considerable expense chiefly for this purpose. A sojourn in America sometimes develops tastes which render an Asiatic discontented with the financial support which his own people or the board can give him, and involves him in many difficulties, and, in some cases, has created a superiority complex that has embarrassed his relations with his fellow ministers who have not been abroad.

Indiscriminately encouraging young men to come to America thwarts wise plans for higher education on the fields, creates irritation among ministers of the national churches, stimulates a worldly ambition, cuts off patriotism and race sympathy, and really cripples the influence which it is supposed to increase. Not infrequently, too, it leads to imposition upon the home churches and to the diversion of funds to personal uses which are supposed to go for missionary objects. Many Orientals have made a good living in this way, and some have been able to buy property and to loan money on bond and mortgage. It is always wise to refer all appeals for assistance to the board, which can judge better than any one in the churches whether a given native can be employed to advantage.

Another problem that is assuming large proportions grows out of the new consciousness of power that was noted in the preceding chapter. While some peoples are so lacking in independent vigour, or are so accustomed to be dominated by foreigners, that they look up to the missionary as a superior being; others, notably the Japanese, Chinese and East Indians, are of a more virile and haughty type. The attitude of a convert towards a missionary is naturally influenced by this racial spirit. He is still an Oriental, and he shares, to some extent at least, the irritation of proud and ancient races as they see the white man everywhere striving for the ascendancy. The growth of the native Church in numbers and power has developed within it a strong nationalistic feeling, a conviction that the natives should be independent of foreign control in religion as in government. This is, of course, natural; but it involves some readjustments that are not easily made.

It will help us here if we remind ourselves that the self-government of the native Church is an essential part of the missionary aim, and that the missionary should, therefore, frankly say of the native Church what John the Baptist said of Christ: "He must increase, but I must decrease."[1] If there is ever to be a self-supporting, self-governing and self-propagating native Church, the missionary must anticipate the time when it will be in entire control. More and more definitely should missionary policy recognize the part that this growing Church ought to have in the work. In the past, the typical missionary has been primarily an evangelist to non-Christians. He had to be, for his was often the only voice from whom the message could be heard. The mission has been paramount and expected to run everything. Whatever was wanted, the board was asked to supply. But a native Church has now been created, and from now on we must concede its due share of responsibility for making the gospel known and for directing the general work. Many things need to be done in non-Christian lands which it is not the function of the boards to do. Our business is to plant Christianity and help to get it started, and then educate it to take care of itself. Even the officers of a local church can often handle cases of discipline more effectively than a foreigner. A missionary wrote from Siam:

"Last week there came a report that one of our women had been gambling in the market. I had already been talking up the matter of self-government, and now I said: 'You four men take up and settle this case.' Well, they took it up, and I was mightily pleased with the patience, kindliness and skill they showed in bringing the woman to a full confession and expression of sorrow without citing witnesses. Then, without passing judgment or making a record, they exhorted

[1] John 3 : 30.

her to make a public confession and renew her covenant before the Church and watch herself carefully ever afterwards, and assured her of their and the disciples' prayers and help. I said to myself: 'These men can do this kind of thing better without me and the sooner I drop it the better.'"

It is true that, in some lands, the native Church is yet in its infancy and that it should have aid and counsel; but we should hold resolutely in view the principle that the mission is a temporary and diminishingly authoritative body and that the native Church is a permanent and increasingly authoritative body. Even though the mission remains a century or more, as it must in some lands, this fundamental distinction should not be overlooked. A policy which builds up a big, all-powerful and all-embracing foreign mission is inherently and radically unsound.

It takes a great deal of grace for the missionary, after having been the supreme authority, to accept a place subordinate to that of the natives whom he has trained. Missionaries in some fields already find themselves in this position, and they would hardly be human if they did not feel uncomfortable. The spirit of independence has become so intense in Japan that many of the native leaders would have the Church refuse to recognize a congregation or preacher that receives foreign aid. Dr. Uemura, the leader of this party, writes:

"Apart from Christ and the Spirit, Japanese Christianity has no need to rely on any one whatever. Sufficient unto itself, resolved to stand alone, it must advance along the whole line towards the realization of this ideal. . . . To depend upon the pockets of foreigners for money to pay the bills is not a situation which ought to satisfy the moral sense of Japanese Christians. Likewise in the realm of religious thought, is it not shameful to accept opinions ready-made, relying on the experience of others instead of one's own?"[1]

[1] *Fukuin Shimpo* Nov. 3, 1904.

"Those of us who are earnestly insisting on the independence of the Church in our country are not moved by narrow nationalistic ideas. . . . We are moved by the positive power of a great ideal. Every nation has its special characteristics. . . . Is it not a great duty which we owe to God and to mankind to develop the religious talent of our people and to contribute our share to the religious ideas of the world? We cannot believe that the natural talents of our people are of mediocre order. At the present time the thought-world of Europe and America is in a state of ferment and uncertainty. Chaos reigns and 'darkness broods over the face of the deep.' Is it not our duty at such a time to develop our heaven-bestowed gifts and shed new light in the world?"[1]

This is rather an ambitious program, but we applaud such a spirit of self-sacrificing independence as far more hopeful than flabby and supine acquiescence in external leadership. We cannot, however, view some phases of the situation without anxiety, nor can we fail to discern how embarrassing the position of the missionaries must be.

What shall be the creed and polity of the native Church, and how far shall the missionary seek to shape them according to his own ideas? This is one of the related problems which is becoming more and more difficult and delicate. The missionary from the West, trained in the tenets of a particular denomination, born and bred to regard its creed and polity as the ones most in accord with the Word of God, is very apt to feel that they should be repeated on the foreign field. But we must more clearly recognize the right of each autonomous body of Christians to determine certain things for itself. We cannot, indeed, ignore the risks that are involved. There is sometimes ground for grave anxiety. Will the rising churches of Japan, of China, of India, be soundly evangelical? God grant that they may be. But who is to be the judge of soundness? And in

---

[1] Prospectus of the Tokyo Theological Society.

respect of undoubted doctrines, to what extent should we impose our western terminology upon eastern churches? We must be fair enough to remember that, in the course of nearly two thousand years, Christianity has taken on some of the characteristics of the white races, and that missionaries, inheriting these characteristics, have more or less unconsciously identified them with the essentials. Perhaps this is one reason that Christianity is so often called by the Chinese "the foreigner's religion," a saying which indicates an entire misconception of its real character.

Our creeds were formed in times of heated controversy, and their statements are massed in such a way as to be effective against the particular errors which were prevailing at those times. The result is that some of these creeds are impregnable fortifications on sides from which no special attack is likely to be made in present-day Asia or Africa, while other positions, which are seriously menaced, are unguarded. It is difficult for us to realize to what an extent our modes of theological thought and our forms of church polity have been influenced by our western environment and the polemical struggles through which we have passed. The Oriental, not having passed through those particular controversies, knowing little and caring less about them, and having other controversies of his own, may not find our forms and methods exactly suited to him. It seems, therefore, not only just to the Asiatic Christians but in the interest of evangelical truth, that the creed and polity of the native Church should be reasonably adapted to the exigencies of Asia, just as our creed and polity have been adapted to the exigencies of Europe and America.

The Presbyterian Board had to face this problem in connection with the movement to form an independent Church in Korea. The question at once arose: Shall approval be conditioned upon the adoption of the creed of the Presbyterian Church in America? This being a theological question which was not within the jurisdiction of the board, it was referred to the General Assembly with the expression of the board's opinion that no such condition should be imposed, but that there should be confidence that the missionaries and Korean Christians were loyal to the Word of God and would form a creed which would be both evangelical and adapted to the needs of the Church. The Assembly approved this view. The secretary of another board said:

"I should be glad to see the experiment tried with the Korean native ministers and elders of all denominations which Dr. Lane tried with some people in Brazil, who wrote to him for instructions as to how to organize themselves into a church. He declined to give them any specific instructions, but advised them to study very carefully Paul's Epistles and find out what they could from their own study of them as to the best way to organize a church. The result was that they organized a ——— Church."

Why should not the Orientals who have accepted Christ as Lord have some liberty in developing for themselves the methods and forms of statements which logically result from His teaching? Possibly some of our methods and statements are not so essential as we imagine. With all due insistence on the essential elements of our faith, let us accord national churches the same freedom which we have demanded for ourselves and refrain from imposing upon other peoples those externals of Christianity that are distinctively racial.

When, however, this position is agreed to, the problem is by no means solved. There is practical unanimity among missionaries that the native churches should be self-governing in time; but when is that time? There is room for wide difference of opinion as to whether a particular Church has attained that maturity and soberness of judgment which fit it to manage prudently its own affairs and to shape its own theological and ecclesiastical development. It is to be feared that in some places this independence is coming before the Church is really fitted for it. And yet it is perhaps only right that, in respect of polity as of doctrine, we should consider whether we are to be the final judges of fitness. Our Anglo-Saxon ancestors would not permit other churches to decide when they were competent to govern themselves. They felt that they were the proper persons to determine that. Nor did American Christians allow their mother churches in Europe to settle this question for them. Everywhere in the history of Protestant Christianity, the principle has been recognized that any considerable body of believers has the right to decide for itself whether or not it should be dependent upon others. Shall we deny to the churches of Asia a principle which we cherish as fundamental?

In considering this matter we must take into consideration the natural disposition of man, from which even grace does not emancipate, to hold on to power as long as possible. It is notoriously difficult for parents to realize that their son is growing up to manhood and is entitled to settle some questions for himself. This is even more apt to be true of the home Church and the mission in dealing with native Christians of a different race, who never will see some things as we see them or be disposed to do some things as we have always done them. It is extremely difficult, in such circumstances, for the missionary to pursue a wise course between the extremes of prematurely hastening and unduly retarding the independence of the native Church. We must balance our own judgment with the clearly expressed judgment of the native Christians themselves, and with our belief in the common guidance of the Spirit of God.

The rather extraordinary objection has been urged that if the native Church becomes self-supporting and self-governing, the missionary cannot control it. But why should he control it? Because the native brethren are not fitted for independence? When will they be, if they are not given a chance to learn? Shall we wait until they equal the American and European churches in stability? Will a century of dependence develop those qualities which wise self-government requires? We must remember that certain essential qualities of character can be developed only by the exercise of autonomy. "It is liberty alone," said Gladstone, "which fits men for liberty. This proposition, like every other in politics, has its bounds, but it is far safer than the counter doctrine, wait till they are fit." The way to teach a child to walk alone is not to carry him until he becomes a man, but to let him begin to toddle for himself while he is still young. He will learn faster by practice and tumbles than by lying in his mother's arms.

What if the native churches do make some mistakes? The Epistles of Paul show that some of the early churches fell into grievous errors; but he did not refuse them independence on that account. The churches of Europe and America have made colossal blunders, some of them resulting in dire calamities. The native churches can hardly do worse and may do better. We can give them the benefit of our experience without keeping them perpetually in leading strings. They need a certain amount of restraint and counsel; but that restraint and counsel are most effective when they are moral rather than authoritative. Better far a few falls and bumps than continual babyhood. The Rev. Dr. George Alexander reported after his visit to Brazil:

"In creating the Synod of Brazil, our American Presbyterian Churches adopted a bolder policy than any of the other churches at work there and incurred risks which they have hitherto avoided. Among a people sensitive, excitable and ready to fly asunder at the slightest provocation, they have planted a self-governing Church and left it to develop in accordance with the genius of the nation. It is now passing through perils and disorders which the other churches must face later. . . . The last Synod was officered wholly by Brazilians and conducted its business in as orderly, intelligent and forceful a way as one of our own Church courts at home. . . . I am persuaded that the policy to which we are committed will prove to be a wise one."

The Missionary and the Native Church

Fear of the independence of the native Church may sometimes have justification, but too often it appears to be based upon four fundamental errors:

First: That we need to be afraid of our avowed aim to establish a self-supporting, self-governing and self-propagating Church.

Second: That the Church in Asia must be conformed to the Church in England or America.

Third: That we are responsible for all the future mistakes of a Church which we have once founded.

Fourth: That Christ who "purchased"[1] the Church and who is its "Head"[2] cannot be trusted to guide it.

"Is there never to be a period when the Christianity which we plant shall be able with God's help to stand alone? Is it like some sickly plant that must forever be tied up to a stick? These Protestant Christians are not exposed to any more dangers than are the Nestorian Christians. Christianity has been left to stand under the awful shadow of Islam for ages in all those Eastern lands, and it has stood, having only itself to blame for its inherent corruption. The Church at Mosul was left to itself for twenty years. The Madagascar Christians were probably benefited by being thrown upon their own resources. The first Tahiti converts stood the fires of persecution. . . . We must assume that Christ is able to care for His Church after we have planted it and duly nurtured it. We cannot be forever responsible for the orthodoxy of Japan. We must leave the Japanese Church under the direction of God's omnipotent Spirit to work out its own religious life. We cannot proceed on any other principle."[3]

We would not minimize the gravity of this question or the perils of a premature independence; but we believe with Dr. Thomas S. Barbour that there should be thoughtful considera-

---

[1] Acts 20 : 28.
[2] Col. 1 : 18.
[3] The Rev. F. F. Ellinwood, D. D., LL. D.

tion of the question "whether some sections of our great mission lands should not now have developed independence of missionary direction," and whether we should not plan "practical steps by which this end may be more swiftly promoted." Let us have faith in our brethren and faith in God. When Christ said that He would be with His disciples alway, He meant His disciples in Asia and Africa as well as in Europe and America. The operations of the Holy Spirit are not confined to the white races. Are we to take no account of His guidance? He is still in the world and will not forsake His own. We should plant in non-Christian lands the fundamental principles of the gospel of Jesus Christ, and then give the native Church reasonable freedom to make some adaptations for itself. If, in the exercise of that freedom, it does some things that we deprecate, let us not be frightened or imagine that our work has been in vain. Some of the acts of the native Church which may impress us as wrong may not be so wrong in themselves as we imagine, but simply due to its different ways of doing things. When a question arose regarding the theological trustworthiness of the Church of Christ in Japan, Mr. Robert E. Speer wrote: "I believe that the Church of Christ in Japan is sound on the great evangelical convictions. . . . The leaders stand for what is central and fundamental. Their battle is with atheism and materialism, with agnosticism and unitarianism. We must not insist on raising issues within the ranks of those who are fighting these battles which are not essential to fidelity to the great central convictions. Having confidence in the Church and its leaders, I think we must be very careful not to antagonize them on issues that are not absolutely fundamental."

The Bible was written by Asiatics and in an Asiatic language. Christ Himself was an Asiatic. We of the West have perhaps only imperfectly understood that Asiatic Bible and Asiatic Christ, and it may be that by the guidance of God's Spirit within the rising churches of Asia a more perfect interpretation of the gospel of Christ may be made known to the world.

> "Our little systems have their day;
> They have their day and cease to be;
> They are but broken lights of Thee,
> And Thou, O Lord, art more than they."

A peculiarly difficult phase of the relationship of the missionary to the native Church is becoming acute in lands where an exceptionally high grade of men are entering the service of the Church. Present methods appear to make all native ministers subordinate to the foreign missionary, to the irritation of the former and sometimes to the embarrassment of the latter. President Arthur Ewing of India says: "I cannot conceive of anything more unfortunate than the lot of the native preacher, who is all his life under the beck and call of the missionary, and with no opportunity to judge of the problems which concern him." Mr. F. S. Brockman, of China, writes:

"The Chinese ministers see that a foreign missionary, no matter how young and inexperienced in Chinese affairs he may be, is always put at the head of something, whereas a native, no matter how long he has been in the service or how able he has proved himself to be, is always playing the second rôle, a helper or assistant to somebody."

We asked some of the leaders of the Indian churches at Lahore, whether the present policy gave sufficiently free scope for the talented Indian leaders. The Rev. K. C. Chatterjee, D. D. replied at length. His manner was courteous. He declared that his personal relations with the missionaries were most cordial, that they had shown him even more consideration than they had shown to one another, that after forty-one years of service he was too old to think of himself and that he only spoke because we had asked him to and for the sake of those who were to come after him. He then stated his view as follows:

"There are two classes of workers in the mission. (1) Americans and Europeans and (2) Indians. The former are associated in counsel and administration and have the power of voting on all matters connected with missionary work. The latter have none of these privileges. They simply carry out the will and the order of the former. A foreign missionary is like a son in his father's house, while the native missionary is like a servant in that house. The servant knoweth not his master's will, but simply carries out his master's orders, often mechanically and without any intelligence, and is apt to acquire the spirit of a hireling and lose all real interest in the work. This system was inaugurated upwards of sixty-six years ago, and worked very well as long as the native ministers were recruited from the orphanages and from the illiterate and half-educated classes of people. They were content to be in a subordinate position. Now the state of things has become different. The Church has grown in knowledge and enlightenment and in Western ideas of working and governing. There are several graduates in the Church of recognized Indian universities and a few of the universities of America and Great Britain. Some of these are gifted young men of fine Christian character and anxious to do missionary work. They ought not to be put in a subordinate position. As they have the same educational qualifications and training as the foreign missionaries, they ought to have the same status and privileges,—they ought to be associated in counsel and administration and allowed to vote in all mission matters, or in other words, they ought to be made full members of the mission. Fairness requires this."

Some of the missionaries sympathized with their Indian brethren in this matter. They asserted that such men are the equals of any foreign missionary in India in ability and culture, that they have greater influence over the Indians than any foreigner can possibly have, that the appointment of even one or two would be a recognition of the Indian churches which would have a most happy effect in conciliating the resentment which some of them now feel, that the present policy practically makes the foreigners a close corporation and a higher caste, and that the missionary and the talented Indian leader ought to meet on the same official level.

If the question were simply one of ability or equality, we should promptly favour this position; but is this all there is to it? It seems to us that the following considerations are also involved:

First: The mission is amenable to foreign control. This policy appears to be inevitable as the home churches are now constituted. The Church which supports a mission will insist on being, through the board, the final authority in the settlement of its larger questions. Therefore to put the leaders of the native Church into the mission is not to give them the liberty which they desire, but to rivet the bonds of dependence, since they would become members of a body which never can be independent.

Second: A large part of the money which a mission distributes is for the support of the missionaries themselves—their salaries, children's allowances, houses, furloughs, itinerating, language teachers, etc., while another large part is required for the management of institutions which, in their present stages, are necessarily under the control of the foreign missionary, such as colleges, boarding schools, hospitals, presses, etc. An analysis of the report of one large board shows that about three-quarters of its total expenditures are for these two purposes. Native ministers have repeatedly complained of this, insisting that the money sent from Europe and America is primarily for them and that they are not getting their fair share. It is impossible to pay them the salaries that are paid to missionaries. The reasons for this are apparent to every one who is conversant with the situation. The missionary who is the product of American civilization, who requires many things that the native has not learned to require, who is a foreigner and who cannot live upon the food or wear the clothing or occupy the house of the native, must be supported on a more liberal financial scale than a native of the country. But the reasons for this distinction, so evident to us, are not evident at all to the Asiatic minister. If the native leaders were made members of the mission, there would almost certainly be embarrassment at this point. We were told in several places that a desire to have a voice in handling the large sums which the mission is known to control has something to do with the eagerness of some of the native ministers to become members of the mission. Dr. Chatterjee would be far above such a motive. However, it would not necessarily be improper, for money represents a certain power over the work, and those who are engaged in that work might quite naturally wish to share in the power. But it is a sound principle that money should be handled by those who can be held to accountability for their use of it. Foreign money must be controlled by foreigners, but the native churches should be allowed to manage whatever funds they themselves raise. Dr. H. K. Carroll, formerly of the Methodist Episcopal Board, expressed the following opinion:

"The participation of the native ministers in the act of distributing missionary funds would have the effect of retarding the progress of self-support and autonomy. They would probably insist that they should receive the same salaries as the missionaries. They might not do so at first, but the drift would be in that direction. This would be a death-blow to the idea of a self-supporting, self-propagating, autonomous Church."

If it be said that the natives would always be in the minority in the mission, we reply that if we adopt the principle of appointing them, we cannot be sure of that. The time will come when, in accordance with our aim, the mission will decrease before the growing native Church. It might easily be that the number of properly qualified natives, developing among the millions in a given field, would in time outnumber the dozen or score of foreigners; while if the mission insisted on keeping them in the minority, the friction would be greater than it is now, for that would be a direct avowal of jealousy and distrust.

Third: The appointment of native ministers as members of a mission is not a local matter. If the arguments for it are valid for one field, they are for others, and the question is reduced to the determination of qualifications. The boards should consider whether the missionaries as a whole favour it. We have frequently raised the question in conferences with missionaries, but we do not recall a single place where missionaries have desired the appointment of native ministers as missionaries, except in the two fields where the object was apparently to secure recognition of particular individuals. The question, however, is not simply the recognition of one or two remarkable men, but the adoption of a principle which will be applicable to any number of such men. Is there not danger that personal regard for a few isolated individuals will warp the judgment as to the larger policy which should be adopted? We believe that the sentiment of the missionary body as a whole was fairly expressed by the Syria Mission when, in response to our inquiry, it unanimously voted "that the Syria Mission regards it as unwise that native ministers who are not responsible ecclesiastically or financially to the board and Church in the United States should be made voting members of a mission."

Fifth: It is doubtful whether membership in the mission would be satisfactory to the majority of the natives themselves. Experience has shown that in proportion as a native pastor becomes foreignized in his associations and habits, he loses influence with his countrymen. It is notorious that many of the Orientals who have been educated in America are regarded with ill-concealed jealousy by their own people. Dr. James L. Barton, of the American board, writes:

"In some countries, like Japan, the influence of the native would be greatly lessened by his appointment as missionary. I am sure that in Turkey his spiritual and moral influence would be weakened. This might be true also in India. I cannot but feel that such a move would mar the high spiritual influence of those who are set to be the spiritual leaders of the native churches. It would be opening a flood gate of difficulty which can be avoided best by keeping the lines between the native and missionary distinctly drawn, so far as the handling of mission funds and the name missionary is concerned."

Sixth: It is often necessary to remind ourselves of fundamental principles, lest we allow sporadic and exceptional cases to drift us into policies which are antagonistic to our true aims. We have already stated several times, and we can hardly state too often, that while the immediate object of the missionary is to present Christ to men with a view to their personal acceptance of Him as Saviour and Lord, the ultimate object is the establishment of a self-supporting, self-governing and self-propagating native Church. No heathen land will ever become Christian as long as its Christianity is an exotic, propagated by foreigners and dependent upon them. There must be in India, for example, an autonomous Indian Church with its own leaders and its own financial resources. The foreign missionary must preach the gospel, establish schools, found hospitals, create a Christian literature; but he must also recognize that the time will come when he should go on to other fields. The sphere of the mission in any field is temporary; that of the native Church is permanent. Though it may be necessary for the mission to remain in a given country for a long period, we must never for an instant forget that our object is not to establish the American Church in Asia, or the English Church, or the German Church, but the Asiatic Church, and that the time will come when that Church will and should control itself.

These are the axioms of missionary policy which are universally accepted as sound. Have they no bearing upon the proposition now before us? Surely, they mean that we should endeavour to build up a permanent and authoritative native

Church, and transfer work and responsibility to it as it is able to receive it, until the mission shall have abdicated all its powers and the Church shall have assumed them. It follows that the native leaders should find their sphere in the Church rather than in the foreign mission. In every conference and association and presbytery, the native minister is on a parity with the missionary who joins it, and with the growth of the churches, the native ministers and elders will in time form the majority. It is unavoidable that the mission should have control in the earlier stages of the work; but it is the deliberately avowed policy of the boards and the missions to turn over to the native churches, as rapidly as they are fitted for it, the authority which now resides in the mission. If we are to transfer the coming leaders of the churches in Asia from the permanent Church to the temporary mission, where they will be directly amenable to the authority of a board in Europe or America, and in a position to exercise a power over trust funds for which they cannot be held responsible, we might as well abandon hope of ever realizing our aim of a self-supporting and self-governing Church in Asia.

It is objected that the Church on the foreign field has no real power. Why not? Manifestly, for one or all of three reasons: first, because the Church is not yet capable of wisely using power; or second, because its work is still chiefly dependent on foreign funds; or third, because the missions and the boards have been too slow to recognize the proper functions of the native Church. Where the first two reasons prevail, it is inevitable that the mission should be the superior body. Self-support and self-government are indissolubly joined. It is as idle in Asia as it is in America to suppose that men can live on the money of others without being dependent upon them, or that business men in our home churches will ever place large sums in the control of men, ninety-nine one-hundredths of whom have had no experience whatever in handling funds, who have but recently emerged from a heathenism notorious for its utter lack of business standards, and who are not responsible to the givers or to anybody whom the givers can reach for the use which they make of the sums which are placed at their disposal. It should require no discussion that such a policy, even if adopted, would infallibly demoralize the churches of Asia. Were the Kings of England independent of France so long as they received French money? Why does the Constitution of the United States peremptorily forbid any officer of our country receiving even gifts from another government without the special consent of Congress, and why did that body prohibit "free and independent" Cuba from borrowing of any other nation than our own? Foreign subsidies mean foreign dependence, and it is folly to suppose that the churches of Asia can regularly receive the former without the latter. It might be well to press self-support more strongly from this viewpoint, in order that the native churches may more clearly realize that if they want to manage themselves, they must more largely maintain themselves, and that as long as the board and the mission foot the bill, they must have a definite voice in determining the character of the bill.

Where the third reason prevails, both the board and the mission should immediately attempt to rectify their error. Is it not true, in some places at least, that the missionary continues to exercise the whole power after the native Church has become able to assume a part of it? Are there no self-supporting churches whose pastors are still obliged to obey a missionary? Do the ministers of Asia understand, from actions as well as declarations, that we intend to give them autonomy as fast as practicable? Native ministers have repeatedly told the author that the native Church has no real authority. This could hardly be said of some churches, especially of the Methodist conferences; but we have heard Presbyterian ministers characterize the presbytery as "a fifth wheel to the coach," "a weak echo of the mission," "innocuous only because it merely registers the missionaries' conclusions in another form." A policy which undervalues the proper jurisdiction of the native Church is fundamentally wrong, and we cannot concede the validity of an argument based upon such undervaluation without vitiating an important element in our mission aim.

We are constrained to believe, therefore, that to make the native leaders members of the mission would not only make matters worse, but would involve some fatally defective policies. "The best results of mission work will be attained only when right lines of distinction are observed between the functions of the native churches and the functions of the foreign missions; the missions contributing to the establishment of the native churches and looking forward to passing on into the regions beyond when their work is done, and the native churches growing up with an independent identity from the beginning, administering their own contributions and resources, unentangled with any responsibility for the administration of the missions or of the funds committed to the missions."[1]

The question logically follows: If the native should not be a member of the mission, should the missionary be a member of the native Church? The native ministers feel that this question is involved in our policy. A statement of the objections to their membership in the mission, and a reminder that their sphere was in the Church as the permanent and ultimately authoritative body, almost invariably elicited the retort: "If the presbyteries are ours, why do not the missionaries leave them to us? If you will not permit us to join the mission, your men ought not to join our presbytery. As it is, both presbytery and mission are under your control, so that the native minister has no authority whatever, but is at the beck and call of the foreigner at every turn. If missionaries are members of the presbytery, we ought to be members of the mission."

Many missionaries, who would cordially agree to all that has

[1] Deliverance, General Assembly of the Presbyterian Church in the U. S. A., 1898.

been said about trusting the native leaders and magnifying the functions of the Church, nevertheless believe that they are needed in the native Church, that they ought to be under its jurisdiction, and that if they were to withdraw, the natives would feel that the missionaries and missionary money and policy would be wholly beyond their reach.

The organization of autonomous churches in India, Japan, Korea, and several other lands has, however, forced the missionaries in those countries to choose between the home and the native Church. The average missionary does not want to sever his connection with the home Church and he ought not to do so. His brethren at home will be more deeply interested in him if he retains his membership with them. They will hear his name in every roll call and have a pride in knowing that one of their number is on the foreign field. When he returns on furlough, he may be chosen to preside over their meetings. Twice, Presbyterian missionaries have been elected Moderators of the General Assembly, the highest honour within the gift of that Church. All this is an advantage to a missionary in strengthening his ties with the home-land, in enabling him to feel that his brethren are thinking about him and praying for him, and it is also a great advantage to the cause of missions in the home churches. These substantial advantages are sacrificed if the missionary cuts loose from the home Church and joins the Church on the field.

Realizing this, recourse has been had to the plan of belonging to both the Church in America and the Church on the field. This plan has been sanctioned by some of the home churches, but it places the missionary in an anomalous condition which is unsatisfactory in many ways. The editor of the *Indian Standard* observes: "The missionaries think that they have cut themselves off from the home Church and fully identified themselves with the Church in India, but of course they have really done nothing of the kind. They are all under their respective mission boards, which are committees of the home churches. The true

The Missionary and the Native Church

presbytery knows nothing of a body of ministers from a foreign land, outnumbering the native ministry and independent of it, and yet dominating all presbyterial action by their vote, and the expedient of cutting the ecclesiastical tie with home does not solve the problem. . . . At present the missionaries are virtually in the position of the House of Lords, with this advantage, that they sit and vote in both houses." [1]

The native leaders are not slow to see that the missionary is not really subject to the native Church. When a missionary in Japan said that he regarded himself as under the jurisdiction of the Japanese Church, Dr. Uemura replied: "The missionaries who have joined our presbyteries are in no true sense integral parts of the Japanese Church. They are members in name, but in fact they are under the control of an outside organization. The churches which are maintained by mission aid are likewise only nominally under the control of presbytery. The real power over them is the mission. Nothing can be done either by the Church or the presbytery without the consent and approval of the missionary in charge. The time has come to have done with all this pretense at coöperation."

The details of the problem differ in various fields, so that all that we have said does not apply with equal force to every body of missionaries. Some ecclesiastical polities and mission methods give less power to the mission and more to the Church than others. But the fundamental problem is still acute in several fields: namely, the domination of the foreign missionary in the native Church, and whether he exercises that domination through a mission outside of the Church or as a leader inside of it, the result is practically the same.

What then should be the relation of the missionary to the native Church? We reply, that of a corresponding member, with a voice in discussion, but without a vote. All the guidance that it is good for the missionary to exercise, and good for

[1] April, 1904.

the native Church to have exercised, can be given just as well if the missionary is in advisory relations. One of the ablest of the Indian ministers says: "I think it would be better if the missionaries were not members of the local presbyteries. Every presbytery in north India could go on as well as now if the missionaries were to be simply corresponding members. Such a policy would help to relieve the present feeling of undue subordination."

It is unwise to organize a Church out of missionaries and their families before there are native Christians, and a presbytery or conference out of foreign missionaries before there are native pastors. This has been done in some fields. Such a policy is apt to force the premature organization of ecclesiastical machinery on the mission field. It creates a Church that will always be foreign in spirit. The natives come in one by one to find foreigners in control, and they regard the whole institution as alien. No harm is usually done by the members of missionary families joining the local church, especially as there may be no other way for their children to confess Christ and be enrolled as communicants; but the ordained missionary loses nothing of value and avoids much that is dwarfing to the native Church by leaving his membership at home.

Consistent procedure would confine mission membership to the missionaries and church membership to the natives. The organization of an autonomous native Church should not, of course, be effected until there is a suitable body of native clergy and laymen to man it. The mission itself can usually determine when the proper time has come, for its members ordain the natives and constitute the Church. The Church once organized, however, should be given an opportunity to exercise its proper functions. This will give all of its ministers a due sense of responsibility, train them to a self-reliant care of their own work, and lead them to value the Church as the expression of their own religious convictions and activities. The Presbyterian Board, with the approval of the General Assembly, has officially recognized this policy. It rescinded, in 1899, its former manual rule that missionaries should unite with presbyteries on the field, and it has since unofficially advised leaving ecclesiastical membership in America. The Southern Presbyterian Church has also formally approved this position.[1] Not without opposition, but slowly and surely, this is coming to be regarded as the logical outcome of sound views of the relation of the missionary to the native Church.

It is not a matter upon which the boards can legislate, as they are not ecclesiastical bodies. It must be left largely to the missionaries themselves. Meantime, it is gratifying to know that all over Asia missionaries are earnestly considering the question of the status of the native Church and are desirous of finding some plan which will give a freer field to it. The *Indian Standard* voices the growing feeling as follows:

"The more we eliminate ourselves and give our native brethren a chance the better. We complain of their lack of independence, and then outvote them whenever they do show a spark of it. Would it not be well if we all took the position of consultative members and left our native brethren more largely to manage their own affairs? Ought we not to cultivate a habit of self-suppression, interfering as seldom as possible, and seeking to make our Indian brethren realize that this is their Church, with its development largely in their own hands? It would be very difficult for some of us to unlearn the habit and practice of years, but it would be a wholesome discipline, and might even be a means of grace."[2]

The whole question of the relationship of the missionary to the native Church should be handled in the spirit of genuine sympathy with the native ministers. Their lot is often a trying one. In addition to the financial embarrassments to which

---

[1] Report of Executive Committee of Foreign Missions to the General Assembly of 1886.

[2] April, 1904.

we have referred, they often encounter the hatred of hostile priests and the contemptuous anger of the official classes. Many of these devoted men have endured the bitterest persecution. They have been disowned by their families, deprived of their property, scourged, imprisoned and killed. If the story of thousands of them could be written, it would be one of the most inspiring records in the development of the Church of God. Making all due allowance for those who have been actuated by improper motives or who have shown themselves lazy or incompetent, the fact remains that multitudes have been loyal, humble, and loving servants of God. The missionary will make no mistake in trusting them and honouring them.

XVI

THE MISSIONARY AND HIS CRITICS[1]

THE purity of the missionary's motive and the unselfishness of his work do not exempt him from criticism, nor should they. Any enterprise which depends upon public support is a fair object of criticism. Boards and missionaries are human and have their share of human infirmities. They have a right to insist that criticism shall be honest; but within that limit, any one has a right to scrutinize their methods and work and to express his conclusions with entire frankness.

Criticisms of missionaries and their work may be roughly divided into four classes:

First: Those which come from friends of the work who see defects, or think that they do. Some of these criticisms are undoubtedly just and should be heeded. Others are based on misapprehensions and should elicit temperate explanations. The attitude of the boards and the missionaries towards this whole class of critics should be that of the inspired writer who said: "Faithful are the wounds of a friend."

Second: Criticisms which spring from conflicting interests. Such are the objections which originate with traders who sell gin and rum in Africa and opium in China, who traffic in the virtue of native girls, or entice away coolies under specious "contracts" which result in virtual slavery. Some regions

---

[1] This chapter was completed before the publication of Dr. James L. Barton's book with the same title. The reader is referred to that admirable little volume for another discussion of this subject and for the quoted opinions of many competent observers. Consult also "The Challenge to Christian Missions," by the Rev. R. E. Welsh.

have long been infested by men of this infamous type, and while some of their nefarious practices have been broken up, others still continue. Almost every port city in non-Christian lands has dens of vice which are kept by white men or women and which pander to the lowest passions. Men of this kind are, of course, virulent haters of missionaries. Charles Darwin asserted that "the foreign travellers and residents in the South Sea Islands, who write with such hostility to missions there, are men who find the missionary an obstacle to the accomplishment of their evil purposes." There are, too, native priests who, like the silver-smiths of Ephesus, find their craft in danger and circulate falsehoods regarding missionaries as political plotters or adepts in witchcraft. In Chinese cities, it was once common for placards to be conspicuously posted, charging missionaries with boiling and eating Chinese babies. The massacre of the Presbyterian missionaries at Lien-chou, China, in 1905, was primarily caused by the finding of a skeleton of a man and the body of a still-born child preserved in alcohol in the mission hospital, the mob parading these grewsome finds through the streets as evidence of the way that missionaries treated the Chinese.

Third : Criticisms which are based on want of sympathy with the fundamental motives and aims of the missionary enterprise. It is sometimes wholesome for those who live in a missionary environment to ascertain how their methods appear to people who are outside of that environment. Attention may thus be called to defects which would otherwise escape notice. Men, however, who are opposed, not merely to certain methods, but to the essential character of the movement itself can hardly be considered fair critics. They will never be silenced, because they are inaccessible to the Christian argument. Their criticisms have been demolished over and over again, but they reappear unabashed within a month. Even when their objections are overcome, their opposition remains. Critics of this class will always ridicule the effort to propagate a religion which they do not practice. Their criticisms are not confined to the missionary, for they sneer at the churches at home, declaring that ministers are hirelings and communicants hypocrites. It does not necessarily follow that the criticisms of such men are unfounded; but "it is within the right of the missionary to protest against being arraigned against judges habitually hostile to him, and it is within the right of the public to scrutinize the pronouncements of such judgments with much suspicion."[1]

Some of the critics of this class live in Europe and America, but many of them reside in the treaty ports of non-Christian lands. We do not mean that the foreign colonies in the concessions are wholly composed of such men. These colonies include some excellent people to whose sympathy and helpfulness the missionaries are greatly indebted. We are not quoting missionaries, however, but widely travelled laymen in the statement that the life of the typical foreigner in Asia is such that a missionary cannot consistently join in it, no matter how cordial his desire to be on friendly terms with his countrymen. Colquhoun declares that foreigners in China go to get money and then return, do not learn the language, have little intercourse with natives and know little about them.[2] Mr. Frederick McCormick, for six years Associated Press correspondent in China, says that "the foreign communities are not in China, but at China," simply "ranged on the shore"; that "they carry on their relations with China through a go-between native"; that their "society is centred about a club, of which the most conspicuous elements are the bar, race-track and book-maker;" and that "the life, for the most part, of the communities is in direct antagonism to that of missionaries" who live and work among the Chinese.[3] Griffis, then of the

[1] Capt. Brinkley, Editor of the *Japan Mail*.
[2] "China in Transformation."
[3] Article in *The Outlook*.

Imperial University, Tokyo, says: "It is hard to find an average man of the world in Japan who has any clear idea of what missionaries are doing or have done. Their dense ignorance borders on the ridiculous."[1] Maclay states that the foreign communities in that country are very immoral.[2] Mr Donrovan, who once filled an important position under the Chinese Government, declares that the foreign residents of that Empire are either ignorant of the work of missionaries, or their lives are so immoral that they studiously avoid them. Such men by their lust and greed, their brutal treatment of the natives and their remorseless pushing of their own selfish interests, create the very conditions of hatred and unrest which critics ignorantly ascribe to the missionaries.

Many naval officers are Christian gentlemen who know how to value missionary work and who have publicly testified to their appreciation of it. But sometimes when a vessel enters a foreign port, the sailors, impatient of the restraints of shipboard, proceed to "paint the town red." The natives are astonished by the conduct of representatives of an alleged Christian nation, and the missionary, in self-defense, finds it necessary to disavow their acts and, perhaps, rebuke them. Then the sailors go away, cursing the missionaries. Prof. E. Warren Clark writes that he once "took two of our most earnest Christian converts on a visit to the foreign resident quarter of Yokohama, and the first thing they saw, in front of the English Episcopal Church, was a drunken British tar assaulting an equally intoxicated American sailor, and both of them were being arrested by a 'heathen' Japanese policeman!" Several years ago, a Rear-Admiral of the American Navy wrote that "the missionaries in Turkey are a bad lot." Investigation developed the fact that of the hundreds of American missionaries in the Turkish Empire, that Admiral had met only three, that these three had

---

[1] "The Mikado's Empire."
[2] "Budget of Letters from Japan."

The Missionary and His Critics

conducted themselves like the gentlemen they were, but that the Admiral himself was notorious for profanity and roughness of behaviour, and that the conduct of his men on shore was in violation of all decency.

When a man who returns from a foreign land maligns missionaries, it is safe to assume, either that he has been making a fool of himself so that he had to be rebuked by the missionaries, or that he has gotten his information from men whose corrupt habits give them personal reasons for disliking consistent Christian men. When "a noted English traveller stated in one of his books that the missionaries at a certain place in Africa accomplished nothing, the missionary retorted that his station could hardly be considered entirely useless, as it had been a refuge for the native women from the drunken attacks of the travelling companions of this censor."

Fourth: Criticisms which come from those who are ignorant of the real character, aims and work of the missionary and the methods of mission boards. This is a large class. There are many people who have never seen missionary work, or met a missionary, or read a missionary book, but who, seeing in the newspapers or hearing from some friend the class of criticisms to which reference has just been made, jump to the conclusion that they are true.

The increasing interest in Asia and the comparative ease with which it can now be visited are rapidly enlarging the stream of foreign travellers. Unfortunately, many of them are mere globe-trotters, knowing little and caring less about missionaries, people who at home are only languidly interested in church work and do not know what religious work is being done in their own city. Abroad, they usually confine their visits to the port cities and capitals, and become acquainted only at the foreign hotels and clubs. They seldom look up foreign missions and missionary work, but get their impressions from more or less irreligious and dissolute traders and professional guides. What they do see of missions sometimes misleads them. Typical mission work can seldom be seen in a port city. The natives often exhibit the worst traits of their own race, or are spoiled by the evil example of the dissolute foreign community. The mission buildings are apt to be memorials or other special gifts, and give a misleading impression as to the scale of missionary expenditure. Hearing the sneers at the clubs and hotels and without going near the missionary himself, the globe-trotter carries away slanders, which, on his return, are sensationally paraded in the newspapers and eagerly swallowed by a gullible public. The Hon. Edwin H. Conger, former American Minister to China, writes: "The attacks upon missionaries by sensational press correspondents and globe-girdling travellers have invariably been made without knowledge or investigation, and nine-tenths of them are the veriest libel and the grossest slander."[1]

It is often interesting to propound some questions to such a critic. An American merchant returned from China to say that missions were a failure. Whereupon his pastor proceeded to interrogate him. "What city of China did you visit?" "Canton," was the reply. "What did you find in our mission schools which impressed you as so faulty?" The merchant confessed that he had not seen any schools. "And yet," said the pastor, "our board alone has in Canton a normal school, a theological seminary, a large boarding school for girls, and several day schools, while other denominations also have schools. Well, what was there about the mission churches which so displeased you?" Again the merchant was forced to confess his ignorance; he did not know that there was a church in Canton till his pastor told him that there were, in and near the city, scores of churches and chapels, some of them very large, and with preaching not only every Sunday but, in some instances, every day.

"But surely you were interested in the hospitals," queried

[1] Address, Kansas City, Mo., May 16, 1906.

the pastor. "One of the largest hospitals in Asia stands in a conspicuous position on the river front, while the Woman's Hospital in another part of the city is also a great plant, with a Medical College and a Nurses' Training School connected with it." Incredible as it may seem, he knew absolutely nothing about these beneficent institutions. Further inquiries elicited the admission that the critic knew nothing of the Orphanage or the School for the Blind or the Refuge for the Insane and that he had made no effort whatever to become acquainted with the missionaries. He was a little embarrassed by this time, but his questioner could not refrain from telling him the old story about the English army officer and the foreign missionary who met on an ocean steamer. The army officer had contemptuously said that he had lived in India thirty years and had never seen a native Christian. Shortly afterwards he recited with gusto his success in tiger-hunting, declaring that he had killed no less than nine tigers. "Pardon me," gently said the missionary, "did I understand you to say that you have killed nine tigers in India?" "Yes, sir," pompously replied the colonel. "Now that is remarkable," continued the missionary, "for I have lived in India for thirty years and have never seen a tiger." "Perhaps, sir," sneered the colonel, "you didn't go where the tigers were." "Precisely," was the bland answer of the missionary, "and may not that have been the reason why you never saw any native converts?"

"Will you kindly tell me where the Lafayette Avenue Presbyterian Church is, Dr. Cuyler's," I asked a street-car conductor on my first visit to Brooklyn. "Well," he replied as a puzzled look came over his face, "I've been runnin' on this here line ten year, but I never heard tell of such a church." I found the great church and more than a thousand worshippers within three blocks of the place where I had asked that question, and I entered it, not with an unfavourable impression of Dr. Cuyler's work, but of that conductor's intelligence.

When Mr. Stead got the impression that "If Christ came to Chicago," with its thousands of churches and Christian institutions of every kind, He would find little but vice and crime, it is not surprising that the casual traveller sees few external signs of Christianity in a populous pagan city. It was Christ Himself who said, "The kingdom of God cometh not with observation," or as the margin reads, "not with outward show."

Let us now take up some current criticisms. Several of the most common have already been considered in connection with the subjects of other chapters, while others have been discussed in the author's "New Forces in Old China." In order that this chapter may be more complete for reference and at the same time repetition avoided, these objections are simply stated in footnotes and the reader is referred to the discussion elsewhere.[1]

1. "Missionaries are inferior men."[2] The man who makes this objection simply shows that he does not know missionaries or that he is generalizing from some exceptional individual. There are undoubtedly missionaries who say and do foolish things, just as some of us at home do, and once in a while a missionary proves to be incompetent. Ninety-four per cent. of the business men of the United States are said to fail at some time in their lives. Why, then, should a few mis-

---

[1] "Missionaries live in luxury." Cf. Chapter VII.

"Missionaries live in idleness." Cf. Chapter VI.

"The houses of missionaries are needlessly expensive." Cf. Chapter VII.

"Missionaries unnecessarily interfere with native customs." Cf. Chapter XIV.

"Missionaries do not acquire the language of the natives." Cf. Chapter V.

"Missionary administration is costly and unbusinesslike." Cf. Chapter III.

"Asiatics do not want our religion." Cf. "New Forces in Old China," pp. 356, 357.

[2] Cf. Chapter IV.

The Missionary and His Critics

sionary failures be deemed an adequate ground for condemning the whole class? The reader who hears criticisms which impress him as serious should demand names and particulars and forward them to the board with which the missionary is connected. The boards have neither desire nor motive to shield misconduct. They will promptly investigate and take such action as the facts may justify.

Travellers and officials like Charles Darwin, Lord Lawrence, Sir Harry Johnston, Sir Robert Hart, Sir Mortimer Durand, the Hon. John W. Foster, the Hon. William Jennings Bryan, Mrs. Isabella Bird Bishop, the Hon. Charles Denby, and scores of others have borne high testimony to the worth of missionaries. Those who do not confine their observations to treaty-port hotels or draw on their imagination for facts, but who have eyes to see and ears to hear the mighty forces which are gradually inaugurating a new era in Asia, report that the real missionary is an educated, devoted man, the embodiment of the highest type of Christian character, and that in the spirit of the Master, he heals the sick, teaches the young, translates the Bible, creates a wholesome literature and inculcates those great truths of the Christian religion to which Europe and America owe whatever of true greatness they possess. No one is perfect, not even a critic, but the man who can write only evil of such men and women does so at the expense of either his intelligence or his candour.

2. "Converts are not genuine, but are attracted to the missionary by the hope of employment or support." The whole number of national Christians in connection with churches in the mission field is 3,614,154, and the total number of their employed leaders is 151,735, many of whom are paid either wholly or in part by the Christians themselves. Making all due allowance for others who are employed as servants or who receive assistance in schools, the number who are aided in any way by the foreigner is relatively insignificant. The great body of native Christians have no financial

motive whatever for confessing Christ. The Hon. Charles Denby, for thirteen years American Minister at Peking, has reminded the world that, during the Boxer uprising, " the province of Chih-li furnished 6,200 Chinese who remained true to their faith in spite of danger, suffering and impending death. It is said that 15,000 converts were killed during the riots, and not as many as two per cent. of them apostatized. In the face of these facts, the old allegation that the Chinese converts are treacherous, venal, and untrue, must be renounced. Let us not call them ' rice Christians ' any more."[1]

3. " Missionaries were responsible for the anti-foreign feeling in China which culminated in the Boxer uprising of 1900."[2] The Chinese themselves have repeatedly denied this and assigned the cause to the political aggressions of Western nations. In an imperial edict of July of that year, the Chinese Government officially declared: "Since the first days of our dynasty, all the foreigners coming to China have been invariably treated with liberality, and, coming down to the eras of Taokwang (1821) and Hienfung (1851), we concluded with them treaties of commerce and intercourse and conceded to them the right of propagating Christianity. Latterly, however, the foreigners have come to encroach on our territories, to rob us of our good people and to plunder by force our properties, thus trampling under their feet this favoured land of ours. Thus have they deeply wronged us, and the results have been the destruction of their churches and the murder of their missionaries."

The Hon. John Barrett, who travelled widely in China, says: "Whenever it was my privilege to discuss anti-foreign sentiment with intelligent Chinese, I found invariably that they placed the chief blame upon the land-grabbing spirit of the European countries."

---

[1] Cf. "New Forces in Old China," Chapter XXII.
[2] *Ibid.*, Chapter XXI.

The Missionary and His Critics

The following opinion of the late Hon. Charles Denby is significant: "On an analysis of the bitter anti-Christian movement, we find that it is largely to be explained as primarily anti-foreign; that is, largely directed against missionaries solely as foreigners, not solely as teachers of a foreign religion."

4. "Missionaries needlessly irritate the Chinese by interfering with native lawsuits."[1] A difference should be observed here between the practice of the European Roman Catholic missionaries and the American Protestant missionaries. The former champion the cause of their converts, particularly when they believe that lawsuits are instigated by the opponents of Christianity. Viceroy Tuan Fong asked the boards to "forbid the interference of missionaries with Chinese courts in cases in which their converts are parties."[2] The Roman Catholics were so much more numerous than Protestants in his vice-royalty that when complaints came to him that missionaries were interfering, he quite naturally thought of the missionaries as a class and failed to distinguish between the Roman Catholics and the Protestants. As long as Chinese courts are so hopelessly corrupt that native Christians cannot usually secure justice in suits which are inspired by their enemies, it is too much to ask that the missionary shall always stand aloof; but it is the policy of the Protestant boards and missions to discourage such interference, and the missionaries themselves are more and more clearly seeing the imprudence of it. Comparatively seldom now does a Protestant missionary give offense in this matter.

5. "Missionaries are universally hated by the natives, while the ordinary foreigner is tolerated." This is grossly untrue.[3] The missionaries are far more popular with the people than any other foreigners. They travel freely, unarmed and unprotected,

---

[1] Cf. "New Forces in Old China," Chapter XIX.
[2] Address, New York, February 2, 1906.
[3] Cf. Chapter XIV.

and it is comparatively seldom that they are molested. When they are attacked, it is by a class of ruffians who, in the slums of an American city, attack a Chinese gentleman on the streets. Official edicts have specifically declared that "the Chinese Government . . . is not opposed to the work of the missions." It would be easy to fill pages with extracts from edicts commending the missionaries and their work. One of the most notable of these was issued by the Emperor in 1844. In 1862, the Rescript of Prince Kung says: "The missionaries are well-disposed men, and are in their own country greatly respected by others, and whereas their first object is to instruct men to do good, they must be treated with more than usual high consideration." In 1895, the Prefect of Nanking invited the missionaries to a feast at his yamen, and afterwards issued a proclamation which included the following passage:

"Now having examined the doctrine halls in every place pertaining to the prefecture, we find that there have been established free schools where the poor children of China may receive instruction; hospitals where Chinamen may freely receive healing; that the missionaries are all really good; not only do they not take the people's possessions, but they do not seem to desire men's praise. Although Chinamen are pleased to do good, there are none who equal the missionaries."

During their visits in America, both Viceroy Li Hung Chang and Viceroy Tuan Fong freely expressed their gratitude for the services of the missionaries, the latter declaring that "the awakening of China may be traced in no small measure to the hands of the missionaries; they have borne the light of Western civilization to every nook and corner of the Empire."[1] In 1900, the people of Paoting-fu murdered the missionaries; but they soon realized their mistake, gave land for a better station site and presented to the new mission hospital a silk banner on which was worked in letters of gold: "This place bestows grace

[1] Address in Boston.

The Missionary and His Critics

on the Chinese people." In the same city, a high official visited the mission church and, seeing the ten commandments upon the wall, said to the missionaries: "If you can get that teaching into the minds of my soldiers they will be good soldiers. I see now one notable characteristic of Christianity: it seems to have the power to go out from oneself to others; it is not self-centred, but works for others."

The Hon. Charles Denby probably was as competent to pronounce upon this question as any one and he wrote: "We find that some of the specific charges made against the missionaries have no reference to their teachings. . . . Few, if any, accusations of aggressiveness and personal violence on the part of missionaries against Chinese can be substantiated, while there are authentic cases of bad conduct against Chinese by foreigners of other classes. The missionaries, in the vast majority of cases, are loved by those Chinese with whom they succeed in establishing intimate relations, and they are almost universally respected by all classes in the communities in which they are well known."

An author, who has achieved the questionable distinction of having written the most unreliable book that has yet appeared on Korea, declares that the people of that country dislike the missionaries. Every one in the Land of the Morning Calm knows better. The missionaries have to an extraordinary degree the confidence and the affection of the people from officials to peasants. The Koreans know well enough who their real friends are, and they testify to the accuracy of their knowledge by loving the missionaries, but by hating the "Puffsnaubers" and mobbing the "Wintershines,"[1] whom Mr. Hamilton would probably regard as congenial friends and high authorities, even if he was not "Wintershine" himself.

A whole volume would be required to quote the appreciative words of Asiatic and African princes, nobles, magistrates and

---

[1] Characters in James S. Gale's Novel, "The Vanguard."

people, wherever they have become acquainted with the real character and objects of the missionaries and have been able to separate them from the white men who have political or commercial designs. Hardly a month passes without some substantial token of this appreciation in the form of gifts to mission institutions. Cabinet ministers in China, Japan and Persia, provincial governors in Korea, the King and Queen of Siam, East Indian, African and South Sea princes without number, and even Moslems have made such gifts, while scores of officials, like the Chinese Governors of Shantung and Formosa and the Siamese Minister of the Interior, have tried to secure missionaries for the presidency of government colleges or for other responsible posts.

6. "Missionaries make trouble for their own governments."[1] Well informed government officials do not complain about missionaries as a class, though they may sometimes object to the indiscretion of a particular individual. Suppose the missionary does occasionally need protection; he is a citizen, and what kind of a government is it which refuses to protect its citizens in their lawful undertakings? No one questions the right of a trader, however dissolute, to go wherever he pleases and to be defended by his country in case of danger. Has not a missionary an equal right to the benefits of his flag? The Hon. John Barrett, formerly American Minister to Siam, says that 150 missionaries gave him less trouble in five years than fifteen merchants gave him in five months. The American Government protects merely nominal citizens, who, though natives of foreign lands and with no intention of residing in the United States, have naturalized themselves to escape military conscription or to secure immunity from criminal prosecution or official exactions in their native land. Many Syrians and Armenians in Turkey are thus protected by the American Government at no small cost and trouble. In 1904, a bashi-ba-

---

[1] Cf. "New Forces in Old China," Chapter XX.

zouk in Morocco kidnapped an American citizen who, for many years, had preferred to make his home in that country and who was an American only in name. Instantly the American press was in an uproar, vociferously demanding warships and marines to "avenge the insult to our flag." Shortly afterwards, a few cruisers of the Mediterranean squadron steamed from Tangier to Smyrna, while negotiations were being carried on with the Sultan of Turkey regarding damages to some mission schools, and the very same papers began to sneer at "the gospel of the gunboat." "It is not easy for the common mind to understand why a luxurious idler, who had long since practically abandoned his country, was entitled to such immediate relief, while the best blood of America, given freely for the amelioration of the wretched of the Far East, should not, even after years of delay, be entitled to some consideration."[1][2]

7. "Missionaries denationalize their converts." Christianity never injured or denationalized any one. It simply made him a better man—more honest, more intelligent, more charitable, more loyal to his own country. The Chinese Government made a large grant for indemnity for the lives of the Chinese Christians who were murdered during the Boxer uprising. How much it meant to the poor survivors will be understood from the fact that the share of the Christians in a single county was 10,000 taels. But none of the Christians in that county would accept the indemnity. They took compensation only for the property they had lost; but they gave one-tenth of that to support several Chinese evangelists to preach the gospel to their former persecutors, and afterwards they tried to raise a fund to pay back to the government the indemnity that they did receive. Such a course indicates both genuineness of faith and loyalty to the Emperor.

[1] *The Interior*, September 1, 1904.

[2] For an answer to the frequent question why the missionaries do not leave their posts when danger threatens, cf. Chapter XVIII.

8. "Missionaries preach sectarianism instead of fundamental Christianity." This is precisely what they do not do. There is far less sectarianism on the foreign field than at home. Denominational lines are often virtually obliterated. Where they are prominent, the fault is usually with the home Church. The missionaries have already united in several lands and they would do so in some others, if the authorities at home would permit them.[1]

9. "There is so much evil in Christian lands that we should not presume to teach others." We do not deny the existence of this evil, much less extenuate it. Rather do we frankly admit it and say that we are heartily ashamed of it. Iniquity in the home land, however, is not because of Christianity, but in spite of it. The religion of Christ is not a national faith to be accepted by men in bulk. It is a personal relationship to God. The man who follows Christ is a Christian, whether he lives in America or in China. The man who does evil is not a Christian, whether he is white or black or yellow. The white men in Asia and Africa who are profane, immoral and intemperate are not Christians, and they no more represent the Christians of Europe and America or the gospel of Christ than the Highbinders of San Francisco represent the people of China or the maxims of Confucius. The standard of judgment should be Christ and those who conform their lives to His teachings, not those who reject Him.

10. "There is much to be done in our own land and charity begins at home." One might urge with equal truth that education begins with the alphabet, but it ends there only with the feeble-minded. We grant that there is a great deal to be done at home, but there are a great many people to do it. A New York pastor says that he "never could understand why we think so much more of a heathen abroad than at home," and he intimates that we ought to give less for foreign missions

---

[1] Cf. Chapters II, VI and XV.

The Missionary and His Critics

and more for the conversion of " the foreigners within the shade of our churches,"—a sentiment which was editorially endorsed by several newspapers. If, however, he had looked into the Report of the Charity Organization Society of New York, he would have found a list of 3,330 religious and philanthropic agencies in his own city. " If these churches and their auxiliary buildings were placed side by side, they would reach in one unbroken frontage of long-meter godliness from the Battery to Yonkers, twenty miles.[1] The first time I visited New York's slum district, I was amazed by the number of missions. A high authority declares that "there is no other city in the world, except London, where more is being done to point the lost to the Son of God than in New York.[2]

A widely published article once stated that St. Louis had one church for 2,800 of population, Chicago one for 2,081, Boston one for 1,600, and Minneapolis one for 1,054. In the United States as a whole, there were said to be 187,800 churches, or one for every 400 people, one Protestant minister for 700, one Christian worker for forty-eight, and one communicant for five.[3] Talk about the relative needs of the United States! In a typical town of 8,000 people, there are three Presbyterian churches, three United Presbyterian, three Methodist, two Episcopal and one Christian Church. " For every missionary the Church sends abroad, she holds seventy-six at home." [4] A million Americans are engaged in distinctively religious work, about 150,000 of whom devote themselves to it as a separate profession.[5] In the light of these facts, the statement that " the Church cannot see the misery which is under her own nose at home " appears rather absurd.

How is it abroad? It is said that in Siam there is only one ordained missionary for 300,000 people, in India and Africa

---

[1] *The Church Economist.*   [2] The Rev. W. T. Elsing.
[3] *The Chautauquan.*   [4] The Rev. Walter R. Lambuth, D. D.
[5] *The Missionary Review of the World.*

for 250,000, in China for 270,000, and in South America for 300,000. Dr. Arthur Mitchell wrote of a journey of only twenty-four hours from Hang-chou to Shanghai: "I was absolutely awestruck and dumb as I steamed past city after city, great and populous, one of which was a walled city of 300,000 souls, without one missionary of any Christian denomination whatever, and without so much as a native Christian helper or teacher of any kind. That silent moonlight night, as I passed unnoticed by those long, dark battlements shutting in their pagan multitudes, was one of the most solemn of my life; and the hours of daylight, when other cities, still larger than many of our American capitals, were continually coming into view, and the teeming populations of the canals and rivers and villages and fields and roads were before my eyes, kept adding to the burden of the night."

As for money, the John Price Jones Corporation, New York, reported in 1930 that gifts to philanthropy in the United States during 1929 reached the tremendous total of $2,450,720,000, an increase of $120,120,000 over 1928, the previous highest year. This colossal sum was distributed as follows: religion, $996,300,000; education, $467,500,000; gifts for personal charity, $279,760,000; organized charitable relief, $278,710,000; health, $221,510,000; foreign relief, $132,000,000; the fine arts, $40,000,000; play and recreation, $20,900,000; miscellaneous reform organizations, $14,040,000. Munificent benefactions are reported almost daily. A generation ago, a church edifice costing $100,000 was exceptional. To-day, we read of churches costing $300,000 in several cities of 10,000 or 12,000 inhabitants and of plants in large cities representing expenditures ranging from $500,000 to $2,000,000. We recently made a list of a dozen educational institutions that were conducting campaigns for sums varying from $3,000,000 to $12,000,000.

Meantime, the total annual receipts of all the boards of foreign missions in the United States are less than $40,000,-

000, including gifts for current work and new property. The Presbyterian Church U. S. A. is probably a fairly representative denomination, and in 1931 the Minutes of its General Assembly reported total contributions of $58,171,381, of which $3,623,186 were given to its Board of Foreign Missions.

In the light of such figures, there is something pitiful in the ignorant criticism that money is given for foreign missions that ought to be spent at home. In general, our home churches spend ninety-four cents in America for every six cents that they give for the evangelization of the world.

It is true that there are unconverted people at home; but what would be thought of a business man who declined to sell goods outside of his own city until all its inhabitants used them? The fact that some Americans are irreligious does not lessen our obligation to give the gospel to the world. If the early Church had refused to send the gospel to other nations until its own nation was converted, Christianity would have died in its cradle, for the land in which it originated was never really Christianized and is to-day Mohammedan. The argument that our own land is not yet evangelized would have made the Church at Antioch disobey the command of the Holy Spirit to send forth Paul and Barnabas. It would have kept Augustine of Canterbury from carrying the gospel to England. It would have prevented the founding of churches in America, and would, to-day, cripple all our home missionary work, since there is no other part of the United States more godless than the eastern states. Christ did not tell His disciples to withhold His faith from other nations until they had converted Palestine; He told them to go at once into all the world and preach the gospel to every creature, and it is because they obeyed that command that we have the gospel to-day.

Indeed no nation ever will be wholly Christianized, for not only will there always be individuals who refuse or neglect to accept Christ, but before any one generation can be converted, a new generation of young people will have grown up and the work must thus be ever beginning anew. The argument, therefore, that we should not preach the gospel to other nations until our own has been converted issues in an absurdity, since it would perpetually confine Christianity to those nations which already have it and forever forbid its extension. Is the Church to be forever moving around and around in a circle, because some white men refuse to become Christians? If, after all these centuries of effort, there is still so much evil at home, it is not a reason for discontinuing foreign missionary effort, but for saying, in the words of Paul: "It was necessary that the word of God should first have been spoken to you: but seeing ye put it from you and judge yourselves unworthy of everlasting life, lo, we turn to the Gentiles."[1] If Christ is "good tidings of great joy . . . to all people," what right have we to withhold Him from "all people"? He belongs to them as well as to us. Indeed, America could no more keep its Christianity to itself than it could keep the telegraph or than the Chinese could keep the art of printing. Christianity is like the sunshine, for all. The moment it is shut up, it ceases to be sunshine and becomes darkness.

11. "Missionaries have introduced a civilization which has destroyed some native races." It is extraordinary that any one should believe such a charge. What is there in the gospel of Christ that shortens life or weakens character? The native races are not being destroyed, however. There are more Indians in North America now than there were when the continent was discovered. The negro multiplies faster in the United States than in Africa. The population of Egypt and India is rapidly increasing under British rule. "The well-clad civilized citizen will out-walk, out-fight and out-live the savage every day in the year, and the missionary brings to barbarian races a physical redemption as well as a spiritual one."[2]

[1] Acts 13 : 46. [2] *The Interior*, October 6, 1904.

The few tribes that are being decimated are being rotted out by vicious white men's lust and whiskey, not by the missionary's religion.[1]

12. "Missionaries' children are usually bad." This is a twin brother of the venerable falsehood that ministers' sons are usually scapegraces. Statistics have repeatedly shown that no other class has produced so many eminently useful men as ministers and particularly missionaries. The black sheep is a rare exception; but just because his conduct is so at variance with the standards of his class, he attracts attention, and shallow or malicious critics jump to the conclusion that he is a type. Considering the number of missionaries' children that have had to grow up in the demoralizing environment of a heathen land or away from parental control in America, the number that have risen to prominence is extraordinarily large.

The critic usually takes as his stock illustration missionaries' sons in the Hawaiian Islands. Dr. Bishop found on inquiry that there are now in the Islands fifty-five sons of missionaries; that forty-four are members of the Congregational Church; that not one of the fifty-five has ever been arrested for crime or fallen into vice; that six are ministers, eight sugar-planters, eight farmers, three merchants, three physicians, three lawyers and one is in each occupation of manufacturer, interpreter, publisher, teacher, surveyor, and scientific instructor. Fifteen are in the government service—one each as president, chief justice, minister of finance, attorney-general, surveyor-general, assistant-general, collector-general, marshall, president of public instruction, superintendent of public works, circuit judge; two are department clerks and two are sheriffs. It would be difficult to find an equal number of men anywhere else in the world who average higher in "moral character, in education, and in general capability."

13. "Missionaries take advantage of their position to en-

---

[1] Cf. "New Forces in Old China," pp. 124 *sq.*

rich themselves." This is simply false. When one critic paraded this charge in a daily paper, we called upon him to name the missionaries whom he had in mind. He did not respond to the challenge, for the simple reason that he could not. We know the missionaries, and while we do not know this particular critic, we know his breed and its proneness to malicious criticisms of men the latchet of whose shoes he is not worthy to unloose.

One critic alleges that "American missionaries in Korea were formerly closely associated with the more important export houses in the leading industrial centres of America." The facts are that when the first missionaries went to Korea, they found a people who were quite destitute of even the commonest conveniences of life. Christianity means much in civilization as well as in religion. It invariably begets a desire for a higher physical life. It was quite natural that when a Korean caller saw a clock or cook stove or sewing machine in the missionary's house, he should ask the missionary to get him one. This was done in some instances by a very few of the missionaries. They did not do it for financial profit, but simply out of kindly interest in the people; and now that foreign business firms are introducing American and European goods, the missionaries do not do such things at all, except in rare individual instances as a matter of personal friendship, or, perhaps, to prevent an extortionate profit by an unscrupulous trader. It is grossly unjust to charge mercenary motives upon a whole body of self-denying men and women simply because three or four gave such assistance as has been indicated in the earlier years of the work.

14. "Wise foreigners avoid employing native Christians." A certain traveller returned from Korea with this dictum, declaring that in employing servants, "it is safer in every case to take men who are not converts." Inquiry showed that his reason lay in the refusal of his Christian servants to minister to his intemperance and lust and to submit to his brutality.

"Converts make poorer servants than heathen" only for those foreigners who abuse them or want them to aid in evil things. Why should it injure a Korean to stop worshipping demons and to begin worshipping the true God; to renounce drunkenness, immorality and laziness, and become a sober, moral and industrious citizen? The fact is that native Christians in Asia and Africa are the very best element in the population. In all our travels in Asia, we had no trouble with native servants, Christian or otherwise; and we did not "curse" or "flog" them either, as the traveller in question says that he was frequently obliged to do.

We grant that not all natives educated in mission schools turn out well. Some show inordinate vanity and some absorb the intellectual benefits of a school without yielding to its spiritual influences. Even so, most of these men are better for their missionary training. Undoubtedly, however, some are not; but this is only saying what is true of the very best of home colleges. Many of the idle and dissolute rich of London and New York, some of the most unscrupulous commercial and political leaders and a fair proportion of the swindlers and adventurers of England and America are college graduates; but no sensible person on that account condemns our home colleges.

15. "Missionaries buy or kidnap native children for their schools." "They do more harm than good." "They are a positive evil." "They are the most futile and the most costly failure in modern history." "Natives who have never come in contact with the missionary are more honest and moral than those who had been under missionary influence." "We should not deceive ourselves by attempting to believe that our religion benefits those who have not been born to it." These criticisms were actually printed in a New York newspaper. A gentleman, not a missionary, replied that he had been a student of missions for nearly forty years, that he had read much in behalf of them and against them and had visited

and inspected Christian missions all over Asia, and that he did not remember ever to have seen compressed within an equal space so much ignorance, prejudice and misrepresentation on the subject as in this criticism. We might say of such critics what Mr. Dooley said of a certain young man: "If he knew a little more, he would be half-witted." Perhaps it would be unkind to speak harshly of this class of objectors. To borrow the words of Ruskin: "They deserve the respect due to honest, hopeless, helpless imbecility. There is something exalted in the innocence of their feeble-mindedness. One cannot suspect them of partiality, for it implies feeling; nor of prejudice, for it implies some previous acquaintance with their subject. I do not know that even in this age of charlatanry, I could point to a more barefaced instance of imposture on the simplicity of the public, than the insertion of these pieces of criticism in a respectable periodical. We are not insulted with opinions on music from persons ignorant of its notes; nor with treaties on philology by persons unacquainted with the alphabet; but here is page after page of criticism, which one may read from end to end, looking for something which the writer knows, and finding nothing."[1]

It is hardly worth while for the friends of missions to reply to such critics. "Do you think I don't understand," said Oliver Wendell Holmes, "what my friend, the Professor, long ago called the hydrostatic paradox of controversy? Don't know what that means? Well, I will tell you. You know that if you had a bent tube, one arm of which was of the size of a pipe-stem and the other big enough to hold the ocean, water would stand at the same height in one as in the other. Controversy equalizes fools and wise men in the same way, and the fools know it."

16. "Single women missionaries often create scandal by ignoring native ideas as to propriety." A Mr. Sidney Brooks

---

[1] "Modern Painters," 1: XXI.

says that "the Chinese cannot for a moment be brought to believe that women who worship in the same church alongside of men can possibly be moral." Even Lord Curzon, who expresses a high opinion of the missionary's "devotion and self-sacrifice, his example of pious fortitude, the influence of the education and culture thus diffused in kindling the softer virtues and in ameliorating the conditions of life," adds: "In a country like China, the institution of sisterhoods planted alongside of male establishments, the spectacle of unmarried persons of both sexes residing and working together both in public and in private, and of girls making long journeys into the interior without responsible escort, are sources of a misunderstanding at which the pure-minded may afford to scoff, but which in many cases has more to do with anti-missionary feeling in China than any amount of national hostility or doctrinal antagonism."[1] Lord Curzon was probably not referring to Protestants, for they do not "plant" "sisterhoods" "alongside of male establishments," nor do their "girls" "make long journeys without responsible escorts." It is admitted that single women missionaries of mature age, in the security of their own conscious rectitude and humanity of purpose, occasionally make journeys to outlying villages to teach classes of Chinese women or to visit the sick, and that some prurient Chinese or foreigner may comment unfavourably upon it; but it is inexcusable that any decent white man should reiterate such sneers. Nor are the Chinese so much offended by these things as some have alleged. In all China, there is no such thing as a separate temple or a separate hour of worship for women. Men and women go to the temples together, as men and women go to churches in Europe and America. The Hon. Charles Denby was in China long enough to know, and he wrote: "Much has been said about sending ladies as missionaries. Possibly, if I had never seen the ladies at work, I might agree with these critics,

[1] "Problems of the Far East."

but the truth is that they do the hardest part and the most of the work in China. The teaching of the children and the nursing and treating of the sick women and children, surgical and medical, fall to their lot. I have not space to praise them here, and I could not say sufficient good of them if I had."

17. "Missionaries are forcing another civilization on lands which already have civilizations of their own that are adapted to their needs."[1] No other objection is more common and no other is more baseless. A higher type of civilization does indeed follow the labours of the missionaries;[2] but this is an incidental result, not an object. Even if it were otherwise, Colonel Denby expresses the opinion that "if by means of gentle persuasion we can introduce western modes and methods into China, we are simply doing for her what has been done, in one way or another, for every nation on the globe."[3]

18. "Revealing to the heathen the higher standards of Christianity only increases their moral responsibility." It has been well rejoined that if we did nothing in this world by preaching the gospel but increase the sense of moral responsibility, we should be doing a good thing. That sense is so wanting among the peoples of Asia and Africa that indulgence is given free reign and efforts to check abuses receive little response. It would be an enormous gain if a keen sense of moral responsibility could be aroused. Christ does this. Moreover, He gives the power which is needed to meet the higher demands. Everywhere the gospel purifies the purpose and strengthens the moral fibre. Many a man who knows better than to yield to sin, but who lacks the ability to fight it, finds in Christ the help that he needs. To say that we should withhold this help from multitudes lest we add to the condemnation of

---

[1] Cf. Chapter II and XIV, also "New Forces in Old China," pp. 31, 32 126 sq., 327, 328, 354, 355.

[2] Cf. Chapter II.

"China and Her People," p. 233.

some who will refuse to accept it is like arguing that the sun is injurious to the world because its light and warmth hasten the decay of dying vegetation.

19. "The religions of other races are good enough for them." Then they are "good enough" for us, for the peoples of "other races" are our fellow men, with the needs of our common humanity. We have not heard, however, of any critic who believes that Islam and Hinduism and Buddhism are "good enough" for Europeans and Americans, and we have scant respect for the Phariseeism which asserts that they will suffice for the Persians and East Indians and Chinese. The fact is that the best of the ethnic faiths have utterly failed to produce high character or social purity. The people of India are undoubtedly the most religious of all non-Christian peoples, but Kipling, who knows the country as well as any white man living, says: "What's the matter with this country (India) is not in the least political, but an all-round entanglement of physical, social, and moral evils and corruptions, all more or less due to the unnatural treatment of women. It is right here where the trouble is, and not in any political consideration whatever. The foundations of their life are rotten, utterly rotten. The men talk of their rights and privileges! I have seen the women that bear these very men, and again, may God forgive the men."

The Chinese are considered one of the strongest of the non-Christian races, but Chang Chih-tung, Viceroy of Hupeh and Hunan, wrote with sorrow of "lethargy," "sensuality and vice." He laments the ignorance and corruption of many officials and the lack of anything to stimulate the mind. He criticises the "bugaboo of custom," and a conservatism "stuck in the mud of antiquity," and he frankly adds: "Confucianism, as now practiced, is inadequate to lift us from the present plight."[1] The Emperor himself recognized the justice

---

[1] "China's Only Hope," pp. 74, 75, 95, 96, 123 and 145.

of this characterization, for he declared in an Imperial Rescript that he had "carefully inspected the volume" and that "it embodies a fair and candid statement of facts." Answering a question whether it is worth while to send foreign teachers to supplant the old religions by Christianity, Colonel Denby wrote: "As Buddhism undoubtedly exercises a salutary influence on the national life of China, so the introduction of Christianity now will instruct, improve and elevate the Buddhists. The adoption of Christianity means to the Chinese a new education. He becomes mentally regenerate. He abandons senseless and hoary superstitions. His reasoning powers are awakened. He learns to think. The world has not yet discovered any plan for the spreading of civilization which is comparable to the propagation of Christianity."

It is difficult to understand how an American or European, who inherits all the blessings of our Christian faith, can deny those blessings to the rest of the world. Christianity found the white man's ancestors in the forests and swamps of northern Europe, considerably lower in the scale of civilization than the Chinese and Japanese of to-day. Jerome wrote that when "a boy, living in Gaul, he beheld the Scots, a people in Britain, eating human flesh; though there were plenty of cattle and sheep at their disposal, yet they would prefer a ham of the herdsman or a slice of the female breast as a luxury." The gospel of Christ brought us out of the pit of barbarism. Why should we doubt its power to do for other races what it has done for ours? The notion that each nation's religion is best for it and should therefore not be disturbed is never made by those who have a proper understanding of Christianity or of its relation to the race. It is based upon the old paganism which believed that each tribe had its own god who was its special champion against all the other gods. Such an idea is not only false in itself, but it is directly contrary to the teachings of Christ, who declared that His gospel was for all men and that it was the supreme duty of His followers to carry it to all men.

20. "We have no right to force ourselves upon other peoples." Why, then, did we do it in politics and commerce? Why did western nations force diplomatic intercourse upon Asia at the mouth of the cannon? Why did they send soldiers to shoot down the natives who protested against the building of railways by foreign companies? Why did they force opium upon China in a bloody war? Why did they send regiments and gunboats to support their traders who were alarming the natives by digging for minerals and by introducing foreign goods which drove multitudes into ruin? Western peoples have taught Asiatics and Africans how to form trusts and labour unions, to swear and drink whiskey and to kill one another by the wholesale. Shall they not teach them also how to be honest and pure and temperate and merciful? "Force our religion upon them?" We are not forcing it upon them. No native is obliged to become a Christian against his will. The missionary simply offers and explains the gospel. Surely he has as much right to do this as English and American manufacturers have to offer and explain their flour and cotton and machinery and liquor.

"To talk to persons who choose to listen; to throw open wide the doors of chapels where natives who desire may hear the Christian faith explained and urged upon their attention; to sell at half-cost or to give the Bible and Christian literature freely to those who may care to read; to heal the sick without cost; to instruct children whose parents are desirous that they should receive education—surely none of these constitute methods or practices to which the word 'force' may be applied, under any allowable use of the English language."[1]

21. "It is much more expensive to convert a heathen than a white man." Shylocks, who grudge their scanty doles to missions, never weary of computing the money cost of converting non-Christians. Their comparisons overlook the fact that the

[1] The Hon. Chester Holcombe.

convert in America is the product, not only of the local church to which he belongs, but of the Christian forces of the whole community and of centuries of Christian teaching. The society developed by Christianity, all the multiform and allied activities of the Christian Church, have had a part in the influences which lead an individual to Christ. Few of us realize how many spiritual influences operate upon us. The expenditure represented by those influences rises into millions of dollars. The cost of producing a convert at home is therefore many times greater than on the foreign field, where the institutions of Christianity are simpler and less expensive.

Consider, too, that in every enterprise there is an initial stage in which large returns are not to be expected. Dr. Nevius planted some apple seeds in his garden at Chefoo, China. He did not of course expect apples the first year, or the second; and when a dozen apples did appear, it would have been foolish for him to divide all the toil and expense of the first five years by the small number of apples and exclaim that the effort did not pay. He anticipated, what is now actually the fact, that those apple seeds would become an orchard, bearing abundant fruit every season. Each of the thousands of apples of to-day is, in a sense, a product of all the preceding years. So it is in mission work. The fruits have begun to appear, but they will be far more numerous in the future than in the past.

We can meet the critic, however, on his own ground. Some years ago, a Chicago editor said that in the forty leading churches of Chicago, the average cost of each convert varies from $580.00 in the Congregational Church, to $285.00 in the Baptist, while the cost of converts by their foreign missionary societies averages $194.00 each. Counting annual expenditures alone, each Presbyterian convert in America represents a disbursement of $260.00 while on the foreign field each convert represents only $158.00; that is, it costs Presbyterians sixty-five per cent. more to convert a man at home than abroad. The principal of a famous school for negroes in the

The Missionary and His Critics 349

United States says that it requires $200,000 a year to maintain it; but a Christian university in China, which is doing quite as important a work, does not get a quarter of that income. It takes more to maintain a single one of our great universities at home than the Presbyterian Board spends in maintaining the 2,279 schools and colleges under its care on the foreign field. Dr. George F. Pentecost declares that "the fruits on foreign missionary fields are from twice to ten times greater, in proportion to the means expended, than at home."

But, after all, we do not estimate other things in this way. It costs $100.00 to fire a twelve-inch gun; but no one complains when several hundred thousand dollars' worth of ammunition is used every year for target practice. Americans eat $14,000,000 worth of turkeys at Thanksgiving, and in a year pay for poultry and eggs $560,000,000; but no one objects. The women of the United States spend $25,000,000 annually for kid gloves. Chewing gum absorbs four times as much every year as foreign missions and candy eight times as much; but regarding expenditures of this kind the voice of the critic is silent. The money that our largest denomination puts into foreign missions would not build a second class war vessel, or run a metropolitan newspaper half a year, or keep young people in soda water for a month. If we ungrudgingly pay such prices for other things, how much ought we to pay for souls?

Moreover, what shall be said of the purifying influence of Christian ideals in the community—the uplifting of woman, the abolition of slavery and infanticide, the inculcation of higher moral standards, the growth of the spirit of charity and sympathy. Can the value of these blessings be computed in dollars and cents? When Christian men persuaded the King of Siam to abolish gambling and slavery, was not a result achieved that was worth all the missionary expenditure in Siam for a generation, even if no converts at all had been made? When some shipwrecked sailors, who feared that they had fallen among cannibals, heard one of their comrades shout: "Come on, lads, it's all right; I see a church!" their immediate feeling of safety testified more eloquently than words to the meaning of foreign missionary work.

How much is a soul worth anyway? " Ye were redeemed, not with corruptible things, with silver or gold, . . . but with precious blood, . . . even the blood of Christ."[1] He did not count the cost, and shall we haggle about the expense of saving others for whom He died and for whose salvation He gave us what money we have?

We protest against this method of computing the cost of converts not only as belittling, but as essentially false. It is materialism in its meanest form. It comes from the spirit which prompted Satan to sneer that Job served God for gain, and which inspired Judas Iscariot to complain that the alabaster box might have been sold for three hundred pence and given to the poor. Are selfishness and greed to dominate everything? Must we buy our love, sell our faith and measure our hope with a yardstick? Is there to be no effort without worldly reward? Even if it were true that foreign mission work is comparatively expensive, what of it? War always costs money. Nations never count it in their conflicts. America spent $482,000,000 in the short war with Spain and the World War cost $37,873,908,499. Why should the Church be parsimonious in this most gigantic and God-inspired of all wars? Instead of apologizing that they have spent so much, it is the frankly-avowed intention of the boards to spend more, for not only is the work growing, but its growth enlarges the scale of expenditure. The pioneer evangelist preaching is the cheapest of all; but with converts must come schools, hospitals, printing presses and a variety of institutions which are always and everywhere the necessary concomitants of a Christian community and which require large sums. We believe that the churches will sustain the boards in this policy, and that while

---

[1] 1 Peter 1: 18.

they will continue to demand reasonable care in administration, they will shame the critic who parades an objection worthy only of a Shylock.

22. "Missionaries are accomplishing very little." This objection might fairly offset the objection that missionaries are making revolutionary changes. Both cannot be true. The fact is that missionary work is remarkably successful and more so now than ever before. An influential Chinese, Ng Poon Chew, declares that "the success of mission work among our people is not an open question, but is an accomplished fact. Every fair-minded person who has investigated for himself comes to no other conclusion."

A sceptical white trader gained some useful information as to the benefits of missionary effort when he sneeringly said to a Fiji chief: "It is really a pity that you have been so foolish as to listen to the missionaries." The chief retorted: "Do you see that great stone over there? On that stone we smashed the heads of our victims. Do you see that oven yonder? In that oven we roasted the human bodies for our great feasts. Now, if it hadn't been for the good missionaries, we should have killed you, roasted you in yonder oven and have feasted upon you in no time."

The justification of foreign mission effort is not dependent upon tabulated results, but it is nevertheless interesting to note them. The natural presumptions would be that Christianity would make very slow progress in a heathen land, for it is regarded with suspicion as an alien faith. It is opposed by a powerful priesthood and at variance with long-established customs. Family ties, social position, caste prejudice, combine to keep one from confessing Christ. The persecution of converts is common and some can speak of dungeons languished in and point to welts and scars which tell of agony endured for Christ. It is literally true in many fields that Christ sets "a man at variance against his father, and the daughter against her mother," and that "a man's foes 'are' those of his own household." Few will suffer these things save under strong conviction of duty. It would not be reasonable, therefore, to expect as high a percentage of increase as at home, where centuries of Christian work have prepared the soil and created an atmosphere, where Christianity is popular and worldly motives blend with religious to attract men to the Church.

But what are the comparative facts? The government census in India shows that while the population increased one and a half per cent., the Protestant church membership increased fifty per cent. The gain in China was from 112,808 in 1900 to 446,631 in 1929. In 1886, the Korea missionaries reported the first baptism. Seven years later, there were only about 100 in the whole country. In 1927 there were 106,884 communicants, and 137,402 enrolled catechumens, children and other adherents. Not all mission fields have been as fruitful as these, but the general rate of progress is high. A typical denominational board in a recent year reported more baptisms on the foreign field than in the largest state of its home constituency. "The influence of Jesus Christ was never so widespread, so penetrating, and so transforming as it is to-day. It is impossible to furnish accurate figures, but it is probably a conservative estimate, based on such returns as are available, to say that fully twenty millions of men and women in non-Christian areas of Asia and Africa are now looking to Christ for guidance, for redemption, and for power infinitely greater than human, where there were less than two millions looking Christward thirty years ago."[1]

Nor do such comparisons tell the whole truth. Take, for example, the board which reports 1,491 foreign missionaries and 152,387 communicants on the foreign field. It would be unfair to divide 152,387 by 1,491 in order to get an idea of

---

[1] John R. Mott, *The Present-Day Summons to the World Mission of Christianity*, pp. 49–50.

results. The dividend should be increased by adding a large number of catechumens who wish to be baptized and who would have been baptized ere this if they lived in America. We should add, too, converts who have died, for if a missionary baptizes sixty persons and buries ten, he reports an increase of fifty; and yet those who died were as truly converts as those who lived. While these considerations increase the dividend, others diminish the divisor. Of the 1,491 missionaries, over a hundred were recruits who were learning the language and, therefore, had no part in the work of the year. Two hundred and ninety were at home on furlough or sick leave, leaving a force on the field of only 1,171. About one-third of these were wives, some of whom did full missionary work, but others of whom were obliged to devote most of their time to the care of their children and households. Some of the men, too, had to spend much time in erecting buildings; while others, both men and women, had to teach schools, conduct hospitals, dispensaries and printing presses, supervise the large number of churches and institutions, and perform many other duties from which home pastors are usually free. These changes in dividend and divisor greatly increase the quotient.

It is, therefore, unjust to estimate the missionary's success by simply dividing the number of converts by the number of missionaries. We do not forget that some of the factors mentioned, such as illness and teaching, diminish to some extent the evangelistic force at home; but after making all due allowances, the remarkable fact remains that in spite of the advantages in Europe and America—historic associations, favourable public opinion, splendid churches, numerous workers—Christianity is making more rapid progress on the foreign field than in the home field. We have been working in foreign lands only about a hundred years, in most fields far less than this, and yet the number of converts is already greater than the number of Christians in the Roman Empire at the end of the first century. No other work in the world is so successful and no other yields such large returns for the expenditures made.

"To sneer at missionaries," said Canon Farrar,—"a thing so cheap and so easy to do—has always been the fashion of libertines and cynics and worldlings. So far from having failed, there is no work of God which has received so absolute, so unprecedented a blessing. To talk of missionaries as a failure is to talk at once like an ignorant and faithless man."

XVII

THE REAL STRAIN OF MISSIONARY LIFE

THE physical hardships of missionary life are less than are commonly supposed. Steam and electricity have materially lessened the isolation that was once so trying. Mail, which a generation ago arrived only once in six months, now comes once or twice a week. Swift steamers bring many conveniences of civilization that were formerly unobtainable. The average missionary has a comfortable house and sufficient food and clothing. His labours, too, have been lightened in important respects by the toil of his predecessors. He finds languages reduced to written form, text-books to aid him in his studies and a variety of substantial helps of other kinds.

Experience too, has taught many things as to the care of health. A generation ago, it was not at all uncommon for a missionary to break down because he did not know how to live amid tropical conditions. But now the young missionary finds older men who can advise him as to what he should eat and drink, the clothing he should wear, the sanitary precautions he should adopt, the kinds of exposure he should avoid and where and how he should build his house. The boards have learned how to care for missionaries, what salaries they ought to have, what buildings to provide for them, what furloughs they ought to take and what medical and surgical attendance is required. Still further, in most lands beginnings of work have been made and foundations firmly laid. Churches and schools and hospitals have been established. A Christian literature has been created and the people have become more or less accustomed to the presence of the foreigner and to the work for which he has come. The lot of the missionary is therefore easier than it was a generation ago. Indeed from the viewpoint of physical hardship, the missionary in some of the large cities of Asia is quite as well off as the average Christian worker at home.

There are many fields, however, where conditions are not so pleasant. Those who complain of a London or New York August can hardly realize the meaning of an India hot season when life is almost unendurable by night as well as by day for months at a time. Kipling represents an English civil engineer as breaking down and dying under the fearful tension of circumstances amid which many a missionary uncomplainingly lives. The western world is appalled by a case of bubonic plague on an arriving ship, and it frantically quarantines and disinfects everything and everybody from the suspected country; but during all those awful months when plague raged unchecked in India, the missionaries steadily toiled at their posts. We are panic-stricken if cholera is reported in New York harbour or yellow fever in New Orleans; but cholera nearly always prevails in Siam, and yellow fever in Brazil, while smallpox is so common in many heathen lands that it does not cause remark. Sanitation means much to the Anglo-Saxon; but, save in Japan, the Asiatic knows little about it and the African nothing at all. What would be the condition of an American city if there were no sewers or paved streets, if all garbage were left to rot in the sun and all offal thrown into the streets? That is actually the condition in the villages of Africa and in most of the cities of Asia, except where the foreigner has forced the natives to clean up. Several years ago, a Methodist bishop solemnly affirmed that he identified seventy-two distinct smells in Peking. The city is cleaner now, but it cannot be called sanitary yet, while the native cities of Chefoo and Shanghai appall the visitor by their nastiness. Everywhere in the interior, vermin literally swarms in the native inns, and usually in the homes of the people. A missionary found sixty fleas on her dress after an afternoon's evangelistic work in Persia. A tent in the Brazilian forest is an attractive place after a weary day; but the traveller may be awakened by the sensation of a thousand hot needles, for the red ants have come to see him. A Siam itinerating tour will take one among stately palms and luxuriant tropical vegetation; but it is well to examine shoes and clothing in the morning, lest a scorpion or centipede may have taken possession of them in the night. India presents the wonders of "the gorgeous East"; but it also presents snakes that it is difficult to keep out of the house. They cozily cuddle in the bed. They boldly crawl into open drawers and coil themselves about exposed rafters. Mr. Goheen of Kohlapur rose one night to get a drink of water and found a cobra lying on the floor just where he must have stepped on it if he had not taken the precaution to carry a light and to walk circumspectly. Syria is supposed to be one of the most attractive of all missionary lands, but Dr. Mary Pierson Eddy wrote from one of her tours: "The people are all sleeping in booths on stilts over their flat roofs because the houses are not safe—scorpions, snakes and centipedes are so numerous. I measured a snake brought to me yesterday and it lacked half an inch of seven feet! We went to take the bandages out of the box of supplies and found a centipede five inches long. No one dares move along our terrace here, even to go to the spring, without a stout stick. Saturday I was about to mount my horse and the man holding my bridle bade me wait a moment while he killed a snake not two feet from me. Every kind of crawling insect, bug and beetle abounds here."

Mr. E. J. Glave, the English traveller, wrote of life in Africa: "Big moths flutter noisily about your lamp or try to commit suicide in your soup, leaving the fluff of their wings floating on the surface. The jigger burrows into your flesh, and starts in to raise a family in a little white bag beneath your skin. The large brown driver ant marches in swarms of millions, with giant ants as leaders and officers, devouring everything they meet from a grasshopper to a goat. They will enter your house; no matter how well filled your larder was before the visit, it will contain nothing but bones afterwards. The white ant destroys your most valuable property, your best trunks, your favourite shoes. In one night, he will so attack a wooden box that when you lift it in the morning the bottom will drop out; he will eat a living eucalyptus tree, and when he is in the district, the poles of your house in a few months' time will crumble into dust. Large beetles come from long distances to see you, and end their journey by striking you in the face. Many insects of smaller calibre settle on your neck, and when you try to brush them off, sneak down your back."

These discomforts do not occur everywhere, nor every day in any place; but they are common enough in many fields to make life far from pleasant. The missionaries usually laugh at them as of minor consequence. We refer to them only because some imagine that missionary life is now a very comfortable one.

But while the physical hardships are less than are commonly supposed, the mental hardships are greater.

First among these, is loneliness. This is not felt so much in the port cities, for there are foreign communities, occasional visitors and frequent communication with the rest of the world. And yet even there, it is pathetic to see how eager not only missionaries but other Americans are to see a visitor. After a hard day's work in a certain capital, we dined with a friend to whom we had brought letters of introduction, but as we were very tired, we rose at ten o'clock. Our host implored us so urgently to stay longer that we did so; but an attempt to leave at eleven brought such importunities not to go that again we yielded. Along towards midnight, we felt that we simply must leave; but as we were still urged to stay, we said that we were greatly enjoying the evening, but that we had spent a wearisome day and that we were to have another to-morrow. Our host apologized for having kept us, but pathetically added: "If you only knew how hungry we get over here for a chance to talk to some one

The Real Strain of Missionary Life

from home, you would understand what it means to have a visitor come."

In many places on that tour, our arrival caused as much excitement as a baby in an old-time mining camp on the American frontier. This, of course, was not due to anything in us, but simply to the fact that we were travellers from the loved native land. "Just think," exclaimed one missionary, "friends from home have actually come to see us!" Our hosts were willing to bear indulgently with all our weaknesses, on the principle, we suppose, of the miner who protested against the request of a minister that a mother should take a wailing child out of the church on the ground that he had not heard a baby's voice for twenty years and that he would rather hear that baby cry than to hear all the sermons the minister could preach.

How few of us who daily gaze indifferently upon our country's flag at home can appreciate the thrill of the missionary who sees that flag flying in Asia or Africa. When we saw it streaming from the flag-pole of the American Consulate in Canton, we thought it the most beautiful object in the world. A moving scene can be witnessed on the Lunetta in Manila almost any evening. It is a spacious and beautiful park, bordering the blue waters of the harbour. Throngs of gaily dressed people and uniformed soldiers and sailors stroll about, while the official and wealthy ride in handsome equipages. The military band plays inspiring airs to which nobody pays special attention. There is a babel of laughing and chatting voices. Suddenly the band strikes up "Home, Sweet Home." Instantly a hush falls upon the throng. Men stop in the midst of half-uttered jests. Laughter dies away while the strains sweetly sound through the evening air. The gaiety of the evening is at an end and the crowd silently wends its way homeward.

Nansen, in his journal of his travels in the Arctic regions, reveals the pathetic fact that he and his men conquered every obstacle which the far North could offer, except the sentimental one of homesickness. They had every comfort which money could buy. They successfully withstood hunger and cold and dreaded ice floe. "But the one enemy they could not down was homesickness. Half their labours and three-fourths of their amusements were to escape the clutch which threatened to stifle the heart. They celebrated the king's birthday, their own birthdays, the ship's birthday, and even the birthdays of their dogs, all to drown remembrance and simulate happiness. Nansen confesses in his journal that there were evenings when, had they relaxed for a moment their efforts to keep up their spirits, they would have broken down in tears like children away at a school. No little time was spent by the stout captain himself writing in his journal dreams of home, and again and again he exclaims that all the honours of the schools and all the plaudits of the world are not worth the price he pays in his isolation. In the midst of their boisterous horse-play, those great-limbed Norsemen looked into each other's eyes and grew suddenly still; for each read in another's face what he felt in his own heart, the desperate 'Heimweh,' that like some neuralgia of the vital organs threatened to crush out life itself with its remorseless hand."[1] Yet Nansen and his associates had no thought of being away for more than two or three years. The missionary, save for an occasional furlough, isolates himself for life.

The reports of army surgeons in the Philippines, during the war of occupation, included in the list of diseases of which soldiers died "nostalgia"—homesickness. The correspondent of the New York *Tribune* wrote, even from Cuba: "Aside from the illness that is incidental to acclimation, the trouble among the soldiers is chiefly mental rather than physical. The men, more or less enervated by the climate and deprived of communication with their homes and families, worry, grow despondent and sicken from suspense. Homesickness seems to be

[1] *The Interior.*

the chief ailment of the majority of those who are in quarters' hospitals. It is a common thing to see daily one or more of the soldier lads break down and cry like children. They just cannot help it."

This was in a campaign of only a few months and so near home as Cuba. Imagine, then, what must be the nervous strain, the nostalgic agony of devoted missionaries, women as well as men, amid far more uncongenial surroundings and for a far longer term of service. Letters from home friends, which were at first numerous, gradually become less frequent, till relatives and board secretaries become almost the only correspondents and the lonely missionary feels that he is forgotten by the world of which he was once a part, "out of sight, out of mind." He is not forgotten, for many at home follow him with sympathy and prayer; but it is not very easy for him to realize this when he is immersed in an African jungle or in the depths of a South American wilderness.

At home, too, while we are conscious of a downward pressure, we are also conscious of a sustaining and uplifting force. Few of us realize to what an extent we are upborne by environment. There is everything to buoy us up—the companionship of friends, the restraints of a wholesome public sentiment, and the inspiration of many meetings and conferences. We are situated morally, as one is sometimes situated physically in a crowd, so wedged in that he cannot fall. But on the foreign field there is little to hold one up and much to push him down. There is no public Christian sentiment to sustain, few associations to cheer, no support from large numbers of neighbouring friends and ministers. The home pastor has his church officers for counsel, but many a missionary must carry heavy responsibility almost unaided. It is desperately hard to stand alone, and the missionary must often stand alone. As for the natives, whatever their excellencies, they are so radically different not only in language, but in manners and customs and prejudices that it may be difficult to find congenial companionships among them. Many customs of the country are against him; all its standards below him. He receives little, but is expected to give everything. There is a constant strain upon his sympathies and his spiritual vitality, with scanty external support for his own spiritual life. The tendencies are down, down, always down. The man who lives in an interior city of Asia or Africa may be compared to the workmen who toiled in the caissons of the great bridge over the East River, New York, where the pressure of the unnatural atmosphere affected the heart and lungs and imagination to the point of utter collapse. In the words of Benjamin Kidd:

"In climatic conditions which are a burden to him; in the midst of races in a different and lower stage of development; divorced from the influences which have produced him, from the moral and political environment from which he sprang, the white man does not in the end, in such circumstances, tend so much to raise the level of the races amongst whom he has made his unnatural home, as he tends himself to sink slowly to the level around him. In the tropics, the white man lives and works only as a diver lives and works under water. Alike in a moral, in an ethical, and in a political sense, the atmosphere he breathes must be that of another region than that which produced him and to which he belongs. Neither physically, morally, nor politically, can he be acclimatized in the tropics. The people among whom he lives and works are often separated from him by thousands of years of development."[1]

Then there is the weary monotony of missionary life. The novelty of new scenes soon wears off, and the missionary is confronted by prosaic realities. It is impossible for the minister in the United States to understand the depressing sameness of life in the interior of China. The few associates of the missionary are subject to the debilitating influences which depress him. It is difficult for any woman in America to know what it

[1] "Control of the Tropics."

The Real Strain of Missionary Life 363

means for Mrs. A to live from one year's end to another without seeing another white woman except Mrs. B, who, though a devoted missionary, is not exactly the person that Mrs. A would have chosen for an intimate associate if she had been consulted. We at home can choose our friends, and if Mr. X is not congenial, we do not have to be intimate with him; but abroad, there is no choice. The missionary must accept the intimacy of the family assigned to his station whether he likes it or not.

The separation from children is harder still. There comes a time in the life of every missionary parent when he realizes that he cannot properly educate his child amid the appallingly unfavourable conditions of a heathen land. Schools for foreign children may not be within reach, and local schools are usually out of the question, not only on account of the language and curriculum, but of the different moral standards of native children. Some mothers have learned to their grief and dismay that it is not even safe to leave children in the care of native women nurses. The whole tone of society is so low that it is all that the missionary can possibly do to keep himself up to the level of the home land. Indeed, he is painfully conscious that he frequently fails to do it, and that one of the urgent necessities of a furlough is not so much to get physical rest, as to tone himself up again mentally and spiritually in a Christian atmosphere. What then can be expected for his immature child but degeneration? There is deep meaning in Edward Judson's dedication of his "Life of Adoniram Judson:" "To the children of missionaries, the involuntary inheritors of their parents' sufferings and rewards."

The average missionary therefore must send children to the home land to be educated. This can easily be done, in one sense. So far as physical care, moral surroundings and educational opportunities are concerned, the missionaries' children can be well provided for in either England or America. But we hope that none of the mothers who read these pages will ever have occasion to know what a heart strain is involved in placing ten thousand miles in distance and years in time between a parent and a child. There are chambers of the human heart that are never opened save by a baby's hand. There are experiences in life that are never felt until the voice of a child is heard. After the tendrils of the soul's affection have wound round that child, after the baby hand has been felt on the face, the baby smile has appealed to the eye, and the little one's life has literally grown into that of the parent, separation is a fearful wrench.

Many missionary mothers feel that they cannot endure it, and when the time comes for the education of their children, they go home with them. This brings the husband face to face with the crisis of his life. Shall he go, too, or shall he remain on the field without wife and children? There is a growing feeling among missionaries that it is not right for them to resign for such a reason, that the separation of families is a probability of the missionary career which should be frankly faced before going to the field, and that after one has voluntarily applied for appointment, has accepted it and has been maintained by the Church at heavy expense during the years of language study and missionary immaturity, it is not fair to the home Church or to his colleagues or to Christ to lay down his work just as he has come to that stage of experience when he is most useful. The missionary rightly feels that his enlistment was for life, and that nothing but ill-health or the judgment of the board and his associates as to the expediency of his retirement can justify him in turning back after he has once set his hand to the plow. The soldiers and sailors of our country separate themselves from their families for years at a time, and shall the soldier of the Cross do less?

The decision of the husband that it is his duty to stay with his work brings the wife in turn to a crisis in her life, for she must choose between her husband and her children. Many wives feel that, in view of all the circumstances, it is better for

The Real Strain of Missionary Life

the children to be placed in the care of some relative or in one of the homes for missionaries' children that friends have provided, and for the wife to remain with her husband. All the considerations of the missionary call are supposed to apply to her as well as to him. She, too, knew before she went to the field that sooner or later this very question would probably arise. Her husband and the missionary work need her as much as her children, and her consecration to both husband and work were prior to the coming of children. The lot of the solitary husband on the foreign field is almost as bad as the lot of children separated from parents in America. But how can we criticise any mother who feels that she must choose her children in preference to husband and mission work? The agonies of such a choice are too sacred for others to presume to decide that question. Each husband and wife must settle it for themselves in the secret of their closets before God. Whichever alternative is chosen will probably be well-nigh unbearable.

There is, too, the distress which every sensitive mind feels in looking upon suffering that one is unable to relieve. Sir William Hunter said that there are a hundred millions of people in India who never know the sensation of a full stomach. An equally great number in China live so near starvation that a drought or a flood precipitates an appalling famine. All over Asia, one sees disease and bodily injury so untended, or what is worse, mistended, that the resultant condition is as dreadful as it is intolerable. Dr. John G. Kerr of Canton was so overcome by the sufferings of the neglected insane in that great city that he could not endure them, and when he could not get help from America, he started an asylum at his own risk. Mrs. A. T. Mills of Chefoo felt driven to the same course by the pitiful condition of deaf-mute children. Heathenism is grievously hard on the poor and the sick and the crippled, while the woes of woman in maternity are awful beyond description. Yet, amid such daily scenes, the missionary must live.

Then there is the mental suffering which comes to any pure-minded man or woman in constant contact with the most debasing forms of sin. Most Asiatics have no sense of wrong regarding many of the matters that we have been taught to regard as evil. They are untruthful and immoral. The first chapter of the Epistle to the Romans is still almost a literal description of heathenism. Its society is utterly rotten, and nowhere else in all Asia is it more licentious than in Japan, which is lauded as the most intelligent and advanced of all Asiatic nations. We do not forget that there is immorality in America, but here it is compelled to lurk in secret places. It is opposed not only by the churches, but by civil law and by public sentiment. In Asia, vice is public and shameless, enshrined in the very temples. We saw the filthiest representations of it in the great Lama Temple in the capital of China. India, which boasts of its "ancient civilization," makes its most sacred places literally reek with vice. The missionary often finds his own motives grossly misjudged by hostile priests and prurient people. The typical Asiatic scoffs at the idea that the missionaries come to him for an unselfish purpose. In many lands, a single man is often misunderstood; a single woman is nearly always misunderstood. Social customs do not provide for the pure unmarried woman, and charges are freely circulated, and sometimes placarded on walls or buildings, in ways that are most trying.

The soul in such an atmosphere feels as if it would suffocate. The pressure of abnormal conditions tends to debilitation. They set nerves on edge and expose to diseases, mental as well as physical. "Many of the missionary's heaviest burdens," observes Lawrence, "are summed up in the one word, whose height and breadth and length and depth none knows so well as he, that word exile. It is not merely a physical exile from home and country and all their interests; it is not only an intellectual exile from all that would feed and stimulate the mind; it is yet more—a spiritual exile from the guidance, the instruc-

The Real Strain of Missionary Life

tion, the correction, from the support, the fellowship, the communion of the saints and the Church at home. It is an exile as when a man is lowered with a candle into foul places, where the noxious gases threaten to put out his light. Yet he must explore it all and find some way to drain off the refuse and let in the sweet air and sun to do their own cleansing work. The missionary is not only torn away from those social bonds which sustain, or even almost compose, our mental, moral and spiritual life, but he is forced into closest relations with heathenism, whose evils he abhors, whose power and fascinations, too, he dreads."

Another phase of the real strain of missionary life is the spiritual burden. To look upon myriads of human beings who are bearing life's loads unaided and meeting life's sorrows unhelped, to offer them the assistance that they need for time and for eternity, and to have the offer fall upon deaf ears —this is a grievous thing. One may stand on the slopes of Tai-shan, the sacred mountain of north China, and look upon almost innumerable villages whose inhabitants do not know that God loves them and that Christ came into the world to save them. The thought of the dull, plodding poverty and wretchedness of those lives, unilluminated by a single ray of hope, gives one an oppressive feeling of what it is to be " without God in the world."

Sorrowful scenes rise to the vision of one who has journeyed through non-Christian lands. The superstitious Koreans toss a stone to the foot of a wayside tree or tie a rag to a branch, in the hope that they may be able to dodge past while the demon of the tree is satisfying his curiosity as to what the stone or rag is. A Hindu woman approaches the hideous, blood-stained image of the goddess Kali, offers a sacrificial lamb and beats her head upon the hard pavement, in the hope that the goddess will reward her by granting her heart's desire for her child. In the capital of enlightened Japan, a suffering woman pitifully rubs her cancerous breast against the corresponding part of a bronze statue in the Temple of Asakusa, in the pathetic belief that she may thus be cured of her malady. In Canton, the proud city of China, another woman is in tears because the bit of paper, which a priest has shaken out of a box in return for her widow's mite, reads bad fortune instead of good. As one recalls these and similar scenes all over Asia, he enters more tenderly into the woe of the Master when He stood on the slope of the Mount of Olives and wept over Jerusalem, stretching out His hands towards the people and crying in the bitterness of His anguish: "Ye will not come unto Me, that ye might have life!"[1] "The travail of His soul!"[2] What does it mean; what tears and agonies and sore cryings? Verily,

> "None of the ransomed ever knew,
> How dark were the waters crossed,
> Nor how dark was the night that the Lord passed through,
> Ere He found His sheep that was lost."

Nothing in the missionary life is harder than this for the man or the woman who has gone to the foreign field from true missionary motives. It is akin to the strain that broke Christ's heart in three years; for it was this that killed Him, and not the nails or the spear.

[1] John 5: 40.   [2] Isaiah 53: 11.

XVIII

THE SPIRIT OF THE MISSIONARY

WE join the missionary in protesting against the impression that he is essentially different from other good men. There is no halo about his head. He is not a saint on a pedestal. He does not stand with clasped hands and uplifted eyes, gazing rapturously into heaven. We have met more than a thousand missionaries, and we have been impressed by the fact that they are neither angels nor ascetics, but able, sensible and devoted Christians workers. The typical missionary is more like a high-grade Christian business man of the homeland than a professional cleric. He is preëminently a man of affairs. He makes no pathetic plea for sympathy for himself, but he wants coöperation in his work and to have people at home feel that the work is theirs as well as his. He unhesitatingly accepts the exhortation of Kipling:

> " Go to your work and be strong, halting not in your ways,
> Balking the end half-won for an instant dole of praise.
> Stand to your work and be wise—certain of sword and pen,
> Who are neither children nor gods, but men in a world of men."

The woman who becomes his wife is like him in the strength and purity of purpose and character. The world does not contain nobler, sweeter women than the wives of missionaries. More sensitively organized than the men, they feel more keenly the loneliness and privations of missionary life. But their courage seldom falters. Indeed, they often nerve their husbands to more resolute effort. When nine years of toil in Bechuana had failed to produce any visible result, Dr. Moffett might have been discouraged if it had not been for his heroic wife; but her faith was so unflinching that, in reply to an inquiry from Mrs. Greaves of Sheffield as to what she needed, she wrote: "Send us a communion service; we shall need it sooner or later." They did, for by the time it arrived, six men were ready to come to the Lord's Table. A wife of that spirit would no more think of giving up than Lincoln, who, when taunted with the defeat of his plans, exclaimed: "Defeat! if it were not one but one hundred defeats, I should still pursue the same unchanging course."

Nor would we withhold the meed of praise from the single woman who goes to the foreign field. We are sometimes solemnly assured that "a man can't stand it to remain single in a heathen land," that "he can't take proper care of himself," and that "he imperatively needs the companionship and sympathy of a helpmeet." And then we think of the hundreds of single women on the mission field, who presumably need companionship and sympathy as much as the men, whose sex places them at a decided disadvantage in many ways, but who manage to "take proper care" of themselves, exhibit energy and self-reliance, do splendid work, and never utter a whimper about the difficulty of living single.

Near Beirut, Syria, there is a region inhabited by fanatical Maronites, who boasted that no Protestant could enter it and live, and who erected a cross to mark the point beyond which neither missionary nor convert must pass. Dr. Mary Pierson Eddy boldly walked into the forbidden territory, rented a house and opened a dispensary. When the furious priests forced the landlord to cancel her lease and no one dared to let her have another house, she coolly brought lumber from Beirut and erected a building of her own. His Holiness, the Maronite Patriarch, angrily protested, but she replied: "There are thousands of Maronites in the United States and the American Christians are not afraid of them. Why should you be afraid of one Christian girl?"

Where is the man who has shown greater courage than Miss

Cameron, who for years has fought the High-binders' traffic in Chinese slave girls in San Francisco? "That shame stood for half a century. Tourists, going through the quarter to admire its picturesque beauty, heard of the traffic from the guides and held up Pharisee hands; but they passed it by on the other side. The police knew of it, lived near it day after day; but they, too, passed it by. The rulers of California and of San Francisco knew it; but slave-women and rescue-workers have no votes, so they debated on railroad oppression and passed it by. The Federal Government heard of it; but Washington is a long way from San Francisco, and Washington passed it by. Only a few women, chief among them a young Scotch-American gentlewoman, passed on the Jericho road and faced down the thieves and gathered in the unfortunates of Chinatown—and behold! the slave-trade in America is no more."[1]

Such women remind us of President Roosevelt's words: "If there is any one thing that I respect more than a good man, it is a good woman. I think she is just a trifle more useful, and she has a harder time in life, and she is a little more entitled to our respect than even the best man."

It is not easy to work in a distant region, unnoticed by the world and without the conveniences of the home-land. But many a missionary does this and makes the best of it. One wrote from Persia: "We have given our lives for the people and work, and our hearts are here. We suffer countless discomforts. We live in houses amid dirt, and often we go hungry because of unpalatable food. We walk in the midst of diseases without numbers. I have come back with the itch and my body broken out in ulcers, showing a run-down system. But we do want to see the Kingdom of God come quickly and the people enlightened in His law."

Some missionaries have given up brilliant prospects at home for a life abroad. Mr. Arthur L. Shumway says that one day

[1] *Everybody's Magazine*, July, 1904.

he was walking the streets of Canton, China, with Mr. Charles Seymour, then American Consul-General, when they passed a quiet, modest looking man. Said Mr. Seymour: "That is Dr. Kerr. He is in charge of the great missionary hospital yonder. The hospital, founded in 1838, has already treated three-quarters of a million patients. I consider that he is the peer of any living surgeon in the world to-day. To my personal knowledge, he undertakes almost daily cases which our most distinguished surgeons at home hesitate to attempt. I suppose that humble man might just as well as not be enjoying an income of from $50,000 to $75,000 a year, instead of his present small salary, if he was only practicing in the city of New York on his own account."

Many a missionary is preaching in the open air to halfnaked Africans, who, if he had stayed at home, might have had a noble church where he could

> ". . . love the high embowed roof,
> With antic pillars massy proof,
> And storied windows richly dight,
> Casting a dim religious light!"[1]

But the true missionary does not make a virtue of these things; rather does he exalt the dignity of his labour. "I like the work immensely," wrote a physician from Hainan. "I would rather wash old leg ulcers daily in my hospital than to be struggling after some worldly fame in the profession at home; for my work here will bring more souls to Christ and help more to advance God's Kingdom."

Sometimes the home Church tries to tempt the missionary by offering him an attractive position; but unless health conditions are involved, the call is usually declined. Dr. Henry H. Jessup, of Syria, who himself refused a secretaryship of his board, voiced the general feeling of the missionary body when he gave the following advice to a company of new missionaries:

[1] Milton, *Il Penseroso*.

"Regard your work as a life-enlistment. You may have offers from home churches or professors' chairs or diplomatic office or lucrative commercial posts, but 'set your face steadfastly' forward. Let it be understood that nothing but the hand of God can separate you from the work. I knew a young missionary who was invited to a theological professorship at home. They said to him: 'We want a man of a genuine missionary spirit in this seminary.' He replied: 'I could not open my mouth on missions if I took this post; for when I would say to the students: 'You ought to go abroad,' they would say: 'Why didn't *you* go?' I would reply: 'I did go.' 'Then why did you return?' 'To take this professorship.' 'Very well, we'll stay and take professorships without all that expense to the churches.'' No man should leave the missionary work unless driven out of it by the clear indications of God's Providence."

When the true missionary finds himself in a hard field, he thinks with Nathan Brown:

> ". . . never was it his design
> Who placed me here, that I should live in ease
> Or drink at Pleasure's fountain.
>   Henceforth then
> It matters not if storm or sunshine be
> My earthly lot, bitter or sweet my cup;
> I only pray, 'God fit me for the work;
> God make me holy, and my spirit nerve
> For the stern hour of strife.'"

Many a missionary is a hero though he knows it not. Abroad, as well as at home, practical, hard-working men and women are sometimes brought face to face with emergencies which demand the highest qualities of wisdom, decision and leadership; and abroad as well as at home, too, men are meeting these emergencies. William Lloyd Garrison has been immortalized because, amid opposition and obliquy, he uttered the words that are inscribed on the pedestal of his statue on Commonwealth Avenue, Boston: "My country is the world;

my countrymen are all mankind. . . . I am in earnest. I will not equivocate. I will not excuse. I will not retreat a single inch, and I will be heard." But hundreds of missionaries have faced hatred, persecution and disease with like indomitable courage. When Judson was lying in a foul jail in Burma, with thirty-two pounds of chains on his ankles and his feet bound to a bamboo pole, a fellow prisoner sneeringly asked: "Dr. Judson, what about the prospect of the conversion of the heathen?" Judson calmly answered: "The prospects are just as bright as the promises of God." Canon Taylor Smith of Sierra Leone, in England on furlough in 1896, was warned of the risk which he ran in going back to his field, but he declared: "If I had ten lives, I would gladly lay them down for Christ in Sierra Leone, the white man's grave, but, by the grace of God, the black man's resurrection." A missionary in a land which is accounted perfectly safe killed a cobra on his piazza, nursed his cook who was dying of bubonic plague, and her son who was dying of cholera—all within twenty-four hours. In a temperature of 130° he made coffins with his own hands and buried the dead that night by the flickering light of a candle. Then he went quietly on with his work, never dreaming that he was doing a heroic thing.

There are martyr's graves in India, China, Africa, Persia, Turkey and the South Sea Islands. In some lands to-day, missionaries are insolently denied the rights guaranteed by treaty to every American citizen. Their property is destroyed, their work hampered, their freedom of movement limited, their very lives menaced.

The critic impatiently asks: "Why do missionaries persist in remaining at their posts, when they know that they are jeopardizing their lives, bringing anxiety to their relatives and embarrassment to their government? Why do they not fly to the safer ports, as the British and American Consuls often advise them to do?"

The Spirit of the Missionary

Why? Partly for the same reason that the Spartans did not retreat at Thermopylæ, that the men of Massachusetts did not run away at Lexington and Bunker Hill, that the engineer does not jump when he sees that death is ahead, that the mother does not think of herself when her boy is stricken with diphtheria. Shall the missionaries leave the native Christians to be scattered, the mission buildings to be destroyed, the labour of years to be undone, the Christian name to be disgraced? The missionary is a soldier; his station is the post of duty. James Chalmers of New Guinea, of whom Robert Louis Stevenson said: "He's as big as a church," and who was finally clubbed to death and eaten by cannibals, declared that "the word 'sacrifice' ought never to be used in Christ's service." And in a speech in Exeter Hall fifteen years before his death, he exclaimed: "Recall the twenty-one years, give me back all its experiences, give me its shipwrecks, give me its standings in the face of death, give it me surrounded with savages with spears and clubs, give it me back with the spears flying about me, with the club knocking me to the ground—give it me back, and I will still be your missionary."

Such missionaries form the "far-flung battle line" of the Church of God. It crosses the mountains of Asia Minor, threads the valleys of Syria and Palestine, traverses the uplands of Arabia and Persia, descends the entire length of China, encircles Korea and Japan and bends around Hainan and the Philippines. It follows the Menam southward to the Gulf of Siam, pierces the plains of India and enters deeply the jungles of Africa; while in the western hemisphere it parallels the Chilean Andes and the Brazilian Cordilleras, runs into Colombia and Venezuela and sweeps through Guatemala and Mexico to California. The patriotism of Briton and American is stirred by the thought that the sun never sets on their dominions; but a holier inspiration should thrill them as they realize that the sun never sets on their missionaries, who journey through heat and cold and dust and mud, burned by the midday sun, drenched by sudden storms, eating unaccustomed food, sleeping in vermin-infested huts, enduring every privation incident to travel in an uncivilized land—and yet, in spite of all, instructing new converts and church officers, settling disputes, visiting the dying, comforting the sorrowing, and above all and in all preaching the glad tidings of the Kingdom of God. It can be truly said of them:

> " There is no place they have not been,
>   The men of deeds and destiny;
> No spot so wild they have not seen,
>   And measured it with dauntless eye.
> They in a common danger shared,
>   Nor shrunk from toil, nor want, nor pain."

Very few points on that long line are adequately manned. Indeed it is a picket, rather than a battle line, and with dangerously wide gaps. There is only a handful of devoted men and women at the average station. They are arrayed against apparently overwhelming foes. Every form of error and superstition, all the vices and follies of the human heart, are backed by the hoary religions of the East, as well as by race prejudice, social custom and hereditary tendency. There, as nowhere else, are "the wiles of the devil" and "the spiritual hosts of wickedness."

We have heard much of the spirit of the British and American soldier and sailor, uncomplainingly eating hardtack and alleged canned roast beef, watching in muddy trenches, soaked with tropical rains, coolly sailing over torpedoes and submarine mines, charging with ringing cheers up the slopes of cannon-crested hills and through fever-breeding swamps. But they had the relief of action, the consciousness of being armed, the pulse-quickening bugle and drum, the sight of thousands of comrades. They were sustained by the knowledge that millions of determined people were ready to give them every possible support, that thousands of newspapers were blazoning their deeds to the world and that prayers were being offered for them in a hundred thousand pulpits and around innumerable family altars. They knew, too, that if they were stricken by bullets or by disease, a grateful and sorrowing nation would revere their memory and care for their loved ones.

But the soldiers of the Cross have few of these outward supports of the soldier. They spend their lives amid the climatic and sanitary conditions which so quickly sapped the vitality of American troops in Cuba and the Philippines. Such silent, invisible foes as cholera and bubonic plague sometimes test the nerves as severely as the whistling of bullets, especially as they menace for months, while a battle lasts only a few days. If a mob forms, the missionary is often alone, far from succour, surrounded by brutal foes, absolutely unarmed, forbidden to fight and scorning to run. To stand calmly at the post of duty in such circumstances and look Death squarely in the face requires fortitude surpassing the demands of any battle-field. When some imperilled British missionaries in Africa declined to desert the native Christians and accept the protection of a ship of war, the admiral in command gazed at them a moment in astonishment. Then, taking off his cap, he exclaimed: "Gentlemen, your courage is magnificent; men have been given the Victoria Cross for less heroism than yours."

And so the forlorn hope of four or five men and women quietly, patiently stand there. A little grayer, a little more careworn, they have what James Lane Allen calls that "stark audacity of faith," that "burning spiritual heroism," which inspire men to wander through the wilderness, "carrying from cabin to cabin, through darkness and snow and storm, the lonely banner of the Christ, and preaching the gospel of everlasting peace to those who had never known any peace on earth."[1] Missionary annals abound with inspiring instances of devotion. The last act of Dr. Eleanor Chesnut, one of the

[1] "The Choir Invisible," p. 80.

martyrs at Lien-chou, China, was to tear off a portion of the skirt of her dress and bind up an ugly gash on the head of a Chinese boy who had been accidentally injured by the mob. The dying words of Mrs. Machle were a plea to her murderers to accept Christ. The last letter of Mr. Peale was such a large-hearted expression of sympathy with the Chinese that the Chinese minister at Washington wrote: "His words seem to me to have a prophetic ring; in his untimely death, America has lost a noble son and China a true friend." The first message of Dr. Machle, after the tragedy which cost the lives of his wife and daughter, was not a demand for revenge, but a vow to consecrate the remainder of his life to the welfare of the Chinese.

Nor does the missionary have the soldier's support at home. Many sneer at him. Some in his own church take no interest in him. Even pastors often forget to pray for him. When the news flashed over the cables that the American army in the Philippines needed reinforcements, long trains of soldiers and supplies thundered to San Francisco and crowded transports and splendid battle-ships sped across the Pacific, till General Otis had the largest army since the Civil War and Commodore Dewey a fleet which was the pride of every patriot. Everybody knows that the valour of soldiers, however great, is not enough; that behind them must be a nation, united, enthusiastic and generous in the conduct of the war; otherwise valour is simply sacrifice. But our Christian army in Asia has been telling the Church for weary years that it is suffering for want of men and supplies. "Hear them begging at home," exclaims Dr. Henry Van Dyke, "these brave, lonely soldiers—for the money to sustain and equip them for the fight. Hear them calling from across the sea for men to help them hold the fort. And then see the Church in Christian lands, rich and increased in goods and in need of nothing, cutting down its contributions and reducing the number of its missionaries!"

And yet how superbly these missionary soldiers fight for God! Some moral triumphs are greater than the physical

The Spirit of the Missionary

victories of war. A medical missionary in Persia refused a palace and a princely income as personal physician to the Shah, saying: "I came to Persia to relieve the distresses of the poor in the name of Jesus." An educator in China declined the high-salaried presidency of an imperial university, giving as his reason: "I want to translate the Bible and to preach the gospel and to train up Christian ministers." An old man in Syria rode horseback eight hours in a wintry storm to administer the communion in a mountain village. Another in Siam pushed his little boat up lonely rivers swarming with crocodiles and tramped through snake and tiger-infested jungles, that he might preach Christ. Still another in Siam forgot his threescore and ten years and made a solitary six months' journey that he might take to distant peoples the tidings of the gospel; twenty-six days he was drenched with dew and rain, ten times he had to swim his pony across rivers, four days he wearily tramped because his horse was too jaded to bear him. A young woman in India walks painfully from house to house under a blazing sun, but writes: "This is delightful work, it is good to be footsore in such a cause." Another in Syria stands in a little gallery of a room containing about ten people, beside cows and goats; the mud floor reeking with dampness, the roof dripping tiny waterfalls of rain, the air heavy with smoke, the missionary herself racked with cough and flushed with fever; but tenderly treating two hundred patients a week and writing: "I am very thankful to record God's goodness to me; I do not believe that ever before into one person's life came such opportunities as I enjoy." A physician in Korea cleanses loathsome ulcers, opens the eyes of the blind and makes the lame to walk. A refined woman in China makes regular visits to a leper colony and ministers lovingly to repulsive sufferers with sightless eyes and rotting limbs.

And then the scene changes and a sick husband in Turkey asks that the photograph of his wife and children may be hung close to his bed, that he might gaze with inexpressible yearning into the faces of far-off dear ones whom he never expects to see again in the flesh. Alfred Marling, seventy miles from a physician, dies in the furnace of African fever, singing:

"How sweet the name of Jesus sounds!"

A mother in a Syrian shed lines a rude box, places in it the still form of her child, sends it away for distant burial; and then goes back to her sick husband and tries to keep up a brave face and not let him know that her heart is breaking. There are little groups of moving people—husbands following to far-off cemeteries the hallowed dust of their wives, widows walking behind the coffins of their husbands, Rachel mothers weeping for their children and "refusing to be comforted because they were not." "Six weeks after my arrival in China," a missionary writes, "my wife, though but shortly before in America adjudged physically sound, died after only a week's illness. The memories of the cold, bleak, January morning when we laid her in that lonely grave upon the hillside will not soon fade from my mind. What a mournful little procession it was that passed through the streets of hostile Tsinan-fu that day! With but half a dozen of my new-found friends, I followed the plain coffin borne by coolies whose jargon seemed all the more unsympathetic because I did not understand it. Oh! the unspeakable desolation that sweeps over a little community such as many of our mission stations are, when death invades its feeble ranks. And then the stifled wail that reëchoed from America three months later!"

Who can think unmoved of that missionary widow, who, when her husband died at an interior station of Siam and there was no place nearer than Bangkok where the body could be buried, caused the coffin to be placed in a native boat, leaving a space eighteen inches wide and eight feet long on each side. She sat on one side and a friend on the other, and the native boatmen pushed the craft out upon the river. That was eight o'clock Friday morning. All day they journeyed under the blazing tropical sun—and the reader can imagine what that meant both to the living and the dead. When darkness fell, the stars surely looked down in pity upon that stricken widow crouching so close to the dead body of her husband that she could not avoid touching his coffin. It was not until two o'clock Saturday afternoon, that the pitiful ride ended at Bangkok. Flesh and blood could not have borne such a strain, if God had not heard the dying petition of the husband, who, foreseeing the coming sorrow, had brokenly prayed: "Lord, help her!"

All along the missionary picket line are the graves of the fallen. Since, two generations ago, Dr. Lowrie buried his wife in India and Mrs. Reed saw her husband's body weighted with shot and lowered into the ocean, hundreds have laid down their lives. When the soldiers of our country die in a foreign land, a grateful nation brings their bodies home at public expense. After the Spanish-American War, a funeral ship entered New York harbour to the booming of minute guns from forts and ships. Two days later, public buildings were closed and ensigns drooped at half-mast, while the honoured dust was borne through the nation's capital to historic Arlington. A vast multitude thronged the beautiful city of the dead. As the flag-draped coffins appeared, a ghostly voice seemed to say to the silent host: "Hats off, gentlemen! for yonder come the riderless steeds, the reversed arms, the muffled drums. Something is here for tears." The President, admirals, generals, statesmen, diplomats, bared their heads. The weird music of "The Dead March" melted into the sweeter strains of "Nearer, My God, to Thee." The parting volleys were fired. Clearly and solemnly the bugler sounded taps, and the multitude turned away with tear-dimmed eyes to talk of a noble monument to commemorate the lives of heroes.

But the dead soldiers of the Cross lie where they fell on our lonely missionary outposts—amid the jungles of Africa, in the swamps of Siam, beside the rivers of China and under the palm-trees of India. From the grave of a Labaree or a Pitkin, as well as of the English general, a poet might have written:

> "Not a drum was heard, not a funeral note,
>   As his corse to the rampart we hurried:
> Not a soldier discharged his farewell shot
>   O'er the grave where our hero we buried.
>
> "Slowly and sadly we laid him down,
>   From the field of his fame fresh and gory,
> We carved not a line and we raised not a stone —
>   But we left him alone with his glory."

Well might a Persian Christian cry: "O winds, that sweep over those who have died for a cause they loved more than life, touch lightly, we beg, the sacred dust! O sun, touch gently with thy burning rays the lives of those who still live and toil! Let the story of their untiring energy and unwavering faith and hope in Jesus Christ be proclaimed in coming generations, to stimulate, encourage, and inspire the children of God!"

Such missionaries are the true heroes and heroines of our modern life. Some of them could say with Paul that in the service of Christ they have been "in perils by the heathen, in perils in the city, in perils in the wilderness, in weariness and painfulness, in cold and nakedness." It can only be "through ignorance" that some minimize the worth of their achievement. When, in the British Parliament, the Duke of Wellington heard the Irish soldiers maligned, he sprang to his feet and exclaimed: "Hold! I have seen the Irish do their duty!" Many a man to-day can bear like testimony to foreign missionaries. They are men and women of ability and culture, who, for love of Christ and of their fellow men, have denied themselves the sweet relations of home, the conveniences of civilization and the opportunities of American life, and gone to distant and inhospitable lands, to toil among people of another race and language and often of barbarous and depraved habits. They are doing the hardest and most thankless of pioneer work. They are fighting at the forefront of the battle where the danger is greatest and the inspiration least. Like that man of whom Victor Hugo wrote in the "Toilers of the Sea," they stand on the point of solitude and of danger; but they stand for a loftier purpose than his and with a nobler courage. If the eleventh chapter of the Epistle to the Hebrews were to be brought down to date, the writer would surely speak of scores of missionaries, who "through faith subdued kingdoms, wrought righteousness, obtained promises, escaped the edge of the sword, out of weakness were made strong, waxed valiant in fight, had trial of cruel mockings and scourgings, were stoned, were tempted, 'and' of whom 'also' the world was not worthy!"

In the spring of 1897, in front of the State House and overlooking the historic Common, the people of Boston witnessed a memorable scene—the dedication in the presence of a vast throng of a monument to the memory of Colonel Robert G. Shaw, who, during the Civil War, accepted the command of a regiment of coloured troops and fell at their head in the storming of Fort Wagner. The inscription reads:

> "Right in the van on the red rampart's slippery swell,
> With heart that beat a charge he fell,
> Forward, as fits a man.
> But the high soul burns on to light man's feet,
> Where death for noble ends makes dying sweet."

The daily press teemed with eulogistic articles and the *Century Magazine* said: "It is fitting that the art of the new world should culminate in this tribute to one who dedicated his pure young life to his country, to freedom, to the uplifting of a people in bondage, to the ennobling of the whole race of man."

We gladly join in honouring the name of that gallant patriot. But "what honour and dignity" shall be done to the foreign missionary, who, in obedience to the call of his country's God and out of love for the self-same race, has made the greater sacrifice of journeying alone to a distant land, living among an alien people, and, amid perils and privations equal to those of any battle-field, seeking "to bind up the brokenhearted and to proclaim liberty to the captives" of evil and superstition? Is his heroism less thrilling than that of the Boston soldier, his achievement less worthy? If we may adapt the words of Mary H. Kingsley to a class that she did not have in mind: "I trust that those at home will give all honour to the men still working in Africa, or rotting in the weed-grown, snake-infested cemeteries and the forest swamps—men whose battles have been fought out on lonely beaches far away from home and friends and often from another white man's help, sometimes with savages, but more often with a more deadly foe, with none of the anodyne to death and danger given by the companionship of hundreds of fellow soldiers in a fight with a foe you can see, but with a foe you can see only incarnate in the dreams of your delirium, which runs as a poison in burning veins and aching brain—the dread West Coast fever."[1]

Edward Everett Hale's poem, "All Souls," eloquently voices the debt which succeeding generations owe to the courage and fidelity of the forgotten missionary as well as to the pioneer settler:

> "What was his name? I do not know his name:
> I only know he heard God's voice and came.
> Brought all he loved across the sea,
> To live and work for God—and me;
> Felled the ungracious oak,
> Dragged from the soil
> With torrid toil
> Thrice-gnarled roots and stubborn rock,
> With plenty piled the haggard mountainside,

[1] "Travels in West Africa," Appendix II.

And at the end, without memorial, died;
No blaring trumpet sounded out his fame;
He lived, he died; I do not know his name.

16 No form of bronze and no memorial stones
Show me the place where lie his mouldering bones.
 Only a cheerful city stands,
 Built by his hardened hands,
  Only ten thousand homes,
   Where every day
   The cheerful play
Of love and hope and courage comes.
These are his monument and these alone;
There is no form of bronze and no memorial stone.[26]

XIX

THE MISSIONARY'S REWARD

REWARD is not the object of the true missionary. He understands that he who seeks to "save his life shall lose it." The motives which constrain one to missionary service should be free from the taint of self-aggrandizement. Nevertheless, there is a reward, and its richness illustrates the other part of Christ's aphorism: "Whosoever will lose his life for My sake the same shall save it."

There is a reward of men. It is true that some ridicule the missionary and that others are indifferent to him. But there are multitudes who believe in his work and who honour and love him. He begins to experience this reward as soon as his appointment becomes known. He finds himself a marked man. He is praised by his friends, commended in the local newspapers and is bade God-speed in a farewell meeting in which the dominant thought is expressed in the words of James Lane Allen: "The world will always be a battle-field to you, but the victory will be worth the fighting. And my last words to you are: fight it out to the end; don't compromise with evil; don't lower your ideals or your aims. If it can be any help to you to know it, I shall always be near you in spirit, . . . and if my poor prayers can ever bring you a blessing, you shall have it."[1] These prayers from those who have frequent audience with God are offered around thousands of firesides after he leaves for the field. In his loneliness and isolation, he does not realize how many pastors preach about him, how many young people discuss his work and how many godly women

[1] "The Choir Invisible," p. 285.

give their richest sympathies to him and to the cause which he represents.

His return on furlough, years later, is usually welcomed with every mark of esteem and admiration. At the large annual assemblages of the home churches, foreign missions nearly always develop an enthusiasm greater than that for any cause. It is not uncommon for the foreign missionaries present to be called to the platform and for the whole Assembly or Conference to rise and greet them with generous applause and the waving of handkerchiefs. Many readers will remember the remarkable manifestation at the Missionary Conference of 1900 in New York. Spacious Carnegie Hall was packed at every session for nine consecutive days, and so many were unable to gain admission that the largest churches were required for overflow meetings. One hundred and sixty-three thousand people attended that Conference, an average of about 18,000 a day. The Hon. Benjamin Harrison, former President of the United States, said that in all his experience in public life, he had never known any political or other secular convention which maintained its interest on so high a plane for so long a time. The daily press devoted whole pages to the proceedings and the Conference was the talk of the world for weeks. And yet the sole subject was foreign missions, and the central figure was the foreign missionary. It is undeniable that the missionary has a large place in the hearts of God's people and that only the prayers of Paul for his beloved Philippians adequately express the breadth and depth of their affection.

This reward of men comes on the field as well as at home. There are exceptions, as in Japan and among the higher classes of several other lands; but in most mission fields the missionary is regarded as a superior being. The educated Christian leaders, although less subservient than formally, treat him with respect. Many a missionary wields large powers of administrative leadership. The kings and princes of Siam and

Korea make missionaries their personal friends, and not only in Africa, but in Syria, Persia and India the people count them among the great men of the land.

It would be easy to fill a volume with tributes which have been paid to missionaries by governors, diplomats, admirals, generals, travellers and foreign potentates. Indeed, so great sometimes is the reward of men, that there is occasionally danger that it will affect the missionary's modesty. It does not often do this, but when it does, it is doubly unfortunate; for there is an increasing number of good men and women who hold the missionary in high regard, and if he keeps himself sweet and modest, he will find in their sympathies and prayers a real reward.

Then there is the reward of conscience. Independently of any recognition of men, the missionary knows that he has obeyed the call of God and that his life is an integral part of the eternal purpose regarding the world. Probably he has undergone a marked spiritual experience in becoming conscious of this conclusion. He may have had ambitions in other directions. Perhaps relatives protested, or church or business enticed. But on his knees before God he thought and prayed the question through, and the victory brought him what Shakespeare calls "that peace above all earthly dignities; a still and quiet conscience." "Joy does not happen," said Maltbie Babcock; "it is the inevitable result of certain lines followed and certain laws obeyed and so a matter of character." Every one who has tried it can truly say: "Vainly I sought Happiness, but she fled before me constantly. Sadly I turned to duty's path, when Happiness sought me, saying: 'I walk this road, to-day, I'll bear thee company!'" No greater inspiration can come to any man than the conviction that he is in the line of God's purpose and call.

There is great reward in knowing that one is using life to the very best advantage. If there is a God, if He is a Being of infinite justice and compassion, if He has given His only begotten Son that whosoever believeth in Him should not perish but have everlasting life, if the knowledge of that Son gives deliverance from sin, adds dignity and power to human life and fits for eternal companionship with God—then the noblest task to which man can address himself is to make known that faith to those who have never heard it. We do not undervalue the importance of Christian work at home. There is much to be done in our native land; but the preaching of the gospel to those who have heard it from their infancy and who can easily hear it from other lips if they do not from ours, the development of work already well under way, the joining of oneself to the already mighty host of Christian workers, cannot compare in importance with the consecration of one's life to the millions in unevangelized lands who have never heard the gospel, and who, but for us, may never hear it. And to the missionary has this dignity been given. To him have the words been spoken: "As the Father hath sent Me, even so send I you."[1] He goes forth, therefore, as an accredited "Ambassador" of the King of Kings.[2] Rich reward is in this thought. It is glorious to work for God in this favoured age. The missionary would say, with Theodore Roosevelt at the Conference in New York: "Woe to him who pities the worker!" He feels that he is to be congratulated, not condoled with. The greatest of all tasks has been committed to him and in the performance of it, he is making

> " . . . every nerve and sinew
> Tell on ages, tell for God."

He knows, moreover, that in this work he is laying foundations for future nations. No one can look back over the march of world empires and then consider the nations of Asia and Africa to-day, without being confident that they are to have a

[1] John 20: 21.   [2] 2 Cor. 5: 20.

more vital relation to the world than they have yet had. **God** did not create these countless millions simply to come and go like the leaves of the forest. He had some purpose. The Christian world is just becoming conscious of this. Books and magazines teem with discussions of it. It is apparent to every one that some of these nations are yet to exert a mighty influence. Japan is already a world power. China is passing through the same transition on a vaster scale. The troubles that from time to time break out are simply the new wine bursting the old bottles, the throes of the new birth. Their consequences may be disastrous to individuals; but he who believes that God is ordering the affairs of men and that all things are working together for good is confident that the disturbances of this present time will result in the enlargement of the opportunity of the gospel. The foreign missionary is the chief human factor in this majestic movement. Patrick in Ireland, Augustine of Canterbury in England, Columba in Scotland, Boniface in Germany, Livingstone in Africa, Judson in Burma, Morrison in China, Duff in India, and dozens of others, living and dead, illustrate this. No historian can ever write of these countries without assigning large place to the services of such men. To them, in the providence of God, was committed the royal task of going to heathen nations, preparing their own materials and laying foundations broad and deep. Similar opportunities await the missionary to-day. No other class of men has the privilege of working on so vast a scale. And in that opportunity itself is reward.

And then the missionary has the reward of knowing that his work is upliftng men temporally. A higher civilization always results from his work, though it is not his object. The alleviation of physical suffering, the promotion of education, cleanliness and morality are all inseparable concomitants of missionary effort. It is encouraging to know that one is contributing to such blessings. To see the community in which he labours becoming more orderly and temperate; to see husbands respecting their wives, woman elevated, children becoming truthful and homes becoming pure—these are great things.

A greater reward, however, comes from the knowledge that the missionary is blessing men spiritually. True, God alone can save a soul; but God uses human instruments and the foreign missionary may be, must be, if he is true to his work, such an instrument. Christ said that there is "joy in heaven over one sinner that repenteth."[1] There is also joy in the heart of the man who is saved. But only he who has been used in the saving knows the ineffable peace which comes to the one who has been thus honoured of the Holy Spirit. He can only say, as he ponders the mystery:

> "O matchless honour, all unsought,
> High privilege surpassing thought,
> That Thou shouldst call me, Lord, to be
> Linkt in work-fellowship with Thee;
> To carry out Thy wondrous plan,
> To bear Thy messages to man;
> In trust with Christ's own word of grace
> To every soul of human race."

There is, too, the reward of success. Sometimes it is given to the missionary to see large results with his own eyes. The remarkable development of the work in Uganda, Korea and the Philippines and among the Karens of Burma and the Telegus and low castes of India are familiar illustrations. Hundreds of missionaries in other lands have had the satisfaction of reaping as well as the toil of sowing. Dr. Corbett and Dr. Mateer, two of the pioneer missionaries of Shantung, China, lived to see that vast and populous province dotted with mission stations and Chinese churches. The former personally baptized more than 3,000 converts and the latter saw the college that he founded become a great university with

---

[1] Luke 15:7.

hundreds of students and academic, medical and theological departments. Indeed, the missionary movement has now gained such headway in most fields, that almost every missionary may now confidently expect to have some visible evidences of success in converts, in changed lives, in developing institutions and in gradual but definite recognition of higher moral standards in the community. It is inspiring to watch day by day the development of Christian character. The Apostle John had many spiritual joys, but in his old age he wrote: "Greater joy have I none than this, to hear of my children walking in the truth." [1]

Some missionaries, however, are not so fortunate, at least from a human viewpoint. Death or ill health removes them before any substantial results appear. Others know the bitterness of many years of apparently unrequited toil. But they know that results will come, if they put their love into their work. We have all heard of the old man who toiled patiently upon one of the arches of a European cathedral, and how nobody paid any special attention, as it was believed that he was too aged and feeble to accomplish anything of value. "But one day the old man was found asleep in death, the tools of his craft beside him, the cunning of his hand gone and his face upturned to a marvellous face which he had wrought. And when men looked upon it, they said: 'This is the grandest work of all, for love wrought this.'" Many a missionary who died in obscurity is remembered to-day by the imprint of divine Love that he made on human lives.

But whether the missionary ever sees it or not, success is sure to come. The mighty truths of God, once implanted in a heathen land, never die of themselves nor can they be exterminated by man. Though they may take centuries to do their work, for God is seldom in a hurry and a day with Him is as a thousand years, they are as certain in their operation as

[1] 3 John 4.

the movements of the planets. We cannot conceive of God failing in anything that He undertakes, and He has undertaken the conquest of the world.

The lonely, half-discouraged worker may therefore take courage. His toil is not in vain. "Whether men heed or reject, not a word spoken, not a kindly act, not an earnest effort, not a prayer, not a tear, not a sigh, is lost or forgotten before God." [1]

> "Be sure, no earnest work
> Of any honest creature, howbeit weak,
> Imperfect, ill-adapted, fails so much
> It is not gathered as a grain of sand
> To enlarge the sum of human action used
> For carrying out God's end. No creature works
> So ill, observe, that therefore he's cashiered." [2]

Like Bishop Morris of Oregon, we have toiled painfully up that majestic pile of perpetual snow in the Cascade Range known as Mount Hood, and have crossed dry-shod on our upward way the bed of a stream in which there were but trickling rivulets of water and occasional shallow pools. But when we have turned, towards evening, we have found the dry bed of the morning filled to the banks with rushing, roaring water. "The sun had risen in his strength, and penetrating every cañon and crevasse with his warm and genial rays, had loosened the snowbound waters, which, flooding the empty channels, poured down their mighty currents to cheer and refresh the mountain slopes and the broad valleys, on to the great sea. And I have said, Is not this an allegory? Thus far, we have been toiling in the morning and the life-giving waters have but trickled forth from the vast but icy reservoirs, while our souls have been much discouraged because of the way.

---

[1] The Rev. F. E. Hoskins, D. D. [2] Mrs. Browning.

But soon the glorious sun will rise and bring the gracious thaw which will fill to the brim all these broad and deep channels, and 'the rivers of the flood thereof shall make glad the holy place of the tabernacle of the Most High.'"

We are not prophets, but as we face the future, may we not see a vision, not the baseless dream of the enthusiast, but the reasonable expectation of those who believe that the divine Hand guides the destinies of men. This vision is that the movement for the evangelization of the world will grow to more and more majestic proportions until all men shall know the Lord. Reports from widely separated fields amply justify this vision. Every mail is burdened with them. Apart from the rapidly increasing number of converts, there are unmistakable signs that a great movement has begun. The very fact that heathen systems are passing from indifference to hostility and feel obliged to conceal their coarser practices and to emphasize their better features is a tribute to the growing power of Christianity. Society in Asia is becoming more ashamed of open vice. Standards of conduct are growing purer. The character of Christ is universally conceded to be the loftiest in history. What Benjamin Kidd calls the altruistic ideas of Christianity have been liberated in heathen nations and they are slowly but surely transforming them. The traveller in those vast continents becomes conscious of the working of mighty forces that are creating conditions more favourable to the rapid triumph of the gospel. He is impressed, not so much by the actual number of those already converted, as by the strength of the current which is sweeping majestically toward the goals of God. He feels, with Gibson, that the situation is satisfactory; not that we are contented with ourselves or with our work, but that "a crucial experiment has been made. We know what can be done and can predict results." We see that we are in the trend of the divine purpose and that "His day is marching on."

There is, too, divine authority for this vision. Paul says

The Missionary's Reward

that it is the purpose of God "to sum up all things in Christ,"[1] that "in the name of Jesus every knee should bow" and that "every tongue should confess that Jesus Christ is Lord."[2] John declares that he heard "great voices in heaven" speak of the future triumph as a certainty so absolute that it should be reckoned as a present fact. "The kingdom of the world is become the kingdom of our Lord and of His Christ, and He shall reign forever and ever."[3] In Khartoum, a fine statue has been erected of General Gordon seated on a dromedary, with his face set towards the vast desert of the Soudan. A traveller asked a guide whether the statue ought not to have faced the city. "O, no, sir," he replied: "they set him looking not towards the palace where he lived, nor towards the Nile where he might have escaped, but towards the Soudan for which he died; and he is waiting, sir, for morning to dawn over the Soudan."[4] And so the missionary faces the future with faith in its promise because with faith in God, looking with clear, untroubled eyes towards that

> ". . . one far-off divine event,
> To which the whole creation moves."

And there is the reward of the Master Himself. This, also, is a reward which comes in this life. "Lo, I am with you alway," said Christ. Those who repeat that promise often forget that it is distinctly associated with the missionary command and that the condition of its fulfillment is obedience to it.[5] This reward is the greatest of all. It would be sufficient of itself, if there were nothing else. The missionary can go anywhere, do anything if Christ is with him. Then one is "strengthened with all power, according to the might of his glory, unto all patience and longsuffering with joy."[6] If there

---

[1] Eph. 1: 10.   [2] Phil. 2: 10, 11.   [3] Rev. 11: 15.
[4] Mabie, "The Meaning and Message of the Cross," p. 167.
[5] Matt. 28: 19, 20.   [6] Col. 1: 11.

are hard places, He will reach them first and help us through. "When thou passest through the waters, I will be with thee; and through the rivers, they shall not overflow thee."[1] Because Madame Guyon felt this, she could say even in a prison:

> "O Lord, how full of sweet content
> Our years of pilgrimage are spent!
> Where'er we dwell, we dwell with Thee,
> In Heaven, in earth, or on the sea.
>
> "To us remains nor place nor time:
> Our country is in every clime:
> We can be calm and free from care
> On any shore, since God is there."

This has been the experience of every devoted missionary. Paul left fame and fortune to follow Christ "in weariness and painfulness, in hunger and thirst, in cold and nakedness";[2] but he said: "I reckon that the sufferings of this present time are not worthy to be compared with the glory which shall be revealed to us-ward. Yea verily, and I count all things to be loss for the excellency of the knowledge of Christ Jesus my Lord: for whom I suffered the loss of all things, and do count them but dung, that I may gain Christ and be found in Him."[3] Peter toiled for Christ in poverty and persecution; but he fervently exclaimed: "Blessed be the God and Father of our Lord Jesus Christ, who according to His great mercy begat us again unto a living hope by the resurrection of Jesus Christ from the dead, unto an inheritance incorruptible, and undefiled, and that fadeth not away."[4] Xavier endured almost incredible hardships as a missionary and finally died on a bleak and forbidding coast; but his roommate heard him cry out in the night: "Yet more, O my God! more toil, more agony, more suffering, for Thee!" After Livingstone had suffered in-

---

[1] Is. 43: 2.
[2] Phil. 3: 8, 9.
[3] 2 Cor. 11: 27.
[4] 1 Peter 1: 3, 4.

numerable hardships in the savage jungles of darkest Africa—hunger, loneliness, sickness, danger, he wrote: "Is that a sacrifice which brings its own blest reward in healthful activity, the consciousness of doing good, peace of mind and a bright hope of a glorious destiny hereafter? Away with the word in such a view and with such a thought! It is emphatically no sacrifice. Say rather it is a privilege. . . . It is utterly unfair to magnify the little we do for Him by calling it a sacrifice, or pretend we are doing all we can by assuming the tones of poor widows. . . . Our talk of sacrifices is ungenerous and heathenish. Can that be called a sacrifice which is simply paid back as a small part of the great debt owing to our God? I never made a sacrifice."[1] Paton lived for years in such peril from savages that an officer of England's navy marvelled at a heroism unparalleled in the annals of war; but he said: "Let me record my immovable convictions that this is the noblest service in which any human being can spend or be spent; and that if God gave me back my life to live over again, I would without one quiver of hesitation lay it on the altar to Christ, that He might use it amongst those who have never yet heard the Name of Jesus."[2]

These citations are representative ones. Said a missionary in China after a day of toil and trial: "A missionary's life is the happiest in the world." "It may be," as Mrs. Isabella Bird Bishop warned a party of young missionaries, "that advancement in the professions at home may be sacrificed by going to the foreign field; but in the hour when the soldier lays his dinted armour down after the fight has been fought, and the hands which were pierced for our redemption crown his brow with the crown of life, and the prize of the high calling of God is won, will there be one moment's regret, think you, for the abandoned prizes of the professions at home?"

---

[1] Blaikie, "Personal Life of David Livingstone."
[2] "Autobiography," Vol. II, p. 381.

It is not in riches, not in power or position to buy such joy as comes to the faithful missionary. "I am born for God only," joyously exclaimed Henry Martyn, "Christ is nearer to me than father or mother or sister—a nearer relation, a more affectionate friend; and I rejoice to follow Him and to love Him. Blessed Jesus! thou art all I want; a forerunner to me in all I ever shall go through as a Christian, a minister or a missionary. . . . I do not wish for any heaven on earth besides that of preaching the precious gospel of Jesus Christ to immortal souls." Can such men be defeated?

"Speak, History, who are life's victors? unroll thy long annals and say—
Are they those whom the world called the victors, who won the success of a day?
The martyrs, or Nero? the Spartans who fell at Thermopylæ's tryst,
Or the Persians and Xerxes? his judges, or Socrates? Pilate or Christ?"

And at the end come the rewards of heaven. "Well done, good and faithful servant," are the welcoming words of Christ, "thou hast been faithful . . . enter thou into the joy of thy Lord."[1] John says that he beheld "a great multitude . . . standing before the throne and before the Lamb, arrayed in white robes and palms in their hands,"[2] and that in answer to the question: "Who are they and whence came they?" he was told: "These are they which come out of the great tribulation, and they washed their robes and made them white in the blood of the Lamb. Therefore are they before the throne of God, and they serve Him day and night in His temple: and He that sitteth on the throne shall spread His tabernacle over them. They shall hunger no more, neither thirst any more, neither shall the sun strike upon them, nor any heat: for the Lamb which is in the midst of the throne shall be their Shep-

[1] Matt. 25 : 21. [2] Rev. 7 : 9.

The Missionary's Reward

herd and shall guide them unto fountains of waters of life: and God shall wipe away every tear from their eyes."[1]

With such present and prospective rewards, physical trials are not worthy to be mentioned. It is better to burn out for Christ in a decade in some Nineveh, than to enjoy life for a generation in a Tarshish. One must die anyway some time, somewhere, and can there be any better place than at the forefront of the battle and at the moment when the Lord calls? If ever missionary life came to a disastrous, unrewarded end, it was on that awful 28th of October, 1905, at Lien-chou, China, when four missionaries were murdered by a frenzied mob. Dr. Eleanor Chesnut had lovingly ministered to suffering Chinese women and girls for eleven years. Mrs. E. C. Machle, whose little daughter Amy perished with her, was widely known as a tactful and indefatigable worker. Mr. and Mrs. J. R. Peale had arrived only the day before. Suddenly a mob arose, looted and burned the mission-buildings, hunted down all resident members of the station, except Dr. Machle and Miss Patterson who could not be found, stripped them, killed them and threw their bodies into the river. Where was their reward? The following poem eloquently voices man's despairing question and Christ's convincing reply:

> "Didst Thou observe Thy promise, Nazarene,
> That last and solemn troth which Thou didst plight
> With Thy disciples, that at every time
> And in all places Thou wouldst walk with them,
> Unto the age's end? Wast Thou with them
> That cruel yesterday in Lien-chou?
> Didst thou behold them, angels of Thy Word,
> Exiles for Thine and for Thy gospel's sake,
> Die so hard death to make a jackals' feast,
> Prey to the pitiless fangs of ravening wolves?
> When the wild-oxen gored them, when the dogs,
> Swarming from all their filthy kennels forth,

[1] Rev. 7: 13-17.

Tore off their raiment, and with frothing jaws
Defiled their Christian bodies: wast Thou by?

"What had they wrought to merit such despite?
Had they not wrought Thy will for all men's good?
Their feet, for Thine, had threaded reeking lanes
Of alien cities, seeking out the lost.
They said, 'They are the Shepherd's wandered ones.'
Their hands, for Thine, had healed whom others spurned,
Counting it joy to lay their palms, for Thine,
On the foul outcast, deeming him brother to Thee.
Their lips, for Thee, o'ercame the alien speech,
That they, for Thine, might voice Thy words of life
Which mend the sorrows and the sins of men.
Is it for this that they are done to death,
And down past death to loss of human form?
And when they perished, Master, where wast Thou?

"Or speak they truth who limit Thine intent
To the white nations of the happy West
And shut Thy mercy off from half the world,
Counting but fools who for no gain of gold
Lead lives laborious under Asian skies,
Vexing the simple Pagan with strange creeds?
Has then Thy pity bounds, and may it be
That all the yellow races live and die
Beyond the healing shadow of Thy cross?
When Thou commandedst, 'Into all the world!'
Didst Thou intend a narrower world than ours?
When on that Mount of Vision Thou didst see
The kingdoms of the world, and undertake
To win them by Thy sorrow, may it be
These coasts were sunk in mists beyond Thy ken,
Beyond Thy heart's horizon and Thy hope?
Or art Thou weary of a wicked world
Which swings so slowly sunward from its night?
Or have the ages sapped Thine ancient strength?
Or has Thy covenant lapsed with lapse of years?
Hast Thou kept faith, 'Thou Man of Galilee'?
So spake one in a bitterness of soul
That life so fair should fall to death so foul.

The Missionary's Reward

"'Hush, child!' He chode, smiling thro' face of tears,
'For when was furnace heated sevenfold
For one of Mine, but through its roaring flame,
Albeit unseen, there walked the Son of God?
Was I beside them, merely! Gave I not
A word of closer comfort to Mine own?
Upon their feet I walked those Sodom streets
To bring My fallen brothers back to God.
My hands in theirs, by couch of mortal pain,
Brought solace and the healing touch of love.
. . . . Thro' their hearts,
Wide with the wide compassion of the Cross,
I gave to all My pity and My love;
I lived in them and laboured, and was glad
And grieved in them, and in them suffered pain,
And thro' death's deepest shadow died in them.
Was I but by them, when that yelping pack
Tore down their lives to death! The rabble's gibes
Found target in My heart. The brutal blows
That rained upon them spent their force on Me.
Again, as in Mine own Gethsemane,
I bowed Myself in them to shadow of death,
Holding a bitter cup that might not pass.
The blood which crimsoned them was holy blood
Of the slain Christ.'

. . . 'Such blood as theirs
Sinks not forgotten into nether earth,
But lieth red upon the 'during rock
And crieth to Jehovah night and day
With blood of Holy Cross, for sinful men
Whose wicked hands have shed it.
. . . . . . Where they fell,
Dragged forth to death by idol worshippers,
Shall the great congregation worship God.
In Sabbaths of sweet peace shall holy bells
Summon the waiting villages to prayer.
That better Eden which God gives to earth
Shall blossom from the desert, for their sake,
In lilies and in roses. Death's red stream
And sorrow's silver rain of sweat and tears

> Shall nourish healing herbs and trees of life
> For earth re-paradised.'
>
>   " ' Ay, Master, ay ;
> But they for tears of whom those lilies blow,
> Shall they behold them ? They above whose dust
> The Sabbath bells shall ring shall never hear
> The minster's music.'
>
>   " Then there came
> A voice that fell from starry silences;
> 'So long as men shall live and die in Him,
> They living in Him die but to toil and tears,
> They dying in Him to undreamed glories live
> That shall outlast the stars.'
>
> " And one saw them walking close with Him
> In festal robes beyond the sunrise fair
> And dowered with the beauty of the Lord.
> And thus He led them up the smiling streets
> Thronged for their triumph, to the Sapphire Throne,
> To bring them to the presence of the King.
> And all the Holy Ones who bade them hail
> Said : ' Blessed are the dead in whom He died!
> They died, and live in him forever more.
> From all their toils for Him they rest in Him,
> And all their works for Him do follow them.'
>
> " And one who heard and saw was comforted." [1]

[1] The striking poem from which these extracts have been quoted was written by the Rev. Charles K. Harrington, D.D., a Baptist missionary at Yokahoma, Japan, and was first published in *The Japan Mail*, December 15, 1905.

REFERENCES FOR SUPPLEMENTARY READING

For the convenience of readers who desire to look more fully into the subjects treated in this volume, the following books and magazine articles are suggested. For valuable assistance in the preparation of this list, I am indebted to Dr. Charles H. Fahs, Curator, and Miss Hollis W. Hering, Librarian, of the Missionary Research Library, 3041 Broadway, New York. The literature is voluminous and it is deemed wise to limit the appended list to a few of the books that are now in print and therefore readily available. This rule excludes some important volumes that are, unfortunately, out of print. Readers who desire information regarding such works may write to Dr. Fahs, or the Secretary of their missionary Board, or the Librarian of a theological seminary, any one of whom would doubtless be glad to suggest titles and the places where they may be borrowed or consulted.

ALLEN, ROLAND—
 Missionary Methods: St. Paul's or Ours?
 The Spontaneous Expansion of the Church and the Causes Which Hinder It.
  Both by World Dominion Press, London, 1927.

BLISS, H. S.—
 The Modern Missionary.
 Atlantic Monthly, May, 1920.

CLARK, CHARLES ALLEN—
 The Korean Church and the Nevius Method.
 Fleming H. Revell Co., New York, 1930.

COREY, STEPHEN J.—
 The Preacher and His Missionary Message.
 Missions Matching the Hour.
  Both by Cokesbury Press, Nashville, 1931.

DOBSON, J. O.—
 Why Christian Missions?
 Student Christian Movement, London, 1930.

402B References for Supplementary Reading

FLEMING, DANIEL J.—
Helping People Grow. 1931.
Marks of a World Christian. 1920.
Whither Bound in Missions? 1925.
All by Association Press.

GOLLOCK, G. E., ED.—
An Introduction to Missionary Service.
Milford Press, London, 1921, or Oxford University Press, N. Y.

HAUGHWOUT, LEFFERD, M. A.—
The Missionary and His Work.
Morehouse Press, Milwaukee, 1927.

HOOPER, J. S. M.—
Spiritual Health of the Missionary.
International Review of Missions, Oct., 1928.

LENNOX, W. G.—
The Health of Missionary Families in China; a Statistical Study.
University of Denver, 1921.

LYON, D. W.—
Some Atheisms to Which a Missionary Seems Susceptible.
International Review of Missions, April, 1923.

MCAFEE, CLELAND B.—
Changing Foreign Missions.
Fleming H. Revell Co., New York, 1927.

MORGAN, E. R.—
Essays Catholic and Missionary.
S. P. C. K., London, 1928, or Macmillan Co., N. Y.

MONTGOMERY, HELEN BARRETT—
The Preaching of Missions.
Judson Press, Philadelphia, 1931.

MOTT, JOHN R.—
Present-day Summons to the World Mission of Christianity.
Cokesbury Press, Nashville, 1931.

PATON, WILLIAM—
The Missionary Motive.
Student Christian Movement, London, 1913.
A Faith for the World.
Edinburgh House Press, London, 1929.

References for Supplementary Reading

PATTON, CHARLES H.—
  Foreign Missions Under Fire.
    Pilgrim Press, Boston, 1928.

PINSON, W. W.—
  Missions in a Changing World.
    Cokesbury Press, Nashville, 1928.

PRESBYTERIAN CHURCH IN THE U. S.—
  Our Church Faces Foreign Missions.
    Executive Committee of Foreign Missions, Nashville, 1931.

SHAW, W. E., ED.—
  Missionary Motivation.
    Methodist Book Concern, New York, 1931.

SMITH, EGBERT W.—
  The Desire of All Nations.
    Ray Long and Richard R. Smith, New York, 1930.

SPEER, ROBERT E.—
  "Are Foreign Missions Done For?" 1928.
  Christianity and the Nations.
    Both by Fleming H. Revell Co., New York, 1910.
  The Church and Missions.
    Ray Long and Richard R. Smith, 1926.

WALTER, H. A.—
  The Spiritual Requirements of the Missionary.
    International Review of Missions, Oct., 1921.

WARBURTON, S. R.—
  The Making of Modern Missions.
    Fleming H. Revell Co., New York, 1931.

WARK, H. E.—
  New Era in Missions.
    Fleming H. Revell Co., New York, 1929.

Report of World Missionary Conference, 1910.
  Edinburgh House Press, London.

Report of Jerusalem Missionary Conference, 1928.
  International Missionary Council, London and New York.

The International Review of Missions (quarterly).
  Edinburgh House, London.

The Missionary Review of the World (monthly), New York.

The Moslem World (quarterly), New York.

World Dominion (quarterly), London.

The Chinese Recorder (monthly), Shanghai.

The denominational missionary magazines (monthlies).

Index

ACCIDENTS, 159, 160
Accountants, 54
Addresses, missionary, 219 *sq.*, 230
Adherents, number of, 7
Administration, missionary, 44 *sq.*; cost of, 55 *sq.*
Africa, 84, 110, 122, 127, 147, 148, 149, 150, 152, 158, 160, 172, 205, 260, 264, 276, 284, 319, 335, 338, 384
Age of candidates, 69, 78
Agents, business, 70; native, 36–39, 42, 60, 103, 256, 291 *sq.*, 305–318
Agricultural schools, 70
Aim, 29 *sq.*, 296, 310 *sq.*
Alexander, The Rev. Dr. George, 302
Allen, James Lane, 377, 386
America, 265, 268, 276, 280
American Board, 48, 49, 169
Amusements, 242
Ancestors, 286
Anglo-Saxons, early, 346
Anti-foreign feeling, 260 *sq.*, 295, 296, 328
Antioch, Church of, 68, 224, 337
Ants, 357, 358
Apostles, 20
Applications, 76, 80 *sq.*
Appointments, 67 *sq.*
Appropriations, see Grants
Architecture, 281, 282
Armenians, 332
Armstrong, Gen. S. C., 247
Asia, 260, 264, 265 *sq.*; Asiatics, 260 *sq.*, 265, 280
Assembly, Presbyterian General, 46, 48, 49, 300, 313, 314, 316, 317
Assignments, 81, 82, 89, 90
Associates, 362, 363
Astronomy, 172

Asylums, 115
Augustine, 390
Avarice, 294

BABCOCK, REV. DR. MALTBIE D., 99, 388
Baird, Mrs. Wm., 95, 127, 178, 179, 188
Baller, Rev. Dr. F. W., 269
Baptisms, 112, 250, 255
Baptist, 225, 336; missionary societies, 48, 49
Barbour, Rev. Dr. Thomas S., 303, 304
Barrett, Hon. John, 328, 332
Barton, Rev. Dr. James L., 309, 319
Bathing, 150
Beach, Rev. Dr. Harlan P., 163, 273, 274, 276
Beds, 275
Bible, 27, 32, 103 *sq.*, 183 *sq.*, 265, 267, 304
Bible societies, 105
Bible translations, see Translations
Biographies, 164
Bird, Rev. Wm., 194
Bishop, Mrs. Isabella Bird, 235, 327, 397
Bishops, 48, 90
Blind, school for, 325
Boards, 44 *sq.*, 67, 134, 197 *sq.*, 249–251, 278, 295, 296, 308, 311, 312, 317, 319, 329, 336, 337
Bookkeeping, 78
Books, 103, 104, 162 *sq.*, 264, 292
Boston, churches in, 335, 336
Bovaird, Dr. David, Jr., 157
Bowels, diseases of, 155, 156
Boxer Uprising, 328, 333
Boycott, American, 266
Brahmans, 117, 170

Index

Brainerd, David, 193, 233
Brazil, church in, 300, 302
Brinkley, Captain Frank, 321
Brockman, Mr. F. S., 292, 305
Brooks, Sidney, 342
Brotherhood of man, 15, 18, 22
Brown, Nathan, 373
Browning, Elizabeth Barrett, 19, 174, 180, 393
Browning, Robert, 118, 195
Bryan, Hon. Wm. J., 265, 270, 327
Bryant, Wm. Cullen, 173
Bryce, Hon. James, 244, 288
Buckley, Rev. Dr. James M., 52
Buddhists and Buddhism, 21, 103, 105, 117, 286, 346
Buildings, 324
Burma, 83, 128, 391
Burns, Robert, 283
Business agents, 70
Butterflies, 172

CALHOUN, REV. SIMEON H., 194
Call, to missionary service, 79
Calls of natives, 273
Calvert, James, 193
Cameron, Miss Donaldina, 371
Canterbury, Archbishop of, 223
Candidates, 67 sq.
Canton, 324, 325, 372
Carey, William, 30, 84, 190, 233
Carlyle, Thomas, 177, 192, 193, 283
Carroll, Dr. James, 153
Carroll, Rev. Dr. H. C., 308
Caste, 125, 189
Catechumens, 109, 112
Cathartics, 156, 157–159
Celibacy, see Marriage
Cess-pools, 151
Chairs, 275
Chalmers, Rev. Dr. James, 375
Chang Chih-tung, Viceroy, 280, 345
Chapel-preaching, 111, 112
Charity, 246, 247, 253, 254, 282, 283, 290
Chatterjee, Rev. Dr. K. C., 305, 306, 308
Chefoo, 111, 136, 173

Chesnut, Dr. Eleanor, 377, 399 sq.
Chester, Rev. Dr. S. H., 60
Chicago, churches in, 335, 336
Children, 76, 77, 99, 100, 110, 119, 124, 273, 274, 275, 339, 341, 363 sq.
China, 113, 116, 122, 125, 128, 147, 151, 167, 168, 170, 173, 204, 264, 266, 270, 280, 286, 292, 330, 336, 347, 365, 366, 368, 390; Church in, 305, 352
Chinese, 26, 27, 45, 105, 260, 265, 267, 272, 273, 275, 276, 277, 294, 295, 299, 328–330, 332, 333, 343, 345, 346, 367
Cholera, 356, 377
Christ, 13–21, 22, 26, 28, 29, 33, 34, 93; a missionary, 111; compassion of, 17; example of, 289, 290; miracles of healing, 106; quoted, 16, 17, 18, 19, 20, 21, 31, 368, 386, 395
Christianity, effects of, 14, 23, 24, 25, 39, 40; for all, 15, 17–21, 42, 346; how to be presented, 21, 29–33, 34
Christianization, 34
Christians, American, 299 sq.; European, 299 sq.; native, 33, 36, 38 sq., 89, 95, 98, 109, 299 sq., 327, 328, 333, 340, 341, 351 sq., 387
Church, 13, 19, 20; apostolic, 42, 233, 302; home, 19, 20, 37, 44, 45, 46, 47, 48, 57, 113, 135, 201, 202, 214, 215, 216 sq., 218, 219–234, 293, 299 sq., 334 sq., 352; native, 33 sq., 38–43, 109, 112, 234, 250, 251, 291 sq., 299–318; of England, 48
Cisterns, 154
Civilization, 22–24, 25, 26, 29, 32, 33, 38, 338, 340, 344, 390; Western, 126, 129
Clarke, Rev. Dr. Wm. N., 45, 46, 51, 64, 65, 227
Climate, 68, 89, 146, 149, 160, 239, 356, 362, 377
Clothing, 121, 145, 151, 152, 275, 276, 280, 283
Coan, Rev. Titus, 172

Index

Cobras, 357
Cochran, Dr. J. P., 121
Colleges, 69, 100, 205, **222**; medical, 144, 145
Colporteurs, 33
Colquhoun, Archibald R., 321
Columba, 233, 390
Comity, 254-258, 334, 335
Commentaries, 163
Commerce, 22, 23, 234, 263, 264, 347
Committee, executive, 48, 49; Southern Presbyterian Executive, 317
Common sense, 71, 72
Complaints, 248
Concert, monthly, 230
Concubinage, 115
Conferences, 188; ecumenical, 387; general, 48, 50; joint of United States and Canada, 66; Methodist, 311, 312; with new missionaries, 81, 82
Confucius, 103, 117, 274, 286, 345
Conger, Hon. E. H., 324
Congregationalists, 225
Conscientiousness, 246, 254, 255
Constipation, 156
Consuls, 259, 268, 374
Controversies, theological, 299, 300
Convention, Southern Baptist, 49
Conversion, 30, 31, 190
Converts, native, 33 sq., 112, 218, 250, 255, 327, 328, 333, 340, 341, 351 sq., 391 sq.; number of, 7; made by native helpers, 36; cost of, 348-351
Conveyances, 109
Corbett, Rev. Dr. Hunter, 111, 121, 136, 391
Courtship, 276, 277
Creeds, 298, 299 sq.
Criticisms, 64, 207, 221, 280, 319 sq., Chapter XVI
Curzon, Lord, 343
Cust, Robert Needham, LL. D., 45
Customs, 217, 273, 274, 275, 276, 280
Cuts, 55, 252

Dana, James Dwight, 172

Darwin, Charles, 24, 320, 327
Deaf-mutes, 365
Debt, 56, 77
Demons, 22, 106
Denby, Hon. Charles, 327, 328, 329, 331, 343, 344, 346
Dennis, Rev. Dr. James S., 24, 168, 169
Dentists, 153
Deputations, 219 sq.
Diarrhœa, 156
Dickens, Charles, 164
Diplomacy, 168, 169, 259, 268, 347
Disciples, first, 20
Discipline, church, 296, 297
Diseases, 22, 68, 82, 106, 128, 140 sq., 153, 155, 356, 367, 368, 371, 377
Disinfectants, 159
Dispensaries, 22, 108, 144
Doane, Right Rev. William, D. D., LL. D., 228
Doctrines, 74, 254 sq.
Dress, 275, 276, 283, 286
Druses, 194
Duff, Alexander, 190, 390
Dunlap, Rev. Dr. Eugene P., 115, 144, 290
Durand, Sir Mortimer, 94, 287, 288, 327
Dysentery, 148, 149, 156

Eddy, Dr. Mary Pierson, 357, 370
Eddy, Rev. Wm. K., 172
Edkins, Rev. Joseph, 168
Education, secular, 25, 101; of missionaries, 69; mission, 22, 32, 33, 38, 99 sq., 108, 110, 166, 168
Egypt, 265, 338
Elephants, 262, 263
Ellinwood, Rev. Dr. Frank F., 303
Ellis, Mr. Wm. T., 46
Elmwood, Thomas, 245
Emerson, 174
Emperor of China, 104; of Korea, 332
Empress Dowager of China, 104, 332

Engineers, 70
England, 204, 205, **265**, **270**, 337; in India, 204, 205
Entomology, 171, 172
Estimates, 55, 61, 198
Etiquette, 273, 274
Europe, 265; conversion of, **117**
Evangelistic missions, 14 *sq.*, 32, 35 *sq.*, 38, 108 *sq.*
Evangelization, 34
Ewing, Rev. Dr. Arthur, 305
Examinations, language, 94
Executive committee, see Committee; council, 53
Exercise, 150, 161
Expenditures, 201 *sq.*, 211
Eyes, 152, 153

FABER, REV. E., 26, **168**
"Face," 271, 272
Fairbanks, Rev. Dr. S. B., 173
Faith, 189, 232, 304; healing, 75; missions, 66
Families, missionary, **274**
Famine, 365
Fatherhood of God, **17**
Farrar, Canon, F. W. 354
Fees, 121
Fevers, 148, 153, 154, 157 *sq.*
Fiction, 164, 165
Filters, 148
Finley, Dr. Carlos, **153**
Finney, Rev. Dr. Charles, 190
Fishes, 173
Fitch, Mrs. George F., 116
Fleeson, Miss Katharine N., 173
Flies, 153
Food, 88, 89, 121, 122, 123, 128, 146, 160, 307
Foreigners in Asia and Africa, 258 *sq.*, 319 *sq.*, 324, 328, 329–331, 334, 339, 362
Forman, Rev. Dr. John, 131
Foster, Hon. John W., 327
Francke, August Hermann, 233
Fraser, Rev. Donald, 186
Freight, 86
French, in Asia, 261
Friction, 73, 238 *sq.*, 244 *sq.*
Fruit, 173, 348
"Fukuin Shimpo," 297

Fulton, Rev. Dr. A. A., 37
Furloughs, 160, 219 *sq.*, 363, 387
Furniture, 85
Fusan, 136

GALE, REV. DR. JAMES S., 331
Gambling, 115, 116, 349
Garrison, William Lloyd, 373
Geil, Wm. E., 155, 156
Geology, 172
Gibson, Rev. Dr. J. Campbell, 394
Gifts, 293; special, 57 *sq.*, 251, 252
Gilder, Richard Watson, 193, 194
Gilmour, Rev. James, 30, 80, 113
Giving, 57 *sq.*, 123, 220, 222 *sq.*; at home, 336, 337, 348, 349
Gladstone, Hon. Wm. E., 302
Glasses, 145, 273
Glave, E. J., 357
God, term for, 90, 91
Good, Dr. Adolphus C., 172
Goodell, Rev. Dr. Wm., 284
Gordon, General Charles George, 395
Gordon, Rev. Dr. A. J., 190
Gospel, how to be presented, 21, 29, 33, 34; effects of, 14, 23, 24, 25; for all, 17–21
Gossip, 244, 245
Government, church, 298, 300–318; national, 169, 204, 205, 234, 263, 268, 278, 279, 332, 333
Grants, 41, 55, 61, 63, 66, 137, 138, 209 *sq.*, 251, 252, 293, 311, 312, 314
Greek Church, 234
Griffis, Dr. Wm. Elliot, 321, 322
Gulich, Rev. Dr. John T., 172
Gutzloff, Rev. K. F. A., 168
Guyon, Madame, 396

HAINAN, 89
Hale, Rev. Dr. Edward Everett, 384
Hall, Rev. Dr. John, 56
Hamilton, Angus, 260, **261**, 331, 340, 341
Hardships, 355 *sq.*
Harrington, Rev. Dr. Charles K., 399 *sq.*

Index

Harrison, President Benjamin, 228, 387
Hart, Sir Robert, 327
Hawaiian Islands, 339
Health, 68, 78, 82, 140 *sq.*, 219, 239, 355; trips, 160
Heat, 356
Heathen, need of Christ, 15; salvation of, 15, 16, 19, 20; state of, 15, 16, 189; qualities, 27
Heathenism, 87, 88, 106, 289, 365 *sq.*, 367, 368
Hendrix, Bishop C. R., 274
Hepburn, Dr. James, 167; Mrs., 124
Heresy, 19, 21
High-binders, 371
Hindus and Hinduism, 21, 27, 103, 267, 367
Histories, 164
Holcombe, Hon. Chester, 347
Holmes, Oliver Wendell, 342
Holy Spirit, 31, 42, 66, 83, 84, 189 *sq.*, 232 *sq.*, 304
Home Missions, 121, 226, 227, 228
Homesickness, 358 *sq.*
Hoskins, Rev. Dr. F. E., 172, 393
Hospitality, 124, 126
Hospitals, 22, 32, 33, 70, 98, 108, 160, 181, 325, 372
Houses, 307, 308, 355; missionary, 120, 135 *sq.*, 149, 160, 270, 274, 281, 282; native, 128, 135, 270
Hugo, Victor, 164, 383
Hulbert, Prof. Homer B., 278
Humanity, 15, 20, 22
Hunter, Sir William, 365
Huxley, Thomas H., 180
Hygiene, 143

IMMORALITY, 259, 268, 276, 277, 363, 366, 371
Impressions, first, 85 *sq.*, 87 *sq.*
Indemnity, 333
Independent agencies, 45, 47, 55, 130, 132 *sq.*
India, 25, 35, 36, 40, 41, 83, 84, 100, 107, 120, 121, 125, 132, 133, 147, 149, 157, 170, 189, 204, 205, 263, 265, 270, 273, 285, 295, 325, 335, 338, 345, 352, 356, 365, 366, 367, 391; Church in, 305 *sq.*, 310, 314, 316, 317
Indian Standard, 314, 315, 317
Indians, American, 338
Industrial missions, 70, 97
Infanticide, 115, 349
Inns, 356
Inquirers, see Catechumens
Insane, 323, 365
Insects, 171, 172, 356, 357
Intemperance, 115, 259, 265
Itineration, 109 *sq.*

JAPAN, 25, 39, 46, 91, 101, 102, 144, 151, 205; Church in, 303, 304, 309, 314, 315, 366, 367, 390
Japanese, 27, 44, 45, 141, 142, 160, 267, 293, 294, 295, 297, 298, 346
Jerome, Hieronymus, 346
Jessup, Rev. Dr. Henry H., 51, 93, 121, 172, 194, 279, 287, 372, 373
Jesuits, 172
Johnson, Rev. Dr. Herrick, 231
Johnston, Sir Harry, 327
Judson, Rev. Dr. Adoniram, 83, 94, 188, 363, 374, 390

KALIGHAT, Temple of, 285
Karens, 83
Keith-Falconer, Ion, 80
Kerr, Dr. John G., 365, 372
Kidd, Benjamin, 116, 362, 394
Kingsley, Miss Mary H., 125, 147, 148, 159, 384
Kipling, Rudyard, 345, 356, 369
Knowledge, contributions of missionaries to, 22, 27, 32
Korea, 91, 107, 111, 148, 151, 188, 204, 205, 260, 330, 391; Church in, 299, 300, 314, 340, 341, 352, 367

LAMBUTH, DR. WALTER R., 145
Languages and language study, 69, 90 *sq.*, 105, 166, 168, 355
Lāo, 274
Lawrence, Lord, 327
Lawrence, Rev. Dr. Edward A., 33, 91, 133, 366, 367

Index

Lawsuits, 266, 329
Laymen, 50, 223, 226, 229, 230; "missionary movement," 223
Lazear, Dr. Jesse, 153
Legge, Rev. Dr. James, 168
Lepers, 108
Letters, 53 sq., 197 sq., 207, 216 sq., 361; from natives, 58, 59
"Letters of a Chinese official," 265
Liberty, 279
Libraries, 162, 169
Lien-chou, massacre of, 320, 377, 399 sq.
Li Hung Chang, Viceroy, 104, 330
Lincoln, Abraham, 370
Liquor, 143, 155, 265, 319, 321, 323
Literary work, 103 sq., 108, 166
Living, cost of, 119, 122 sq., 264; scale of, 127 sq., 131 sq.
Livingstone College, 144
Livingstone, David, 77, 84, 186, 390, 396, 397
Loans, 271
Loneliness, 358 sq.
Longley, Archbishop, 105
Lowrie, Rev. Dr. Thomas, 169
Lowry, Rev. Dr. H. H., 121
Lull, Raymond, 172, 233

Mabie, Rev. Dr. Henry C., 395
Macaulay, Thomas B., 120
Machle, Mrs. E. C., 378, 399 sq.
Mackay, Alexander M., 70
Maclay, "Budget of Letters from Japan," 322
McCartee, Dr. Divie Bethune, 168
McCook, Rev. Dr. Henry C., 171, 172
McCormick, Frederick, 321
McGilvary, Rev. Dr. Daniel, 109
Madagascar, Church in, 303
Magazines, 165, 166, 167, 292
Malaria, 143, 147, 153, 157
Malays, 267
Managers, boards of, 48, 49
Manila, 359
Manners, 271 sq.
Manuals, 203
Maps, 230
Marling, Rev. Alfred, 380

Marriage, 75, 76, 131, 370
Martin, President W. A. P., D. D., LL. D., 69, 169
Martyn, Henry, 233, 398
Maronites, 370
Martyrs, 374, 375, 377
Massachusetts, General Association of, 49
Mateer, Rev. Dr. Calvin W., 91, 95, 391
Medical missions, 22, 32, 33, 106 sq., 108, 110; missionaries, 141, 372, 379; colleges, 144, 145
Medicines, 155, 156, 157 sq.; schools of tropical, 144, 154
Methodists, 225, 233, 335, 336; board of, 48, 52; secretaries, 50; woman's society, 47
Methods, apostolic, 42; mission, 113, 185, 289, 290
Michie, Alexander, 169, 170
Mikado of Japan, 332
"Mikado's Empire, The," Griffis', 322
Mills, Mrs. R. T., 365
Milne, Rev. Dr. William, 168
Milton, 177, 372
Ministry, native, 291 sq., 305 sq.; cf. agents
Minneapolis, churches in, 335
Mission, The, 60, 61, 90, 198 sq., 212, 249-251, 255, 256, 296, 297, 305-318
Missionaries, ability of, 326 sq.; number, preface, 34 sq., 97; and natives, 329-332; meaning of word, 20; new 34 sq., 82; distribution of, 80, Protestant, 131; women, see women; citizenship, 332, 333; see table of contents
Mitchell, Rev. Dr. Arthur, 229, 233, 336
Mobs, 377
Modesty, 243, 244, 276 sq
Moffat, Robert, 103, 369
Moffett, Rev. Dr. S. A., 111, 112, 177, 284
Mohammedans and Mohammedanism, 21, 40, 41, 104, 117, 189, 234, 265, 273, 277, 285-288, 332, 337

Index

Money, 38 sq., 41, 44, 53 sq., 59 sq., 137, 222 sq., 234, 293, 307 sq., 311, 312, 314
Monotony, 362
Morals, 276, 277
Moravians, 225, 233
"Morning watch," 188
Morphine, 157
Morrison, Robert, 30, 168, 390
Mosquitoes, 153–155
Mosul, Church in, 303
Mothers, missionary, 364, 365, 380
Motives, Chapter I, 228, 229
Muirhead, Rev. Dr. William, 168
Mullahs, 287, 288
Murray, Rev. D. A., 293
Music, 78

NANSEN, FRIEDJOF, 359
Nassau, Rev. Dr. Robert H., 172
Natives, 36, 89, 170, 171, 338, 339, 366, 387; cf. Churches, Christians
Nature, love of, 173 sq.
Naval officers, 322, 323
Negroes, 260, 338
Nestorians, 303
Nevius, Rev. Dr. John, 91, 173, 348
"New Forces in Old China," Brown's, 258, 260, 264, 326
New missionaries, 34 sq., 237 sq., 243, 244
Newspapers, 26, 165, 166, 168, 229, 230, 264
New York, religious work in, 334, 335, 336
Nightingale, Florence, 145
Nurses and nursing, 70, 143, 145, 325

OBJECTS, special, 57 sq., 209 sq., 251, 252
Oculists, 152, 153
Offerings, 222 sq.
Officials, 258, 260 sq.
Opium, 114, 115, 319
Optimism, 74, 242
Orchards, 173
Ordination, 70

Orientals in America, 294, 295, 309
Orphanages, 325
Outfit, 85

PAOTING-FU, 330
Parents, 274, 286, 363 sq.
Parish abroad; see Station Plan
Parkhurst, Rev. Dr. Charles H., 186, 187
Pastors, 71, 222, 226 sq.; home, 19, 20, 45, 123, 134, 201, 239
Patience, 274
Patrick, 390
Patriotism, 279, 280
Patteson, Bishop John Coleridge, 195, 196
Paul, 14, 21, 26, 31, 34, 42, 68, 79, 83, 180, 184, 191, 224, 247, 253, 278, 285, 337, 338, 382, 395, 396
Peale, Rev. J. R., 378, 399 sq.
Pentecost, 190, 232, 233
Pentecost, Rev. Dr. George F., 349
Persia and Persians, 122, 137, 151, 270, 287, 288, 371
Peter, 26, 190, 215
Philadelphia, 336
Philanthropy, 21, 32, 115, 123
Philippines, 25, 131, 148, 172, 391; Church in, 352
"Philippines, The New Era in," Brown's, 256, 258
Physicians, 68, 69, 70, 77, 85, 94, 107, 110, 143, 144, 153, 154, 155, 156, 163, 165, 372, 379
Pietism, 233
Plague, 107, 356, 377
Pledges, 226
Poetry, 164
Policy, mission, 65, 66, 206, 250, 310 sq.
Politeness, 271, 272
Politics, 264, 278, 279; western, 347
Polity, church, 298, 299 sq.
Post, Dr. George E., 168, 173
Ports, treaty, 321, 323, 324
Poverty, 59, 123, 204, 271, 291, 292, 367; of natives, 38, 40
Prayer, 185 sq., 230, 231 sq., 386; meetings for, 188

Index

Prejudice, race, 26, 27, 260 sq., 295
Presbyterian Board, 46, 48, 54, 82
Presbyterians, 46, 225, 299, 300, 302, 316, 317, 320, 335, 336
Presbytery, 311, 312, 313, 315, 316
Presents, 273
Press, 26, 229, 264; mission, 32, 70, 104 sq., 391 sq.
Priests, Roman Catholic, 131, 266, 279; heathen, 105, 320
Princeton, Theological Seminary, 67
Privacy, 238, 269, 270
Professionalism, 182
Progress of missions, 116–118, 348 sq., 391 sq.
Property, 250, 281, 282
Propriety, 273, 274
Prostitutes, 116
Protestant Episcopal Missionary Society, 48, 336
Protestantism, 131, 234, 329

QUALIFICATIONS, for appointment, 67 sq., 243
Quinine, 157, 158

RACES, 260, 269, 294, 295
Ralph, Julian, 127
Reading, 162 sq.
Receipts of boards, 53, 54, 134
Recreations, 171, 217, 242
Reed, Dr. Walter, 153, 154
Reform movements, 114–116
Reformed Church, board of, 48
Refuse, 151, 356
Religions, non-Christian, 87, 88, 106, 117, 217, 284–289, 345, 365 sq.
Reports, 53, 54
Resignation, 364, 372, 373
Results, of missions, 24, 26, 29, 31, 218, 348 sq., 391 sq.
Revivals, 233
Roman Catholics, 75, 131, 184, 234, 266, 279, 329, 336
Romans, Epistle to, 246, 247
Roosevelt, President, 268, 371, 389
Ross, Dr. Donald, 154
Ross, Rev. Dr. John, 36
Riis, Jacob, 227
Ruskin, 174, 220, 342

SACRIFICES, 355 sq., 369 sq., 379 sq., 396 sq.
Sailors, 322, 364, 376, 377, 378
Salaries, missionary, 57, 77, 119 sq., 307, 308; native, 292 sq., 307, 308
Salvation, 15, 16, 17, 19, 20, 27
Salvation Army, 132
San Francisco, Chinese in, 371
Sanitation, 106, 151, 153, 281, 356
Schools, mission, 22, 32, 33, 58, 59, 60, 98, 99 sq., 108, 110, 168, 181, 277, 294, 295, 324, 341, 363; secular, 25, 363; technical, 70
Schwartz, Christian F., 233
Sciences, contributions of missionaries to, 22, 32
Scott, Walter, 164
Seaman, Dr. Louis L., 142
Secretaries, 50, 53, 197 sq., 207, 227
Sectarianism, 254–258, 334, 335
Secular life, 179 sq.
Sedan chair, 273
Self-government, 33, 296, 299–318
Self-propagation, 33 sq., 303, 310
Self-support, 33, 38–43, 59, 123, 291 sq., 301 sq., 308 sq., 310, 311, 312
Selwyn, Bishop Geo. A., 195, 196
Seminaries, theological, 70, 230
Sensitiveness, 242
Sermons, missionary, 230
Serpents, 357
Servants, 124–127, 261, 269
Sewers, 151
Seymour, Charles, 372
Shakespeare, 266
Shaw, Barnabas, 83
Shaw, Colonel Robert G., 383
Sheffield, Rev. Dr. D. Z., 121
Shoes, 151, 152, 275
Shumway, Arthur L., 169, 371
Siam and Siamese, 99, 101, 115, 116, 122, 149, 158, 261, 264, 267, 286, 292, 333; King of, 332, 379
Slavery, 115, 349
Smallpox, 152, 356
Smith, Canon Taylor, 374
Smith, Rev. Dr. Arthur H., 168, 169

Index

Smith, Rev. Dr. Eli, 103, 167
Society for the Diffusion of Christian and General Knowledge among the Chinese, 167
Societies; see Boards
Soldiers, 141, 142, 347, 360, 361, 364, 376, 377, 378, 381, 383
Sorcerers, 106
Soudan, 395
South America, 123, 131, 144, 217, 276, 316
Southern Baptist Convention; see Convention
South Sea Islands, 320
Speer, Mr. Robert E., 304
Spener, Philipp J., 233
Spiders, 171
Spirituality, 77, 177 *sq.*, 191 *sq.*, 232 *sq.*
Stanley, Henry M., 184
Stars, 173, 174
Station plan, 63
Stations, number of, Preface, 70, 73, 238, 239, 252, 269
Steamers, 86, 87
Stephen, 26, 31, 180
Stereopticons, 230
Stevenson, Robert Louis, 375
Stimulants, 143, 155, 161
St. Louis, churches in, 335
Street preaching, 111, 112
Strong, Rev. Dr. E. E., 62, 63, 64, 212
Students, 35, 67 *sq.*, 72, 79, 80, 103, 222, 231, 275; theological, 293, 294
Subscriptions, 226
Suffering, 365, 366
Sultan of Turkey, 217
Sun, 145, 153, 356
Sunday, observance of, 265
Superstition, 106, 116, 341, 367, 368
Surgery, 143, 144, 159, 160
Swamps, 154
Syria and Syrians, 103, 104, 126, 131, 151, 204, 205, 271, 309, 332, 357, 370

TACT, 271, 272, 274, 287-290
Tahiti, 84; church in, 303

Tea, 273
Teachers, 70, 77, 163, 166
Technical schools; see Schools
Teeth, 153
Temperament, 73, 74, 239-242, 247, 274
Tennyson, Alfred, 395
Text-books, 167
Theology, 27, 74, 254
Thoburn, J. M., Bishop, 285
Tokyo Theological Society, 298
Tract Societies, 167
Trade, 22-24, 25
Traders, 75, 258, 260, 264 *sq.*, 332, 347, 351
Translations, 103 *sq.*, 166-170
Travel, 86, 87; expenses of, 85
Travellers, 258, 260 *sq.*, 323, 324
Treasurers, 50, 54, 70, 137 *sq.*
Tropics, 150, 151, 362
Tuan Fong, Viceroy, 329, 330
Turkey, 217, 332, 333; Church in, 309
Tyler, Josiah, 30
Typhoons, 172

UGANDA, 39, 391
Ulfilas, Wulfila, 233
United States, 332, 333; churches in, 335, 336
"United Study of Missions," 222
Universities, 306
Uemura, The Rev. Dr., 297, 298, 315.

VACCINATION, 152
Van Dyck, Dr. C. V. A., 103, 167, 168
Van Dyke, Rev. Dr. Henry, 56, 181, 378
Veils, 277
Vermin, 356, 357
Vice, 116, 265, 319-321, 323, 366, 371, 394
Volcanoes, 172
Volunteers, 70, 72; Student Volunteer Movement, 35, 46, 222, 223

WAR, BOER, 142; Spanish-American, 142, 350, 381; Russia-Japan, 141, 142, 160, 266

Water, 146–149, 154, 159, 161
Watson, Rev. Dr. John, 18, 195
Wellington, Duke of, 21, 224, 382
Wells, 147
Welsh, Rev. R. E., 319
Wesley, Rev. Dr. John, 233
Whittier, 108, 236, 241, 255, 290
Williams, Dr. S. Wells, 169
Witte, Count, 246
Wives, 76, 94, 95, 124–127, 273, 274, 276, 363–365, 369, 380, 381
Women, single, 277, 342–344, 366, 370, 371, 379; missionaries, 70, 363 *sq.*; in boards, 49; heathen, 100, 115, 128, 269, 270, 278, 345, 349; societies, 47, 223, 224

XAVIER, FRANCIS, 396

YEAR-BOOKS, of missions, 232
Yellow fever, 153, 154, 356
Young People's Missionary Movement, 222

ZENANAS, 278
Ziegenbalg, Bartholomew, 233
Zinzendorf, Count N. L., 193, 233

Printed in the United States of America